DISCOVER ACTIVEX

Visual Basic Keyboard Shortcuts

Run and Restart

F5	Run the project. Or, if in Break Mode, restart from the breakpoint.
Shift+F5	Restart the project *from the beginning* after an interruption.

Miscellaneous

Ctrl+N	Start new project.
Ctrl+Z	Undo

Maneuvering

Ctrl+F	Find (F3 to Find Next)
F7	Display Code Window
Ctrl+Down Arrow	Move to next procedure
Ctrl+Up Arrow	Move to previous procedure

Display Windows

F4	Display Properties Window
Ctrl+R	Display Project Explorer
F2	Display Object Browser
Ctrl+T	Display Components dialog

Debugging

F8	Single-step through your source code ("Step Into")
Shift+F8	Same as single-step, but ignores any procedure calls ("Step Over")
Ctrl+BREAK	Stop a running Visual Basic project
F9	Toggle Breakpoint
Ctrl+Shift+F9	Clear all Breakpoints
Shift+F9	Quick Watch (query a variable's value)
Ctrl+G	Display Immediate window
Ctrl+L	Display Call Stack

Immediate Window

Enter	Run the current line of code
F6	Toggle between Immediate and Watch windows

Instancing Options

This table shows you which settings of the Instancing Property can be used with each of the three primary kinds of ActiveX components.

Instancing	ActiveX EXE	ActiveX DLL	ActiveX Control
Private	X	X	X
PublicNotCreatable	X	X	X
MultiUse	X	X	
GlobalMultiUse	X	X	
SingleUse	X		
GlobalSingleUse	X		

Native-Code Compilation Options

If you decide to compile into native code, you're offered the following set of six options:

* **Optimize for Fast Code.** This means the compiler will choose speed over file size whenever that tradeoff comes up during the compilation process.

* **Optimize for Small Code.** The opposite of Optimize for Fast Code, this produces the smallest possible executable file, at the expense of execution speed.

* **No Optimization.** You should avoid this choice, unless you want a compromise between the two previous optimizations.

* **Favor Pentium Pro.** If you're sure that your component will be used only on a Pentium Pro machine, go ahead. Otherwise, you'll create a component that runs inefficiently on other computers — though it will still run.

* **Create Symbolic Debugging Info.** This option can be useful if you use Visual C++ or a debugger that can work with the .PDB files that are deposited on your hard drive.

* **DLL Base Address.** When your component is loaded into memory, Windows will try to insert it into the address specified. If Windows can't put it there, it will put it elsewhere in memory.

DISCOVERY CENTRAL

DISCOVER
ACTIVEX™

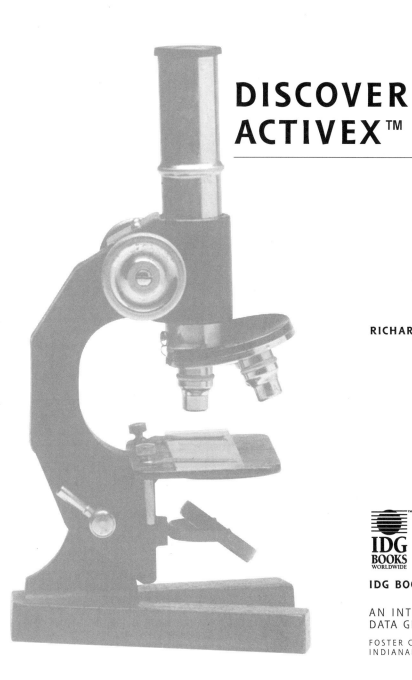

DISCOVER
ACTIVEX™

RICHARD MANSFIELD

IDG
BOOKS
WORLDWIDE

IDG BOOKS WORLDWIDE, INC.

AN INTERNATIONAL
DATA GROUP COMPANY

FOSTER CITY, CA • CHICAGO, IL •
INDIANAPOLIS, IN • SOUTHLAKE, TX

Discover ActiveX™

Published by
IDG Books Worldwide, Inc.
An International Data Group Company
919 E. Hillsdale Blvd.
Suite 400
Foster City, CA 94404
http://www.idgbooks.com (IDG Books Worldwide Web site)

Library of Congress Catalog Card No.: 97-74808

ISBN: 1-7645-3150-6

Printed in the United States of America

10 9 8 7 6 5 4 3 2 1

1E/SX/RQ/ZX/FC

Distributed in the United States by IDG Books Worldwide, Inc.

Distributed by Macmillan Canada for Canada; by Transworld Publishers Limited in the United Kingdom; by IDG Norge Books for Norway; by IDG Sweden Books for Sweden; by Woodslane Pty. Ltd. for Australia; by Woodslane Enterprises Ltd. for New Zealand; by Longman Singapore Publishers Ltd. for Singapore, Malaysia, Thailand, and Indonesia; by Simron Pty. Ltd. for South Africa; by Toppan Company Ltd. for Japan; by Distribuidora Cuspide for Argentina; by Livraria Cultura for Brazil; by Ediciencia S.A. for Ecuador; by Addison-Wesley Publishing Company for Korea; by Ediciones ZETA S.C.R. Ltda. for Peru; by WS Computer Publishing Corporation, Inc., for the Philippines; by Unalis Corporation for Taiwan; by Contemporanea de Ediciones for Venezuela; by Computer Book & Magazine Store for Puerto Rico; by Express Computer Distributors for the Caribbean and West Indies. Authorized Sales Agent: Anthony Rudkin Associates for the Middle East and North Africa.

For general information on IDG Books Worldwide's books in the U.S., please call our Consumer Customer Service department at 800-762-2974. For reseller information, including discounts and premium sales, please call our Reseller Customer Service department at 800-434-3422.

For information on where to purchase IDG Books Worldwide's books outside the U.S., please contact our International Sales department at 415-655-3200 or fax 415-655-3295.

For information on foreign language translations, please contact our Foreign & Subsidiary Rights department at 415-655-3021 or fax 415-655-3281.

For sales inquiries and special prices for bulk quantities, please contact our Sales department at 415-655-3200 or write to the address above.

For information on using IDG Books Worldwide's books in the classroom or for ordering examination copies, please contact our Educational Sales department at 800-434-2086 or fax 817-251-8174.

For press review copies, author interviews, or other publicity information, please contact our Public Relations department at 415-655-3000 or fax 415-655-3299.

For authorization to photocopy items for corporate, personal, or educational use, please contact Copyright Clearance Center, 222 Rosewood Drive, Danvers, MA 01923, or fax 508-750-4470.

is a trademark under exclusive license to IDG Books Worldwide, Inc., from International Data Group, Inc.

ABOUT IDG BOOKS WORLDWIDE

Welcome to the world of IDG Books Worldwide.

IDG Books Worldwide, Inc., is a subsidiary of International Data Group, the world's largest publisher of computer-related information and the leading global provider of information services on information technology. IDG was founded more than 25 years ago and now employs more than 8,500 people worldwide. IDG publishes more than 275 computer publications in over 75 countries (see listing below). More than 60 million people read one or more IDG publications each month.

Launched in 1990, IDG Books Worldwide is today the #1 publisher of best-selling computer books in the United States. We are proud to have received eight awards from the Computer Press Association in recognition of editorial excellence and three from *Computer Currents'* First Annual Readers' Choice Awards. Our best-selling *...For Dummies®* series has more than 30 million copies in print with translations in 30 languages. IDG Books Worldwide, through a joint venture with IDG's Hi-Tech Beijing, became the first U.S. publisher to publish a computer book in the People's Republic of China. In record time, IDG Books Worldwide has become the first choice for millions of readers around the world who want to learn how to better manage their businesses.

Our mission is simple: Every one of our books is designed to bring extra value and skill-building instructions to the reader. Our books are written by experts who understand and care about our readers. The knowledge base of our editorial staff comes from years of experience in publishing, education, and journalism — experience we use to produce books for the '90s. In short, we care about books, so we attract the best people. We devote special attention to details such as audience, interior design, use of icons, and illustrations. And because we use an efficient process of authoring, editing, and desktop publishing our books electronically, we can spend more time ensuring superior content and spend less time on the technicalities of making books.

You can count on our commitment to deliver high-quality books at competitive prices on topics you want to read about. At IDG Books Worldwide, we continue in the IDG tradition of delivering quality for more than 25 years. You'll find no better book on a subject than one from IDG Books Worldwide.

John Kilcullen
CEO
IDG Books Worldwide, Inc.

Steven Berkowitz
President and Publisher
IDG Books Worldwide, Inc.

Eighth Annual Computer Press Awards ≥1992

Ninth Annual Computer Press Awards ≥1993

Tenth Annual Computer Press Awards ≥1994

Eleventh Annual Computer Press Awards ≥1995

IDG Books Worldwide, Inc., is a subsidiary of International Data Group, the world's largest publisher of computer-related information and the leading global provider of information services on information technology. International Data Group publishes over 275 computer publications in over 75 countries. Sixty million people read one or more International Data Group publications each month. International Data Group's publications include: **ARGENTINA:** Buyer's Guide, Computerworld Argentina, PC World Argentina; **AUSTRALIA:** Australian Macworld, Australian PC World, Australian Reseller News, Computerworld, IT Casebook, Network World, Publish, Webmaster; **AUSTRIA:** Computerwelt Österreich, Networks Austria, PC Tip Austria; **BANGLADESH:** PC World Bangladesh; **BELARUS:** PC World Belarus; **BELGIUM:** Data News; **BRAZIL:** Annuário de Informática, Computerworld, Connections, Macworld, PC Player, PC World, Publish, Reseller News, Supergamepower; **BULGARIA:** Computerworld Bulgaria, Network World Bulgaria, PC & MacWorld Bulgaria; **CANADA:** CIO Canada, Client/Server World, ComputerWorld Canada, InfoWorld Canada, NetworkWorld Canada, WebWorld; **CHILE:** Computerworld Chile, PC World Chile; **COLOMBIA:** Computerworld Colombia, PC World Colombia; **COSTA RICA:** PC World Centro America; **THE CZECH AND SLOVAK REPUBLICS:** Computerworld Czechoslovakia, Macworld Czech Republic, PC World Czechoslovakia; **DENMARK:** Communications World Danmark, Computerworld Danmark, Macworld Danmark, PC World Danmark, Techworld Denmark; **DOMINICAN REPUBLIC:** PC World Republica Dominicana; **ECUADOR:** PC World Ecuador; **EGYPT:** Computerworld Middle East, PC World Middle East; **EL SALVADOR:** PC World Centro America; **FINLAND:** MikroPC, Tietoverkko, Tietoviikko; **FRANCE:** Distributique, Hebdo, Info PC, Le Monde Informatique, Macworld, Reseaux & Telecoms, WebMaster France; **GERMANY:** Computer Partner, Computerwoche, Computerwoche Extra, Computerwoche FOCUS, Global Online, Macwelt, PC Welt; **GREECE:** Amiga Computing, GamePro Greece, Multimedia World; **GUATEMALA:** PC World Centro America; **HONDURAS:** PC World Centro America; **HONG KONG:** Computerworld Hong Kong, PC World Hong Kong, Publish in Asia; **HUNGARY:** ABCD CD-ROM, Computerworld Szamitastechnika, Internetto online Magazine, PC World Hungary, PC-X Magazin Hungary; **ICELAND:** Tolvuheimur PC World Island; **INDIA:** Information Communications World, Information Systems Computerworld, PC World India, Publish in Asia; **INDONESIA:** InfoKomputer PC World, Komputek Computerworld, Publish in Asia; **IRELAND:** ComputerScope, PC Live!; **ISRAEL:** Macworld Israel, People & Computers/Computerworld; **ITALY:** Computerworld Italia, Macworld Italia, Networking Italia, PC World Italia; **JAPAN:** DTP World, Macworld Japan, Nikkei Personal Computing, OS/2 World Japan, SunWorld Japan, Windows NT World, Windows World Japan; **KENYA:** PC World East African; **KOREA:** Hi-Tech Information, Macworld Korea, PC World Korea; **MACEDONIA:** PC World Macedonia; **MALAYSIA:** Computerworld Malaysia, PC World Malaysia, Publish in Asia; **MALTA:** PC World Malta; **MEXICO:** Computerworld Mexico, PC World Mexico; **MYANMAR:** PC World Myanmar; **NETHERLANDS:** Computer! Totaal, LAN Internetworking Magazine, LAN World Buyers Guide, Macworld Netherlands, Net, WebWereld; **NEW ZEALAND:** Absolute Beginners Guide and Plain & Simple Series, Computer Buyer, Computer Industry Directory, Computerworld New Zealand, MTB, Network World, PC World New Zealand; **NICARAGUA:** PC World Centro America; **NORWAY:** Computerworld Norge, CW Rapport, Datamagasinet, Financial Rapport, Kursguide Norge, Macworld Norge, Multimediaworld Norge, PC World Ekspress Norge, PC World Nettverk, PC World Norge, PC World ProduktGuide Norge; **PAKISTAN:** Computerworld Pakistan; **PANAMA:** PC World Panama; **PEOPLE'S REPUBLIC OF CHINA:** China Computer Users, China Computerworld, China InfoWorld, China Telecom World Weekly, Computer & Communication, Electronic Design China, Electronics Today, Electronics Weekly, Game Software, PC World China, Popular Computer Week, Software Weekly, Software World, Telecom World; **PERU:** Computerworld Peru, PC World Profesional Peru, PC World SoHo Peru; **PHILIPPINES:** Click!, Computerworld Philippines, PC World Philippines, Publish in Asia; **POLAND:** Computerworld Poland, Computerworld Special Report Poland, Cyber, Macworld Poland, Networld Poland, PC World Komputer; **PORTUGAL:** Cerebro/PC World, Computerworld/Correio Informático, Dealer World Portugal, Mac*In/PC*In Portugal, Multimedia World; **PUERTO RICO:** PC World Puerto Rico; **ROMANIA:** Computerworld Romania, PC World Romania, Telecom Romania; **RUSSIA:** Computerworld Russia, Mir PK, Publish, Seti; **SINGAPORE:** Computerworld Singapore, PC World Singapore, Publish in Asia; **SLOVENIA:** Monitor; **SOUTH AFRICA:** Computing SA, Network World SA, Software World SA; **SPAIN:** Communicaciones World España, Computerworld España, Dealer World España, Macworld España, PC World España; **SRI LANKA:** Infolink PC World; **SWEDEN:** CAP&Design, Computer Sweden, Corporate Computing Sweden, Internetworld Sweden, it.branschen, Macworld Sweden, MaxiData Sweden, MikroDatorn, Nätverk & Kommunikation, PC World Sweden, PCaktiv, Windows World Sweden; **SWITZERLAND:** Computerworld Schweiz, Macworld Schweiz, PCtip; **TAIWAN:** Computerworld Taiwan, Macworld Taiwan, NEW ViSiON/Publish, PC World Taiwan, Windows World Taiwan; **THAILAND:** Publish in Asia, Thai Computerworld; **TURKEY:** Computerworld Turkiye, Macworld Turkiye, Network World Turkiye, PC World Turkiye; **UKRAINE:** Computerworld Kiev, Multimedia World Ukraine, PC World Ukraine; **UNITED KINGDOM:** Acorn User UK, Amiga Action UK, Amiga Computing UK, Apple Talk UK, Computing, Macworld, Parents and Computers UK, PC Advisor, PC Home, PSX Pro, The WEB; **UNITED STATES:** Cable in the Classroom, CIO Magazine, Computerworld, DOS World, Federal Computer Week, GamePro Magazine, InfoWorld, I-Way, Macworld, Network World, PC Games, PC World, Publish, Video Event, THE WEB Magazine, and WebMaster; online webzines: JavaWorld, NetscapeWorld, and SunWorld Online; **URUGUAY:** InfoWorld Uruguay; **VENEZUELA:** Computerworld Venezuela, PC World Venezuela; and **VIETNAM:** PC World Vietnam. 3/24/97

Welcome to the Discover Series

Do you want to discover the best and most efficient ways to use your computer and learn about technology? Books in the Discover series teach you the essentials of technology with a friendly, confident approach. You'll find a Discover book on almost any subject — from the Internet to intranets, from Web design and programming to the business programs that make your life easier.

We've provided valuable, real-world examples that help you relate to topics faster. Discover books begin by introducing you to the main features of programs, so you start by doing something *immediately*. The focus is to teach you how to perform tasks that are useful and meaningful in your day-to-day work. You might create a document or graphic, explore your computer, surf the Web, or write a program. Whatever the task, you learn the most commonly used features, and focus on the best tips and techniques for doing your work. You'll get results quickly, and discover the best ways to use software and technology in your everyday life.

You may find the following elements and features in this book:

Discovery Central: This tearout card is a handy quick reference to important tasks or ideas covered in the book.

Quick Tour: The Quick Tour gets you started working with the book right away.

Real-Life Vignettes: Throughout the book you'll see one-page scenarios illustrating a real-life application of a topic covered.

Goals: Each chapter opens with a list of goals you can achieve by reading the chapter.

Side Trips: These asides include additional information about alternative or advanced ways to approach the topic covered.

Bonuses: Timesaving tips and more advanced techniques are covered in each chapter.

Discovery Center: This guide illustrates key procedures covered throughout the book.

Visual Index: You'll find real-world documents in the Visual Index, with page numbers pointing you to where you should turn to achieve the effects shown.

Throughout the book, you'll also notice some special icons and formatting:

A Feature Focus icon highlights new features in the software's latest release, and points out significant differences between it and the previous version.

Web Paths refer you to Web sites that provide additional information about the topic.

Tips offer timesaving shortcuts, expert advice, quick techniques, or brief reminders.

The X-Ref icon refers you to other chapters or sections for more information.

Notes provide additional information or highlight special points of interest about a topic.

The Caution icon alerts you to potential problems you should watch out for.

The Discover series delivers interesting, insightful, and inspiring information about technology to help you learn faster and retain more. So the next time you want to find answers to your technology questions, reach for a Discover book. We hope the entertaining, easy-to-read style puts you at ease and makes learning fun.

Credits

ACQUISITIONS EDITOR
Greg Croy

DEVELOPMENT EDITOR
Katharine Dvorak

TECHNICAL EDITORS
Rich Schwerin
Laura McCarthy

COPY EDITORS
Judy Brunetti
Barry Childs-Helton

PRODUCTION COORDINATOR
Katy German

BOOK DESIGNERS
Phyllis Beaty
Kurt Krames

GRAPHICS AND PRODUCTION SPECIALISTS
Linda J. Marousek
Shannon Miller
Maureen Moore
Christopher Pimentel
Trevor Wilson

PROOFREADER
Jenny Overmyer

INDEXER
Nancy Anderman Guenther

About the Author

Richard Mansfield has written over fifteen books, including the bestsellers *Machine Language for Beginners, The Second Book of Machine Language, The Visual Guide to Visual Basic,* and *The Visual Basic Power Toolkit.* His books have sold over half a million copies worldwide and his most recent title is *The Comprehensive Guide to VBScript.*

To Jim, Butch, and David Lee

PREFACE

Thank you for choosing *Discover ActiveX* to learn more about ActiveX technology. Readers of this book should have at least a little programming experience. Although some of the topics covered are advanced (particularly in Part IV, "Specialized ActiveX"), the book is designed and written so that virtually anyone, regardless of his or her level of programming expertise, will succeed in creating and understanding the many step-by-step examples.

Discover ActiveX is written in clear, nontechnical language and the examples were chosen because they solve real-world problems or result in useful ActiveX controls. You should be able to use these examples and the associated descriptions as the basis for crafting ActiveX solutions to your own Windows, NT, or Internet programming tasks.

What Is ActiveX?

ctiveX is a general term covering a variety of initiatives from Microsoft. ActiveX is a technology, a set of operating system features, a programming technique, and a collection of objects you can plug into programs or Web pages.

The word *ActiveX* made its first appearance in December, 1995, as Microsoft was repositioning itself in response to the exploding popularity of the Internet. ActiveX is an umbrella term that covers the various concepts and technologies of Dynamic Data Exchange (DDE) and Object Linking and Embedding (OLE). It adds color, animation, sound, and, above all, efficient interactivity to Web pages. But ActiveX, as you will see, is hardly limited to Internet programming.

Focus on Visual Basic

n this book you'll learn how to use two versions of Visual Basic: VBScript for Internet programming and the commercial version of VB for creating ActiveX components and controls for use in Internet pages, or for use in Windows and NT applications in general. Visual Basic was chosen as the programming language in this book for the same reason millions of programmers and developers have chosen it as their preferred language for Windows programming since 1991: VB is probably the easiest, most efficient programming language ever developed. And it's almost always fun to work with.

Two free Microsoft products are explored in this book — the ActiveX Control Pad and Visual Basic Control Creation Edition (VBCCE). The ActiveX Control Pad makes it easy to insert ActiveX controls into a new or existing Web page. VBCCE makes it easy to create new ActiveX controls. Both of these applications are on the CD-ROM that accompanies this book.

How This Book Is Organized

*D*iscover ActiveX is divided into four primary sections, organized so that the topics build from the basics of ActiveX in the early chapters to sophisticated programming in the final chapters.

Quick Tour

Discover ActiveX opens with a section called *Quick Tour* that is intended to plunge you right into the thick of things. In the first few pages of the book you'll fire up the ActiveX Control Pad and insert a Layout control into a Web page. No point in wasting any time. You'll get a brief sample of how easy Microsoft has made it for you to enliven your Web pages and other programming with ActiveX controls. The result: You'll want to go deeper into this book to learn more about the exciting world of ActiveX technology.

Part One: Using ActiveX Controls

Part One of *Discover ActiveX* covers the fundamentals of ActiveX controls. You'll learn where to find ready-to-use, commercial ActiveX controls and how to insert them into word processor documents and Web pages. You'll also find out how to customize controls using VBScript and Microsoft's ActiveX Control Pad.

Part Two: Creating Compound Controls

Part Two explores the powerful features of Visual Basic Control Creation Edition. You'll discover how to create your own custom ActiveX controls, and how and when to use the assistance of the built-in Wizards. Finally, you'll find out how to effectively integrate your controls into Web pages using VBScript.

Part Three: Classes and Objects

Part Three delves more deeply into the world of objects, developing your understanding of the principles of object-oriented programming (OOP) and its implementation in Visual Basic. You'll try writing a program using traditional procedure-oriented programming, and then writing the same program all over again using OOP techniques. Finally, you'll create a useful and sophisticated

ActiveX control, teaching you how to design and code more advanced ActiveX components.

Part Four: Specialized ActiveX

Discover ActiveX concludes with a final section that extends your understanding of ActiveX technology in two ways. First, you'll review — and enhance your proficiency in — several important topics introduced in earlier chapters, such as polymorphism and encapsulation. And, second, you'll learn several additional advanced ActiveX techniques. For instance, you'll learn how to create and test the new document-style components as well as how to build user-drawn controls (you design their *appearance* as well as their behaviors). You'll also find out how to optimize compilation, and which setup and security options are best for your particular projects. Finally, you'll experiment with several sophisticated OOP and ActiveX features, tap into the vast collection of functions in the Windows operating system, and discover ways to apply containment techniques to your components.

Discovery Center

Near the end of *Discover ActiveX*, you'll find the *Discovery Center*, an illustrated guide to many of the significant points and step-by-step instructions that are key to mastering ActiveX. You'll also find page references to help you locate any additional information you might need on a particular topic. The Discovery Center can be useful as a way to review some of the main points of a chapter before going on to the next, or as a quick reference to ActiveX programming.

The CD-ROM

*D*iscover ActiveX includes a companion CD-ROM attached to the inside of the back cover. The CD-ROM includes all of the programming code in this book, Microsoft's ActiveX Control Pad, Visual Basic 5 Control Creation Edition, and a select group of commercial ActiveX controls in demo versions.

ACKNOWLEDGMENTS

Special thanks to Greg Croy and Laura Moss for seeing merit in my proposal for this book and for their support during its writing. Thanks, too, go to my agent, Matt Wagner, who always seems to know best what should be done next.

Particular gratitude goes to Development Editor Katharine Dvorak for her insights; thoughtful and helpful editing throughout the process of her review and improvement of this manuscript; several instances of kindness; and her understanding of how some authors work.

I also appreciated the constructive suggestions of Technical Editors Rich Schwerin and Laura McCarthy, and the careful copyediting done by Barry Childs-Helton and Judy Brunetti.

Finally, I'd like to acknowledge the patience of my close friends.

CONTENTS AT A GLANCE

CONTENTS

PART IV—SPECIALIZED ACTIVEX, 275

13 FROM THE CLIENT SIDE, 277

ACTIVEX QUICK TOUR

PRACTICE USING THESE SKILLS

W elcome to ActiveX!

Microsoft offers three tools you can use to work with — or create — ActiveX controls: the ActiveX Control Pad, Visual Basic Control Creation Edition (VBCCE), and the commercial versions of Visual Basic 5.0. Amazing as it seems, the first two tools are free. You can download them from Microsoft's Web site at http//www. microsoft.com or find them on the CD-ROM that accompanies this book.

Find It. Use It. It's Free.

T here's been a breakthrough. Several years ago, most programs for the Windows operating system were written in the difficult C language. Then, in 1991, Microsoft introduced Visual Basic. Suddenly, writing Windows applications and utilities wasn't all that hard any more. Since then, millions of programmers — from casual amateurs to experienced professionals — have migrated to this easy-to-use and highly efficient programming language.

Something similar has happened again this year. With the introduction of Visual Basic 5.0, VBCCE, and the ActiveX Control Pad, creating ActiveX objects for use with Windows applications or for Internet programming has become much easier. With these three tools, Microsoft has made it possible for anyone to efficiently design ActiveX controls. We're going to cover all three tools in this book, starting with the simplest "monkey-see, monkey-do" use of existing controls to creating your own controls from scratch. But why not get your feet wet right now?

How to Install and Run the ActiveX Control Pad

Microsoft's ActiveX Control Pad offers you the easiest way to add ActiveX controls to your Web pages. The Control Pad is free and it's sitting there just waiting for you to start energizing your Web pages with it. If you don't have it already, it's included on the CD-ROM that accompanies this book.

Follow these steps to install the ActiveX Control Pad:

1. Locate the ActiveX Control Pad on this book's CD-ROM.

2. Run the ActiveX Control Pad setup program and then double-click on the ActiveX icon and you'll see the ActiveX Control Pad ready to run, as shown in Figure QT-1.

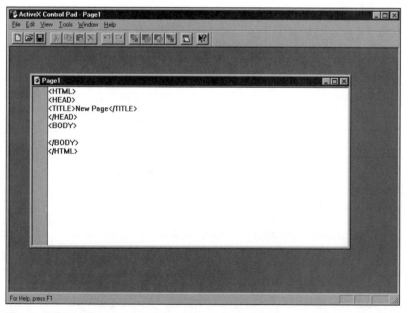

Figure QT-1   When you start the ActiveX Control Pad running, it provides you with this default page.

The empty document you see in Figure QT-1 is ready for you to build a Web page from scratch if you wish. Alternatively, you can load in a page you've already created (or someone else's page that you want to modify). Just look for .HTM files (short for HyperText Markup Language) on your hard drive.

How to Add Controls to a Web Page

It's easy to use the ActiveX Control Pad to add ActiveX controls to your Web pages. The Control Pad even comes with a set of commonly used controls built into the Pad itself. And most important, there's a specialized control called a Layout control that behaves like a Form in Visual Basic. Onto the Layout control you put other controls — making it easy to drag those other controls around to position and size them visually. You don't have to adjust Width, Height, Top, or Left properties.

Here's how to add a Layout ActiveX control to a Web page:

1. Position the insert cursor (the blinking vertical line in the document window) between the HTML commands `<BODY>` and `</BODY>`. This is where the Layout control will be located.

2. Right-click and choose Insert HTML Layout.

3. Type in **TB** as the filename for your new Layout control.

4. Click Open, then click Yes to create this new file named TB.ALX.

You've now created a Layout control and embedded it within your HTML document. Notice the new programming code that's now been inserted into your document:

```
<OBJECT CLASSID="CLSID:812AE312-8B8E-11CF-93C8-00AA00C08FDF"
ID="TB_ALX " STYLE="LEFT:0;TOP:0">
<PARAM NAME="ALXPATH" REF VALUE="file:C:\ContlPad\tb.alx">
</OBJECT>
```

HTML is the page-description language used to specify how Web pages look. Most of the time, HTML commands are plain English and easily understood, such as TITLE or FONT. However, ActiveX objects require a CLASSID, a long string of characters and digits that uniquely identify the object. When you insert an ActiveX control using the ActiveX Control Pad, the Pad creates the CLASSID for you. That's one of the signal advantages of using the Pad.

Now for a surprise. Click the icon ⬛ in the left margin, right next to the `<OBJECT CLASSID` tag. There it is: your new Layout control, and a Toolbox full of ActiveX controls you can place onto the Layout. If you've ever tried to add ActiveX objects to a Web page using an ordinary HTML editor, you'll appreciate

the simplicity and logic of the ActiveX Control Pad. Now that you've gotten your feet wet, we'll continue this example in Chapter 1.

TIP   ActiveX controls are sometimes referred to as ActiveX objects or ActiveX components. Feeling that objects is too general a term (there are other kinds of objects in the computer world), I'm using *controls* or *components* in this book.

USING ACTIVEX CONTROLS

This first section of the book covers the fundamentals of ActiveX controls. You'll learn where to find ready-to-use, commercial ActiveX controls and how to insert them into word-processing documents and Web pages. You'll also find out how to customize controls by using VBScript and Microsoft's ActiveX Control Pad.

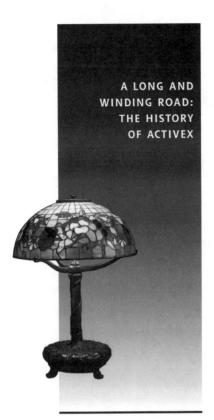

ActiveX is neither a new technology nor a single technology. And it didn't spring fully formed one day from the mind of Bill Gates, either. ActiveX has gone through three basic phases: DDE, OLE, and, finally, ActiveX.

The earliest incarnation of ActiveX was called Dynamic Data Exchange (DDE). This concept surfaced in 1990 as a way of permitting two documents to share data. It was like an automated Windows Clipboard—DDE-capable programs were able to trade information while they were running; exchanging text, pictures, and even simple commands with no user intervention.

For instance, instead of the user selecting text, clicking the Edit menu, clicking Copy, switching to the target application, clicking Edit, and then clicking Paste, you could automate all these steps with DDE. This automation had broad implications. In essence, it meant that one program could control the behavior of another. This feature was Microsoft's first major step toward object-oriented programming.

DDE was quickly superseded over the next three years by Object Linking and Embedding (OLE). OLE expanded the facilities of DDE, and added several new concepts. Complex communication between applications became possible with OLE Automation. For example, a Visual Basic application could access and trigger nearly all the features in Word for Windows. This way, an application written in Visual Basic could, for instance, "borrow" Word's spelling checker, using it to examine the text in a TextBox.

In addition, through OLE the distinction between programming and data became less rigid. A new concept was introduced called *in-place editing*. While in a Word document, if you embedded a graphic that was created in Paint, Word's menus and toolbar icons could be temporarily replaced with the menus and icons in Paint.

Finally, the term *ActiveX* made its appearance in December, 1995. ActiveX is an umbrella term that covers the various concepts and technologies of DDE and OLE, and adds the idea that ActiveX Controls can also be embedded into Web pages. ActiveX adds color, animation, sound, and, above all, efficient interactivity to Web pages.

This book focuses on the latest incarnation of ActiveX as embodied in three programming tools: the ActiveX Control Pad, Visual Basic Control Creation Edition, and Visual Basic 5. This book also covers the use of ActiveX in programming for the Internet as well as the use of ActiveX with ordinary applications that are ActiveX-capable, such as Office 97.

Until recently, most Web pages were quite static: You'd see text and pictures, but not much really *happened.* Enter ActiveX controls. You can find hundreds of ActiveX controls out there that can add animation, 3D effects, attractive user-input devices, high-quality audio, and much more to a Web page.

In this chapter you will learn how to use Microsoft's ActiveX Control Pad to insert ActiveX controls into your Web pages. After you finish this chapter, you'll know how to drop pre-built ActiveX controls right into your Web pages and, with very little effort, bring your Web site alive.

Rolling Your Own Controls

In the Quick Tour at the start of this book, you installed Microsoft's ActiveX Control Pad and inserted a Layout control. The Layout control is a primary benefit offered by the ActiveX Control Pad. The user never sees a Layout control, but you, the Web page programmer, can use it as a container to hold *other* ActiveX controls. With the Layout control it's easy to resize or reposition other ActiveX controls, and to modify their properties. That's what you should experiment with now.

Adding ActiveX Controls to a Web Page

Follow these steps to add TextBoxes and a Label to a Web page:

1. Start the ActiveX Control Pad. Follow the steps described in the Quick Tour at the beginning of this book to insert a Layout control into a Web page. Now display the Layout: Click the small icon 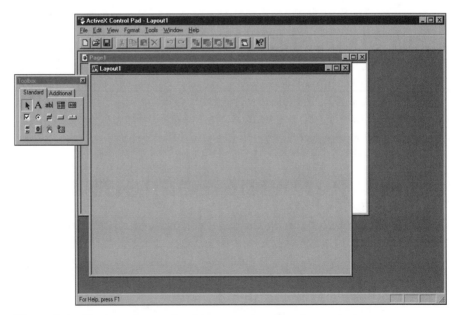 next to the words OBJECT CLASSID in the document in your ActiveX Control Pad.

2. You'll see a Toolbox and a Form pop up. Pause your mouse pointer over the various controls in the Toolbox to see their names.

3. Click the TextBox icon, the item third from the left in the top row of the Toolbox. Then drag your mouse on the Form to create a new TextBox. (Note that the icon will be third from the left if you haven't resized the Toolbox.)

4. Repeat this three more times so that you have four TextBoxes on the Form.

5. Click the Label icon, the item second from the left in the top row of the Toolbox. Drag a Label control onto the Form. Repeat three times for a total of four Labels.

6. Now drag and resize these TextBoxes and Labels so they're in the positions shown in Figure 1-1. (You can also resize the Layout if you wish.)

Figure 1-1 The Layout control acts as a container for other controls.

7. To adjust the font and font size of each Label and TextBox, hold down the Ctrl key while clicking each of the eight controls. This selects them all.

8. Right-click one of the controls and click Properties.

9. In the Properties window, double-click Font and change it to Arial. Then select 12 for Size. Click OK, then click the x icon in the upper right to close the Properties window.

10. Close the Layout control. Then save the entire Page1.Htm file by clicking `File` → `Save All`.

Adjusting Properties

TIP **In the Properties window you can adjust the color, border, typeface, and many other qualities of a control. Right-click the control, then click Properties. As a shortcut, you can just double-click a control to bring up the Properties window.**

X-REF **For a detailed discussion of creating new controls out of existing controls, see Chapter 6.**

Now you want to edit the Labels' Caption property so they describe the purpose of each TextBox. Click the Layout control (on the background, outside of any other control) to deselect the controls. Then double-click the first Label. Locate Caption in the Properties window, click it to select it, and change it to *Name* (in the TextBox at the top of the Properties window). Likewise, change the other Captions to *Address; City; State, Zip;* respectively, as shown in Figure 1-2.

You've now constructed a useful address-entry component by cobbling together several controls that are built into the ActiveX Control Pad. In effect, you've made a new ActiveX control out of several existing ActiveX controls.

To make the address-entry component you built actually submit the user's address information to you over the Internet requires a bit of VBScript programming. Coverage of this useful yet easy-to-learn language begins in Chapter 4. However, at this point you can see how the address component looks in the browser. And, as you'll see next, you can also test this address control in your Web browser. Save the address component and remember the filename you use — you'll use this file in the next example when you test the address component.

Testing Web Pages

I t's easy to test ActiveX controls — just load them into your Internet browser and try them out. You don't even have to log onto the Internet if you don't want to. Start Internet Explorer and choose Open from its File menu. (If you're asked whether you want to connect to the Internet, it's up to you. Click OK or Cancel. It doesn't matter.) Click the Browse button and locate the Page1.HTM file that you saved from the ActiveX Control Pad. Load it into the browser and type in your name.

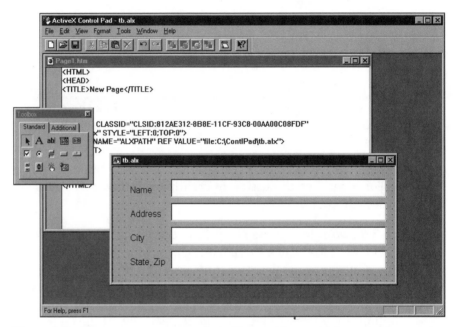

Figure 1-2 It's easy to create a new ActiveX control by combining existing controls.

Testing Right in Your Browser

Even complicated Web pages can be tested directly in your browser. You don't have to post the pages onto an Internet site to test most features of Internet pages. When you load a page into your browser you'll see precisely how it looks, hear any audio, view any animation, interact with any controls or programming, and so on.

An Efficient Testing Loop

Throughout this book you'll see how to take advantage of this useful and efficient testing loop: Make an adjustment in the ActiveX Control Pad (or another page-creation editor), save the document to disk as an .HTM file, load it into the Internet Explorer browser, test it, make further adjustments in your editor, and so on until the control works precisely the way it should. This testing cycle is quite efficient, as you'll see in future chapters. You can quickly test changes you made by clicking the Refresh button in Internet Explorer (or pressing F5). This will reload and display the latest version of your page, including your recent changes.

Exploring Existing Web Pages

One of the best ways to spur your creativity and think up fresh ideas for your Internet pages is to look at pages created by other people. You can surf the Web, then when you find a page you like, choose Save As File from the browser's File menu. This creates an Internet document file on your hard drive. These files have an .HTM extension (for HyperText Markup Language).

There's a Cache on Your Hard Drive Aready

Alternatively, you can locate .HTM files that are already on your hard drive. They've been cached by your browser during previous surfing expeditions and are waiting for you to view them. To do this, click the Windows Start button `Start` → `Find` → `Files or Folders`. In the TextBox labeled Named, type ***.HTM** and click the `Find Now` button. If you've been at all busy on the Internet recently you're likely to find hundreds of .HTM files.

Right-click an .HTM filename and choose Open. The file is then loaded into your browser. (If you've installed the ActiveX Control Pad you'll also see an option to Edit with ActiveX Control Pad.) But assuming that you've simply loaded a page into Internet Explorer, you can see the various effects created by the designer of that page. Likely the graphics are missing — they're usually not stored on your hard drive because that would quickly take up too much space. But you can see in the browser the place markers where the graphics used to exist within the page.

Find Out How They Did That

If you see an effective design element or other special effect that you like, you can find out exactly how it was done. Right-click the page and choose View Source. (This means view the *source code*, the HTML and other programming that created the page.) Windows places the source code for that page into Notepad where you can look at all the HTML code and, if you wish, copy and paste some of it into a page of your own to reproduce a special effect.

THE VELVET ELVIS

Fashions come and go. Sophisticates in the cities of Victorian Europe had their hair twisted into elaborate, delicate puffs to distinguish themselves from their country cousins. When the rustics began copying that hairstyle, the city folk started attaching expensive pearls to their clothing and hats. The worldly always take pains to distinguish themselves.

For the past few years, many people have been dressing entirely in black — black coats, shoes, even black eyeglass frames and scarves — as a way, perhaps, of making themselves appear worldly. Others, however, may favor vivid colors and rarely dress in black — except maybe for funerals.

You will find that this black look is also currently popular on some of the most sophisticated Web sites. The background is completely black and you see only a few foreground accents. Fortunately, the effect is usually superior to those black velvet paintings of Elvis and tigers sold at yard sales. In particular, the Microsoft Network (`http://www.msn.com`) currently features some extraordinarily attractive page designs. Notice in the following screen shot how the word *Communicate* is blown up and subtly spotlighted when you click it. Some of these clever lighting effects are possible with ActiveX controls; others depend on a black (or at least a very dark) background.

THE VELVET ELVIS

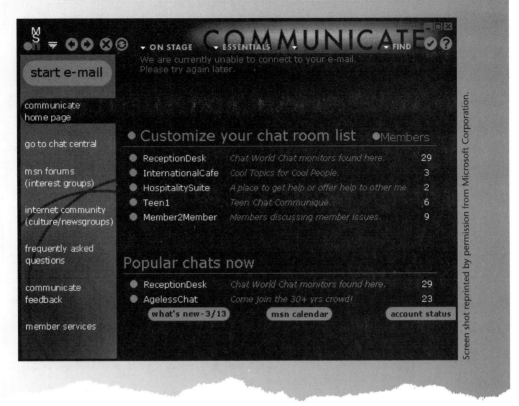

Screen shot reprinted by permission from Microsoft Corporation.

Using Commercial ActiveX Controls

At the end of Chapter 2, you'll find a detailed description of how to download and register commercial ActiveX controls. But here's a sneak peek if you want to take a look at what's currently available.

Microsoft's ActiveX Component Gallery is the first place to look. You'll find a select list of sites from which you can download demos and even purchase ActiveX controls. These controls have been checked for viruses and are digitally signed (see Chapter 15) to verify that they won't wreak havoc on your computer when you download them for testing. Nor will they cause problems for other people who access your Web page after you've included the control.

Scroll the List of Available Controls

Start Internet Explorer and locate Microsoft's ActiveX Component Gallery:

```
http://www.microsoft.com/activex/controls
```

You'll see a list of the partner sites, as shown in Figure 1-3.

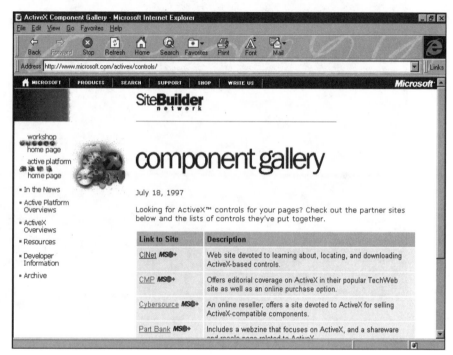

Figure 1-3   Microsoft displays a list of partner sites that contain many ActiveX control demos as well as controls for sale.

At the partner ActiveX control sites, you'll find download instructions for each control.

When you request a download from the Internet, you're sometimes asked if you want to *run* or *save* the control. If you're given this choice, it's generally best to save it to your disk. Then open Windows Explorer and double-click the file to install it. However, if you choose to download an ActiveX control from a Microsoft partner site, you'll be instead presented with an *Authenticode* certificate, as shown in Figure 1-4. It certifies that the control is safe to use, that it contains no virus and is guaranteed clean by the manufacturer. *You*, though, must complete the authentication process by clicking the two links provided within the certificate. They are supposed to take you to an Internet site supported by the manufacturer of the control, then to the company (such as VeriSign) that provides the authentication. If they don't, hit the deck!

When you're satisfied that a control is authentic, click the button labeled Yes and the control is added to your hard drive and also displayed.

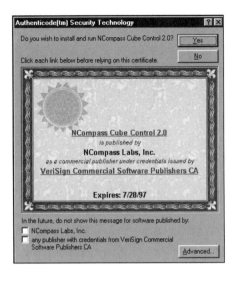

Figure 1-4 This certificate helps the user avoid damage from viruses.

A *working sample* isn't yours for free. Generally it only works until a specified date, can't be incorporated into your own Web pages, or perhaps lacks a feature or two. It's like shareware — you can try it out, but if you want to use it in your own Internet Web pages, you'll have to pay for the commercial version of the control. The sample version just lets you see all the cool things the control does.

Running It Registers It

After the control is downloaded and run, you'll find that it has been *registered* on your computer. This means that Windows 95 or NT has added it to the list of controls you can plug into Web documents.

A set of ActiveX controls is automatically added to your hard drive when you install the ActiveX Control Pad. Other ActiveX controls are downloaded when you visit a Web page where one of them is being used (Internet Explorer saves such a control to your hard drive while displaying that Web page). And yet other sets of controls or insertable objects are installed when you set up Microsoft Office, Internet Explorer, Visual Basic Control Creation Edition, Visual Basic 5.0 and other applications.

Here's how to see what ActiveX controls are currently registered on your computer:

1. Start the ActiveX Control Pad running.

2. Click **Edit** on the menu bar and then click **Insert ActiveX Control**. The dialog shown in Figure 1-5 pops up.

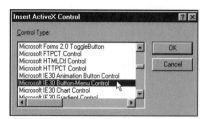

Figure 1-5 This dialog box displays a list of all ActiveX controls available on your computer.

3. Scroll through the list to see all the ActiveX controls available for your use.

BONUS

How Controls Get to the User

If you're technically inclined, you might be asking yourself, Just how does an ActiveX control get to the user? Assume that you decide to include, in one of your Web pages, the ActiveX address-entry control we built earlier in this chapter. Then some stranger, while surfing the Web, comes upon your Web page. How does that address control get from your Web site onto the user's hard drive? And why does the ActiveX control have to be on the user's hard drive anyway?

The Great Divide

In computers — as in real life — things can be divided into two states: information and action. Another way of expressing this division is *qualities* versus *behaviors* or *data* versus *processing*. You see this partitioning everywhere. For example, open a cookbook and look at most any recipe. You'll see a list of ingredients (the data) followed by the steps you take (the processing) that turn the data, the apples, sugar, butter, and flour into a steaming pie.

This same division occurs when you create a Web page. HTML, the language that is used to create Internet Web pages, is known as a *page-description language*. Most of the commands in HTML are merely related to formatting and are thus pure data (not processing). The HTML command <FONT SIZE =6> specifies that text should be a larger font size than 3, the default body text size in HTML. This is quite similar to the data instructions in a recipe: 1/2 stick butter. This is pure data; it doesn't *do* anything (like melt the butter). It merely describes an entity that will later be acted upon (whipped into the flour, in a food processor).

HTML, then, contains many instructions that describe size, position, color and the raw text that will eventually be sized, positioned and colored (by the user's browser) before it is displayed in a Web page. However, very few HTML instructions describe an actual *behavior*. About the only action you'll find available in the HTML command set is one that starts a piece of text feebly blinking.

If you want interactivity, multimedia, *action* — you'll have to go beyond HTML to programming languages like Java and VBScript, or to ActiveX controls.

When a Control Is Requested

What, technically, happens when Internet Explorer (IE) finds an ActiveX control embedded within a Web page? If a user is maneuvering around the Web and comes to a page containing an ActiveX control (or several), IE immediately looks in the user's Registry to see if the control is already available on the user's hard drive. If the control is found, IE goes ahead and starts the control running on the user's machine and displays the page. If the control is a marquee, then text begins scrolling through it. If the control displays video, then a little TV clip starts running for the user to watch.

TIP **The Registry is a huge database of information about a computer's peripherals, applications, user preferences and other details about the configuration of the machine. The Registry is Windows 95's and Windows NT's replacement for the SYSTEM.INI, WIN.INI and miscellaneous other .INI files in previous versions of Windows.**

If a control is not registered, IE goes out onto the Web and locates it and, right then, installs the control on the user's computer. A few controls, though, may be installed automatically when IE itself (or another application) is installed. These controls can come with IE: Label, Marquee, Menu, Popup Menu, Popup Window, Preloader, Stock Ticker and Timer. (Which controls are installed with IE depends on which version of IE you're using.) But most ActiveX controls have to be downloaded the first time the user comes upon a Web page containing the control.

When you insert an ActiveX control into a Web page that you're designing, you specify the location of the control with the CodeBase property of that control. If you start the ActiveX Control Pad running, and then choose Insert ActiveX Control from the Edit menu, you'll see a Properties window displayed after you've chosen the control you're interested in. In the Properties window you can select CodeBase and type in the location (or several locations). In other words, you provide a URL (Uniform Resource Locator), an Internet address, where your control can be found. This is just as if you were adding a link to a Web page that the user could click. However, the user never sees the CodeBase address. The browser automatically contacts that address and downloads the control.

Local Control Is Superior

Why does a control have to be stored on the user's hard drive, anyway? In fact, it doesn't. Until Java and ActiveX, interactivity on a Web page consisted of messages sent back and forth between the user's browser and the Web page's server. Perhaps a map of the USA was displayed. The user clicks California. The coordinates of that click within the map graphic are then messaged back to the server, where the identity of California is calculated. Then some text describing California is messaged back to the user's browser. This is a rather a messy arrangement and quite time-consuming.

This approach is inefficient in several ways. It's difficult to write programs that require messaging. Local response (it all takes place within the user's computer) is both faster and simpler. In the next chapter, for example, you'll see how easy it is to divide a graphic into zones that respond *locally* to user-clicking. Microsoft has come up with a HotSpot control that you can just place onto a graphic. The coordinates are calculated for you automatically. You, the Web page designer, merely drag the controls around to size and position them. Everything else is handled for you by the controls themselves.

Repetitive communication between a Web site on a server and the user's computer is inherently cumbersome, particularly when graphics are involved (as they increasingly are). So the solution is to download controls that can be run — at high speed — within the user's computer. And, as a bonus, a control only has to be downloaded once. Most of them are compact for quick transfer.

The Danger of Viruses

 What about viruses? Security issues are covered in depth in Chapter 15, but IE includes some defenses against a poisonous ActiveX control. Sure, HTML is a mere page-description language — capable of displaying text and little else. But at least it's harmless. An ActiveX control, by contrast, could easily be designed by some venomous programmer to trash the user's hard drive. By default, IE displays a message when a new ActiveX control is about to be downloaded. (The user can change this precautionary measure by selecting Options from IE's View menu, then clicking the Security tab.) At that point the user has the option of refusing the download.

Where Are They Stored?

Finally, where are ActiveX controls stored? You'll find those that were downloaded over the Internet in the \Windows\Occache directory. Others are built into files that come with IE, versions of Visual Basic, Microsoft Office applications, or other sources.

Summary

This chapter covered the basics of ActiveX. You learned how to use the ActiveX Control Pad to insert controls into a Web page, and how to load and test controls within a browser. You also found out how to examine Web pages created by other people, how to deploy third-party ActiveX controls, and what happens when a control must be sent over the Internet to a user's computer. In the next chapter, you'll find an in-depth discussion on how to use the valuable set of controls that come free with Microsoft's ActiveX Control Pad, and other controls that are available from third-party control developers.

THE STANDARD CONTROL SET

This chapter provides an overview of ActiveX controls. You'll find out how to use the set of 13 controls that come with the ActiveX Control Pad. These controls provide what Microsoft considers to be the essentials for creating useful, highly interactive Web pages.

You'll also learn how to add additional controls to the Layout control's Toolbox. Then the doors will be thrown open to the hundreds of third-party ActiveX controls. You'll find out where to locate them, how to be sure they're virus-free, and how to evaluate them.

The Thirteen Standard Controls

In the Quick Tour, you saw where to locate and how to run Microsoft's ActiveX Control Pad. Start it up again so that you can take a closer look at each of the controls that come with the Control Pad. They are the basic controls, the ones you'll use most often when adding interactivity to your Web pages. Not only that, most of these controls are the same as the basic set of controls supplied with Microsoft's other ActiveX programming tools: the Visual Basic Control Creation Edition (VBCCE) and Visual Basic 5.0. So if you intend to work — at whatever level — with ActiveX, or Windows programming in general, you'll find that taking a close-up look at this set of controls will prove useful.

Follow these steps to get the ActiveX Control Pad Toolbox up and running:

1. Start the ActiveX Control Pad.

2. Click File → New HTML Layout (or press Ctrl+E).

You'll see the Layout control and Toolbox shown in Figure 2-1.

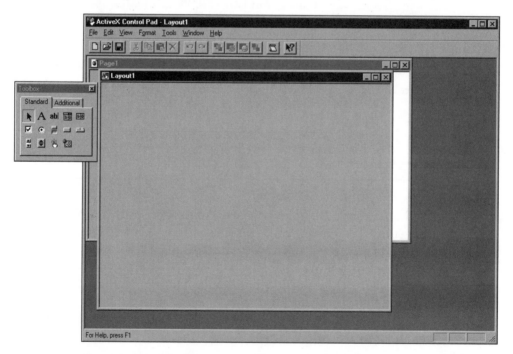

Figure 2-1 When you choose New HTML Layout, the ActiveX Control Pad displays both a blank Layout and the default Toolbox.

Now to see the qualities and uses for each of the built-in controls.

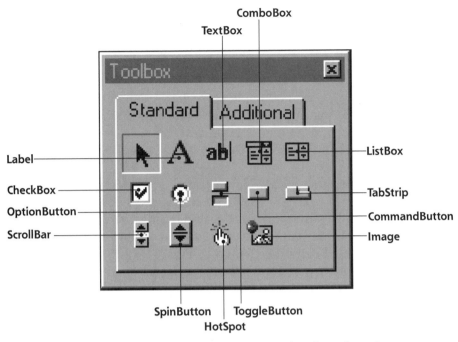

Figure 2-2 These 13 controls might be all you'll need for most of your Web page work.

Displaying Longer Segments of Text

There are two Text controls supplied with the ActiveX Control Pad Layout control. Unlike the List controls described in the next section, use the Text controls when you want to show the user phrases, sentences or longer pieces of text.

Use the Label to describe the purpose of other controls, or otherwise inform the user about zones or elements in your document. The user cannot change the text in a Label. Label text is read-only. When you want to display large amounts of text, or allow the user to enter or edit text, use the TextBox.

Label Controls Describe Other Controls

Use the Label control to present instructions to the user, descriptions of other controls, and captions for graphics. To insert a Label into the Layout control, click the Label icon in the Toolbox, then drag the mouse pointer on the Layout control to position and size the Label. (For more details about creating Label controls, see the Quick Tour at the beginning of the book.)

TIP If you want to clone a control, click a control in the Layout to select that control (a gray frame will appear around the selected control). Then press Ctrl+C to copy the control and press Ctrl+V to paste the clone. The clone will have the same properties as the original (it will be the same size, have the same caption, and so on).

Labels have the usual set of modifiable properties common to most controls: BackColor, Caption, ForeColor (for text), Font, Height and Width, Left and Top (for position on the Layout), Picture (to display an icon or other graphic within the Label), TabIndex (when the user repeatedly presses the Tab key to cycle the focus through the controls on the Layout), and Visible.

In addition, there are some specialized properties available in the Label control: AutoSize (should the Label size itself so it frames the caption?), BackStyle (should the color of the Layout or any background on the Layout show through the Label, or be covered by the Label?), PicturePosition (where, in relation to the caption, should a graphic be displayed?), SpecialEffect (what kind of border — see Figure 2-3), and WordWrap (if a caption is longer than the Label's Width property, should part of it appear on the next line?).

Here's how easy it is to adjust the Label control's border appearance:

1. Double-click a Label on the Layout. This brings up the Properties window.

2. Scroll in the Properties window until you locate the SpecialEffect property.

3. Click the drop-down ComboBox at the top of the Properties window to see all five border options: Flat, Raised, Sunken, Etched and Bump.

4. Click whichever option you want.

There are five possible border effects for a Label, as shown in Figure 2-3.

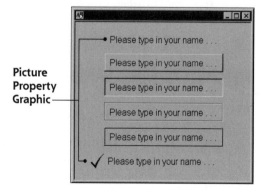

Picture Property Graphic

Figure 2-3 You can choose between these five SpecialEffects properties, and also add a Picture property (bottom).

A TextBox Is a Mini-Word Processor

The TextBox is your all-purpose user-input device — you can let users enter data as brief as a one-letter abbreviation or as lengthy as their life story. TextBoxes are mini-word processors. They feature automatic word wrap (if you set their MultiLine Property to True). However, you or the user cannot make any interior formatting changes; whichever font, font size or font style, such as italic, is used applies to *all* characters within that entire TextBox.

TIP MultiLine is one of the most important Properties of a TextBox. If set to the default single-line setting, no matter how much the user types in, the text will all be placed onto a single, scrolling line. Pressing the Enter key will simply shift the focus to the next control in the TabIndex list (see the next Tip below). However, if you change the MultiLine Property by clicking it in the Properties Window, a new line is created each time the user presses the Enter key. What's more, when the user's typing reaches the right side of the TextBox, additional typing will automatically wrap down and continue on the next line. (It's supposed to work this way, but at the time of this writing, there's a bug: Pressing the Enter key shifts the focus to the next control on the Layout. Only the Tab key is actually supposed to shift focus. The Enter key is currently working incorrectly.)

X-REF In Chapter 8, you'll learn how to extract and examine whatever the user types into a TextBox.

However, at this point you should understand some of the significant Properties of the TextBox that allow you to modify the way it behaves. The AutoSize Property determines whether the TextBox will automatically resize itself to frame the text it contains. This effect can be unsettling to the user and is therefore rarely used. AutoSize defaults to False.

The AutoTab Property, though, is often useful for data entry. With AutoTab set to True, the input cursor (the focus) automatically moves to the next control once the maximum number of characters (as defined by the MaxLength Property) have been typed into a TextBox. For example, if the user is to enter a phone number, you might arrange three TextBoxes in a row, providing the punctuation by using Labels (see Figure 2-4) and displaying the correct spacing. All the user then has to do is type in the digits.

Here's how to use the MaxLength and AutoTab Properties to provide an efficient user-input device:

1. Start the ActiveX Control Pad.

2. Click Edit → Insert HTML Layout . In the Filename box, type **Phone**. Click OK to close the dialog window.

3. Click the icon in the ActiveX Control Pad to open the new Layout.

4. Click the TextBox icon in the Toolbox and draw a TextBox onto the Layout.

5. Repeat twice so you have three TextBoxes lined up as shown in Figure 2-4.

6. Add four Label controls. The first displays the "Please enter . . ." instructions and the remaining three display the ( ) and - punctuation.

Figure 2-4 Make things easy on the user with the AutoTab property.

Set each of the TextBox controls' AutoTab properties to True. Set the first two TextBoxes' MaxLength properties to 3. Click the x icon in the upper right corner of the Layout to close the Layout.

Now, to test this document in your Web browser, choose Save from the File menu and save the .HTM file as PHONE.HTM. Run the Internet Explorer and choose Open from the File menu. Load the PHONE.HTM file and try typing your phone number. You'll notice that as soon as you finish typing the three-digit area code, the input cursor jumps to the next TextBox so you can continue typing the phone number. This not only makes things easier for the user, it makes life easier for you as well. You don't have to worry that users might punctuate their phone numbers in various ways — causing you headaches when you try to store them in a database or otherwise manipulate them.

TIP Most controls on a Layout become part of a list. This list is ordered according to each control's TabIndex property. The TabIndex list describes the order in which the controls receive the focus if the user repeatedly presses the Tab key to cycle among the controls. Having the *focus* means that the control will react to any typing as the user presses keys on the keyboard. For example, there are three TextBoxes in Figure 2-4. The TextBox with the focus at any given time will be the one that displays any typed characters. You can change the TabIndex number for any control. When the example above was created, three TextBoxes were placed on the Layout in order, and the ActiveX Control Pad automatically assigned sequential TabIndex properties to each TextBox.

The AutoWordSelect property determines whether a user-selection jumps word by word or only character by character. *Selection* means that the user is highlighting some text for later cutting or copying. By default, AutoWordSelect is set to True, causing the highlighted zone to leap from word to word when the user presses the Shift+arrow key or drags the mouse.

The EnterFieldBehavior property by default causes the entire contents to be selected if the user tabs to a TextBox. You can, however, change this property so that a previously selected portion of the text will remain selected when the TextBox is tabbed to. Often this will mean that no text is selected (because the last time the user was working with this TextBox, no text had been selected).

When Data Is in Pieces

Sometimes the most useful way to present information to a user is in a list. Perhaps you want to enable the user to see a collection of brief items of information. Or perhaps you want to let the user select a subset of brief items. In either situation, the ListBox or ComboBox are the controls of choice.

ComboBoxes Have Two Styles

The ComboBox and ListBox controls are similar. Both controls display a list of items from which the user can choose. The main difference between the two controls is that a ComboBox saves screen space because it doesn't display its contents until the user clicks it to drop it down. A ComboBox only takes up the space on screen of a single item. A ListBox, however, doesn't drop down; it always remains the same size — its height when you created it.

ComboBoxes come in two styles, which are determined by the Style property. The default style, DropDownCombo, enables the user to type something into the small TextBox at the top. This way, the user isn't forced to choose only from the items you've placed into the list. For example, if you provide a ComboBox filled with the names of all the countries in the world, the user might want to type in a name that's not on the list. Perhaps the user's country changed its name or divided into two countries. With the ComboBox's Style property set to DropDownList, the user cannot type anything into the ComboBox.

As you can see in Figure 2-5, the user can type Choice #22 into the DropDown-style ComboBox on the left. The list only contains choices up to #10, but a DropDown style ComboBox enables the user to create a new item. The DropDownList-style ComboBox in the middle of Figure 2-5 permits the user to choose only from Choices 1-10, as does the ListBox on the right.

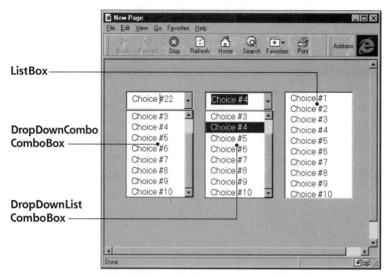

ListBox

DropDownCombo
ComboBox

DropDownList
ComboBox

Figure 2-5 Left to right: A DropDownCombo ComboBox,
a DropDownList ComboBox and a plain ListBox.

How to Fill Boxes with Data

If you're curious, you can fill Combo- and ListBoxes with items by using VBScript to program the contents.

From Chapter 8 to the end of the book, you'll find extensive information on Visual Basic programming.

Here's a brief preview of VB programming. Be sure that you've got two ComboBoxes and a ListBox on your Layout, then right-click the Layout control and choose Script Wizard. Double-click Layout1 in the Select an Event list, then choose OnLoad. (If you've named the Layout control something other than the default *Layout1*, double-click your new name for it.) In the Insert Actions list, double-click ComboBox1 and double-click Font, then double-click Size. When asked to enter a value, type **12** then click OK. Click OK to close the Script Wizard.

Right-click the Layout again and choose View Source Code. The message `Viewing the source code will cause your current layout changes to be saved, and the layout to be closed. Do you wish to continue?` appears at this point. Choose *Yes*. Windows Notepad will open, displaying the HTML programming that describes your Web page. You'll see `<SCRIPT LANGUAGE="VBScript">` followed by the assignment of a FontSize to ComboBox1. Add the VBScript programming shown in boldface to the programming that's already there. When finished, choose Save from Notepad's File menu.

```
<SCRIPT LANGUAGE="VBScript">

Sub Layout1_OnLoad()

ComboBox1.FontSize = 12
ComboBox2.FontSize = 12
ListBox1.FontSize = 12

For i = 1 to 10
ListBox1.AddItem "Choice #" & i
ComboBox1.AddItem "Choice #" & i
ComboBox2.AddItem "Choice #" & i
Next
end sub
</SCRIPT>
```

The source code is a mixture of HTML and VBScript. Only those lines between the <SCRIPT LANGUAGE> and </SCRIPT> tags is VBScript. Note also that you can either assign 12 as the FontSize here in the programming code, or just use the Properties Window for each Box while viewing the Layout. If the Properties Window isn't visible, double-click one of the Boxes.

With the code between For i = 1 to 10 and Next you're telling VBScript to add 10 items to the ListBox and both ComboBoxes. The programming will *loop* ten times, carrying out the AddItem commands each time through the loop. (VBScript interprets the *Next* command to mean: Go back up to the *For* command and repeat this list of commands until the variable *i* has reached 10. When the For . . .Next loop repeats, it automatically increments the variable *i*.

TIP **If you're working on an .HTM document, you have probably used your browser to test the document, as discussed in Chapter 1. You can load it into Internet Explorer by choosing Open from the File menu. Then try out the various features. Next you might want to make some changes to the programming (such as including the AddItem commands in the previous example). After you make some changes, save your edited program by choosing Save in Notepad's File menu. Recall that you can quickly test changes you made by clicking the Refresh button in Internet Explorer (or by pressing F5). This will reload and display the latest version of your page, including your recent changes.**

Using the ColumnCount, ColumnHeads and ColumnWidths properties, you can create Combo- or ListBoxes with more than one list. This way, you have the option of displaying data in a grid, the way it appears in a spreadsheet.

The MatchEntry property of Combo- and ListBoxes determines whether or how the user's typing will affect the selected item within the Box. For example, by default the Box watches each character as it is typed and continually moves the selection to the closest match within the Box to what the user is typing. You can change this property by setting it to FirstLetter, which matches only the first character typed. Repeated typing of that character will cycle through all items that begin with that letter. Or you can set the property to None, no matching at all. Because Windows users are accustomed to the default matching behavior, it's best to leave the MatchEntry Property set to its default. Similarly, you should generally leave the AutoSize, DropButtonStyle, HideSelection, ListStyle and MatchRequired properties set to their defaults as well. (The ListBox doesn't have all these properties.) Their defaults are, not coincidentally, the generic Windows defaults. Unless you have a compelling reason to adjust these Properties, leave them set to the default. Users almost always prefer that controls behave the same way in all applications, including Web pages.

Let Them Click

For many users, particularly when they are surfing the Web, the mouse is always in their hand. Clicking is easier by far than typing. So whenever possible, do the typing for them by providing labels, lists or other data. Then let the user simply make a choice by clicking. Among the most useful of the controls that let users efficiently express their preferences are CheckBoxes and OptionButtons.

OptionButtons Are Mutually Exclusive

The CheckBox and OptionButton controls enable the user to make selections, and see those selections graphically. A selected CheckBox contains a small check and a selected OptionButton contains a black dot.

The difference between these controls is that the items in a set of OptionButtons are mutually exclusive. Only one OptionButton can be selected. If the user clicks another OptionButton, the currently selected one is deselected. By contrast, users can select as many CheckBoxes as they wish. To see this distinction, take a look at Figure 2-6. Text can only be one color, so the OptionButtons are useful in limiting the user to one choice. Text styles, though, can be combined, so it's possible that more than one of the CheckBoxes can be selected at a time. In Figure 2-6, the user has chosen bold, italics, and all caps.

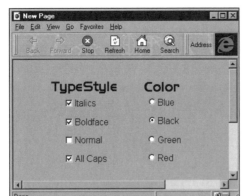

Figure 2-6 CheckBoxes (left) enable as many selections as the user wishes, but with OptionButtons (right), only one item at a time can be selected.

 TIP What if you want to create more than a single group of OptionButtons on the same Web page? By default, all OptionButtons that you place on a Layout will be in the same group — the user clicks one button, and the button that was previously selected will be automatically deselected. Only one OptionButton at a time in a group can be selected. But what if you want to permit the user to choose the FontColor (see Figure 2-6) and, on the same Layout, choose the FontSize? FontSize, like FontColor, is a mutually exclusive quality. The typeface cannot simultaneously be 12 points and 44 points in size any more than it can be both red and black.

You can create separate OptionButton groups by using the GroupName Property. Every time you add an OptionButton to a Layout, the ActiveX Control Pad automatically gives it an empty, default GroupName. This makes all these OptionButtons part of the same group. But if you give several OptionButtons a GroupName in common (such as "ColorGroup," or whatever name you want to use), they will then become part of a separate group. In other words, the user can then select two OptionButtons: one that specifies the user's desired text color (FontColor) and another that specifies the desired type size (FontSize).

ToggleButtons Are CheckBoxes in Disguise

The ToggleButton control is relatively new to the Windows environment. It probably won't last long; it's unlikely to ever become part of the standard set of controls. Why not? The ToggleButton is one of those confounding objects that looks like one thing, but behaves like something else. The ToggleButton looks like a CommandButton, but it behaves like a CheckBox. What's the point? This kind of thing can confuse users. You've already got the functionality of CommandButtons and CheckBoxes. Why this blending of the two? What does the ToggleButton bring to the table that those other two controls don't? Nothing.

When the user clicks a ToggleButton, it remains visually depressed (in the same way that a CheckBox displays a check icon when clicked). This signals to the user that the control is activated. If the control represents italics, then italics are in effect. When the user clicks a ToggleButton a second time, it pops back out and is no longer activated.

TIP TripleState is a new Property of the OptionButton, CheckBox, and ToggleButton controls. It permits a control to exist in three states. For example, by default, the TripleState property is set to False. In that situation, a CheckBox has two states: a check icon, signaling that the Box's Value Property is set to True, or no check, indicating that the Value Property is set to False. However, if you change the TripleState Property to True, that CheckBox now has three states: True, False, and Null. The Null state means that whatever the CheckBox represents is out of context or inappropriate. For instance, a CheckBox representing boldface would be True or False while the user was typing in a TextBox, but would become Null if the user began drawing within a graphic image. The user can click a control that is in the TripleState three times, cycling through the three possible states. Or you can use programming to assign True, False, or Null to the control (CheckBox1.Value = True). Figure 2-7 illustrates that there are four states for these controls. The Disabled state means that if the user clicks the control, the click has no effect. (You disable a control by setting its Enabled property to False.)

Figure 2-7 The TripleState property enables these controls to signal four states: True, False, Null, and Disabled.

CommandButtons Are Useful for Nearly Everything

The CommandButton is Windows's general-purpose control. To the user, it means "click me and something will happen." Typically, on Web pages, you'll see a CommandButton next to a group of TextBoxes. Users type in their name and address, or some other information, then click a CommandButton captioned *Submit* to send the information back to the Web page's author. As you can see in Figure 2-8, CommandButtons can include icons or other graphics. Set the Picture Property to whatever graphic you want, then click the PicturePostion Property to decide where, in relation to the caption, you want the graphic to appear. In Figure 2-8, PicturePosition is set to LeftCenter.

Of the various qualities of the CommandButton, perhaps the one that makes it so popular with programmers and users alike is its animation. When the user clicks, the CommandButton is visually depressed. When the user releases the mouse button, the CommandButton pops back out. CommandButtons look and behave like buttons in the real world. You'll find the CommandButton quite useful when you want to give the user the option to initiate an action.

Figure 2-8 CommandButtons are all-purpose action controls. When the user clicks one, something is going to happen.

An Efficient User-Input Device

A TabStrip control is a useful user-input device. It's a way of organizing a lot of information within a small space. TabStrips are metaphors for a 3x5-card file: The user clicks a tab and is presented with a new "card" of options.

TabStrips for Customization

In general, the TabStrip control is used when you want to enable the user to customize or set personal preferences. In that sense, the TabStrip is similar to the Properties window in the ActiveX Control Pad. However, a TabStrip has the advantage of enabling you to group options into various categories. Figure 2-9 shows the TabStrip that is displayed when the user asks to customize Word 97 in the Options menu.

So far, the TabStrip has rarely been used in Web pages, but this control is quite popular in general Windows applications and utilities. When you select Options from their View or Tools menu, many applications display a TabStrip.

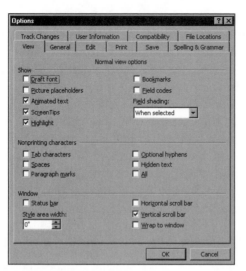

Figure 2-9 TabStrips display many options using an efficient, organized cardfile metaphor.

You program a TabStrip by putting CheckBoxes, ListBoxes and other controls onto the TabStrip control. Then, when the user clicks a tab, you set the Visible property to True for the set of controls that is intended to be seen when that tab is active. Simultaneously, you set the Visible property of all the other controls' to False. For example, if you want only CommandButton1 to be visible when the first tab is clicked, and only CommandButton2 visible when the second tab is clicked, here's how you would program that:

```
<SCRIPT LANGUAGE="VBScript">
<!—
Sub TabStrip1_Click(Index)

If Index = 0 then
CommandButton1.Visible = True
CommandButton2.Visible = False
End If

If Index = 1 then
CommandButton1.Visible = False
CommandButton2.Visible = True
End If

end sub

</SCRIPT>
```

TIP To change or set a tab's Caption property, you use the Tabs collection (much more about collections later in this book). For now, it's enough that you know how to program the Caption property of each Tab:

```
TabStrip1(0).Caption = "First"
TabStrip1(1).Caption = "Second"
```

Notice that the first Tab is referred to as the *zero*th one in the collection of Tabs; the second Tab is 1, and so on.

Put All Controls onto the Same TabStrip Surface

Notice that you pile *all* controls for *all* tabs onto the TabStrip. Then you set the Visible property of each control to False, except for the controls you want to appear on Tab 1. (Notice that a TabStrip isn't a *container* for other controls in the sense that a Layout control contains other controls. Controls placed on a TabStrip are merely *visually* contained. These other controls won't move if you drag the TabStrip.)

Tab 1 is the tab that the user will always see first. When the user clicks another tab within an If...Then structure, you make visible the appropriate controls and hide all the rest. Remember, too, that the Index parameter begins counting with 0 — so the first tab's Index is 0, the second tab's Index is 1 and so on. This zeroth indexing was illustrated previously in the code that demonstrated how to set the Caption properties of a collection of Tabs.

The TabStrip control has a TabOrientation property. It enables you to move the tabs from their expected location (the top) to the right, left or bottom of the control. Also, there's a Style property that enables you to replace the tabs with buttons that look like small ToggleButtons. One of the buttons is always depressed, just as one tab always appears on top of the other tabs — to indicate the currently active page. It's difficult to imagine why you'd ever want to move the tabs to a different orientation, or transform them into buttons. Either maneuver on your part would effectively destroy the useful and familiar visual cardfile metaphor. The only example that comes to mind is a large window with the tabstrip(s) along the bottom, such as in Excel. In any case, if you want to rearrange the tabs, the TabStrip control gives you the option.

Analog Controls Feel Right

Much of the power of Windows and other graphical computer environments derives from analogies to the real world. Purely *digital* environments are computer-friendly, but humans resist simple, cold, binary, black-and-white environments. We want a visually stimulating, colorful milieu. Animation, sound and *analog* controls are powerful stimulants. They're simply more real to us.

Let's say the computer needs to know how many years you've lived at your current address. You could type the digit **4**. That's how you would have answered that question in the blackboard-and-chalk world of DOS. In Windows, though, there are analog objects like SpinButtons that you can click until a 4 is displayed. This approach is more real to us. After all, if you set your kitchen timer to 4 minutes, you don't reach for a typewriter keyboard and type in the digit 4. Instead, you twist a dial on the timer until you reach 4.

Digital keypads *are* making incursions. You'll find keypads on such appliances as dryers and dishwashers. Nearly all microwave ovens require digital user input. But most of the time we work with analog controls. And some analog controls will always be with us. A car's steering wheel will forever provide superior feedback to any digital replacement we could possibly think up.

What's the moral of all this? When you're designing a Windows application or a Web page, and you need information from the user, consider an alternative to their typing something into the keyboard. Perhaps you could display a set of choices in a ListBox that they could click (the computer equivalent of touching). Or you could let them choose between a group of OptionButtons or CheckBoxes. If the choices are in a series — such as the number of years the user has lived at a particular address — you could display the analog SpinButton control and let them hold down the mouse button until the right answer appears. In other words, avoid always requiring that your user type data into TextBoxes. Remember, most users, most of the time, have their hand on the mouse.

ScrollBars and SpinButtons Illustrate Their State

The ScrollBar is the familiar sliding scroll box (the small tab or *thumb* as it's sometimes called) that the user can click or drag to move, for example, through some text that's too long to display all at once in a TextBox window. In Windows, the scroll box within a ScrollBar visually gives the user two items of information. The scroll box's position within the ScrollBar is analogous to the user's current position within the large document. The scroll box's size reveals the percentage of the entire document that is currently displayed (if the scroll box fills half the ScrollBar, the user is viewing half the document).

ScrollBars are sometimes built into a control. If you adjust the ScrollBars property of a TextBox, ScrollBars will automatically be added, as necessary, to the TextBox. If the Text property of the TextBox contains a piece of text that will all fit within the TextBox, no ScrollBar appears. However, if the text is too big, a ScrollBar is placed on the right side or along the bottom of the box.

There is, though, a stand-alone ScrollBar control that you can use. It's rarely done, but you can put a separate ScrollBar onto a Web page or other ActiveX application. It could then be used to page through a set of graphics or, perhaps, enable the user to maneuver a graphic that was larger than the window that contained it.

The SpinButton Is Most Useful

More useful, however, is the SpinButton. When you want to give the user a tool to adjust items in a series, such as the time, use a SpinButton. For instance, if you were selling real estate on your Web site, you could put up a Label reading

"Years Old" and under that put a SpinButton that users could adjust to indicate the oldest house they are willing to consider.

To see how a SpinButton works, follow these steps:

1. Start the ActiveX Control Pad.

2. Click Edit → Insert HTML Layout or press Ctrl+E. Give the new Layout any name you wish.

3. Click its icon on the left side of the ActiveX Control Pad to open the Layout.

4. Click the SpinButton control, then click the Layout control, to add a SpinButton to the Layout.

5. Follow the same procedure to add a Label control to the Layout.

6. Right-click the Layout and choose Script Wizard.

7. In the Event list, double-click SpinButton1, then click SpinDown.

8. In the Insert Actions list double-click Label1, then double-click Caption. Type **SpinButton1**. Click OK on both OK buttons to close the window.

9. Right-click the Layout and choose View Source Code. Remove the " " marks around SpinButton1, and also create a similar Sub for the SpinUp event as well. Your final script should look like the following:

```
<SCRIPT LANGUAGE="VBScript">
<!-
Sub SpinButton1_SpinDown()
Label1.Caption = SpinButton1
end sub

Sub SpinButton1_SpinUp()
Label1.Caption = SpinButton1
end sub
->
</SCRIPT>
```

10. Save the edited Script by clicking File → Save .

11. Now load Page1.Htm (or whatever you've named your .Htm file) into Internet Explorer (see Figure 2-10) and try clicking the SpinButton and watch the Label indicate how old a house must be to interest the user.

Figure 2-10 A SpinButton is useful when the user needs to select from items in a series — such as minutes, years, or dollars.

TIP Notice in the previous VBScript code that every time the user clicks the SpinButton, the script reacts by assigning SpinButton1 to the Label's Caption. You could just as easily assign the Value, like this:

```
Label1.Caption = SpinButton1.Value
```

However, each control has a default Property. If you don't mention the property, VBScript assumes that you mean the default. For a SpinButton, the default property is Value, so you can omit it. And, in fact, the default for the Label is the Caption. So you could use this shorthand: `Label1 = SpinButton1`.

Graphic Controls Are Best

Whenever possible, you should try to provide visual cues to the user. Raging nerds are, of course, always ready and happy to interact with a computer on the computer's terms. The computer likes hexadecimal arithmetic, so a "real programmer" learns that strange math and is glad to type it into a TextBox. But most people would prefer to avoid learning a whole new set of rules or a whole new language or number system, just to be able to make a machine do what they want it to do. Most people would rather choose a color by clicking on a visual rainbow of colors than by typing in #245,111,110. Whenever possible, don't describe the options, *show* them, and let the user *point and click* to make a selection.

Image and HotSpot Controls Work Together

Sometimes you'll want to display a graphic to the user, then allow a click somewhere within the graphic to initiate an action. For example, a travel agency might display a map of the Caribbean and allow users to click the islands they're interested in visiting. Another common technique is to display a row of buttons (they're all part of a single graphic; see in Figure 2-11) that each produce a different reaction.

In plain HTML this technique is cumbersome. It involves complex coordinate definitions and the inefficiency of using the MAP and AREA commands to send information about the user's click back to the home page server. However, thanks to ActiveX controls and VBScript, the process of creating hot spots on graphics is greatly simplified.

In the example Layout control shown in Figure 2-11, the four buttons are in a single .BMP graphic that's been loaded into the PicturePath Property of an Image control. (You can find collections of buttons on the Internet. Just choose *Search the Web* on Internet Explorer's Go menu. To save graphics that you've found on Web pages to your hard drive, choose Save As File from Internet Explorer's File menu.)

Figure 2-11   Place HotSpot controls over any zone within a graphic, or even over other controls.

A Label control is positioned next to each button, describing the category that will be displayed if the user clicks that button. Finally, a HotSpot control surrounds each button-Label pair — so the user can click either on the button graphic or the associated Label to trigger an appropriate response. You can see the highlights around all four HotSpots in Figure 2-11. The HotSpots won't be visible when the user loads your Web page into a browser, but the HotSpots *will* react to clicks.

After you've created your HotSpots, you can then program VBScript to react when the user clicks a particular HotSpot. For example, you could display a message in a TextBox if the user clicks the button labeled *Luxury* in Figure 2-11.

```
Sub HotSpot3_Click()
TextBox1 = "We have a wide selection of luxury vehicles..."
End Sub
```

Image Controls Efficiently Display Graphics

The Image control is also useful whenever you want to display an ordinary graphic. It is significantly superior to the graphics display features of plain HTML. For one thing, an Image can display four graphics file types: .GIF and .JPG (like HTML), but also .WMF and .BMP types. Also, you can easily size or position an Image control on a Layout, so it will be just where you want it. Also, built into the Image control are several useful features. It has a PictureTiling

Property that will repeat a graphic within the Image, filling it the same way that the wallpaper tiling feature can fill the desktop in Windows.

The PictureSizeMode property, when set to Zoom (the default), will stretch or shrink the graphic to fit the Image control's height or width — no matter what size you've made them. However, the aspect ratio of the graphic will be maintained, so it doesn't look distorted and stretched. When set to Clip, the graphic will be chopped off if it's larger than the dimensions of the Image control. Finally, when set to Stretch, the graphic will be made to fit the dimensions of the Image control, even if it distorts the graphic.

BONUS

Try Commercial Controls

There are hundreds of ActiveX controls out there. However, Microsoft maintains an ActiveX Component Gallery that includes links to partner sites with over 100 controls at the time of this writing. Various companies have contributed one or more of their controls that you can try out as demos. The reason that there aren't several thousand ActiveX demos is that only those that have been *digitally signed* are permitted to be listed at these sites. This signature identifies the creator of the control and assures the user that a virus isn't being loaded onto the hard drive along with the ActiveX control.

You'll probably want to visit this site on a regular basis to see what new controls have been added to the partner sites, and to see if you might want to use one of them in your own work.

Downloading Is Easy

To download and test a working version of a commercial ActiveX control from a Microsoft ActiveX partner site, follow these steps:

1. Start Internet Explorer and go to the following Web site:

   `http://www.microsoft.com/activex/controls`

2. From the list, choose a partner site and click it to go to it. Take a look at the various ActiveX controls offered. Note that any control with the prefix *MCSi*, such as MCSiLabel, is supported by Microsoft's Active Template Library. These controls are smaller — often less than 50

percent as big as comparable controls. Therefore, they download to you faster (and download faster to your Web site visitors as well).

3. After you click a control, you'll see a brief description of the control, along with its picture in the right frame.

4. Click the phrase *Download and run*.

5. You'll see the Authenticode security dialog window.

6. To authenticate the control, click the links in the certificate to see if you go to the correct Web pages. When satisfied, click the Yes button to download the control.

7. Many of these controls simply download and then register themselves automatically. You don't have to do anything. If necessary, though, run the setup program to register the control.

8. Run the ActiveX Control Pad.

9. Insert a Layout control by clicking $\boxed{\textbf{Edit}} \rightarrow \boxed{\textbf{Insert HTML Layout}}$.

10. Type in a name for your new Layout, click Open, and answer Yes when asked if you want to create this Layout.

11. Click the icon next to the new Layout OBJECT CLASSID definition in the ActiveX Control Pad.

12. Right-click the Toolbox and select Additional Controls.

13. Look in the list for the ActiveX control that you just downloaded. Click the control to both select it and add it to the Toolbox (as shown in Figure 2-12).

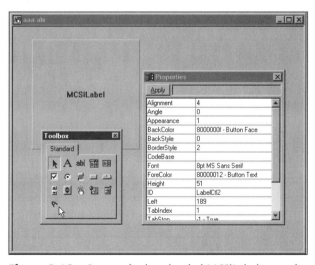

Figure 2-12 Our newly downloaded MCSiLabel control, on the Toolbox and added to a Layout.

Make a List of Those You Trust

TIP On the Authenticode security dialog window is an Advanced button. If you click it, you'll see the window shown in Figure 2-13.

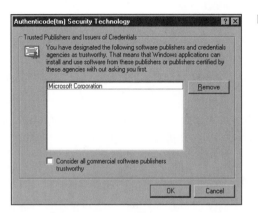

Figure 2-13 Here you can create a list of manufacturers whose controls you're willing to trust.

If you wish, you can make a list of commercial ActiveX control producers that you feel sure won't permit a virus to be loaded into their controls. Controls from these manufacturers can be directly downloaded without making you feel as if you must first check their links. You can even select the option shown on the bottom of Figure 2-13 and open your hard drive to downloads from any commercial software publisher. This isn't as wildly reckless as it sounds. After all, you show the same trust whenever you purchase commercial software in a store or through a mail-order catalog.

Others, though, might think it's quite reckless to "consider all commercial software publishers trustworthy." Installing ordinary, store-bought commercial software allows a discrete number of programs to be loaded onto your hard drive at the time of installation. But checking the Internet Explorer's 'Consider all . . .' option allows a potentially infinite number of controls to be installed, at any time.

Summary

This chapter explored the fundamental set of ActiveX controls provided by Microsoft with the ActiveX Control Pad. The majority of these controls are also the basis of programming in any version of Visual Basic: VBCCE (Control Creation Edition), VBScript (for Internet programming), VBA (Visual Basic for Applications, the macro language in Microsoft's applications, such as Access and Word), and the commercial versions of Visual Basic. As you'll see, this fundamental set of ActiveX controls can be used to build nearly any kind of user interface for Web pages or applications.

CHAPTER THREE

BUILDING A COMPLETE WEB PAGE

IN THIS CHAPTER YOU LEARN THESE KEY SKILLS

I n this chapter, you'll see how to design a Web page using the ActiveX Control Pad and the controls available with its Layout control. In addition, you'll find out where to locate initialization code — code that should be carried out by a browser before the user sees the newly loaded page. You'll also discover the purpose of .ALX files and how you can directly modify them. Finally, you'll learn how to use special visual effects to boost the visual appeal of various ActiveX controls.

Identifying the Goals

W hen you're designing a Web site — whether for yourself or for someone else — the first step is to identify the goals of the site. Is it an advertisement, a sales pitch, a public service, a device to increase awareness of a business or brand name? What do you expect the user to get out of it? What do you expect to get from the user?

To explore the process of Web page design, from the identification of its purpose to the execution of the final document, it's useful to work with an imaginary client. Let's say you got a phone call from Etchings & More, the shop of a local art dealer. Beth, the owner, wants to display some of her wares on a Web page, and also provide the user with a list of all of her currently available etchings and their prices. Finally, she wants to include her 800 number and address.

The goal of this Web page is, ultimately, to sell art. The page must therefore *look* well-designed for the same reason you'd want a banker's Web site to suggest security and a restaurant's site to suggest good food. Further discussions with Beth reveal that the etchings are black and white. You'll therefore want to add some color to the page, so it won't look entirely gray. Beth has a nice logo for her store, in a blue typeface, so you can use that. She provides you with the logo, the two drawings she wants displayed, and the list of all other available drawings.

Starting the Design

Because of the way the Layout control interacts with Internet Explorer, a default margin appears around the Layout when it's displayed in the browser. Thus your first job should be to remove that margin, using the HTML LEFTMARGIN and TOPMARGIN commands.

Start the ActiveX Control Pad and change the default template to include margin settings following the BODY command. Also change the title to Etchings & More. When you've added the margin commands, the default HTML code should look like the following:

```
<HTML>
<HEAD>
<TITLE>Etchings & More</TITLE>
</HEAD>
<BODY LEFTMARGIN=0 TOPMARGIN=0>

</BODY>
</HTML>
```

Balance Graphic Elements

Now select Insert HTML Layout in the Pad's Edit menu. Move the cursor to the blank line between BODY and /BODY.

The primary visual elements on this page are the logo and the two drawings. It's useful to start arranging and balancing them on the page first. However, you don't want to just slap the drawings onto the background. No art dealer in her right mind would tape raw drawings onto the wall. Pictures require frames. You can create attractive frames by superimposing several Image controls. Click the Image control in the Layout Toolbox, then click the Layout itself to place an Image onto the Layout.

Create Custom Frames

Double-click the Image control to bring up the Properties window. Change the SpecialEffect property to Raised. Add two more Image controls to the Layout. Superimpose the Images, positioning them so they are close together and look something like the Image controls in Figure 3-1. Set the middle Image's SpecialEffect property to Sunken and the inner Image's SpecialEffect property to Etched. Change the PicturePath property of the innermost Image so it shows a graphic (provide the full path of a .BMP, .GIF, .WMF or .JPG file, for example: C:\GALLERY\WREN.BMP).

Figure 3-1 Create frames by overlapping Image controls.

You position a control by clicking it to select it, then dragging the control until it resides where you want it. You resize a control by selecting it, then dragging one of the eight small white boxes that appear within the selection frame.

TIP *If you're having trouble sizing or positioning the Image controls, follow these steps to make your job easy:*

1. Right-click the largest Image control (the one in the back) and select Send To Back.

2. Right-click the smallest (innermost) Image control and choose Bring To Front.

3. Click Tools → Options → HTML Layout and deselect (turn off) the Show Grid and Snap to Grid options.

Using only three Image controls, you can create the appearance of matted frames shown in Figure 3-1, but by all means, experiment using additional Images and playing around with different SpecialEffect settings. Likewise, if you change the Images' BackStyle to Opaque, choose a color other than the Windows default battleship gray by adjusting the BackColor property.

Copy and Paste to Save Time

Now, the next job is to display the second drawing. You can save time by copying the entire set of frames that are around the first drawing — then pasting the set elsewhere on the Layout. Try it now. Position the mouse pointer above and to the left of the first drawing's Image controls, click, then drag the pointer down below and to the right of the controls. Release the mouse button; all three controls are now simultaneously selected. (Note that you can also select multiple controls by holding down the Ctrl key while clicking each control.)

Once all the controls are selected, press Ctrl+C to copy them. Then press Ctrl+V to paste the new set. Reposition the new set by dragging it to wherever you want it located on the Layout, as illustrated in Figure 3-2.

Figure 3-2 It's easy to clone a complex set of controls. Just select, copy and paste.

TIP   While a set of several controls is selected, you can resize all those controls simultaneously by dragging on one of the eight white squares on the selection frame. And, if you suddenly become wildly uncoordinated and do something you regret, all is not lost. Perhaps you dragged only one of the three frames, thereby throwing everything out of whack. Just press Ctrl+Z for undo, and the wandering frame should snap back into its previous position.

Remember the Logo

Next comes the "Etchings & More" logo. If your client already has a logo, you might be able to get a graphics file of it on a disk. Just transfer the file to your hard drive and provide the PicturePath to that location. Remember that a *PicturePath* is technically a URL — an address that can be contacted over the Internet. Therefore, when you finish creating a Web page or Web site, you must be sure to provide all the support graphics files to whichever Web server will be used to present the finished documents to the world at large. It's therefore often useful to merely assign the name of the graphics file (for example, LOGO.BMP) rather than a specific path (C:\MYPICS\LOGO.BMP). As long as the LOGO.BMP file is located in the same subdirectory as the .HTM file that needs this graphic, all will be fine. Browsers assume that a filename with no path means that the file can be found in the same location from which the currently displayed page was loaded.

It's often best to center a logo at the top of a Web page, as shown in Figure 3-3.

Figure 3-3 Balance the graphics by positioning the logo at the top center.

TIP If you're working at 800x600 resolution, you'll want to hide the ActiveX Control Pad's Toolbar and Status bar, and maximize the Control Pad itself. That way you can stretch the Layout control so it nearly fills the screen, and you can size and position the various elements on it. From the View menu, deselect the Toolbar and Status bar. The Control Pad will then look as it does in Figure 3-3.

Put the store's 800 number and address at the bottom of the page, and the captions for the two drawings can go directly beneath each drawing. Add three Label controls to the Layout. Move one Label under each drawing, and enter a caption. Note that you don't have to double-click a Label to change the Caption property by bringing up the Properties sheet. Instead you can click the Label twice (slowly) and then type the new Caption directly into the Label, just the way you can change a filename in Windows Explorer. Type the 800 number and the store's address into the third Label and position it at the bottom of the page. Finally, add a ListBox control to the Layout. Change its BackColor property to the same standard gray as the Layout. Then add one more Label and position it above the ListBox, changing the Label's Caption to *Other available drawings*. The final result is shown in Figure 3-4.

Figure 3-4   Our finished Web page, complete with current list of available drawings.

Understanding the Control Pad's Features

Now that you've built a complete Web page visually with the ActiveX Control Pad, it's instructive to examine the results. Where is the programming (the source code) located? Where can you make adjustments to the ActiveX controls? To find out, it's time for you to add the list of drawings and their prices to the ListBox on the Etchings & More Web site.

Adding New Layouts

So far, you've seen how to make some simple adjustments to the main HTML source code. In this example, you adjusted the default TOPMARGIN and LEFT-MARGIN settings. This source code appears as a window within the ActiveX Control Pad and is saved as an .HTM file. This page contains a default template when you choose New HTML from the Control Pad's File menu, or when you first start the Control Pad running. The following code is what the default template looks like:

```
<HTML>
<HEAD>
<TITLE>New Page</TITLE>
</HEAD>
<BODY>

</BODY>
</HTML>
```

You add new Layout controls, or insert existing Layout Controls, between the <BODY> and </BODY> commands. Similarly, you can also add individual ActiveX Controls to the HTML source code (use the Insert ActiveX Control option on the Edit menu). However, it's much easier to position and size Controls while they are on a Layout Control — therefore few people will want to directly insert an ActiveX Control onto an HTML page. Instead, most people will do as you've done in this chapter: create a page by adding ActiveX Controls to a Layout Control.

Layout Controls are saved in separate files ending in the extension .ALX. Therefore, when you insert a Layout into an HTML page, you'll see code similar to the following:

```
<OBJECT CLASSID="CLSID:812AE312-8B8E-11CF-93C8-00AA00C08FDF"
ID="etchings_alx" STYLE="LEFT:0;TOP:0">
<PARAM NAME="ALXPATH" REF VALUE="file:C:\ContlPad\etchings.alx">
</OBJECT>
```

Understanding ALX Files

The ID command identifies the filename with which this Layout object is saved to disk, in this case, *etchings.alx*. The main HTML code itself, though, is saved in an .HTM file. So, what happens when a browser loads the main .HTM page? As soon as the browser sees OBJECT, it looks for the filename of the object and loads the object into the computer's memory. At this point, the user can see or otherwise interact with the ActiveX object.

This is very similar to what happens when HTML source code includes a reference to a graphic. The browser comes upon a filename that it must load in before the user can view the graphic.

However, a Layout Control object contains *other* ActiveX objects, such as ListBoxes, and CommandButtons, and so forth. What's more, a Layout Control can contain its own HTML source code. In other words, the .ALX file that contains the Layout control will always have additional objects defined, and may have programming, too. Adding your programming directly within a Layout Control can be an effective technique, as you'll see.

Inserting Programming into a Layout

Recall that in Chapter 2 you filled a ListBox with items by putting a subroutine directly on the main HTML source code page in the ActiveX Control Pad, like this:

```
<HTML>
<HEAD>
<TITLE>Page</TITLE>
</HEAD>

<SCRIPT LANGUAGE="VBScript">
Sub Layout1_OnLoad()

ComboBox1.FontSize = 12
ComboBox2.FontSize = 12
ListBox1.FontSize = 12

For i = 1 to 10
ListBox1.AddItem "Choice #" & i
ComboBox1.AddItem "Choice #" & i
ComboBox2.AddItem "Choice #" & i
Next
end sub
</SCRIPT>


</BODY>
</HTML>
```

In this example, you used the OnLoad event of the Layout Control. In effect, you said: "When this Layout Control is loaded into a browser, carry out the following instructions: the commands I've entered between the Sub OnLoad and the End Sub commands."

However, any VBScript commands that you put into the .ALX file of a Layout control will *automatically* be carried out when that Layout is loaded into the browser. It's not necessary to use an OnLoad event as a trigger. To fill the ListBox with the names and prices of the drawings, you can add your programming directly to the Layout Control's source code (by default this source code consists of the object definitions of all the ActiveX Controls you've added to the Layout).

Follow these steps to insert code directly into the Layout Control's source code:

1. Right-click the Layout control you created for this chapter's Etchings & More example.

2. Select View Source Code.

3. The ActiveX Control Pad will display a message box informing you that it is about to save any changes you've made to the Layout. Click the button labeled Yes.

4. Windows Notepad will open the .ALX file loaded.

5. Type the following code into the .ALX file, at the end below the final </DIV> command:

```
<SCRIPT LANGUAGE="VBScript">
ListBox1.AddItem "Printemps        $240"
ListBox1.AddItem "Fair Day         $350"
ListBox1.AddItem "Sandy Shores     $800"
ListBox1.AddItem "Alabama         $1200"
ListBox1.AddItem "Shrikes & Wrens  $900"
ListBox1.AddItem "A Mid-day Repast $400"
ListBox1.AddItem "Creatures        $200"
ListBox1.AddItem "Creatures #2     $200"
ListBox1.AddItem "Last Year's Snow $1800"
ListBox1.AddItem "Salamanders      $850"
</SCRIPT>
```

6. Save the results by clicking File → Save . Then close the Notepad.

Browsers React Immediately

Now, when you load your .HTM file into Internet Explorer, the .HTM file will, in turn, load this .ALX file and load all the objects you've placed on the Layout. Finally, the browser will come upon your <SCRIPT> and will faithfully carry out your commands. The important thing to remember is that you can insert script programming into HTML code, without using the Sub OnLoad Event. As soon as the browser comes upon this non-Event programming, it will be carried out. You'll write most of your VBScript within Events, as you'll see in the next chapter. However, initialization behaviors such as filling a ListBox are supposed to be carried out when the browser first loads a page. So you can just drop any startup programming right into a Layout's source code, and that programming will be carried out when the Layout is loaded by a browser. Recall, also, that anything triggered by being loaded into a browser is also triggered if the user refreshes the page. A refresh causes the currently displayed page to be reloaded.

At this point, your .ALX file should look something like the following (your source code will vary a little bit from the following, depending on the size and position you've made your controls):

```
<DIV ID="aa" STYLE="LAYOUT:FIXED;WIDTH:576pt;HEIGHT:406pt;">

    <OBJECT ID="Image4"
     CLASSID="CLSID:D4A97620-8E8F-11CF-93CD-00AA00C08FDF"
    STYLE="TOP:92pt;LEFT:347pt;WIDTH:201pt;HEIGHT:157pt;ZINDEX:0;">
        <PARAM NAME="BorderColor" VALUE="0">
        <PARAM NAME="BackColor" VALUE="12632256">
        <PARAM NAME="BorderStyle" VALUE="0">
        <PARAM NAME="SizeMode" VALUE="3">
        <PARAM NAME="SpecialEffect" VALUE="1">
        <PARAM NAME="Size" VALUE="7091;5539">
        <PARAM NAME="PictureAlignment" VALUE="0">
    </OBJECT>
    <OBJECT ID="Image2"
     CLASSID="CLSID:D4A97620-8E8F-11CF-93CD-00AA00C08FDF"
    STYLE="TOP:92pt;LEFT:29pt;WIDTH:285pt;HEIGHT:206pt;ZINDEX:1;">
        <PARAM NAME="BorderColor" VALUE="0">
        <PARAM NAME="BackColor" VALUE="12632256">
        <PARAM NAME="BorderStyle" VALUE="0">
        <PARAM NAME="SizeMode" VALUE="3">
        <PARAM NAME="SpecialEffect" VALUE="1">
        <PARAM NAME="Size" VALUE="10054;7267">
        <PARAM NAME="PictureAlignment" VALUE="0">
    </OBJECT>
    <OBJECT ID="Image1"
     CLASSID="CLSID:D4A97620-8E8F-11CF-93CD-00AA00C08FDF"
    STYLE="TOP:118pt;LEFT:53pt;WIDTH:235pt;HEIGHT:155pt;ZINDEX:2;">
        <PARAM NAME="BorderColor" VALUE="16512">
        <PARAM NAME="BorderStyle" VALUE="0">
        <PARAM NAME="SizeMode" VALUE="3">
        <PARAM NAME="SpecialEffect" VALUE="2">
        <PARAM NAME="Size" VALUE="8290;5468">
        <PARAM NAME="PictureAlignment" VALUE="0">
        <PARAM NAME="VariousPropertyBits" VALUE="19">
    </OBJECT>
    <OBJECT ID="Image3"
     CLASSID="CLSID:D4A97620-8E8F-11CF-93CD-00AA00C08FDF"
    STYLE="TOP:121pt;LEFT:56pt;WIDTH:230pt;HEIGHT:150pt;ZINDEX:3;">
        <PARAM NAME="PicturePath" VALUE="c:\gallery1\wren.bmp">
        <PARAM NAME="BorderColor" VALUE="16777215">
        <PARAM NAME="BorderStyle" VALUE="0">
```

```
      <PARAM NAME="SizeMode" VALUE="3">
      <PARAM NAME="SpecialEffect" VALUE="3">
      <PARAM NAME="Size" VALUE="8114;5292">
  </OBJECT>
  <OBJECT ID="Image5"
   CLASSID="CLSID:D4A97620-8E8F-11CF-93CD-00AA00C08FDF"
STYLE="TOP:121pt;LEFT:371pt;WIDTH:147pt;HEIGHT:106pt;ZINDEX:4;"
>
      <PARAM NAME="BorderColor" VALUE="16512">
      <PARAM NAME="BorderStyle" VALUE="0">
      <PARAM NAME="SizeMode" VALUE="3">
      <PARAM NAME="SpecialEffect" VALUE="2">
      <PARAM NAME="Size" VALUE="5186;3739">
      <PARAM NAME="PictureAlignment" VALUE="0">
      <PARAM NAME="VariousPropertyBits" VALUE="19">
  </OBJECT>
  <OBJECT ID="Image7"
   CLASSID="CLSID:D4A97620-8E8F-11CF-93CD-00AA00C08FDF"
STYLE="TOP:119pt;LEFT:371pt;WIDTH:152pt;HEIGHT:106pt;ZINDEX:5;"
>
      <PARAM NAME="BorderColor" VALUE="16512">
      <PARAM NAME="BorderStyle" VALUE="0">
      <PARAM NAME="SizeMode" VALUE="3">
      <PARAM NAME="Size" VALUE="5362;3739">
      <PARAM NAME="PictureAlignment" VALUE="0">
      <PARAM NAME="VariousPropertyBits" VALUE="19">
  </OBJECT>
  <OBJECT ID="Image6"
   CLASSID="CLSID:D4A97620-8E8F-11CF-93CD-00AA00C08FDF"
STYLE="TOP:122pt;LEFT:374pt;WIDTH:143pt;HEIGHT:102pt;ZINDEX:6;"
>
      <PARAM NAME="PicturePath" VALUE="c:\gallery1\mill.bmp">
      <PARAM NAME="BorderColor" VALUE="16777215">
      <PARAM NAME="BorderStyle" VALUE="0">
      <PARAM NAME="SizeMode" VALUE="1">
      <PARAM NAME="SpecialEffect" VALUE="3">
      <PARAM NAME="Size" VALUE="5045;3598">
  </OBJECT>
  <OBJECT ID="Image8"
   CLASSID="CLSID:D4A97620-8E8F-11CF-93CD-00AA00C08FDF"
STYLE="TOP:8pt;LEFT:56pt;WIDTH:464pt;HEIGHT:84pt;ZINDEX:7;">
      <PARAM NAME="PicturePath"
VALUE="c:\bookactx\3\etchings.bmp">
      <PARAM NAME="BorderStyle" VALUE="0">
```

```
        <PARAM NAME="SizeMode" VALUE="3">
        <PARAM NAME="Size" VALUE="16369;2963">
        <PARAM NAME="PictureAlignment" VALUE="0">
        <PARAM NAME="VariousPropertyBits" VALUE="19">
   </OBJECT>
   <OBJECT ID="Label1"
    CLASSID="CLSID:978C9E23-D4B0-11CE-BF2D-00AA003F40D0"
STYLE="TOP:301pt;LEFT:143pt;WIDTH:172pt;HEIGHT:18pt;ZINDEX:8;">
        <PARAM NAME="Caption" VALUE="&quot;Spring Song&quot;
$700">
        <PARAM NAME="Size" VALUE="6068;635">
        <PARAM NAME="FontName" VALUE="Times New Roman">
        <PARAM NAME="FontHeight" VALUE="240">
        <PARAM NAME="FontCharSet" VALUE="0">
        <PARAM NAME="FontPitchAndFamily" VALUE="2">
        <PARAM NAME="FontWeight" VALUE="0">
   </OBJECT>
   <OBJECT ID="Label2"
    CLASSID="CLSID:978C9E23-D4B0-11CE-BF2D-00AA003F40D0"
STYLE="TOP:250pt;LEFT:446pt;WIDTH:110pt;HEIGHT:18pt;ZINDEX:9;">
        <PARAM NAME="Caption" VALUE="&quot;The Press&quot;
$1200">
        <PARAM NAME="Size" VALUE="3881;635">
        <PARAM NAME="FontName" VALUE="Times New Roman">
        <PARAM NAME="FontHeight" VALUE="240">
        <PARAM NAME="FontCharSet" VALUE="0">
        <PARAM NAME="FontPitchAndFamily" VALUE="2">
        <PARAM NAME="FontWeight" VALUE="0">
   </OBJECT>
   <OBJECT ID="Label3"
    CLASSID="CLSID:978C9E23-D4B0-11CE-BF2D-00AA003F40D0"
STYLE="TOP:338pt;LEFT:29pt;WIDTH:357pt;HEIGHT:30pt;ZINDEX:10;">
        <PARAM NAME="Caption" VALUE="Call 1-800-887-6554
Etchings &amp; More, 12 Bath St., Cinrane, OH 23553">
        <PARAM NAME="Size" VALUE="12594;1058">
        <PARAM NAME="FontName" VALUE="Times New Roman">
        <PARAM NAME="FontHeight" VALUE="240">
        <PARAM NAME="FontCharSet" VALUE="0">
        <PARAM NAME="FontPitchAndFamily" VALUE="2">
        <PARAM NAME="FontWeight" VALUE="0">
   </OBJECT>
   <OBJECT ID="Label4"
```

```
      CLASSID="CLSID:978C9E23-D4B0-11CE-BF2D-00AA003F40D0"
    STYLE="TOP:278pt;LEFT:401pt;WIDTH:152pt;HEIGHT:18pt;ZINDEX:11;"
    >
         <PARAM NAME="Caption" VALUE="Other available drawings . .
    .">
         <PARAM NAME="Size" VALUE="5362;635">
         <PARAM NAME="FontName" VALUE="Times New Roman">
         <PARAM NAME="FontHeight" VALUE="240">
         <PARAM NAME="FontCharSet" VALUE="0">
         <PARAM NAME="FontPitchAndFamily" VALUE="2">
         <PARAM NAME="FontWeight" VALUE="0">
      </OBJECT>
      <OBJECT ID="ListBox1"
       CLASSID="CLSID:8BD21D20-EC42-11CE-9E0D-00AA006002F3"
    STYLE="TOP:293pt;LEFT:401pt;WIDTH:146pt;HEIGHT:77pt;TABINDEX:3;
    ZINDEX:12;">
         <PARAM NAME="BackColor" VALUE="12632256">
         <PARAM NAME="ScrollBars" VALUE="3">
         <PARAM NAME="DisplayStyle" VALUE="2">
         <PARAM NAME="Size" VALUE="5151;2716">
         <PARAM NAME="MatchEntry" VALUE="0">
         <PARAM NAME="FontName" VALUE="Times New Roman">
         <PARAM NAME="FontHeight" VALUE="240">
         <PARAM NAME="FontCharSet" VALUE="0">
         <PARAM NAME="FontPitchAndFamily" VALUE="2">
         <PARAM NAME="FontWeight" VALUE="0">
      </OBJECT>

</DIV>

<SCRIPT LANGUAGE="VBScript">
ListBox1.AddItem "Printemps          $240"
ListBox1.AddItem "Fair Day           $350"
ListBox1.AddItem "Sandy Shores       $800"
ListBox1.AddItem "Alabama           $1200"
ListBox1.AddItem "Shrikes & Wrens    $900"
ListBox1.AddItem "A Mid-day Repast   $400"
ListBox1.AddItem "Creatures          $200"
ListBox1.AddItem "Creatures #2       $200"
ListBox1.AddItem "Last Year's Snow  $1800"
ListBox1.AddItem "Salamanders        $850"
</SCRIPT>
```

Deconstructing the Source Code

If you examine this source code, you'll see that it can tell you how a browser interprets OBJECTs and how you can modify those objects directly within the source code. No need to call up a Properties window; just edit the parameters directly within the source code.

DIV Means Division

First, notice those `<DIV>` `</DIV>` commands. In HTML, many commands are paired, indicating the start and stop of something. For example, the `<TITLE>` command signifies that what follows is the title of the current document. The companion command, `</TITLE>` with the backslash, says that the title segment of this source code has ended.

The `<DIV>` command is short for *division*. Use this command to subdivide a document. For example, `<DIV>` tags could be used to separate a table of contents, individual chapters and appendices. However, the ActiveX Control Pad uses the `<DIV>` command to enclose the definitions of any objects you place on a Layout control. Note the ID parameter right after the DIV tag. ID identifies the name of the layout. In this case it's *aa*. The FIXED parameter means that the Layout control does not change its size if the user resizes the browser window. Finally, the WIDTH and HEIGHT are defined, in *points*. A point is a unit of measurement used in printing and publishing: There are 72 points in an inch. So the WIDTH:576pt means that this Layout control is 8 inches wide.

An ActiveX Control Pad Limitation

TIP The ActiveX Control Pad enables you to stretch a Layout control only to the width or height of your screen. You can't stretch it any further. But what if you want a double- or triple-page height? Many Web pages are more than a single screen in height, and the browser automatically adds a scrollbar so the user can move up or down through the page.

You can't do this with the ActiveX Control Pad. You might attempt to expand the Layout for the Etchings & More document in the above example to two screens in height, by doubling the HEIGHT definition in the source code. Right-click the Layout, choose View Source Code, click the Yes button, change HEIGHT:406pt; to HEIGHT:812pt. This seems as though it should work, but the next time you attempt to work with the Layout in the ActiveX Control Pad, a message will pop up informing you that at your current resolution (800x600 in my case) the maximum width is 8" and the maximum height is 6". What's more, the ActiveX Control Pad goes ahead and edits your HEIGHT to the maximum, 436pt, in the .ALX file. (The messages you see will depend on your settings.)

```
<OBJECT ID="Image4"
    CLASSID="CLSID:D4A97620-8E8F-11CF-93CD-00AA00C08FDF"
  STYLE="TOP:92pt;LEFT:347pt;WIDTH:201pt;HEIGHT:157pt;ZINDEX:0;">
        <PARAM NAME="BorderColor" VALUE="0">
        <PARAM NAME="BackColor" VALUE="12632256">
        <PARAM NAME="BorderStyle" VALUE="0">
        <PARAM NAME="SizeMode" VALUE="3">
        <PARAM NAME="SpecialEffect" VALUE="1">
        <PARAM NAME="Size" VALUE="7091;5539">
        <PARAM NAME="PictureAlignment" VALUE="0">
    </OBJECT>
```

Following the DIV definitions are the OBJECT definitions, one for each ActiveX control that you placed on the Layout. Notice the first OBJECT, named Image4, one of the Images you used to create a frame around another Image. Following its ID is the CLASSID, a unique and complicated identifier of the ActiveX Image control. The STYLE section includes definitions of the position of this Image control relative to the Layout control. TOP:92pt means that the top of this image is 1.28" down from the top of the Layout. The ZINDEX describes the Z-axis, a *depth* dimension. In other words, the ZINDEX of each control determines which other controls it would cover up, or be covered up by, if they are superimposed. The ZINDEX is normally handled for you. If you want to adjust which control appears *on top* of another, right-click a control and click Send To Back, Move Backward, Move Forward or Bring To Front. The Layout control will automatically adjust the ZINDEX of other affected controls, as necessary.

Most of the PARAM tags define properties that you can change in the Properties window of an object. Just double-click a control in the ActiveX Control Pad, and up comes the Properties window. However, you can also edit the PARAMs directly within the source code, if you wish.

SizeMode is what's called the *PictureSizeMode* in the Properties window. This property determines whether a graphic is stretched, clipped or zoomed when loaded into the Image control. The Size parameter combines the Width and Height properties, separating them by a semicolon. Notice that the Size of Image 4 is described as 7091 wide and 5539 high. The unit of measurement used in the PARAM list is not points or inches. Instead, it's the finest unit of measurement of all in computer programming, the *twip*. There are 1440 twips per inch. Therefore, 7091;5539 translates to 4.92 by 3.85 inches.

BONUS

Adding Sophistication with Faux Controls

There's a quick way to improve the appearance of your Web pages, or any applications you build using ActiveX controls. Creating faux controls is one of the best ways to enliven the look of your pages and make your Web site stand out from the crowd.

For example, everyone knows that controls don't cast shadows. But you can *add* shadows to controls by putting the controls on top of an Image control. If you have a photo editing application such as Photoshop or PicturePublisher, adding special effects can be quite simple.

Add Drop Shadows

First create an ActiveX Control Pad Layout control. Put two Labels and three CommandButtons onto the Layout control, as shown in Figure 3-5.

Figure 3-5 BEFORE: The flat, dull lettering typical of most Web pages.

Then use the automatic selection wand in your graphics application to select the background. Invert the selection so that the CommandButtons and the text in the Labels is selected, as shown in Figure 3-6.

There are many special-effects plug-ins you can purchase for use with graphics applications. In this example, the DropShadow plug-in used is from Alien Skin Software, 1100 Wake Forest Road, Suite 101, Raleigh, NC 27604. You can also contact them at this Web site:

WEB PATH http://www.alienskin.com

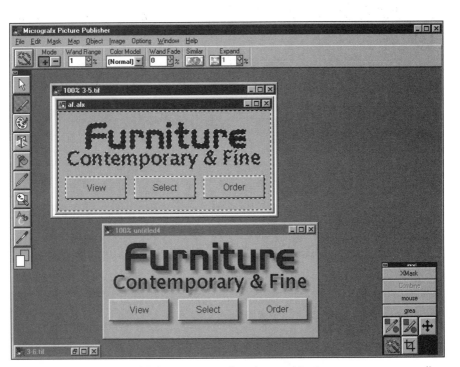

Figure 3-6 In PicturePublisher, you can select the graphic elements you want to adjust. Here a drop shadow is added to the selected elements in our Layout.

The next step is to save the graphic as a .BMP file. Choose Save As from your graphics application's File menu. Now put a new Image control onto your Layout, and load the graphic .BMP into its PicturePath property, as shown in Figure 3-7. Right-click the Image control and choose Send To Back. This way, the real CommandButtons will appear on top of the fake ones in the graphic. Click each of the Labels (holding the words *Furniture* and *Contemporary & Fine*) to select them. Press the Del key to remove these Labels. They're no longer needed, now that the Image control contains a graphic displaying the same information, but with a drop-shadow.

The final result of this graphic tinkering is a more sophisticated, attractive layout and a set of controls that look more realistic. Given that CommandButton features built-in animation when clicked, the resulting behavior in a real-world Web page seems startlingly authentic (see the clicked, "depressed" CommandButton in Figure 3-8).

Figure 3-7 Move the Image directly over the original controls in the ActiveX Control Pad.

Figure 3-8 AFTER: The title lettering is more attractive, and the three CommandButtons now look more realistic.

This same technique can be used in VBCCE or the commercial versions of Visual Basic. In fact, you can even simplify things a little when not using the ActiveX Control Pad, because you can load a graphics file directly into the background in versions of VB. Instead of a Layout control, you'll be using a VB Form. Forms have their own Picture property, so you need not first add an Image control in order to display a graphic.

Add 3D Lettering

Most people prefer the subtle look of 3-D lettering to the usual plain, black characters. You can add drop-shadows and other special effects to captions as well as to larger objects, such as controls. Many ActiveX controls now feature a Picture property, and that's all you need to replace the flat, traditional lettering with any special effects a graphics application can generate. To create the next example, follow the same steps described above to add a drop-shadow, but this time add white rather than a shadow, and create three .BMP files, one for each of the captions of the three CommandButtons. See the sample shown in Figure 3-9.

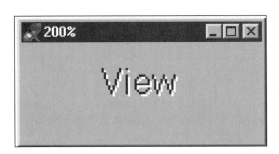

Figure 3-9 To create a 3-D effect, duplicate the letters at a 1-pixel offset, and fill them with white.

Save these three .BMP files and then load them into the Picture properties of each of the three CommandButtons. Erase the original caption, leaving the Caption property blank. Finally, change the PicturePosition property to Center. The results are subtle but handsome, as shown in Figure 3-10.

Figure 3-10 The full effect: drop-shadows on all large lettering and CommandButtons, plus 3-D effects for the three captions.

CAUTION At the time of this writing, some graphics do not display correctly when added to a CommandButton in the ActiveX Control Pad. They do, however, work fine in the versions of Visual Basic covered in this book: VBCCE and the commercial versions of VB. Note, though, that in these other versions you must first change the Style property of a control to Graphical before a picture will be displayed (even though the Picture property contains a bitmap).

Summary

In this chapter, you learned elements of Web page design and saw how to create an effective Web page using only the ActiveX Control Pad, the Layout control, and the basic set of ActiveX controls that come with the Control Pad. You also learned how to write VBScript programming that resides directly within HTML source code, rather than being enclosed inside an event procedure. You explored the structure and purpose of .ALX files and, finally, learned ways to employ graphics applications to add sophisticated visual elements to ActiveX controls. Now it's time to turn your attention to more sophisticated programming — manipulating properties, methods, and events using VBScript.

CUSTOMIZING CONTROLS

I n this chapter, you explore how properties, methods, and events give you (the programmer) considerable authority over the behaviors and qualities of controls. You discover how objects include various kinds of built-in functionality that you can manipulate to customize controls to suit your needs.

As earlier chapters introduced you to *properties;* this chapter introduces you to *methods* and *events.* Methods are tasks an object knows how to do. For example, the AddItem method inserts new items into a ListBox, and the Clear method removes all of a ListBox's items at once. *Events* are things that can happen *to a* control, such as the Click event. All controls contain a set of events, but the events start out empty; they do nothing until you put some programming into them. If you display a TextBox to a user and you haven't written programming in that TextBox's DoubleClick event, nothing will happen if the user double-clicks it. Until you put some programming into it, an event is an empty sensitivity. Think of it this way: Every human contains a tickle event. While some people don't react at all to tickling, others wiggle and writhe. Events are *potential* behaviors, but the programmer must define the actual behaviors, if any.

Internet programming is the true subject of this chapter: how to use Visual Basic Script (referred to as VBScript), how to trigger a control's behaviors (its methods), and how to react to outside actions taken against a control (its events). When you finish this chapter, you'll have a good idea of the purposes and features of VBScript.

The Elements of ActiveX Controls

You can describe just about anything in two ways: what it is and what it does. A list of its qualities, taken together, define what an object *is*. *Large, gray, tusks, prehensile nose* pretty much narrows this object down to an elephant. Those qualities are its *properties*. By contrast: *wanders, trumpets, eats, wallows* is a list of what it *does* — that is, its *methods*.

How a Control Is Constructed

In Part III of this book, you'll learn how to build your own ActiveX controls from scratch. For now, you'll learn how to adjust controls built by someone else. Before you begin, though, you need to understand the meaning of properties, methods, and events, as well as the distinction between them. In this section you will flash forward briefly to consider in general how a control is designed from scratch.

PROPERTIES ARE QUALITIES

To build a control, the designer first defines the set of qualities — the properties — that make up the control, such as color, font size, and width.

METHODS ARE BEHAVIORS

After the designer defines the qualities, the designer next defines a set of behaviors, or methods, for the control. If your control is supposed to be a cash converter, you (the designer) will teach it how to convert dollars into yen, and vice versa, for example. Your converter control will have a DollarsToYen method and a YenToDollars method (or whatever other names you want to give these methods). You'll then teach the converter how to perform the DollarsToYen method by writing some VBScript programming that looks at the digits the user types in, and then does the math to convert the user's dollar figure into yen.

EVENTS ARE SENSITIVITIES

You sensitize your control by giving it a set of events to which it reacts. Common events include: Click, DoubleClick, Change, KeyDown, MouseDown, and MouseMove. You (the creator of a control) don't provide programming within an event. The event is a location where the developers who use your control can insert programming of their own. Perhaps, for example, a user wants your converter calculator to change color every time it's clicked. To do this, the user places a line of VBScript programming into the Click event that will assign a random color value to the control's BackColor property.

Fixed Versus Variable Qualities

Precisely *which* properties, methods and events a given control features depends on what qualities, behaviors, and sensitivities the control's designer wanted to give to it. Notice that a control can contain some qualities and behaviors that are *fixed* and inherent. A CommandButton, for instance, is always rectangular. You can change its height, color, typeface, width, and other visual elements. But it has no Shape property by which you can change it to an oval or a circle. This void means that the creator of this control didn't build in a property that enabled you (the user of the control) to mutate it from its rectangular essence.

Similarly, a CommandButton has a fixed method. The button is automatically animated to appear depressed when the user clicks on it, as shown in Figure 4-1. Unfortunately, the designer of the CommandButton control didn't provide programmers with any provision to turn off this animation. Technically, you can avoid the animation by setting the Enabled Property to False. This setting, however, also grays the button and disables its Click event — side effects you may not want. Therefore, you cannot take the animation away from a CommandButton.

Figure 4-1 A CommandButton always animates when clicked — that's not optional.

Three Levels of Interaction

Three levels of people interact with any given control: the control's creator, the programmer, and the end user. Each successive level apllies more restrictions to how much the control can be modified or manipulated.

Creators

The creator of the control has permission to do anything to the control — no restrictions apply. The creator defines what the control is, what it does, and what any subsequent user can do to or with it. This intimate relationship with all the nuts and bolts of an object is often called *low-level programming*. That doesn't mean the creator's role is simple, or somehow less significant than other levels of interaction. It merely means that, like an auto mechanic, a low-level programmer can get down into and under the object and has the understanding (and the permission) to make adjustments to virtually every aspect of the machine.

Programmers

Programmers (also called *developers*) who use a prebuilt control are at the second level of interaction. Perhaps you're using a control as part of a Web page you're constructing (or maybe you're using the control in a Windows application you're writing). Whatever the case, you can define the control's behaviors and qualities only to the extent the creator gave you permission. The creator decides which elements of the control to make available to programmers who later use this control by defining some properties, events, and methods as *public*. Other elements of the control are not made public and, thus, reside hidden within the control and beyond the reach of programmers other than the creator.

Leaving some elements hidden is called *encapsulation*. For example, when you buy a microwave oven, you (the user) expect to be able to control the power between the settings low, medium, and high. These settings have been made public by the engineer who designed the oven. You're *not* expected to yank off the case and try to double the power of the magnetron tube. Not only would that void your warrantee, it would also endanger all life forms in your vicinity.

When you use a prebuilt control, you can insert your programming into places the creator permitted you access: the events the creator gave to this control. If, for example, the creator gave the control a KeyDown event, you could detect (and react to, by your programming) any keys the user presses on the keyboard. This would enable you, for example, to give the user permission to change the font size employed by the control. You could tell the user that pressing Alt+L will increase the font size and pressing Alt+S will decrease it. Then, in the control's KeyDown event, you could insert programming that reacts to keypresses such as this:

```
Sub MyControl_KeyDown(KeyCode, Shift)
If Shift = 4 and KeyCode = 76 Then
   FontSize = FontSize + 2
EndIf

If Shift = 4 and KeyCode = 83 Then
   FontSize = FontSize - 2
EndIf
End Sub
```

The KeyDown event includes two variables: KeyCode (which tells you which ordinary, alphabetic key was pressed) and Shift (which tells you if the Alt, Shift, or Ctrl keys were pressed at the same time).

Users

On the highest level is the ordinary end user, someone who uses Windows applications or Web pages, but doesn't do any programming. The people on this level can click a control, but cannot define what happens when that control is clicked.

If the programmer has written some VBScript programming within the Click event, that programming defines what happens when the button is clicked. The user can activate, but not define, behaviors. Likewise, if the programmer included a preference or customization feature, perhaps the user could adjust colors or choose fonts or make some other decisions. But all this depends on what permission the programmer has granted the user.

Describing the user as being on the highest level doesn't imply any superiority over the programmer or the creator. The word *highest* in this sense means least involved with and most abstracted from.

Programmatic Versus Design-Time Behaviors

If you glance at the controls that come with the ActiveX Control Pad's Layout Toolbox, you'll notice that some elements (such as the BackColor property and the Click event) are nearly universal. Almost every control permits you to change its color and enables you to react (by writing some programming) to a click. However, other elements (such as the SpinUp event) are unique. Only SpinButton controls have SpinUp and SpinDown events.

Likewise, most controls have a SetFocus method, enabling you to programmatically set the focus to that control. Most controls also have a ZOrder method, enabling you to programmatically bring the control forward or back along the z-axis — that is, you can put the control "on top of" or "behind" other controls that overlap it.

The term *programmatic* refers to *run-time* activity, which means the program carries out some task while the script is running with VBScript or some other programming language. By contrast, *design-time* activity refers to making changes to a control before the program runs. Thus, you can change the Caption of a control in either of the following two ways:

✳ during *design time* by using the Properties window to change, for example, a CommandButton's caption to "Send," or

✳ *programmatically* while the program runs (this is also sometimes referred to as *run-time* activity) by writing some programming such as
```
Command1.Caption = "Send"
```

TIP **VBScript has eight built-in constants you can use with BackColor or other color properties: vbBlack, vbRed, vbGreen, vbYellow, vbBlue, vbMagenta, vbCyan, and vbWhite.**

TIP All versions of VB — Visual Basic Script, Visual Basic for Applications, Visual Basic Control Creation Edition, and all-purpose commercial VB — have exceptionally fine online help systems. For example, if you want to know what properties, methods, or events are built into a control, press F1 in the ActiveX Control Pad. Use the help index to find the control in which you're interested, and you'll find that each control entry includes hypertext lists of that control's properties, methods, and events, as shown in Figure 4-2.

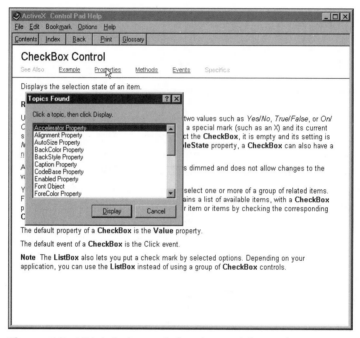

Figure 4-2 VB's help feature is first-class and thorough.

Programming Run-Time Changes

In previous chapters, you learned how to adjust a control's properties by using the Properties window. It's just as easy to change them while a script is running.

Follow these steps to change a CommandButton's backcolor programmatically:

1. Use the ActiveX Control Pad to put a CommandButton on a Layout.

2. Right-click the Layout and choose View Source Code.

3. Click the Yes button.

4. In Notepad, add the <SCRIPT> section to the existing source code:

```
<DIV ID="cc" STYLE="LAYOUT:FIXED;WIDTH:400pt;HEIGHT:300pt;">
  <OBJECT ID="CommandButton1"
    CLASSID="CLSID:D7053240-CE69-11CD-A777-00DD01143C57"
STYLE="TOP:49pt;LEFT:90pt;WIDTH:72pt;HEIGHT:24pt;TABINDEX:0;ZIN
DEX:0;">
    <PARAM NAME="Caption" VALUE="CommandButton1">
    <PARAM NAME="Size" VALUE="2540;847">
    <PARAM NAME="FontCharSet" VALUE="0">
    <PARAM NAME="FontPitchAndFamily" VALUE="2">
    <PARAM NAME="ParagraphAlign" VALUE="3">
    <PARAM NAME="FontWeight" VALUE="0">
  </OBJECT>
</DIV>

<SCRIPT LANGUAGE="VBScript">
commandbutton1.backcolor = 34422
</SCRIPT>
```

5. Click **File** → **Save** to store the revised .ALX file on disk.

6. Go back to the ActiveX Control Pad and save the .HTM file.

7. Load that .HTM file into Internet Explorer and observe that, as soon as it's loaded, the backcolor of the CommandButton turns from gray to green.

Giving Users Permission

Another way to change something programmatically is to give the user permission to make the change, which you can do by inserting some programming into an event. The following code illustrates how to edit the source code listed in the previous steps so that the user can change the backcolor by clicking the Layout control. Note that this method assumes you didn't rename the Layout from the default name given to it by the ActiveX Control Pad: *Layout1*. If you did rename the Layout to, for example, ColorCh, use ColorCh_Click as the title of your event.

```
<SCRIPT LANGUAGE="VBScript">
Sub Layout1_Click()
CommandButton1.BackColor = 34422
end sub
</SCRIPT>
```

Consider the Chameleon

When you insert programming into an event, you're telling VBScript that it shouldn't simply carry out this command when the Layout is first loaded into the browser. Instead, VBScript should wait until (or if) the user clicks the Layout, triggering that event. Remember that programming inside an event (between a Sub and End Sub command) is only carried out if that event is triggered. Programming you place outside an event (but still between the <SCRIPT> and </SCRIPT> commands) is carried out immediately when the browser first loads the document.

Methods Are Rare

You can also use methods to adjust a control. In previous chapters, you may recall adding items to a ListBox by using the AddItem method. Methods, though, are relatively rare in Visual Basic. You have many events and properties, but few methods. In fact, most controls only have two methods: SetFocus and ZOrder.

You may even question the validity of the distinction between methods and properties. After all, changing a control's position on the z-axis by using the ZOrder *method* isn't all that different from changing a control's position on the y-axis by using the Top *property*. Why the depth axis is adjusted via a method, but the horizontal and vertical axes are adjusted via properties, is a mystery.

Methods in Disguise

If you were designing a chameleon object, you would give it the capability to change its color to blend in with the background to avoid being eaten. Should this change of color be classed as a property (a quality) or a method (a behavior)? The difficulty in answering this question may explain why Visual Basic provides only a few methods. What's more, some properties (such as Enabled and WordWrap) seem as if they might really be methods in disguise. The distinction between properties and events, however, is generally valid — and, to the programmer, significant.

Using Events

In Chapter 3, you created a sample Web page for an art dealer. Now, to see how to employ events in your programming, you can expand on that example. Load the ETCHINGS.HTM file into your ActiveX Control Pad. If you didn't save it to disk, you can find it on the CD-ROM that accompanies this book.

Programming Brings Events Alive

The example Web page contains a ListBox displaying all available drawings and their prices. Your goal now is to add some programming that reacts when the user clicks an item within the ListBox. When the user clicks, you'll display a picture of the drawing the user selected. The programming to make this happen changes the PicturePath property of the larger Image control; it also copies the title and price information to the caption beneath the larger image.

In the ActiveX Control Pad, right-click the Layout control and select View Source Code. Type the following code (or copy the file from the CD-ROM). You can put it at the end below the </DIV> tag or at the top — in fact, it doesn't matter where you put it, as long as you don't put it inside one of the <OBJECT> . . .</OBJECT> definitions.

```
<SCRIPT LANGUAGE="VBScript">
ListBox1.AddItem "Printemps       $240"
ListBox1.AddItem "Fair Day        $350"
ListBox1.AddItem "Sandy Shores    $800"
ListBox1.AddItem "Alabama         $1200"
ListBox1.AddItem "Shrikes & Wrens $900"
ListBox1.AddItem "A Mid-day Repast $400"
ListBox1.AddItem "Creatures       $200"
ListBox1.AddItem "Creatures #2    $200"
ListBox1.AddItem "Last Year's Snow $1800"
ListBox1.AddItem "Salamanders     $850"

dim files(11)
files(1) = "c:\gallery1\Printemp.Bmp"
files(2) = "c:\gallery1\Fairday.Bmp"
files(3) = "c:\gallery1\Sandy.Bmp"
files(4) = "c:\gallery1\Alabam.Bmp"
files(5) = "c:\gallery1\Shrikes.Bmp"
files(6) = "c:\gallery1\Repast.Bmp"
files(7) = "c:\gallery1\Creat1.Bmp"
files(8) = "c:\gallery1\Creat2.Bmp"
files(9) = "c:\gallery1\Snow.Bmp"
files(10) = "c:\gallery1\Sala.Bmp"

Sub ListBox1_Click()
r = ListBox1.ListIndex + 1 'adjust for zero
n = ListBox1.List(r-1)
Label1 = n
Image3.PicturePath = files(r)
end sub

</SCRIPT>
```

Compensating for the Zero-Index Problem

When the user clicks an item within the ListBox, the ListBox's Click event is triggered. The ListIndex property tells you which item was clicked — first, second, and so on. This ListIndex, though, starts with a *zero index*. This procedure is awkward. You should make an adjustment in your programming to compensate: Add 1 to the ListIndex number. This way, if the user clicks the fifth item in the ListBox, the variable *r* will contain the index number 5, as shown in the following code:

```
r = ListBox1.ListIndex + 1 'adjust for zero
```

Then the text of the clicked item is put into the variable *n* and copied to the Label under the larger Image box. Finally, the Image's PicturePath property is changed to the path and filename of the graphic file associated with the selected drawing. The result is shown in Figure 4-3.

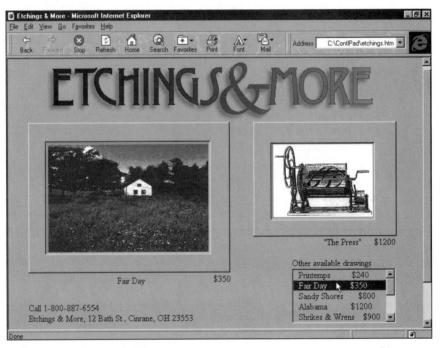

Figure 4-3   Now, when the user clicks an item in the ListBox, a new graphic is displayed.

Notice that in the preceding VBScript programming an array of filenames (one for each drawing mentioned in the ListBox) is dimensioned to 11: `Dim files (11)`. Eleven was used, even though the ListBox contains only ten items. This step enables you to ignore files(0) and list the filenames by using index numbers from 1 to 10. Again, this adjustment from a zero-based to a one-based index system is for the programmer's convenience only. It can, however, help to prevent errors when you or someone else updates the parallel lists of drawing names and filenames. The fifth drawing name will match the fifth filename, and so on. For most people, it's just easier to work with lists if they are one-based rather than zero-based.

TIP All versions of Visual Basic, except VBScript, have an Option Base command that you can use to force arrays to begin with an index of 1 rather than zero. However, VBScript doesn't include this feature. What's more, Option Base has no effect on other zero-based lists, such as the ListIndex property of a ListBox.

Understanding VBScript

VBScript does not contain any commands that enable access to a user's peripherals. You won't find any way in VBScript to save a message or a file to a user's hard drive. This happens by design. If VBScript included disk access features, it would be too easy for a miscreant to insert a command into a Web page, reformatting or wiping out a user's hard drive. People must be able to traverse the Internet without worrying about downloading a Web page that will gleefully trash their computer's memory and storage devices before they can say, "Please, no! No! Stop!" Neither JavaScript nor HTML have hard-drive-access commands either, which may be just as well.

The Essence of VBScript

If you've tried the examples in earlier chapters, you may have already grasped the essence of VBScript. It puts the *active* in ActiveX, when ActiveX controls are added to a Web page. Supplemented by VBScript programming, ActiveX controls make Web pages active and energetic. Stock-ticker displays roll by, music plays, animation attracts the eye, and so on.

An ActiveX control can contain considerable built-in functionality. A ListBox, for example, displays items of data within a vertical grid, and it can tell you which items the user has selected. However, some jobs a ListBox cannot accomplish by itself. As you've seen so far in this chapter, if you want to add items to a ListBox, you must use the VBScript command *AddItem*. And if you want to change a picture in response to the user's click, you have to add VBScript programming to adjust an Image control's PicturePath property.

In other words, VBScript is a *computing* language. HTML, in contrast, is largely a *page description* language. It's mostly devoted to describing size, position, color, typeface, and other formatting issues. HTML contains little that is *dynamic;* it can't even add 2 + 2. HTML isn't designed to compute; it's supposed to describe the details of how a Web page will look. VBScript, however, can add numbers together and accomplish many other jobs that come under the general heading of information processing.

Where Is VBScript Located?

VBScript resides within Internet Explorer (IE). When users install IE on their computers, the VBScript interpreter engine is also installed. IE knows how to interpret the VBScript commands and carries them out when it comes upon the following tag:

```
<SCRIPT LANGUAGE="VBScript">
```

IE stops interpreting VBScript when it comes upon this tag:

```
</SCRIPT>
```

Why VBScript Is Sometimes Only a Remark

Unfortunately, while IE recognizes and runs JavaScript along with VBScript, Netscape doesn't return the favor. This is why you'll often see VBScript written with the HTML REMark symbols. When HTML comes upon the <!– symbol, it knows that it should ignore everything between the <!– symbol and the end symbol –>. Between these two symbols, HTML expects to find a *remark,* a mere descriptive comment that the programmer inserted to clarify the purpose or meaning of the programming. A remark is the HTML equivalent of Visual Basic's REM command. It's not something the browser needs to interpret and act on; a remark is strictly for the benefit of the programmer. However, you'll often see VBScript surrounded by these HTML remark symbols, as shown in the following code:

```
<SCRIPT LANGUAGE="VBScript">
<!–
Sub aa_OnLoad()
Image3.AutoSize = True
end sub
–>
</SCRIPT>
```

Does this mean that the script should be considered just a programmer's remark and, therefore, be ignored by the browser? Yes and no. When IE comes to the <SCRIPT LANGUAGE="VBScript"> tag, it ignores those <!– and –> tags. IE interprets the VBScript and carries out the commands that are listed within the VBScript programming. Netscape, however, thinks of VBScript as a group of remarks. Netscape ignores the VBScript language between the <!– and –> tags. What if Netscape came upon some VBScript language that wasn't surrounded by remark tags? Without those tags, Netscape sometimes displays, *as simple text*, the VBScript commands. What a way to puzzle Internet surfers!

BONUS

Using the Script Wizard

In the last two years, Microsoft has added Wizards to some of its applications and software. These intelligent assistants are designed to ease the process of building tables, creating macros, adjusting formats, and many other tasks that are not all that simple for the unassisted novice to undertake. Sometimes Wizards are also useful to advanced computer users as well.

 In Chapter 10, you'll discover how to work with the highly effective Class Builder Utility, a Wizard in disguise.

Not All Wizards Are Created Equal

Not all Wizards are equally useful, though. You may have noticed that a *Script Wizard* is built into the ActiveX Control Pad. This Wizard is supposed to help you write VBScript, but, alas, the Script Wizard is a poor substitute for knowing the VBScript language and typing it in yourself. VBScript has many commands and features that the Wizard doesn't offer and can't assist you with. It's not really the Wizard's fault. No Wizard can step in and thoroughly simplify a computer language, just as no Wizard can turn a clumsy writer into a good one. Languages are too fluid and complex.

A Strange Tool

The Script Wizard is in some ways a strange tool. It's probably too complicated for a novice to understand, yet far too restrictive to be of use to anyone who knows how to accomplish even a little Visual Basic programming. The Script Wizard is really only useful as a quick way for VBScript to insert a template into an HTML page or a Layout Control in the ActiveX Control Pad. If you don't want to type the `<SCRIPT LANGUAGE="VBScript">` start tag and the `</SCRIPT>` end tag (along with the `<!-` and `->` remark tags) use the Wizard to enter that template for you.

If you're just starting out with Visual Basic programming, the Wizard can at least sometimes guide you in the right direction. It asks you to first select an event, and then to choose an action that will be inserted into the event.

Say you want to modify the Web page example you worked on earlier. To change the BackColor of both Image controls that frame the two drawings to a deep blue, do so programmatically when the Layout first loads (in its OnLoad event). Double-click each of the large frame, and you discover that their ID's are Image2 and Image4.

Here's how to use the ActiveX Control Pad VBScript Wizard:

1. Load the example ETCHINGS.HTM into the ActiveX Control Pad. Click **File** and a list of the most recent .HTM files appears, as shown in Figure 4-4.

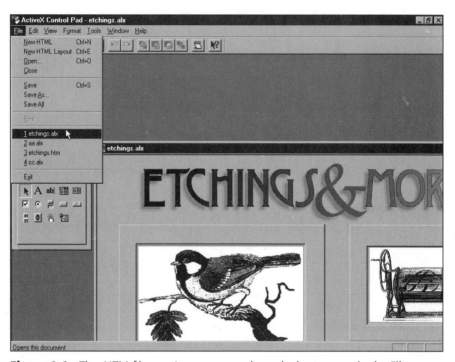

Figure 4-4 The .HTM files you've most recently worked on appear in the File menu.

2. Open the Script Wizard by clicking **Tools** → **Script Wizard** .

3. To change the BackColor of both Image2 and Image4 to blue, in the Select an Event list, click the name you've given the Layout control. In Figure 4-5, the Layout's name is *aa*. Click the OnLoad event.

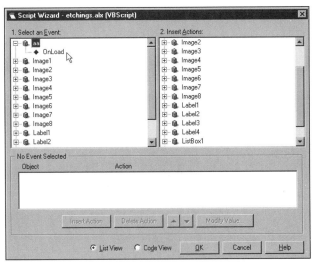

Figure 4-5 The Wizard includes a list of all the ActiveX controls on the current document, along with their events, methods, and properties.

4. In the Insert Actions list, double-click Image2, and then double-click BackColor. The color selector appears, as shown in Figure 4-6.

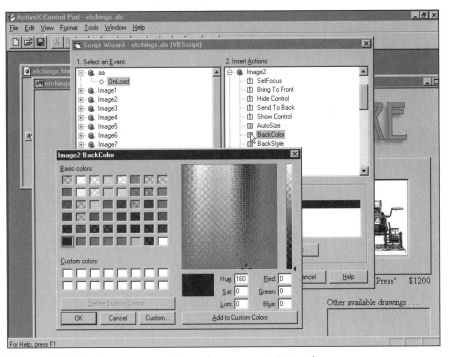

Figure 4-6 The Layout control has only one event: OnLoad

5. Choose a color, and then click OK to close the color selection window.

6. Repeat Steps 4 and 5 with Image4.

7. Click the Code View option button and you should see that the Wizard inserted two lines of programming that adjust the BackColor of the two Image controls, as shown in Figure 4-7.

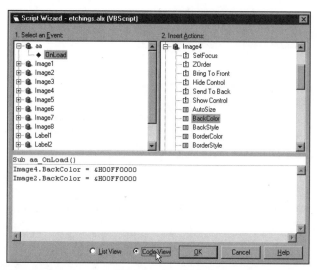

Figure 4-7   The Wizard has created two lines of VBScript programming for you.

8. Click OK to close the Wizard.

If you right-click the Layout after the Wizard is closed, and then choose View Source Code, you'll see that the Wizard has entered two complete lines of programming within the Layout control's OnLoad event:

```
<SCRIPT LANGUAGE="VBScript">
<!—
Sub aa_OnLoad()
Image4.BackColor = &H00FF0000
Image2.BackColor = &H00FF0000
end sub
—>
</SCRIPT>
```

Summary

This chapter concludes your investigation of the ActiveX Control Pad. You've learned how to put it through its various paces, and you've seen how to insert ActiveX controls into HTML Web pages by using VBScript as the glue. At this point in the book, you'll leave the ActiveX Control Pad behind and turn your attention from VBScript to a more robust programming environment: Visual Basic Control Creation Edition, or VBCCE. Like the Control Pad, VBCCE is free; you can find it on the CD-ROM that accompanies this book.

In Part II of this book, you'll discover how to use VBCCE to customize the behavior of existing controls. Then, you can save a customized control as a new control. This new control can be added to the Toolbox and inserted in future projects.

Just as VBScript is a subset of VBCCE, so VBCCE is a subset of Visual Basic. In the next four chapters, you'll explore the potential of VBCCE. Many people find it amazing that such a powerful language is offered, free, from Microsoft.

PART TWO

CREATING COMPOUND CONTROLS

THIS PART CONTAINS THE FOLLOWING CHAPTERS

This second section of the book explores the powerful features of Visual Basic Control Creation Edition. You'll discover how to create custom ActiveX controls and how and when to use the assistance of the built-in Wizards. Finally, you'll find out how to effectively glue your controls into Web pages by using VBScript.

Observers may have wondered why Microsoft is giving VBCCE away. After all, it's a powerful language, a functioning subset of the commercial version of Visual Basic 5.

What's missing? Unlike the commercial version of VB, VBCCE isn't capable of compiling standard .EXE Windows applications — so you can't use it to write a utility that will run by itself in the Windows environment. (You *can* create an .EXE project within the VBCCE for purposes of testing an ActiveX control you're developing. You just can't compile that .EXE project into an .EXE file and save it to disk as an executable program.) You can't create User Documents or Add-Ins to extend the features of the VB IDE (Integrated Design Environment). And VBCCE's help facilities are limited.

But what you *can* do with the VBCCE is fairly astonishing: You can build fully functional ActiveX controls for use in Web pages or in ActiveX-capable applications. What's more, the IDE is virtually identical to the commercial version of VB, complete with powerful debugging facilities, the Object Browser, and helpful Wizard assistance.

With VBCCE you can create a new control of your own, modify an existing control, or collect several existing controls into a single unique control. You can add Property Pages to permit other programmers or users to customize your controls (there's even a Wizard to help you write Property Pages). And the language boasts many other sophisticated features:

* You can have controls behave differently at design time or run time.
* Connecting a control to a database is simplified because controls can be made data-aware.
* You can program your own events into controls you create.
* A Setup Wizard makes it easy to prepare your control for automatic downloading over the Web.
* You can make a control invisible, or make its background transparent.

So why *is* Microsoft giving the VBCCE away? There have been various guesses, but the most likely answer is this: *Java.* Microsoft admits it wasn't first out of the gate with Internet products. And Sun Microsystems' had already developed Java years ago for use in household appliances and microcontrollers.

Microsoft has responded by providing a competing technology, ActiveX. And to make the migration easy for developers, Microsoft has been giving a powerful ActiveX language away. It's VBScript versus JavaScript and VB versus Java. The winner hasn't been announced, but giving away VBCCE can't hurt Microsoft's chances of eventual victory.

USING VISUAL BASIC CONTROL CREATION EDITION

IN THIS CHAPTER YOU LEARN THESE KEY SKILLS

I n this chapter you begin to experience the full power of the Visual Basic programming language. Until now, you've only explored the capabilities of VBScript. VBScript works well within Web pages as a means of communication between the user and prebuilt ActiveX controls. But if you want to create your own ActiveX controls, VBScript isn't sophisticated enough.

Enter Visual Basic Control Creation Edition (VBCCE).

Until the introduction in 1997 of Visual Basic 5.0 and VBCCE, it wasn't possible for a Visual Basic programmer to build an ActiveX control. Visual Basic and other languages could *use* controls; every version of VB, even VBScript, includes a Toolbox that comes with a standard set of controls (such as TextBoxes and OptionButtons) that you can add to a VB program. But, until now, ActiveX controls themselves had to be written in C or Delphi. At long last, you can have the best of both worlds: the ease and efficiency of programming in Visual Basic, coupled with the power and sophistication of creating your own .OCX objects (another name for ActiveX controls).

The .OCX controls you build can be used by any language, application, or platform that accepts ActiveX controls. This expanding ActiveX-capable universe now includes Visual Basic; Microsoft Office applications such as Word and Access; Internet Explorer; and, in the future, the Windows desktop and even Netscape.

Creating Your First Control

Designing and compiling a unique, standalone ActiveX control is easy with VBCCE. Here's a sample of just how easy it is: Say you're designing a Web page that requires the user to enter a password. You want to create a small, single-line TextBox-type control that will permit the user to type in only nine characters, and display ********* rather than the characters themselves.

 In Chapter 6, you'll find out how to add properties (such as **CharacterCount, Font, and BackColor**) that are customizable by a programmer who uses your control.

To create a simple ActiveX control, follow these steps:

1. Start VBCCE. If you've not yet installed it, you can find a copy of the program on the CD-ROM that accompanies this book.

2. Choose ActiveX control, and VBCCE displays the UserControl template shown in Figure 5-1.

3. In the Properties window, change the Name property to **PWordEntry**. (If you don't see the Properties window, press F4 to bring it up.)

4. Select Properties in the Project menu.

5. Change the Project Name to **Entry**, as shown in Figure 5-2.

6. Click the OK button to close the Properties window.

7. Put a TextBox onto the Form. A *Form* is the VBCCE equivalent of the Layout control you used in previous chapters. A Form is the primary unit of organization in VB, both visually and as a way to segregate a project's programming into various logical containers.

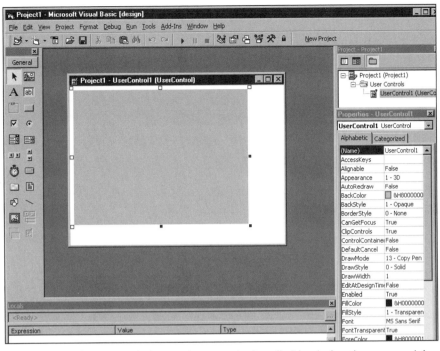

Figure 5-1 The VBCCE design environment is virtually identical to the commercial VB version.

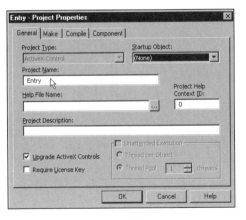

Figure 5-2 Change the Project Name (the filename) here.

 TIP To automatically place the control onto the Form for you, simply double-click a control in the ToolBox. If the ToolBox isn't visible, select it from the View menu.

8. Remove the default Text1 caption inside the TextBox. Just double-click the Text property in the Properties window, and then press the Del key to remove the unwanted *Text1*.

9. In the Properties window, change the TextBox's MaxLength property to **9** and the PasswordChar property to *.

10. Reduce the size of the Form so it just embraces the TextBox, as shown in Figure 5-3.

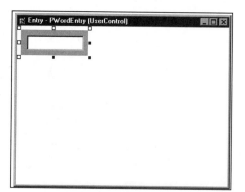

Figure 5-3 You may frequently want to reduce the size of the host Form so that it just frames your ActiveX control.

11. Close the design window by clicking the small x icon in the upper-right corner of the Form.

After you close the design window, look at the Toolbox, down in the corner. It's your new PWordEntry control, sitting there among the other ActiveX controls such as the ListBox and Image control. Now, you can test your new control without even leaving the VBCCE integrated design environment (IDE).

Follow these steps to test the new password-entry control:

1. Start a *regular* VB project (as opposed to an ActiveX .OCX user-control-type project) by clicking File → AddProject .

2. Double-click Standard EXE.

3. Double-click your PWordEntry control on the Toolbox, and it appears on Project1's Form.

4. Press F5 to run Project 1.

You can now type into your PWordEntry custom TextBox. Notice that it only permits you to type nine characters, and that it refuses to display any characters other than the asterisk. Just what you wanted.

Making Your Control Official

When you're satisfied that your new control is well tested and ready for general use, you can compile an official .OCX version. This adds your control to the components that are available for use with the ActiveX

Control Pad or any version of Visual Basic (including VBA, built into Microsoft Office applications such as Word, VBCCE, and the commercial versions of VB).

Compiling Your Control

To compile your control, double-click PWordEntry in the Project Explorer window, so that your user-control design window becomes the active window. Then choose Make Entry.ocx from the File menu (this selection assumes that you named this project *Entry*). Click the OK button.

When VBCCE finishes the compilation, the new ActiveX control is *registered* by Windows and, thereby, becomes available for use by any ActiveX-capable language or application.

 This same registration process is handled during setup when you distribute an ActiveX control to others. You'll see how this is done in Chapter 12.

Verifying Registration

To verify that your control has been registered and is now available for use, choose New Project from the File menu, and double-click Standard EXE. Now right-click the Toolbox and choose Components (or press Ctrl+T) to bring up the Components dialog box shown in Figure 5-4.

Figure 5-4 Your component is properly registered by Windows and can be added to your Toolbox.

Click the OK button. Your custom ActiveX password-entry control appears on the Toolbox, ready to be added to any future Visual Basic application or Web page you design.

Using Your Control in Word and Control Pad

Is this newly registered ActiveX control (called *Entry*) available for use in Word or the ActiveX Control Pad? Sure.

Follow these steps to insert your password-entry control into Word:

1. In Word 97, press Alt+F11 to bring up the Macro Editor window.

2. Click ` Insert ` → ` UserForm `.

3. Click ` View ` → ` ToolBox `.

4. Right-click the Toolbox and select Additional Controls.

5. Scroll the list until you see your ActiveX control, `Entry.PWordEntry`. Select it.

6. This ActiveX control now appears on Word's Macro Editor Toolbox, as shown in Figure 5-5.

Figure 5-5 Your new ActiveX control has been added to the standard Word97 Toolbox.

To add the Entry control to the ActiveX Control Pad's Toolbox, follow the same steps. While viewing a Layout control in the ActiveX Control Pad, right-click the Toolbox and select Additional Controls. (If the Toolbox isn't visible, select it from the View menu.) Then scroll the list until you see `Entry.PWordEntry` and select it.

Using the New VBCCE Standard Controls

In Chapter 2 you learned the purpose and features of the standard set of 13 ActiveX controls that came with the ActiveX Control Pad. If you look at the VBCCE Toolbox, you'll notice that it includes eight additional standard controls: PictureBox, Frame, Timer, DriveListBox, DirListBox, FileListBox, Shape, and Line. Some of these new controls are powerful and important, so if you haven't used them before, you'll want to read the following sections.

The PictureBox: A Heavy-Duty Image Control

The PictureBox serves the same purpose as the Image control — displaying graphics files — but the PictureBox has some special features of its own. For one thing, you can *group* other controls onto a PictureBox. This grouping means that any controls you placed onto a PictureBox will move with the PictureBox when you drag the PictureBox to reposition it. Grouping also has an effect on OptionButton controls: Only one of the group can be selected at a given time. (The Frame control has this same grouping capability.)

In contrast to the Image control, a PictureBox doesn't have a way of automatically stretching or resizing a graphic (as you can do by changing the Image Control's Stretch property). However, a PictureBox does have an AutoSize property that causes the PictureBox to grow or shrink so it becomes the exact size of any graphic loaded into it. An Image control can't do this, though it is of limited usefulness. You don't want elements of a Web page resizing themselves — it's generally better if you, the programmer, organize controls by size and position beforehand. After a document is designed, it would be awkward if a new graphic loaded into a PictureBox caused the PictureBox to expand wildly and, for example, covered up a Label control intended to display a caption.

Unless you need some of the features of a PictureBox, you should use an Image control instead — the Image control is a simpler, smaller control and takes up fewer system resources. It also loads faster into a user's browser.

Frame: Zoning Your Pages

The Frame control has two uses. Like the PictureBox, a Frame can group other controls, such as a set of OptionButtons. Of more value, though, is that a Frame is often useful as an attractive way to organize documents into logical sections. For instance, if you're displaying the results of state elections, you can divide the Web page into the 12 counties. HTML, of course, also has a FRAME command, but this command can be overkill when you don't need individually scrollable virtual documents within the main document. If all you want to do is divide a document into visually logical sections, use the VB Frame control.

VB Frames are superior to HTML FRAMEs in several ways. To begin with, it's easier to position and size a VB Frame — just drag it around until you get it where you like it. Secondly, that same ease of design applies to any text labels or other controls that you've placed within the Frame. Finally, a VB Frame has a Caption property with which you can label and identify the contents of the area enclosed by the Frame. Even better, a Frame isn't just a plain line. It's a 3D effect and makes a subdivided document look slick and sophisticated, as you can see in Figure 5-6.

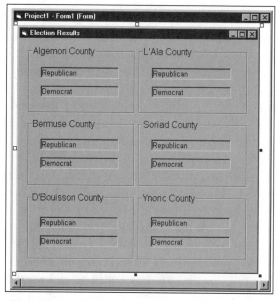

Figure 5-6 When you want to divide a document into logical sections, consider using the VB Frame control.

Timer: High-Precision Timing

The Timer control is often essential for such tasks as animation, reminder utilities, and other applications when the accurate measure of passing time is important. The Timer is one of the most useful of all the VB controls.

Think of the Timer control as a super kitchen timer. You give it an amount of time by setting its Interval property, as in the following code:

```
Timer1.Interval = 10000
```

Then the timer will "go off" in ten seconds. In other words, whatever programming commands you've placed within the Timer event will be carried out when the time comes (that is, when the Interval has passed).

TWO PROPERTIES INTERACT

Note that two properties of a Timer control must be correctly set before the Timer will begin its countdown. The Interval must be other than the default zero and the Enabled property must be set to True (it defaults to True).

If you make no changes to these two properties, nothing will happen. By default, Enabled is turned on, but Interval is zero. Nothing will happen unless you provide some Interval. The Interval is measured in milliseconds, so an Interval of 2,000 is two seconds.

To see how a timer works, start a new VBCCE project by pressing Ctrl+N and selecting Standard EXE. Put a CommandButton and a Timer on the Form. In the

CommandButton's Click event, type: **Timer1.Interval = 20000** and in the Timer's Timer event, type the following code:

```
Private Sub Timer1_Timer()
MsgBox "Time is up!"
Timer1.Interval = 0
End Sub
```

Press F5 to start the program running and, after 20 seconds have elapsed, a message appears. If you hadn't set the Interval back to zero, the message would appear every 20 seconds as long as this program continues running. The Interval continues to count down and the Timer repeatedly goes off, unless you intervene by turning off the timer. You can do this by setting its Interval to zero or its Enabled property to False.

TIMERS HAVE MANY USES

Timers can be used in several ways. You can use one to cause short delays in animations. Perhaps you want a 50 millisecond pause between flashing different graphics, or between increments of a graphic's Top or Left properties, to move the graphic across a Form.

Or, you can use a Timer to cause something to happen after an interval of time has passed (such as a traditional kitchen timer). The Interval property can be set to a maximum of only 65,565 milliseconds — a bit longer than a minute. Nevertheless, it's easy enough to create longer intervals by using a Static variable to count minutes, or even hours. Assume that, in a CommandButton or some other triggering mechanism, you set the Interval of this timer to 60,000. Then, to make the Timer go off after 5 minutes, insert the following code:

```
Private Sub Timer1_Timer()
Static counter
counter = counter + 1
If counter = 5 Then
MsgBox "Time is up!"
Timer1.Interval = 0
End If
End Sub
```

Each time the Interval passes (once every minute), the Timer carries out the instructions you've given it. It raises the counter variable by one. When the counter reaches five, five minutes has passed and the Timer finally "goes off" and displays its message.

An alternative technique is to use a Timer's Interval as a way of regularly checking the computer's clock. Assume that, in a CommandButton or some other triggering mechanism, you set the Interval of this Timer to 30,000 so the time will be checked every 30 seconds. Then, in the Timer's event, you check to see if it's 4:49 p.m. yet. Note that the Hour function provides military time, so 4:00 p.m. is 16.

```
Private Sub Timer1_Timer()
hr = Hour(Now)
mn = Minute(Now)
If hr = 16 And mn >= 49 Then
MsgBox "It's 4:49"
End If
End Sub
```

One final trick: Because the Timer can do things at regular intervals, you can use the Properties window to change a Timer's Interval property to, perhaps, 1,000, and then display a digital clock, as shown in the following code and in Figure 5-7:

```
Private Sub Timer1_Timer()
Label1 = Time
End Sub
```

Figure 5-7 It's easy to create a digital clock with the Timer control.

DriveListBox, DirListBox, FileListBox: Antique File Access

When the DriveListBox, DirListBox, and FileListBox controls are used together, you can offer the user a complete disk-file access interface. However, Microsoft created a CommonDialog control that features a set of standardized Windows 95 user interfaces for printer setup, color preferences, fonts, and opening or saving files. You should, therefore, ignore the old-style DriveListBox, DirListBox, and FileListBox controls.

If you are designing an application or ActiveX object that requires you to let users interact with their hard drive, use the CommonDialog control. To see if you have this control available on your computer, right-click the VBCCE Toolbox and select Components. Scroll the list to see if Microsoft CommonDialog control is listed, as shown in Figure 5-8.

If you don't see the CommonDialog control in the list of available components, you can get it by buying a copy of Visual Basic 5.0.

You don't want to turn back time and piece together your own, inevitably quirky, nonstandard hard-drive access interface. One valuable quality of Windows 95 and NT is that many user interfaces have become standardized. When the user wants to open a file, the identical FileOpen dialog box appears in a word processor such as Word for Windows, and in a photo-retouching application such as Photoshop. This way, users don't have to adjust to different disk-access dialog boxes for each of their applications (as was true prior to Windows 95).

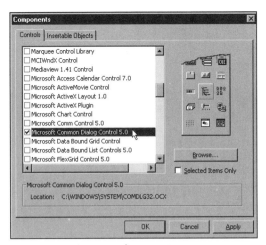

Figure 5-8 Use the CommonDialog control rather than the outdated DriveListBox, DirListBox, and FileListBox controls.

TIP The Common Dialog control is *modal*. This means that, like other dialog boxes and the VB MsgBox and InputBox commands, the CommonDialog will halt your program. A modal window remains up there on the user's screen until the user makes a selection or, at the very least, clicks the OK or Cancel buttons and thereby shuts this dialog box.

If you want to permit users to open a disk file, first show them the standard CommonDialog window (see Figure 5-9), and then use the FileName property of the CommonDialog to find out the path of the file they chose. To see how this works, put a CommandButton, a CommonDialog control, and a TextBox on a Form. Set the TextBox's MultiLine property to True, and then type in the following code:

```
Sub Command1_Click()
On Error Resume Next
CommonDialog1.ShowOpen
Open CommonDialog1.filename For Input As #1
If Err Then MsgBox Error(Err): Exit Sub
n = Input(LOF(1), 1)
Close
Text1 = n
End Sub
```

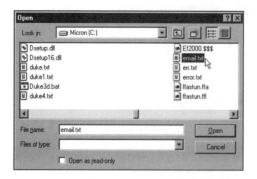

Figure 5-9 Microsoft standardized the user interface for file access.

Notice that after the user selects a filename, the complete path for that filename is available to you (the programmer) in the *CommonDialog.filename*. You can use it to open the file, as illustrated in the preceding programming.

Shape and Line: Simple Designs

The Shape and Line controls are too elementary to be of much use these days. The Line control displays a line; the Shape control displays one of six shapes: square, circle, rectangle, oval, rounded square, or rounded rectangle. You can change the color, width, and other properties of the Lines or Shapes.

If you want these graphic effects, you don't have to use these controls. You can draw lines and shapes programmatically by using VB's Line and Circle commands. However, as usual, it's easier to resize and position controls with the mouse than it is to calculate coordinates programmatically.

The real problem with the Shape and Line controls is that they're not visually sophisticated. As you can see in Figure 5-10, the 3D effect created by the Frame control fits in better with the other 3D effects in the Windows 95 user interface. Note that VB Forms and other Windows 95 windows are themselves framed with 3D lines, not the simple single lines available to the Shape and Line controls.

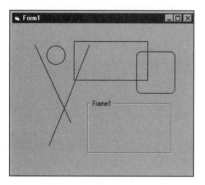

Figure 5-10 Users expect 3D effects (such as the Frame control), not the flat, simple geometrics of Line and Shape controls.

Exploring the Major Features of the IDE

Now that you've learned the primary qualities of the new controls on the VBCCE standard Toolbox, it's time to consider the VBCCE in general. It's a powerful tool.

Recall that the ActiveX Control Pad is an environment in which you can create simple VBScript. And, of course, the ActiveX Control Pad is also useful as a way of adding ActiveX controls to a Web page (the Control Pad automatically generates that necessary, but huge, CLASSID specification). Finally, the Layout control that comes with the ActiveX Control Pad is superior to plain HTML as a way of positioning and sizing controls on a Web page.

However, the integrated design environment (IDE) for creating controls with VBCCE is far more sophisticated than the Control Pad, just as VBCCE is a far more sophisticated language than VBScript. In fact, in many respects, the VBCCE IDE is identical to Visual Basic 5.0 (the full, commercial version of the Visual Basic language).

This book assumes that the reader has a general familiarity with programming. There are, however, aspects of Visual Basic and the VB IDE that are unique or at least somewhat different from other languages' IDEs. These unique or different features are covered in the remainder of this chapter.

An Optional Multiple-Document Interface

FEATURE FOCUS

By default, VBCCE offers a multiple-document interface — windows within windows. This interface makes it seem as if you opened several documents within a word processor. You can resize them and rearrange them, but you can't drag these child windows outside the parent window (see Figure 5-11).

Until VB 5.0 (and VBCCE), the VB IDE was a single document interface — a set of windows that are independent and reside on the Windows desktop as individual windows. If you prefer the single document interface, shown in Figure 5-12, select Options from the Tools menu. Then click the Advanced tab and click SDI Development Environment.

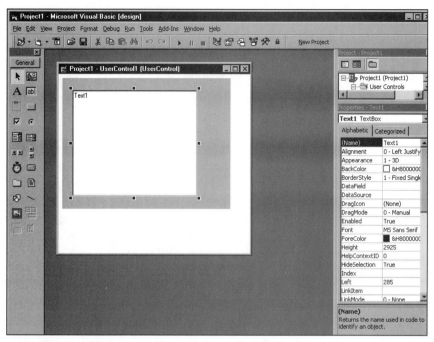

Figure 5-11　None of these child windows can be dragged outside the large parent window.

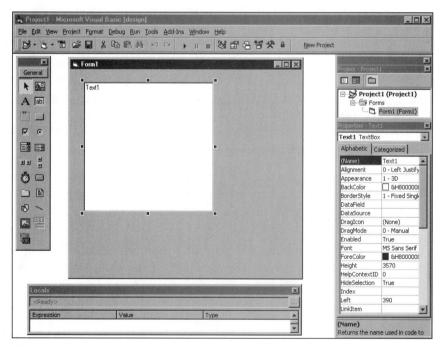

Figure 5-12　You can choose the single document interface (the pre-VB5 default) if you wish.

NUDGING AND RESIZING

VB includes several highly effective design features. To explore them, consider the following figure. Surely you'll agree that the CommandButton is a bit too tall.

You could drag this CommandButton to make it narrower, but that's an imprecise approach. It's difficult to control dragging to make fine, exact adjustments. A better solution when you're positioning or sizing controls is to use the special VB keyboard positioning feature. Click the CommandButton to highlight it. Then press Shift+UpArrow. Each time you tap the UpArrow key, the CommandButton will grow one pixel narrower. To make larger changes, hold down the Shift+UpArrow keys. Likewise, to make the control taller, use Shift+DownArrow; to make it wider use Shift+RightArrow; to make it narrower, use Shift+LeftArrow.

To position a control, click the control to select it, and then press Ctrl+DownArrow to move it down, and Ctrl+LeftArrow, Ctrl+RightArrow and Ctrl+UpArrow to move in those directions. In the figure to the left, the CommandButton has been both resized and repositioned.

Multiple Projects

A program is called a *project* in VB. In other words, any self-contained entity that you can compile into a standalone .EXE file, or an .OCX ActiveX control is called a *project*. What's new in VB5 and VBCCE is that you can simultaneously have more than one project active within the IDE at a given time. And you can make these projects interact.

This feature is useful if you're building an ActiveX control because controls can't be tested or debugged all by themselves. To test a control, you have to provide a client for the control (an application or Web page). That's why it's valuable to be able to create both a Standard EXE project (the client) and a control (the server) in the same Visual Basic IDE.

After you create a User control, follow these steps to test it:

1. Click **File** → **AddProject**

2. Choose Standard EXE as the project type.

3. Close the User control window by clicking the X button in the upper-right corner of the window. Your User control is then placed onto the Toolbox.

4. Double-click your User control on the Toolbox to place it on the Standard EXE Form.

5. Press F5 to run the Standard EXE program (or *project* as it's called in VB) and test the various features of your ActiveX control.

How to Align Controls

To make your projects look well-crafted, related controls should be aligned and of identical size. For example, if you have two CommandButtons (Cancel and OK), they should be aligned vertically (that is, their Top property should be identical) and they should be the same Width and Height. Even small differences are detectable and make your user interface look sloppy, as you can see in Figure 5-13, in which the CommandButton on the left isn't top-aligned with the other button.

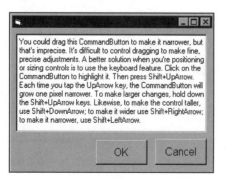

Figure 15-13 The CommandButton captioned OK isn't top-aligned with the other button.

To align (by size or position) a set of controls, follow these steps:

1. Hold down the Shift key while clicking each control you want to align. This selects them all as a group. (You can also drag the mouse around the entire set to collectively select them.)

2. Click `Format` → `Make Same Size` → `Both` to force the controls to be the same size, as shown in Figure 5-14.

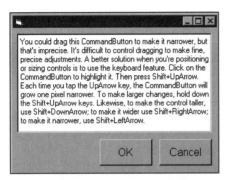

Figure 5-14 After using the Make Same feature, both CommandButtons are the same height.

3. Click `Format` → `Align` → `Tops` to make the controls vertically aligned.

TIP Note the Lock Controls option on the Format menu. When you're satisfied with the alignment and sizing of all the controls on a Form, click Lock Controls. This way, when you're double-clicking a control in the future (to get to its code window), you won't accidentally nudge the control out of alignment.

Understanding Components, Objects, and References

VBCCE divides objects into several categories. The Components dialog box displays controls or "insertable objects" that can be put onto the Toolbox for insertion into Forms. The Object Browser displays libraries of commands and constants that you can use in your programming. The References dialog box enables you to specify the order of precedence of object libraries, or to add new libraries to your current project.

Manage the Toolbox with the Components Dialog Box

Components are ActiveX controls that you can add to the VBCCE Toolbox, and, therefore, use in your projects. Some of these components come with the ActiveX

Control Pad, VBCCE, VB, or Microsoft Office. These "built-in" components are registered (made available) when these languages, IDEs, or office applications are first installed on your computer. Other components can be downloaded from Microsoft's ActiveX Web site at:

WEB PATH **http://www.microsoft.com/activex/controls**

or purchased from ads in magazines or other sources. However you acquire these components, any ActiveX controls that have been installed (registered) on your computer will be listed in the Components dialog box, ready to be added to the Toolbox, as shown in Figure 5-15.

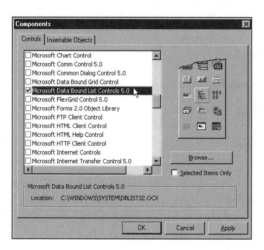

Figure 5-15 Click any of these ActiveX controls to add them to your VBCCE Toolbox.

To bring up the Components dialog box, you can use three different techniques:

* Right-click the Toolbox.
* Choose Components from the Project menu.
* Press Ctrl+T.

TIP If you think that an ActiveX control is available on your hard drive, but it doesn't show up in the list in the Components dialog box, click the Browse button and locate the control. This step adds the control to your Components list, and also registers it with Windows.

Notice that two tabs appear in the Components dialog box: Components and Insertable Objects. Insertable objects are OLE-capable objects that act as servers, such as WordPad or Word documents, MIDI music sequences, PhotoShop images, Microsoft Access's Calendar object, and so on. Unlike ActiveX controls, these insertable objects cannot be directly placed onto a User control that you're creating in the VBCCE.

If you're working on a User control, all insertable objects will remain disabled (grayed out) on the Toolbox. However, you *can* use these objects in your

User controls. Just put insertable objects onto a regular VBCCE Form that is displayed by a User control. To do this while you work on a User control, choose Add Form from the Project menu. Onto this Form you can place an insertable object. Then, perhaps in the User control's Initialized event, you would display the Form using this programming: `Form1.Show`.

The Object Browser

Press F2 and a hidden help feature appears: the Object Browser. It's not listed as help, or organized like most Windows applications' help systems, but it's sometimes quite helpful nonetheless.

When you press F2, you see the Object Browser, as shown in Figure 5-16. Here you can look at lists of all the properties, methods, events, and constants available to your project — including any you've defined in your project itself. The Object Browser displays a set of libraries.

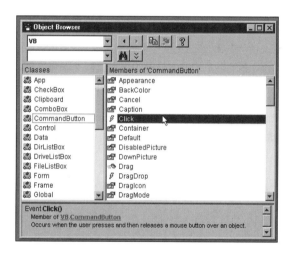

Figure 5-16 Select any of the items in the Classes list to see their syntax and a brief definition.

Some of the libraries are permanent. In the list of libraries you'll always find VB (containing all the default VB controls, and objects such as the App and Printer); VBA (many functions such as date/time and financial commands, the error object, variable handling such as conversion and query commands, and miscellaneous other sets of functions such as disk file commands); VBRUN (miscellaneous sets of constants, such as scalemodes and fillstyles); and Stdole (font and graphics objects).

Any other libraries displayed depend on what controls or insertable objects you've added to the Toolbox, as well as any libraries you've added using the References option on the Project menu.

The primary value of the Object Browser is that it can refresh your memory if you've forgotten the syntax (or purpose) of a particular property, method, event, or constant. For instance, VBCCE includes a group of constants you can use with the FillStyle property. If you forget what they are, press F2, select VBRUN as the library, and locate FillStyleConstants in the Classes list.

Add Libraries with the References Dialog Box

Choose References from the Project menu and the References dialog box appears, as shown in Figure 5-17.

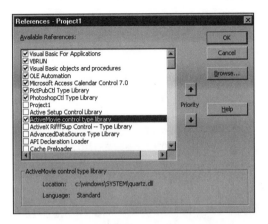

Figure 5-17 In this dialog box you can add, remove, or prioritize libraries.

The References dialog box should probably have been located in the Object Browser as a CommandButton option you could click. Generally, the References dialog box enables you to select new libraries to add to those already in use. You can also deselect libraries if they are not being used by the current project.

Also, the possibility always exists that two properties, methods, events, or constants from two different libraries will share the same name. If this occurs, VBCCE uses the definition in whichever library appears highest in the list of libraries. If you wish, you can rearrange the order of the libraries list by selecting a library, then clicking the arrows above and below the word *Priority*, as shown in Figure 5-17.

BONUS

A Rich Set of Debugging Features

VBCCE provides a generous set of tools to assist you in debugging your projects. When it's time to track down errors in a program, Visual Basic comes to your aid in a variety of ways. And unlike many other computer languages, you can even adjust the source code and immediately test the effects of your changes.

Immediate, Local, and Watch Windows

Something has gone wrong in your programming. You're trying to add 2 + 2 and you keep getting 5. That does it! It's usually easy enough to recognize that a problem exists, but it's the *where* that's often so hard to figure out.

As an example, assume that you put a CommandButton on a VBCCE Form. When clicked, this CommandButton is supposed to add 2 + 2 and display the result in a TextBox. But every time you click the CommandButton, a 1 is displayed in the TextBox. What a head-scratcher!

Start a new project by pressing Ctrl+N. Select Standard EXE. Type **Dim X As Boolean** at the very top of the code window, in the General Declarations section of the Form (before any events, Subs, or Functions).

Then type the following programming inside the CommandButton's Click event:

```
Private Sub Command1_Click()
x = 2
y = 2
z = x + y
Text1 = z
End Sub
```

Seems solid enough. How come when you click the CommandButton you always get 1 as the answer?

The first technique to try in these situations is single-stepping, with a Watch. Press F8 and you will move one line at a time through the programming. Add a Watch for each of the three variables, and you will see when something unexpected happens. A Watch opens a window that shows the current status of any variables you've requested be watched. You can, as you may have suspected, *watch* what happens to these variables and, thereby, perhaps detect when things have gone awry in your program.

Follow these steps to set up a variable Watch and step through the programming:

1. Add a Watch for variable *x* by clicking Debug → Add Watch , as shown in Figure 5-18.

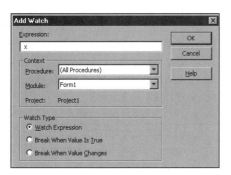

Figure 5-18 Here's where you can tell VBCCE that you want to watch a particular variable.

2. Repeat Step 1 to add Watches for variables *y* and *z*.

3. The Watch window appears.

4. Press F8 to start your program. Click the CommandButton to begin the action. If you don't see the Watch window, click View → Watch Window .

5. Press F8 to step through each line of programming, and watch the Watch window to see the effect on the variables, as shown in Figure 5-19.

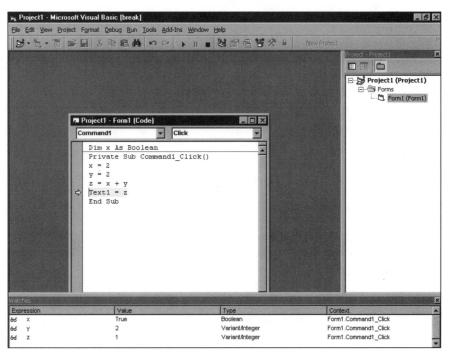

Figure 5-19 Notice the Watch window at the bottom of this figure. Eagle-eyed readers will see an anomaly in this window.

The game is up! As you can see in Figure 5-19, the variable *x* has been defined as Boolean, so it can only hold the values True and False. It cannot hold numbers such as 2. Look up in the preceding code window, and you'll see that the variable *x* was defined as Boolean and, because the Dim was outside of any procedure (that is, it wasn't between a Sub and End Sub or between a Function and End Function command), the definition applies to this entire Form. The definition is in the General Declarations section of this Form and, therefore, is global to the Form. The variables *y* and *z* are local to their procedure — so they are, by default, Variant types and can hold numbers.

Of course, this is an artificial example. The program is so small that it's hard to avoid noticing the problem. In a larger program, though, just this kind of error can occur, and the Watch window and single-stepping technique can help you track it down.

TIP Shift+F9 is a handy shortcut to remember. When a running VB program has been halted, you're in *break mode.* You pressed Ctrl+Break, VB came upon a Stop command in the programming, you're single-stepping through the program, or a breakpoint was encountered — all these situations put a program into break mode. If you highlight a variable or expression in the code window while in break mode, pressing Shift+F9 brings up a Quick Watch window, telling you the value currently held in that variable or expression, as shown in Figure 5-20.

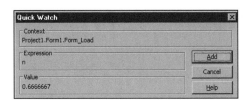

Figure 5-20 The Quick Watch window shows the contents of a single variable or expression.

While the Quick Watch window is displayed, you can click the Add button and the variable or expression is added to the permanent Watch window.

USE THE IMMEDIATE WINDOW FOR QUICK CHECKS

You have an alternative to the Quick Watch. While in break mode, you can use the Immediate window to query the contents of a variable or expression. Just type in **? n** and press Enter to see the contents of variable *n*. Likewise, you can test any procedure from the Immediate window. If you have written a function that turns a string into uppercase letters, as in the following code:

```
Function uppr(t As String)
uppr = UCase(t)
End Function
```

you can test that function while in break mode by typing **? uppr ("thomas")** and pressing Enter into the Immediate window. You'll then see the result: THOMAS.

THE LOCALS WINDOW SHOWS EVERYTHING

FEATURE FOCUS The Locals window is a new feature of VBCCE and VB5. If you want to watch the contents of *all* the variables in the current procedure, you don't have to add each of them to the Watch window. Just click View → Locals Window and press F8 to step through your programming.

All the Rest

VBCCE and VB5 include numerous debugging facilities. For example, you can have VB keep an eye on one or more variables, and break to display a line where something anomalous took place.

Assume that, for reasons you can't figure out, the total employees figure for your company (held in variable *empl*) goes negative while your program is running. This is an impossibility, yet there it is on screen: you have –12 employees.

This kind of error is easy to track down by setting an intelligent breakpoint. Click Debug→Add Watch, and type in your conditions. In this case, you will type in **empl < 0**. Now, when the value in the variable *empl* falls below zero, VB will halt the program and display the offending line where this condition, this impossible condition, became true.

Within the Add Watch dialog box, you can also set the scope of the watch, and define watches that will trap any kind of change or condition. Is something true? Did it change? Is something equal to something else? Whatever condition you want to test for, you can define it in this Watch dialog box.

SEVERAL KINDS OF STEPPING

VBScript also provides several kinds of *stepping*, in addition to pressing F8, to single-step through the program. You can Step Over (Shift+F8), which is like single-stepping, but it skips over a procedure (if you're about to step into one). This way you can skip stepping through a procedure that's been tested and is known to be good.

FEATURE FOCUS New to VBCCE and VB5 is the Step Out (Ctrl+Shift+F8) feature, which speeds through any remaining lines of programming in the current procedure, and then stops on the next line in your program outside the current procedure. If you're within a procedure that you're confident isn't causing the bug, Step Out and then resume single-stepping once you're past the current procedure.

FEATURE FOCUS Also new in VBCCE and VB5 is the Run To Cursor (Ctrl+F8) feature. You can click in the programming code somewhere else other than your current location. This moves the insertion cursor, the blinking vertical line. Press Ctrl+F8 and VB rapidly executes all the lines between your current location in the code and the location where you placed the cursor.

Toggle breakpoints

If you know of a location within the programming code where you want VB to stop during execution, press F9 or click in the left margin of the code window. Either action inserts a breakpoint and displays a red dot. VB will halt execution at this location. You can insert as many breakpoints as you wish. Pressing F9 a second time, or clicking the red dot in the margin, toggles the breakpoint off.

You can clear all the breakpoints in your entire program by pressing Ctrl+Shift+F9 (or clicking Clear All Breakpoints on the Debug menu). Pressing Ctrl+F9 (or selecting Set Next Statement in the Debug menu) will cause VB to restart running from the line you click. This feature is similar to the Run To Cursor feature described previously, but instead of running from the current location to the new cursor point, Set Next Statement instead *skips* all the programming between the current line and new cursor insertion point. It then resumes executing lines at the new cursor point. The Set Next Statement feature would be useful if you have a large For. . .Next Loop, for example, that you want to skip over rather than try to single-step through.

Summary

In this chapter, you learned how to create a simple ActiveX control, and then how to compile it and register it. Following that, you found out the value, or lack thereof, of the new standard controls that come with the VBCCE language. You saw how to use several of the impressive features of the VBCCE's integrated development editor (IDE) — its programming environment. Finally, you learned of the various dialog boxes in the IDE that handle libraries of components, and also how to use the IDE's robust debugging apparatus.

CHAPTER SIX

SUBCLASSING

There's no reason for you to figure out the low-level complexities of displaying a font or color on a UserControl that you create. VB contains loads of properties, methods, and events that can accomplish those jobs and much more. If you want your UserControl to enable users to type in text, for example, you don't need to write the code that accepts and displays text — just plug a VB TextBox into the UserControl. By borrowing features from existing objects, you can get all the functionality that dozens of Microsoft programmers took dozens of years to create. Borrowing features from existing objects is called *subclassing* and is the subject of this chapter.

Subclassing Saves You Time and Trouble

To understand subclassing, you must first read about a more basic topic: *What is a class?*

The concept of a *class* has been compared to a template, a recipe, and a blueprint. In other words, a class is abstract; it isn't a thing in itself. A class is a plan that describes how to create something real and how to create an object such as an ActiveX control that actually does something in the real world.

If you look at a control's icon, such as the TextBox icon on the VBCCE Toolbox, you're looking at a class — a symbol of a description. If you double-click that TextBox icon on the Toolbox, an actual control is then inserted on the current Form. Thus, a class is a plan that describes the qualities and behaviors of an object. From one class you can stamp out as many identical objects as you want.

Subclassing means taking an existing class and modifying it in some way. It's like buying a set of blueprints for a house, but changing the size of the den or adding a sunroom to the original floorplan. You can then use that *subclass* to stamp out as many identical objects — of the new, modified object — as you want.

In its broadest definition, to *subclass* means to create a new ActiveX control out of an existing control.

 In Chapter 5, you created your first ActiveX control, a password-entry box, by modifying a standard TextBox to make it do what you wanted.

The value of subclassing is obvious: Why reinvent the wheel if a few changes to a PictureBox or some other existing control will do what you want?

Visual Basic, in all its versions, offers impressive functionality to the programmer. For example, the programmer has a set of financial functions that return all the answers that could be desired by accountants or anyone else involved in the mathematics of business (VBScript doesn't include these functions). You could gather these various financial functions — depreciation, annuities, rate of return, net present value — into a single ActiveX control of your own devising. Then, by adding this control to a Web page, you immediately provide all these functions to any user of that Web page. Also, you provide these functions to any programmers who insert your control into their Web pages.

Gathering Functionality

Borrowing functionality from existing controls is another form of subclassing. When you borrow functionality, you use elements of the VB language, but gather them together in your own fashion. Perhaps you organize the elements in a special way, or attach a user-interface so that clicking a CommandButton produces a series of questions.

In effect, when you borrow functionality from existing controls, you create a new class (a description of the qualities and behaviors of an ActiveX object). Then, into your class, you place an existing object or set of objects. Your new class, therefore, acts as a shell, enclosing the features of an existing class or set of classes. To the programmer or user who interacts with your new ActiveX control, a subclassed UserControl seems to be just another control. In fact, you've merely borrowed features from existing controls, perhaps modified some of those features or added features of your own, and then wrapped the whole package in a new ActiveX control envelope.

> **TIP** *Subclassing* is another word for a classic element of Object-Oriented Programming (OOP), called *inheritance*. Both terms mean that you take an existing class and modify it by making it more specialized. In this sense, when you extended the existing TextBox in Chapter 5, you made it into a password-entry TextBox — a more specialized form of the original TextBox class. You'll learn much more about OOP in Chapter 9. For now it's enough to know that VB doesn't permit "true" inheritance as defined by strict OOP enthusiasts because no parent-child relationship exists between the original class and the subclass. You can, however, be grateful for this because it avoids certain problems inherent in strict OOP. In VB, for example, the original (or "parent") class is isolated from the subclass (or "child"). This isolation means that if you change an original class, you can't cause problems in the subclass — classes and subclasses have no dynamic relationship in VB.

Creating an Aggregate Control

When you wrap several existing controls or functions into a single, new control, the result is called an *aggregate control*. Perhaps you decide to create a new control that accepts the address and phone number from a visitor to a Web page. You could subclass several TextBoxes into this new aggregate control.

Not only can you cluster a group of existing controls, you can also write programming that ties them together. For example, suppose that the first TextBox is labeled *Name*, the fourth TextBox is labeled *City*, and the fifth, *State*. You can write programming that tests each of these TextBoxes to see if they contain any digits. If they do, you display a message box telling the user there has been an error. This way, your new aggregate control can provide properties, methods, and even events — just like any existing, commercial control.

Drawing Your Own Control

As you can see, it's possible to subclass by modifying the behavior of an existing control, or gathering more than one control (or function) into an aggregate control. Another possibility is to *draw* your own control.

By default, when you create a new ActiveX control, a simple icon is placed onto the Toolbox. You can change this icon by changing the ToolboxBitmap property of the control. For complete instructions on how to create custom icons using Windows' Paint utility, see the "Bonus" section in Chapter 7.

You can also design the appearance of the control itself — how it will look to a developer after it is placed onto a Form or displayed to a user by a running application.

 X-REF You learn how to build a user-drawn control in Chapter 16.

 TIP Given the richness of Visual Basic, it's well worth your time to learn the language — all its features, functions, and controls. That way, when the time comes for you to create your own ActiveX control, you won't necessarily have to start from scratch. The deeper your knowledge of existing Visual Basic capabilities, the less likely you are to overlook existing features you could subclass into your own controls.

 NOTE You may recall from Chapter 4 that three levels of people interact with a control, and that each level has a different degree of permission to define the behavior of that control.

* Creators have complete freedom to define a UserControl.
* Developers put your UserControl into one of their projects or Web pages (or other container), have whatever freedom to manipulate the control the creator permits them (by offering events, methods, and properties that can be adjusted).
* Users can only customize a control to the extent permitted by the developer, via Customize or Options menus, property pages, and so on.

Adding a Method

To understand how to add behaviors to your controls, try modifying the password-entry example you created in Chapter 5. The goal now is to add a method to that password control. When developers access this method you've provided them, the password control will be centered on the screen.

Start VBCCE and load the password control. Then recreate the password control.

To recreate the password control from Chapter 5, follow these steps:

1. Start a UserControl project type in the VBCCE.

2. Put a TextBox onto the UserControl.

3. In the Properties window, change the TextBox's MaxLength property to **9** and its PasswordChar property to *****.

4. Delete *Text1*, the default Text property.

5. Resize the UserControl so it's only slightly larger than the TextBox.

6. In the Properties window, change the UserControl's BackStyle property to **Transparent**. This way, future users of your control can add it to Forms with backcolors other than the standard windows gray — and the UserControl won't show up as a gray frame around the TextBox.

X-REF There are other ways to deal with the issue of keeping properties (such as BackColor) in sync between a container and a UserControl. See the discussion of the Ambient object in the "Bonus" section of Chapter 9.

Now create a Standard EXE project that you can use to test the UserControl.

To create a Standard EXE project to test the control, follow these steps:

1. Click File → AddProject and choose Standard EXE.

2. Close Project1, the UserControl, by clicking the x icon in the upper-right corner of Project1's design window. This step makes it available on the Toolbar.

3. Double-click the UserControl on the Toolbar to add it to the standard EXE (Project2).

Look at the Object Browser to see what properties, methods, and events of the original TextBox survived to become part of your UserControl. Press F2 to bring up the Object Browser. In its Libraries list, select Project1. Click UserControl1 in the Classes list and you see UserControl1's properties, methods, and events (collectively these three elements are called the *members* of the UserControl1 class), as shown in Figure 6-1.

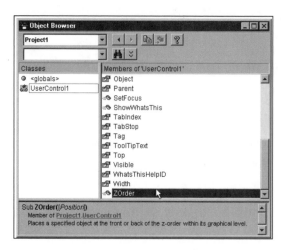

Figure 6-1 Look in the Object Browser if you want to see a list of an object's members.

Drag, Move, SetFocus, ShowWhatsThis, and ZOrder are the only methods that made the transition from the standard TextBox to our modified, subclassed version. The standard TextBox has 11 methods.

TIP To see the members of the standard, built-in controls, select VB in the Libraries list, and then click the control that interests you in the Classes list.

X-REF The Move method is a member of the TextBox class, but doesn't automatically become part of a subclassed TextBox such as the password control. In this chapter, you learn how to create new methods for your subclassed controls. In Chapter 7, you'll see how to force inheritance — how to force properties, methods, or events to remain members when a control is subclassed. This forced inheritance technique is known as *mapping*.

Make a Public Sub or Function

Now you can create a new method for your password control. Close the Object Browser window. In the Project Explorer window, double-click UserControl1 to restore its window. Double-click the password control to get to its code window. You want to define a method that will clear out the contents of the password control. Type the following code into the General Declarations section of the code window (at the very top):

```
Public Sub Reset()
Text1.Text = ""
End Sub
```

Simple enough, no? To create a method, you simply type in a Public Sub or Function and write whatever code accomplishes the job you want the method to do. When you create a method, you're giving a developer, who uses your control, a behavior that the developer can invoke as desired.

To test your new Reset method, double-click Form1 in the design window or in the Project Explorer to get to Form1's code window. Type the following code into the Form Click event:

```
Private Sub Form_Click()
UserControl1.Reset
End Sub
```

Press F5 to run the test. Type something into the password control, and then click the Form. Your typing should disappear, because the Reset method of the UserControl was triggered by the Click event.

Can Objects Collide?

You may wonder what would happen if a developer using your control put another TextBox on Form1 with the name Text1. You would now have two TextBoxes on Form1 with the same name. How would the Reset method know which one should be reset? Would it clear the text out of both TextBoxes? No, because there's no confusion. When you invoke a UserControl method (or property, for that matter), you identify the object as that UserControl (UserControl1 is its name in this example). Recall that the programming above names the UserControl, *UserControl1.Reset*. That UserControl is the object the method will work on, so only the Text1 contained by the UserControl1 object will be affected by UserControl1's methods and properties.

 TIP You can create methods that you (the creator of the UserControl) will use, but that you will not expose to developers. To do this, just make your Sub or Function *Private* rather than *Public*.

Adding an Event

Events aren't much more difficult to add to one of your UserControls than are methods. Remember that events are sensitivities. A Click event means that the object is sensitive to users clicking the object. It's up to a developer using your UserControl to make the event actually do something. The developer writes code that causes an event to, say, display a message when the user clicks. You (the creator of a UserControl) merely provide the developer with the empty Click event that can later be used or left empty.

Maybe you've decided to offer developers an event that is sensitive to user's typing in digits. You want the user to only be able to use alphabetic characters in the password. In the Project Explorer, double-click UserControl1. Then in its design window, double-click UserControl to bring up the code window. At the very top of the window, in the General Declarations section, you can type in your new event that you've decided to name *Wrong*:

```
Public Event Wrong()
```

This announces to any outside application (such as Form1, your test Standard EXE program) that this UserControl has an Event called *Wrong*.

Raise the Event

Now you must *raise* (trigger) this event within the UserControl. *Something* within your object must trigger the event. It could be as simple as the following code, but the Raise command is required:

```
Private Sub Text1_Click()
RaiseEvent Wrong
End Sub
```

However, you want to trigger the event only when the user types in an incorrect character, such as a digit. You could test for digits in the TextBox's Change, KeyPress, or KeyDown events, and then raise the custom *Wrong* event in any of those locations. But the best place may just be the KeyPress event.

The KeyPress event provides a variable called *KeyAscii* that contains the key code for the currently pressed key. The lowest code for an alphabetic character is 65, capital A. You can test for 65 and, if the user is pressing a key with a lower code, you know it's nonalphabetic. In TextBox1's KeyPress event, type the following:

```
Private Sub Text1_KeyPress(KeyAscii As Integer)
If KeyAscii < 65 Then
RaiseEvent Wrong
KeyAscii = 0
End If
End Sub
```

In this example, you're saying that if the code is lower than 65, you must raise the custom event *Wrong* and also put 0 into the KeyAscii variable. That 0 has the effect of canceling the character — that is, it will not be added to the contents of Text1.

Now close the UserControl design and code windows. Double-click Form1 to bring up its code window. Click UserControl in the list on the top-left corner of Form1's code window. Then, in the list on the top-right corner of Form1, locate the new event named *Wrong*. There it is! Type the following code into the Wrong event:

```
Private Sub UserControl1_Wrong()
MsgBox "Please use only alphabetic characters"
End Sub
```

You've now made it impossible for a developer to permit users to enter digits. The programming is hard-coded within your UserControl, saying that if a non-alphabetic key is pressed, the KeyAscii variable is loaded with 0, thereby preventing that character from appearing within the TextBox. The developer cannot prevent this. You put that feature into the UserControl and poured hot black plastic over it so no developer can change it.

Avoid Tyranny

You may not want to be so dictatorial. What if the developer *wants* to permit digits in the password? You've unnecessarily limited the flexibility of your UserControl. It's fine to provide an event that triggers when nonalphabetic characters are entered, but you should allow the *developer* to decide whether to react to that situation. If developers are willing to accept nonalphabetic characters, they can simply ignore your event by not writing any programming within it. On the other hand, if they want to reject nonalphabetic characters, let them (the developers) refuse to add those characters to the TextBox. To give this freedom to the developers, you have to add a Text *property* to your password UserControl.

Properties Are More Complicated

As you've seen, adding events and methods to custom controls is rather straightforward, but adding properties is a bit more elaborate. First, you have the run-time versus design-time issue. A developer can adjust most properties at design time by changing them in the Properties window. But the UserControl must remember and exhibit any of these adjustments at run time. This means that a property the developer adjusts (such as specifying text in a Text property) must be remembered between run times. VB uses a *PropertyBag* to do this. (You find out all about PropertyBags later in this chapter.)

The duality of properties is another issue. Remember that properties, like variables, usually permit two kinds of behaviors: their value can be changed (by setting them), and their value can be queried (by reading them). For example, the developer should be able to set the BackColor (UserControl1.BackColor = vbBlue) and also be able to query what the BackColor currently is (N = UserControl1.BackColor). This will require that you write two separate procedures called *Property Let* and *Property Get*. (See the section "Letting and Getting" later in this chapter for more information about the Property Let and Property Get procedures.)

If you want to create a read-only property, do not create a Property Let procedure, or else make it Private. How about a write-once procedure? Maybe you'll want to use unique ID numbers with items in a collection. (The index numbers of a collection are unreliable; they can shift around as the collection is added to or as items are removed.) An ID number is, however, persistently associated with a particular member of the collection. Use the following code to make a write-once property:

```
Private mID as String

Property Let ID(TheID As String)
 Static IDExists As Boolean
 If Not IDExists Then
 IDExists = True
 mID = TheID
 End If
End Property
```

But back to the password UserControl example you're working on. To finish creating it, you must borrow the Text property functionality from the TextBox, using a process known as *mapping*. In this process, VB passes the TextBox's Text property right through to the new Text property of your UserControl.

X-REF Create the following example by hand, from scratch, to learn about the various elements and behaviors of a property. However, you ordinarily won't bother doing all this by hand. Instead, you'll use the ActiveX Control Interface Wizard, which is covered in detail in Chapter 7.

For now, though, it's worth understanding all the nuts and bolts, so try it out the hard way. To add a Text property to UserControl1, type the following code into the UserControl1 code window:

```
'MappingInfo=Text1,Text1,-1,Text
Public Property Get Text() As String
 Text = Text1.Text
End Property

Public Property Let Text(ByVal New_Text As String)
 Text1.Text() = New_Text
 PropertyChanged "Text"
End Property

'Load property values from storage
Private Sub UserControl_ReadProperties(PropBag As PropertyBag)
 Text1.Text = PropBag.ReadProperty("Text", "")
End Sub
```

```
'Write property values to storage
Private Sub UserControl_WriteProperties(PropBag As PropertyBag)
 Call PropBag.WriteProperty("Text", Text1.Text, "")
End Sub
```

To finish the adjustments that let developers decide which characters to permit and which to reject, remove the KeyAscii = 0 programming from the UserControls KeyPress event. You only want to raise the event named Wrong, not discard the character.

```
Private Sub Text1_KeyPress(KeyAscii As Integer)
If KeyAscii < 65 Then
RaiseEvent Wrong
End If
End Sub
```

Finally, type the following code into Form1's Wrong event to test the new behavior of the Wrong event. In this case, the developer decided to reject nonalphabetic characters. But because you've given developers the option to accept or reject these characters, it's now up to them to write the programming that prevents these characters from being added to the Text within the UserControl. This functionality, you see, has been moved from your UserControl to the "developer's work area," the Standard EXE container, Form1.

```
Private Sub UserControl1_Wrong()
MsgBox "Please don't use numbers"
L = Len(UserControl1.Text)
UserControl1.Text = Left(UserControl1.Text, L - 1)
End Sub
```

Mapping for Inheritance

Several features of the programming that create a property may be new to you. The line

```
'MappingInfo=Text1,Text1,-1,Text
```

is probably the most mysterious. It says that the Text property of Text1 should be mapped to the UserControl. In other words, a TextBox control has functionality built into it that gives it a Text property. This enables programmers to query the contents of a TextBox (X = Text1.Text) or change the contents (Text1.Text = "Bob").

When you *map* a property, method, or event, you pass along the functionality of the original control to the UserControl. This transfer means that neither you (the creator) nor developers (who use your control) have to write the programming that provides the Text property functionality. Instead, you can map it and the UserControl inherits that functionality from the original control.

What happens when you put a TextBox or other control onto a UserControl? By default, most of the TextBox's properties are not made available to developers who use your UserControl. Often, though, you'll want to make a control's original properties available to the developers. After all, even though our custom password control is a specialized kind of TextBox, it still makes sense to offer developers many of the properties of the original TextBox. Developers would appreciate being able to choose the colors, the font, and other qualities. They would also of course appreciate being able to contact and employ the Text property.

The best way to provide mapping is by using the ActiveX Control Interface Wizard (see Chapter 7). However, for now, it's enough to understand the basics of adding a mapped property.

Letting and Getting

The *Property Let* and *Property Get* procedures also add a property to a UserControl. These procedures work together — you always use both of them. Also, they must both employ the same variable type (in the preceding example, they are both *string* types). Property Let enables a developer to change (write to) a property during run time. Property Get enables a developer to query (read) a property during run time.

```
Public Property Get Text() As String
  Text = Text1.Text
End Property
```

This procedure says that if developers wants to read this property's value, they can do it with the following code:

```
Tvalue = UserControl1.Text
```

The Get procedure will provide them with the Text property of the original TextBox (Text1).

If the developer wants to change the Text property of UserControl1, a Property Let procedure accepts the incoming New Text and assigns it to the Text property of the original TextBox control. What's more, each UserControl has a built-in PropertyChanged method. You use this method to let VB know that a property value has changed. You must notify VB of the change so that changes made at design time by developers (using the Properties window) will be remembered. If the developer changes the BackColor to blue during program design, VB must remember that fact (it's not in the programming code of the object or the container). To remember the status of an edited property, the PropertyChanged method triggers the WriteProperties event, as shown in the following code:

```
Public Property Let Text(ByVal New_Text As String)

 Text1.Text() = New_Text
 PropertyChanged "Text"
End Property
```

Bags for Storage

The final job when adding a property is to create another set of paired procedures, ReadProperties and WriteProperties.

```
'Load property values from storage

Private Sub UserControl_ReadProperties(PropBag As PropertyBag)
 Text1.Text = PropBag.ReadProperty("Text", "")
End Sub


'Write property values to storage
Private Sub UserControl_WriteProperties(PropBag As PropertyBag)
 Call PropBag.WriteProperty("Text", Text1.Text, "")
End Sub
```

Although to the creators, developers, and users, controls seem fairly substantial, they repeatedly flicker in and out of existence. When a project is opened in
the IDE (the VB design environment), when you press F5 to test a program, or
when a window is opened or closed by the user, all these and many other situations create or destroy controls. Every time a control is created, the
ReadProperties events are triggered — restoring properties that had previously
been set in the Properties window during design time. Each time a control is
destroyed, VB uses the WriteProperty events to store the current status of a control's properties in a file: .FRM or .FRX files for the controls on a Form; .CTL or
.CTX files for a UserControl.

For example, the following is a list of properties stored for your password
control in the UserControl1.Ctl file:

```
Begin VB.UserControl UserControl1

 BackStyle   = 0 'Transparent
 ClientHeight = 990
 ClientLeft  = 0
 ClientTop   = 0
 ClientWidth = 2550
 ScaleHeight = 990
 ScaleWidth  = 2550
 Begin VB.TextBox Text1
  BackColor   = &H00FFFFFF&
  Height    = 690
```

```
·IMEMode    = 3 'DISABLE
 Left    = 180
 MaxLength   = 9
 PasswordChar = "*"
 TabIndex  = 0
 Top     = 135
 Width   = 2205
End
End
```

The precise values for elements such as the Top property will, of course, depend on where your UserControl was positioned on the Form the last time the UserControl object went out of existence.

The *PropertyBag* is an object that enables properties to remain persistent even though UserControls and their constituent objects often go in and out of existence while a developer is designing a project or a user is opening and closing containers (windows, browsers, or other containers).

The WriteProperty method has the following three arguments:

* The property being saved (described by a string variable).

* The actual value of that property (in the password control example, Text1.Text). You cannot use default properties in this situation. *Text1* won't work; the full description *Text1.Text* is required.

* The default value of the property (empty text "" in the password example). Recall that you changed the default value by deleting *Text1* from the TextBox's Properties Window when you first created the password control. Notice the paradox: You're *writing* (saving) a value, Text1.Text, but you also save the default along with this new value. The reason you do this is because it conserves space (the .CTL file will be smaller). When you save a property value, VB checks to see if the new value differs from the default. Only if it differs does VB save this line into the PropertyBag.

ReadProperties Restores the Values

A UserControl has a ReadProperties event, too. This event finds out the properties of an object when VB needs to recreate that control to bring it back into existence (because you press F5 to test a project, you reopen a Form, and so on). The ReadProperty method includes two parameters: the name of the property (in a string variable) and the default value of that property, shown in the following code:

```
Text1.Text = PropBag.ReadProperty("Text", "")
```

If a property exists in the PropertyBag, ReadProperty returns it. If no property has been saved, ReadProperty returns the default.

TIP   **VB will automatically display to the developer any property you create for your UserControl. The property will be listed in the Properties window during design time.**

If you don't want developers to have access to a property in the Properties window, follow these steps to suppress it:

1. Click ‎ Tools ‎ → ‎ Procedure Attributes ‎. If Procedure Attributes is disabled, double-click the User Control in the Project Explorer.

2. In the Name list, choose the member you want to suppress.

3. Click the Advanced button.

4. Select "Hide this member" in the Attributes section, as shown in Figure 6-2.

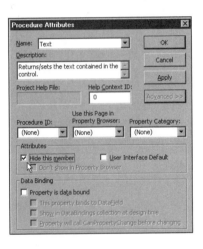

Figure 6-2   You can define various features of UserControl members in this dialog box.

You can relax about all this seemingly complex code required to add a property. As mentioned earlier in this chapter, you'll ordinarily use the ActiveX Control Interface Wizard to assist you in mapping properties. Typing all these procedures (four for each property) is not only tedious, it's unnecessary. In the next chapter, you'll see how to employ the Wizard to save you considerable time and effort. The Wizard does all this housekeeping and clerical coding for you.

However, this is a learning chapter. You should know how to do long division by hand before relying on a calculator. To complete this survey of adding properties to a class (such as a UserControl), you should understand the complete syntax for the Property Let and Property Get procedures, as shown in the following code:

```
[Public | Private | Friend] [Static] Property Let name ([arglist,]
    value)
```

```
    [statements]
    [Exit Property]
    [statements]
```


```
End Property
```

Public refers to the fact that this procedure can be called from anywhere — from any Form or Module, UserControl, or Class Module in this project; or from an outside application (a client) that is making use of this UserControl. For example, the Standard EXE project that you're using to test this UserControl is permitted to access any Public procedure in the UserControl.

Private means that the procedure can be called only from within the Form, UserControl, or Module where the procedure resides.

The new Friend command makes the procedure available to all zones within its own project (all Modules, Forms, and other UserControls), but not available to outsiders such as the Standard EXE project or a client application that's using the UserControl. Friend is a compromise between the total scope of Public and the module-only specificity of Private. Friend enables you to encapsulate a procedure within an object, but make it available from anywhere within that object.

Static preserves the local (within the procedure) variables' values, even when VB is running elsewhere in the project. Without Static, local variables are only persistent while VB is running within the particular procedure where they are located.

The Property Get syntax is similar:

```
[Public | Private | Friend] [Static] Property Get name [(arglist)]
    [As type]
    [statements]
    [name = expression]
    [Exit Property]
    [statements]
    [name = expression]
End Property
```

Note that the As Type definition (*As String* or *As Variant* or whatever) must match the variable type of the Property Let procedure. Likewise, the arglist variable types (the arguments) must be identical in the paired Property Get and Property Let procedures.

Adding Your Own Properties

The preceding example maps the TextBox's Text property onto the new UserControl version of that TextBox. Most of the time, mapping is the technique you'll use to add properties to subclassed controls. As previously stated, why reinvent the wheel when a full set of properties already exists in the original controls, and you can quite easily map them onto your new controls?

However, you'll sometimes want to create a property that doesn't exist in the original control, a custom property of your own devising. You'll have to create that kind of property all by yourself and write the programming that accomplishes it within the Property Let procedure. After all, it doesn't exist in the original control, so you can't very well copy (map) it.

Provide Something Unique for the Developer

To see how this works, try now to add a property named *Center* to the password UserControl. When set to True, the host Form on which the password control resides is centered on the user's screen. Password-input dialog boxes are usually centered on the user's screen, so you can provide this optional feature for your developers by creating a property.

The primary difference between borrowing a mapped property and creating a new property is that in the latter case you must do the programming that makes the property happen. What's more, you must also create a Private variable to hold the value (the current status) of the property, which enables the developer to write programming that will query the property during run time.

To create this new Center property, double-click UserControl1 in the Project Explorer, and then double-click the password control in the design window. The code window appears. Type the following code at the very top of the code window, in the General Declarations section:

```
Private Centered As Boolean
```

You can't map this property because it doesn't exist in the original TextBox. You thought it up all by yourself. The following is the code for your Property Let procedure, which centers the container (the *parent*) that holds the UserControl:

```
Public Property Let Center(N As Boolean)
Centered = N
x = (Screen.Width - Parent.Width) / 2
y = (Screen.Height - Parent.Height) / 2
Parent.Left = x
Parent.Top = y
End Property
```

In this code, the first line assigns the value of *N* to the Private variable *Centered*. This assignment will be True or False, and *Centered* can be queried by the developer to find out whether the parent Form is centered. Then you calculate the horizontal and vertical center position. Finally, you move the *Parent* object into the center of the screen. The Parent will be whatever Form or other container holds the password UserControl. In this example, the Parent is Form1 of the Standard EXE project you're using to test the UserControl.

What to Do if the Developer Queries

To provide a response if the developer's code queries the status of the Center property, type the following Property Get procedure into the UserControl's code window:

```
Public Property Get Center() As Boolean
Center = Centered
End Property
```

To test this new property, type the following code into the code window of the Standard EXE project, Form1:

```
Private Sub Form_Load()
UserControl1.Center = True
End Sub

Private Sub Form_DblClick()
Print UserControl1.Center
End Sub
```

Press F5 to run Project2, the Standard EXE project, and then double-click to test the Property Let and Property Get procedures.

BONUS

Follow the Yellow Brick Road

Now you have a pretty good idea of the code components that, when working together, provide a functioning property, method, or event to a UserControl, or indeed any other kind of object. It's instructive to take this a step further and watch the twisted path that VB takes when running a

UserControl project in along with an outside, container (client) project such as your Standard EXE project.

Load the password-entry Project Group into VB if it isn't there already. Now watch where VB goes and what it does with each step while employing the services of your UserControl object.

Press F8. The first event triggered is the UserControl's ReadProperties event. Initialize is the first Event triggered in any Form; Terminate is the last event. However, you've put no programming into the Initialize event, so VB locates your first programming in ReadProperties. The TextBox is filled with any text left over from a previous session or from the Properties Window. It finds none, so the default "" (blank text) is used.

Press F8 until you get to the next event, the Form_Load event of the Standard EXE test program. This step triggers your Center method in UserControl1, and program execution is transferred right back to the UserControl. Step through the Center method. The Standard EXE's Form1 is the Parent because it contains the UserControl. In this event, the Parent is centered relative to the screen.

Notice that the centering goes on in a vacuum: The Form isn't made visible until the Form_Load event is finished. Now click Form1 to give it the focus and type in the letter **a**. You trigger the UserControl's KeyPress event, but because this is a valid character, it passes the KeyAscii not less than 65 test and nothing happens. The TextBox displays an asterisk.

Try typing the digit **8** now. This time, through the KeyPress event, you trigger the RaiseEvent command and go back to the Standard EXE to carry out any programming within the UserControl1_Wrong event. The MsgBox is displayed, as shown in Figure 6-3.

Figure 6-3 After several messages between client and server, this dialog box is displayed.

After the MsgBox is closed by the user, the following programming first queries, and then assigns a new value to, the UserControl's TextBox:

```
L = Len(UserControl1.Text)
UserControl1.Text = Left(UserControl1.Text, L - 1)
```

Notice that as you keep pressing F8, you go to the Property Get procedure, and then to the Property Let procedure, both within the UserControl. Next, you go back to Form1 to conclude the Wrong event, and finally over to the UserControl to conclude the KeyPress event.

You should now have a good idea of the amount of communication — or *messaging* — that can go on between a client and an ActiveX server object. They work together, cooperatively, to fulfill the needs of the client. Figure 6-4 shows the traffic pattern between the Standard EXE client and the UserControl server.

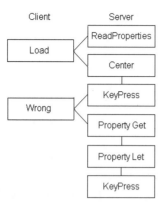

Figure 6-4 The server is doing most of the work in this example, but the client interacts with it.

Summary

In this chapter you learn about the three kinds of UserControls: simple sub-classing, aggregate controls, and user-drawn controls. You also learn how to add a method and an event to a UserControl. Finally, this chapter covered how to add the two types of properties to a UserControl, both mapped and creator-programmed properties. The goal was to get down at the lowest level and code by hand these properties, methods, and events (collectively known as an object's *members*). Finally, you followed the twisted path that is executed during run time when a container and its server object work together to accomplish their task.

Just as it's better to first learn to multiply and divide before you're given a calculator to speed up the process, it's good that you learn the details of adding members before taking the shortcut of using the ActiveX Control Interface Wizard, the subject of the next chapter.

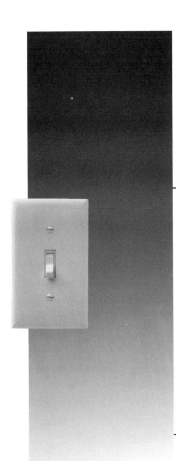

CHAPTER SEVEN

HELP FROM THE WIZARDS

IN THIS CHAPTER YOU LEARN THESE KEY SKILLS

ADDING CUSTOM PROPERTIES TO AN OBJECT
    PAGE 130

PROGRAMMATICALLY RESIZING CONTAINED CONTROLS
    PAGE 132

USING THE ACTIVEX CONTROL INTERFACE WIZARD
    PAGE 136

CREATING PROPERTY PAGES   PAGE 145

COMPILING AND REUSING .OCX FILES   PAGE 148

DESIGNING CUSTOM TOOLBOX ICONS   PAGE 149

I n this chapter you learn how to program your own custom properties and add them to objects. It's often important that you provide programming to ensure that when a user resizes a UserControl, the controls contained within the UserControl are also resized. You also learn which event to use to make contained controls respond intelligently.

Wizards are often extremely efficient at accomplishing clerical or housekeeping jobs for you. In this chapter you learn how to use one of the best Wizards available, the ActiveX Control Interface Wizard that's built into VBCCE and the commercial versions of VB. You also learn how easy it is to create Property Pages — those "index card" dialog boxes that pop up when Custom is double-clicked in the Properties window. Finally, you discover how to create your own, custom-built Toolbox icons.

Adding Properties to a Control the Easy Way

A key feature of any control is the set of properties it permits developers to manipulate. When you give a developer an ActiveX control that you've created, the developer expects to be able to modify and customize the control. Properties are *qualities*, such as the thickness of a border, whether or not the object is visible, the color, and so on.

When you decide to subclass a control, look at the properties of the original control and determine which of the original control's properties you'll want to permit a developer to adjust, and which properties you'll conceal. For instance, if you subclass the standard VB Label control, are you going to allow developers access to the original ForeColor property? If you do, programmers using your control will be able to specify the color of text in your new control. If you don't, programmers will have to accept whatever text color you've specified for the control.

To understand how to restrict or provide properties to the users of your controls, try creating the useful custom frame control in this chapter. You may recall that in Chapter 3 you learned how to frame an image by superimposing several Image controls. Your goal in this chapter is to create a custom UserControl that consists of a PictureBox control superimposed on a CommandButton. The reason for using the CommandButton is that in VBCCE only the CommandButton has a raised 3-D appearance, desirable for the outer frame.

A Special Percentage Property

The primary programming job when creating this frame control is to provide developers with a property that changes the width of the frame. You want to enable them to specify the relationship between the height and width of the outer CommandButton and the inner PictureBox control — from thin to thick. The best way to do this is to provide a Percentage property that can be set from 1 to 99. When the Percentage property is set to 1, the PictureBox control is only 1 percent the size of the CommandButton. The frame is, therefore, very thick. When the Percentage property is set to 99, the frame is very thin.

First, create the new frame visually. Start VBCCE, or if it's running, press Ctrl+N to start a new ActiveX Control. Put a CommandButton on the Form, and then put a PictureBox Control on top of the CommandButton. Delete the CommandButton's Caption property and set its Enabled property to False. This step will prevent it from moving if the user clicks it. Ordinarily, a CommandButton is animated to appear to be depressed when clicked. You don't want that effect.

Move the new frame up near the upper-left corner of the UserControl and size the UserControl so it's just a little larger than the frame, as shown in Figure 7-1. Set the UserControl's BackStyle property to Transparent. This way, only the frame will show up when a developer places it onto a Form.

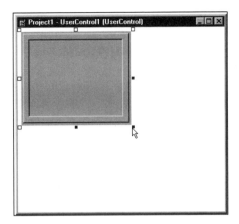

Figure 7-1 Make the UserControl only slightly larger than the frame.

You may recall from Chapter 6 that when creating a custom property, the first step is to put a Private variable in the General Declarations section of the UserControl's code window. This variable holds the current status of the property during run time. (The PropertyBag on the hard drive retains the status of a property when an object has disappeared, such as when the project has stopped running.)

Double-click the UserControl to bring up the code window and, at the top in the General Declarations section, type the following:

```
Private m_Percentage As Integer
```

The next job is to write the programming that will accept changes to the Percentage property. Type the following code into the General Declarations section of the UserControl code window:

```
Public Property Let percentage(ByVal New_Percentage As Integer)
    If New_Percentage > 99 Or New_Percentage < 1 Then
    MsgBox "The percent must be between 1 and 99"
    Exit Property
    End If
    m_Percentage = New_Percentage
    PropertyChanged "Percentage"
UserControl_Resize
End Property
```

Insert Validation Code

Notice the *validation code* in this procedure. Often you may insert some programming into a Property Let procedure that tests what the developer is sending as a value (the argument). You don't want to permit impossible values, a color that doesn't exist, or a size larger than Texas. In this case, you're allowing the inner part of the frame, the PictureBox, to be anywhere from 1 to 99 percent the size of the outer part, the CommandButton. If the developer tries to assign a value outside this range, you display a message explaining why you're rejecting the value. Then you `Exit Property` (leave the procedure at this point), without assigning the New_Percentage value to the m_Percentage (the variable that holds this property's value).

The actual adjustment that resizes the frame takes place in the Resize event of the UserControl, as explained in the section that follows. That's why this Property Let procedure ends by triggering the UserControl's Resize event: UserControl_Resize.

Making Controls Sensitive to Size

In many situations, you'll permit developers to resize a UserControl. That way they can make it look right on their Forms and projects. While designing their programs, they may prefer a different size or aspect ratio than the size and shape you originally created. Programmers expect to be able to drag your control to resize it, just as they can resize any other control (such as TextBoxes or CommandButtons) during design. You even have some cases where controls are resized during run time. Perhaps a set of CommandButtons should become larger if the user makes a project's window larger.

Contained Controls Should Respond to Dragging

You can program the interior controls to respond to the resizing of the container UserControl. Remember that no matter how many controls you place onto a UserControl, the developer will see only a single Width and a single Height property representing *the entire UserControl* — not the other controls inside it. To enable developers to independently adjust contained controls, you have to provide custom properties such as the Percentage property you just created.

At the upper-left corner of the UserControl's code window, drop the list down and choose UserControl. Then select the Resize event in the list box on the upper-right corner. Type the following code into the UserControl's Resize event:

```
Private Sub UserControl_Resize()
Command1.Height = Height - 60
Command1.Width = Width - 60

z = m_Percentage / 100
Picture1.Height = Command1.Height * z
Picture1.Width = Command1.Width * z

'center the PictureBox
X = Command1.Width / 2
Y = Command1.Height / 2
```

```
Picture1.Left = X - (Picture1.Width / 2) + Command1.Left
Picture1.Top = Y - (Picture1.Height / 2) + Command1.Top
End Sub
```

This programming requires a bit of explanation. In many situations it's quite easy to make a control responsive to developers' dragging the contained UserControl to a different size. All you normally have to do is the following:

```
Command1.Height = Height
Command1.Width = Width
```

Then, every time the developer resizes the UserControl, the interior CommandButton is automatically resized along with it.

Make the Container Slightly Larger Than the Contained

Creating a frame is somewhat more complex. To begin with, you want the frame UserControl — though transparent — to be slightly larger than the outer limits of the visible frame. If you don't leave a slight border, the outer edges of the CommandButton will be clipped off, destroying the framing effect. That is why in the Property Let procedure, the CommandButton is 60 twips less high and less wide than the container UserControl. Recall that a *twip* is the finest unit of measurement in Visual Basic: You have 1440 twips per inch.

Next, the current percentage is retrieved from *m_Percentage.* It's divided by 100 so the Height and Width of the CommandButton can be multiplied by the variable *z* to get the correct Height and Width for the PictureBox. This formula takes care of the relative sizes of the two controls, making the overall frame effect as thick as the developer has specified. One problem remains: the relative *position* of the PictureBox within the CommandButton.

If the relative size of these controls changes, the PictureBox must be recentered within the CommandButton so the frame's shape isn't thrown off-kilter. The last four lines in the procedure accomplish the centering. The Width and Height measurements of both controls are divided by 2. This gives you the coordinates for the exact center of both controls. Then those coordinates are used to move the PictureBox into the center of the CommandButton.

To complete the creation of the Percentage property, you should type in the Property Get procedure:

```
Public Property Get percentage() As Integer
percentage = m_Percentage
End Property
```

As usual, the Property Get procedure merely returns (to a querying developer) the value of the Private variable that holds the current value of the property.

Now type in the following two procedures to preserve the value of the percentage between sessions or between instances of the UserControl:

```
'Load property values from storage
Private Sub UserControl_ReadProperties(PropBag As PropertyBag)
  percentage = PropBag.ReadProperty("Percentage", "80")
End Sub

'Write property values to storage
Private Sub UserControl_WriteProperties(PropBag As PropertyBag)
  Call PropBag.WriteProperty("Percentage", percentage, "80")
End Sub
```

The WriteProperties procedure saves to disk any changes the developer made to the Percentage property. This way, when the project is run again in the future, the size of the frame remains whatever the developer wanted it to be.

Finally, you want to ensure that when a developer first places one of your frame UserControls onto a Form, the PictureBox won't disappear. Using the drop-down list boxes at the top of the UserControl's code window, locate the UserControl's InitProperties event, and then type the following code:

```
Private Sub UserControl_InitProperties()
m_Percentage = 80
End Sub
```

With this programming, the first time the developer puts the frame control onto a Form, it will at least look like a frame. Without this programming, the value of m_Percentage is zero when the UserControl is first put onto a Form or otherwise employed by a developer. When a UserControl is first instantiated, its Resize event is triggered. The calculations within the Resize event result in a Height and Width of zero for the PictureBox.

Trying It Out

Now the new frame control is functional. Try testing it. Select Add Project from the File menu to bring in a Standard EXE project. Close the UserControl's code and design windows if they're open. Then double-click the UserControl icon on the Toolbox to put a frame onto the Standard EXE's Form. You should see a frame at 80 percent, like the one shown in Figure 7-2.

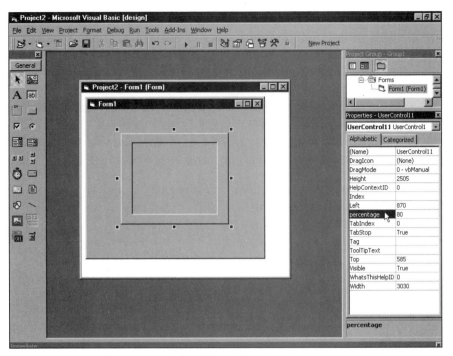

Figure 7-2 Your frame control should look like this with 80 percent thickness.

You'll find an unfortunate perplexity in the VBCCE and the commercial version of VB as well. You must memorize this perplexity to avoid headaches trying to figure out why things are not working. By default, a UserControl, when first created, is given the name *UserControl1* by VBCCE. (That is as you would expect.) However, when you close the design and code windows of the UserControl and then add the UserControl from the ToolBox to a Standard EXE Form to test it, VBCCE renames it to *UserControl11*. This renaming can cause you great confusion. For example, the VBCCE's ActiveX Control Interface Wizard will create programming that will not work because it's using the name UserControl1. And any programming you write to test the UserControl (such as UserControl1.BackColor = vbBlue) will fail because UserControl1 doesn't exist any more. The solution is to use the Properties window to change the Name property of the UserControl back to UserControl1. Note that this isn't technically a bug. VB thinks of UserControl1 as the basic name of the UserControl and, therefore, each time you add a new instance of this UserControl to a Form, each new instance gets the next higher default number: UserControl11, UserControl12, UserControl13 and so on. VB is merely appending 1, 2, 3, and so on (as it always does) to the actual Name of the object.

The Visual Basic Books Online feature suggests that you can avoid this confusing situation by renaming a UserControl as soon as you start working on it. Name it something like *Framer* or *Framit* or whatever, but don't use any digits at the end. This way, when you add them to a Form they'll be named Framer1, Framer2, and so on.

Notice, too, in the Properties window that the UserControl has 16 properties. You have your Percentage property, plus those that VB, in its wisdom, decided to include. The Properties VB gave your control are the size and position properties, plus assorted miscellaneous properties such as index, tag, dragmode, and visible.

X-REF These VB-supplied properties are said to belong to the *extender object*. You'll find out about this object and the related ambient object in the "Bonus" section at the end of Chapter 9.

To see the complete list of members that VB gives the UserControl, press F2 to bring up the Browser Window. Click Project1 in the Libraries list, and then click UserControl in the Classes list. You'll see all the properties, plus five methods: Drag, Move, SetFocus, ShowWhatsThis, and ZOrder. You'll also see four events: DragDrop, DragOver, GotFocus, and LostFocus.

Firing Up the Wizard

Well, let's see. Don't you think developers would appreciate a few more properties, methods, and events? They would likely be grateful if you included BackColor and Picture properties to enable them to adjust the frame's color, or load in a graphic to give the frame a texture if they wish. You'll also have to include the CommandButton's Style property (it should be set to *Graphical* to permit the Picture property to work properly). All this work calls for mapping, borrowing features of the original CommandButton, and giving them to the UserControl. Note that mapping is best accomplished by using the Wizard.

Follow these steps to map the BackColor, Picture, and Style properties from the CommandButton to the UserControl:

1. Click `Add-Ins` → `ActiveX Control Interface Wizard`. If you don't see the Wizard listed, click `Add-Ins` → `Add-Ins Manager` and select VB ActiveX Control Interface Wizard.

2. You see the first screen of the Wizard, as shown in Figure 7-3.

3. Click the Next button, and you see two lists of properties, methods, and events, as shown in Figure 7-4.

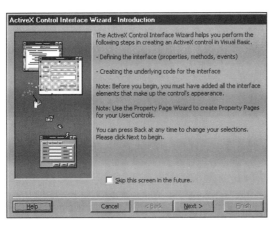

Figure 7-3 This window greets you when you call up the ActiveX Control Wizard.

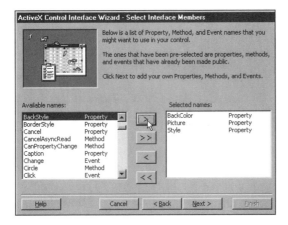

Figure 7-4 Hold down Ctrl and click all the members in the left window that you want to map.

Note that the Wizard has already preselected a group of common properties, methods, and events that it thinks you may want to map.

4. To keep the source code for this example short and simple, click the double-arrowed CommandButton on the bottom of the set of four buttons in this dialog box. This sends all the properties in the Selected Names list (on the right) back to the Available Names list (on the left). This leaves the right list empty. Holding down the Ctrl key, click BackColor, Picture, and Style in the left list. Click the top CommandButton to move these three properties into the right list, as shown in Figure 7-4. Note that you haven't actually *mapped* any of these items yet. You're just choosing names at this stage.

5. Click the Next button. The Custom Interface Members window appears. This is where you can see any unique properties, methods, or events that you've added via programming to your UserControl. Or you can add new custom members in this window.

Your Percentage property is listed. You won't add any new items now, so click the Next button again. The Set Mapping window appears, as shown in Figure 7-5. This is where you tell the Wizard that, indeed, you intend to borrow the BackColor, PictureBox, and Style functionality that's built into the CommandButton control you are subclassing.

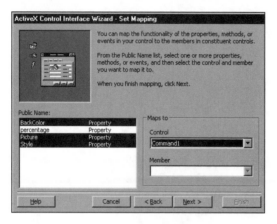

Figure 7-5 Here's where you do the actual mapping.

6. Click BackColor, Picture, and Style to select them, as shown in Figure 7-5. Click Command1 in the Maps to. . .Control list. Note that if you click the properties *individually* in the Public Name list, the Member list automatically displays the CommandButton property of the same name. However, all the properties of the CommandButton are in this Member list, so you could map some other property to a particular Name if you wished. But just leave things as they are.

7. Click Next. The dialog box shown in Figure 7-6 appears. Here you can define the basic elements of your custom property. This member is not mapped, so the Wizard asks you to answer some questions about it. When you defined the Property Let and Get procedures *As Integer*, you specified the property's variable type, and the Wizard knows this.

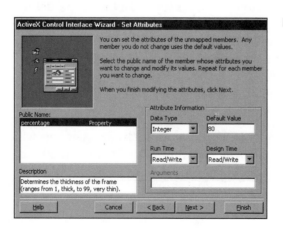

Figure 7-6 Give the Wizard some information about your custom property in this dialog box.

By default, a property can be read (queried) and written to (changed) during both design time (in the Properties window) and run time (by calling on Property Let or Get within the programming). However, you can specify read-only, write-only, or completely unavailable. The Wizard generates the necessary source code to accomplish these variations on the more common read-write behavior of a variable.

Add a description, if you wish. It will be displayed if the developer looks up your object in an object browser or other help feature.

Finally, provide a default value of 80, so the frame will look like a frame when a developer first puts your control on a Form or into an application.

8. Click the Next button. You can choose to view the Summary Report if you wish. It's a list of reminders for you, the creator of an ActiveX control. Click the Finish button.

What Has the Wizard Done?

Now you want to see just what programming the Wizard has inserted into your source code for the frame UserControl. In the Project Explorer, double-click UserControl1 to display the UserControl control design window. Then double-click the UserControl in its design window to get down to the programming level, the code window.

You should see the changes shown in the following code. Notice some new programming, written for you by the Wizard. Notice also that some of the original programming you wrote has been *commented out* (the Wizard put ' characters at the start of some of your lines of code, so VB will ignore those lines when running this programming).

```
Private m_percentage As Integer

'Public Property Let percentage(ByVal New_Percentage As Integer)
'   If New_Percentage > 99 Or New_Percentage < 1 Then
'      MsgBox "The percent must be between 1 and 99"
'   Exit Property
'   End If
'   m_Percentage = New_Percentage
'   PropertyChanged "Percentage"
'UserControl_Resize
'End Property
'
'Public Property Get percentage() As Integer
'percentage = m_Percentage
'End Property
```

```
'Default Property Values:

Const m_def_percentage = 80

'Property Variables:
Dim m_percentage As Integer

Private Sub UserControl_InitProperties()
'm_Percentage = 80
  m_percentage = m_def_percentage
End Sub

Private Sub UserControl_Resize()
Command1.Height = Height - 60
Command1.Width = Width - 60
z = m_percentage / 100
Picture1.Height = Command1.Height * z
Picture1.Width = Command1.Width * z
'center the PictureBox
X = Command1.Width / 2
Y = Command1.Height / 2
Picture1.Left = X - (Picture1.Width / 2) + Command1.Left
Picture1.Top = Y - (Picture1.Height / 2) + Command1.Top
End Sub

'Load property values from storage
Private Sub UserControl_ReadProperties(PropBag As PropertyBag)
  percentage = PropBag.ReadProperty("Percentage", "80")
  Command1.BackColor = PropBag.ReadProperty("BackColor",
  &H8000000F)
  Set Picture = PropBag.ReadProperty("Picture", Nothing)
  m_percentage = PropBag.ReadProperty("percentage",
  m_def_percentage)
End Sub

'Write property values to storage
Private Sub UserControl_WriteProperties(PropBag As PropertyBag)
  Call PropBag.WriteProperty("Percentage", percentage, "80")
  Call PropBag.WriteProperty("BackColor", Command1.BackColor,
  &H8000000F)
  Call PropBag.WriteProperty("Picture", Picture, Nothing)
  Call PropBag.WriteProperty("percentage", m_percentage,
  m_def_percentage)
End Sub
```

```
'WARNING! DO NOT REMOVE OR MODIFY THE FOLLOWING COMMENTED LINES!
'MappingInfo=Command1,Command1,-1,BackColor
Public Property Get BackColor() As OLE_COLOR
  BackColor = Command1.BackColor
End Property

Public Property Let BackColor(ByVal New_BackColor As OLE_COLOR)
  Command1.BackColor() = New_BackColor
  PropertyChanged "BackColor"
End Property

'WARNING! DO NOT REMOVE OR MODIFY THE FOLLOWING COMMENTED LINES!
'MappingInfo=Command1,Command1,-1,Picture
Public Property Get Picture() As Picture
  Set Picture = Command1.Picture
End Property

Public Property Set Picture(ByVal New_Picture As Picture)
  Set Command1.Picture = New_Picture
  PropertyChanged "Picture"
End Property

'WARNING! DO NOT REMOVE OR MODIFY THE FOLLOWING COMMENTED LINES!
'MappingInfo=Command1,Command1,-1,Style
Public Property Get Style() As Integer
  Style = Command1.Style
End Property

Public Property Get percentage() As Integer
  percentage = m_percentage
End Property

Public Property Let percentage(ByVal New_percentage As Integer)
  m_percentage = New_percentage
  PropertyChanged "percentage"
End Property
```

The Wizard Isn't a Genius

This code won't work right off. The Wizard isn't a perfect genius. You have to do some editing to adjust some of what the Wizard has done. The first thing to notice is that the Wizard has commented out your Property Let and Property Get procedures for the Percentage property. The Wizard has replaced them with its own procedures. You can't have two procedures with the same name in the same module, so the Wizard had to comment yours out.

The Wizard added a new definition of the property variable m_percentage. You should delete the following:

```
Dim m_percentage As Integer
```

You can delete this line because you already have a perfectly good definition of it at the top, which you wrote earlier yourself: `Private m_percentage As Integer`. The Private and Dim commands accomplish the same thing.

The Wizard created a Constant to hold the default value (80) for the frame control's thickness. The Wizard has also commented out your programming in the InitProperties procedure and replaced it with a line of its own:

```
Private Sub UserControl_InitProperties()
'm_Percentage = 80
  m_percentage = m_def_percentage
End Sub
```

You can leave this as is. No harm done. Both lines do the same thing, but the Wizard prefers to use the constant it defined as 80 rather than the literal 80 you used. The Wizard has its ways.

Wisely the Wizard left undisturbed all the programming you wrote within the UserControl's Resize event. However, the ReadProperties and WriteProperties procedures have been expanded to include the BackColor and Picture properties.

Two Oddities

Notice that the Wizard created two oddities. The Wizard didn't comment out your lines assigning and retrieving the value of the Percentage property, even though it inserted similar lines to accomplish the same task. Therefore, you should comment out your original programming by inserting ' characters in front of your lines, as shown in the following:

```
Private Sub UserControl_ReadProperties(PropBag As PropertyBag)
   'percentage = PropBag.ReadProperty("Percentage", "80")
   Command1.BackColor = PropBag.ReadProperty("BackColor",
   &H8000000F)
   Set Picture = PropBag.ReadProperty("Picture", Nothing)
   m_percentage = PropBag.ReadProperty("percentage",
   m_def_percentage)
End Sub

Private Sub UserControl_WriteProperties(PropBag As PropertyBag)
   'Call PropBag.WriteProperty("Percentage", percentage, "80")
   Call PropBag.WriteProperty("BackColor", Command1.BackColor,
   &H8000000F)
```

```
   Call PropBag.WriteProperty("Picture", Picture, Nothing)
   Call PropBag.WriteProperty("percentage", m_percentage,
   m_def_percentage)
End Sub
```

The other oddity about these two procedures is that no provision was made by the Wizard for saving or retrieving the Style property by using the PropertyBag. Nor did the Wizard create a Property Let procedure for Style. You can just ignore these omissions because you can leave Style a read-only property that you set to 1 (Graphical) in the Properties window of the original CommandButton when you were first designing the UserControl.

The Wizard inserted two pairs of Property procedures for the BackColor and Picture properties, including the lines that define the mapping (MappingInfo). Follow the Wizard's warning and don't tamper with the mapping data:

```
'WARNING! DO NOT REMOVE OR MODIFY THE FOLLOWING COMMENTED LINES!
'MappingInfo=Command1,Command1,-1,BackColor
Public Property Get BackColor() As OLE_COLOR
   BackColor = Command1.BackColor
End Property
```

Use Property Set for Objects or Variants

Notice, though, that instead of a Property Let procedure for the Picture property, the Wizard inserted a Property *Set* procedure:

```
Public Property Set Picture(ByVal New_Picture As Picture)
   Set Command1.Picture = New_Picture
   PropertyChanged "Picture"
End Property
```

If your property accepts a Variant as an argument, a traditional string or numeric variable type could be passed to your property. It would go to the Property Let procedure. But an object could also be passed. (Variants can be objects as well as integers, strings, floating point, and the other traditional variable types.) Therefore, if your property accepts a variant (VarName As Variant) argument, you should provide both a Property Let procedure (to accept traditional variable types) as well as a Property Set procedure (in case an object is passed as the argument). In the code that calls your procedures, the developer will have to use the Set command to send an object argument, so VB will know to use the Property Set procedure in that case.

You should use *Set* (rather than Let) whenever the variable involved is an *object* (as opposed to an integer, string, or other traditional variable type). There are a few objects (such as Picture and Font) used in this way. Also, remember that you must create both a Property Set and a Property Let procedure when the argument is a Variant variable type.

Restore the Missing Code

Finally, Wizard or not, it remains necessary to call the UserControl_Resize event from within your Property Let percentage procedure. Unless you make this call, the frame won't be resized if the developer changes it from the Properties window. And, as will frequently be the case, you'll want to include boundary-checking or other error-trapping in case the developer tries to assign an inappropriate value to your property. Edit the Property Let procedure until it looks like the following:

```
Public Property Let percentage(ByVal New_percentage As Integer)
  If New_percentage > 99 Or New_percentage < 1 Then
    MsgBox "The percent must be between 1 and 99"
  Exit Property
  End If

  m_percentage = New_percentage
  PropertyChanged "percentage"

  UserControl_Resize
End Property
```

Close any opened UserControl code or design windows now, and double-click Form1 (the Standard EXE project) in the Project Explorer. Put one of your UserControls on Form1 by double-clicking it in the Toolbox. Try adjusting the Percentage property and the BackColor property, and then put a PictureBox inside your frame, as shown in Figure 7-7.

Figure 7-7 The Form behind the custom frame control has a gradient loaded into its Picture property.

Gradients can add an attractive background (in the Form's Picture property) to a Form, as shown in Figure 7-7. To create a gradient, look it up in the Help feature of a graphics program such as Photoshop. Try placing a graphics file into the Picture Property of the UserControl, as shown in Figure 7-8. At the time of this writing, the Picture Property mapping is only partially successful. You can get good grayscale textures, but colors are reduced to grayscale. Perhaps this problem will be fixed by the time you read this. Textures can look good, though, as you can see in Figure 7-8.

Figure 7-8 Add textures to the frame control by loading graphics into its Picture property.

TIP If you decide to modify the behavior of a member, or add a new member, you can rerun the ActiveX Control Interface Wizard any time you want.

Using the Property Page Wizard

Another Wizard that comes with VBCCE is called the Property Page Wizard. This Wizard adds a nice touch to the Properties window, making it more efficient when a developer goes to adjust some of a UserControl's properties.

Follow these steps to invoke and use the Property Page Wizard:

1. Click Add-Ins → Property Page Wizard . If you don't see this Wizard listed, click Add-Ins → Add-In Manager and select VB Property Page Wizard.

2. Click Next to get past the introduction screen. A list of selections appears, as shown in Figure 7-9. Note that the Wizard has chosen to include two classic Property pages: StandardColor (because your UserControl has a BackColor property) and StandardPicture (for the Picture property).

3. Click the Add button so you can add a separate page for the frame size. Type **FrameSize** and click OK. You must use a single word here.

4. Click Next and move *percentage* onto the FrameSize Property page, as shown in Figure 7-10. You can double-click it or drag it to move it.

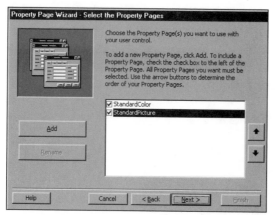

Figure 7-9 The Wizard has decided you'll want these two standard Property pages. Good decision.

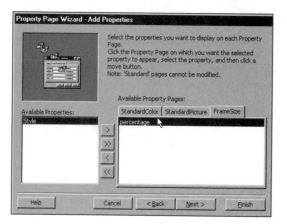

Figure 7-10 Just drag any properties onto any pages.

5. Click Finish and close the Wizard.

Now your Property page is added to the UserControl in your project. You can design the custom FrameSize page at this point, if you wish. In the Project Explorer, double-click FrameSize, the name you gave your custom page. You'll see the default design that the Wizard created for you, as shown in Figure 7-11.

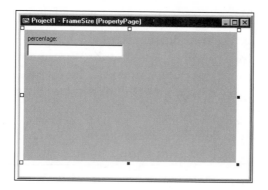

Figure 7-11 You'll probably want to add a brief description to this custom Property page.

Provide Help Information for the Developer

Double-click a Label control in the Toolbox to place it on the Property page, and type in whatever help data you want to provide to the developer to explain the meaning or parameter of this property. Notice that you can adjust the FontSize or any other aspects of the elements on a Property page — they're just ordinary TextBoxes, Labels, or other controls. For example, the frame around the Label wasn't doing much for the page, so it was removed, and the BackColor changed to match the Property page, as you can see in Figure 7-12.

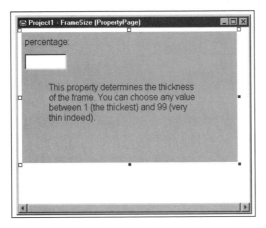

Figure 7-12 You can customize a Property page as much as you wish.

TIP A Property page contains a full set of properties itself, including BackColor and even Picture. It's much like an ordinary Form, so feel free to experiment with it by adding controls to it and adjusting its properties.

To try out this new Property page as if you were a developer, close the Property Page design window and, in the Project Explorer, click Form1, the Standard EXE test project Form. Click the UserControl on the Form, to select the UserControl. Then note at the top of the Properties window that a new item has been added named *Custom*. Double-click Custom, and your Property pages appear, as shown in Figure 7-13.

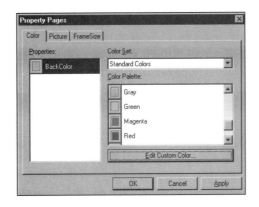

Figure 7-13 Here is your new set of Property pages — an easy way to adjust properties.

Click the custom FrameSize tab to see the effect of your design.

Making the .OCX

Now that you have a tested and working ActiveX control — a control of some utility that you or others might want to use in the future — it's time to save the official .OCX version to disk.

In the Project Explorer, right-click Project1 and choose Project1.Properties. You'll see the dialog box shown in Figure 7-14.

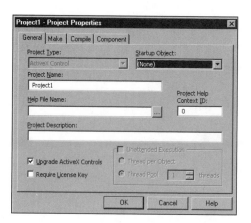

Figure 7-14 Before compiling your official version, make adjustments to your control here.

Name It FFrame

Change the Project Name to *FullFrame* and type in a brief description of the control. Click OK to close the dialog box. Click UserControl1 to select it in the Project Explorer. Then, in the File menu, double-click Make Project1.OCX. The Make a Project dialog box appears. Type FFrame as the Project Name. This name, *FFrame,* will be the actual name of the UserControl and the .OCX file that a developer (or you) will be able to use in future VB projects, ActiveX-capable applications, or Web pages.

Click OK, and the compilation begins. Not only does this compilation process store your FFrame control on disk, but it also registers the control in the Windows Registry. Registration means that you can add it to the Toolbox in VB or VBCCE for inclusion in future projects; to the ActiveX Control Pad Toolbox; or the Toolbox in such applications as Word 97. (In Word, run the macro editor. From the Insert menu, choose User Form. Then, from the View menu, choose Toolbox.)

Add Your Control to a Toolbox

In any of these applications or utilities, you can right-click the Toolbox and choose Additional Controls (or Components). Look in the list for FullFrame.UserControl1 and click it. Your FFrame control will appear on the Toolbox. It may be necessary, however, to use the Browse feature of the AdditionalControls (or Components) dialog box to locate your .OCX file if it doesn't appear in the list of available controls.

BONUS

How to Create Custom Toolbox Icons

When you create ActiveX components that you intend to distribute to others, you'll want to replace the default Toolbox icon, shown in Figure 7-15, with your own.

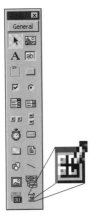

Figure 7-15   Draw your own icon to replace this generic UserControl icon.

It's easy to design one of these icons. They're 16 × 16 pixels large — quite small, really. Ordinary Toolbar and desktop Windows icons are 32 × 32. And you can just use Windows's Paint accessory to create or modify them. You don't need a special icon-designer utility. Paint works fine.

If Paint Damages a DLL

Windows's Paint application has been known to replace a key dynamic link library that Visual Basic and VBCCE require. If, after you run Paint, VB or VBCCE refuse to run when you try to start them up, no major harm done. Just Click START→Settings→Control Panel. Then double-click the Add/Remove Programs icon. Locate Visual Basic 5.0 Whatever Edition in the ListBox and double-click it. Follow the Wizard's instructions to uninstall VB5. After the program is gone from your hard drive, put your CD-ROM back into your CD-ROM drive and reinstall

VB5. (If you're using VBCCE, follow the same steps to uninstall and then reinstall it.) The reinstallation will overwrite the DLL that Paint corrupted.

Follow these steps to design your own ActiveX UserControl icon:

1. Click START → Programs → Accessories → Paint to run Windows' Paint accessory.

2. In Paint, click Image → Attributes and select Pels (means pixels) as the Units.

3. Enter **16** for both Height and Width, as shown in Figure 7-16:

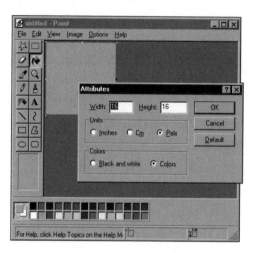

Figure 7-16 Toolbox icons are only 16 × 16 pixels large.

4. Click OK to close the dialog box. Click the Zoom button (the magnifying glass) and select 8x so you can see each pixel.

5. Click the Fill Tool button (the tilted paintbucket), and then select the standard Windows gray (second color from the left on the bottom). Press Ctrl+A if the color box isn't visible. Fill the picture with this gray.

6. Using any of the tools — perhaps the pencil tool is best — create your icon. Any time you want to see it in its real size, click the Zoom button and select 1x.

Give It a 3D Look

Many of Microsoft's icons have shading, giving them a 3D look. For the FFrame UserControl, you could draw something like the shaded frame symbol shown in Figure 7-17.

Figure 7-17 Here's a good design for your enhanced Frame UserControl.

Click File → Save and in the Save as Type ListBox at the bottom of the Save File dialog box, choose 16-color bitmap. Save the file as FFRAME.BMP, and then close Paint.

Now you can insert your new custom icon into the FFrame UserControl. Double-click UserControl1 in the VBCCE Project Explorer to select it. In the Properties window, locate the ToolboxBitmap property and double-click it to bring up the file-browsing dialog box. Find your FFRAME.BMP file and load it into the ToolboxBitmap property. Then, from VBCCE's File menu, recompile your UserControl so it contains the new bitmap.

If you want to see it on the Toolbox right away, close the UserControl design window and it will appear, as shown in Figure 7-18.

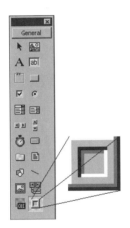

Figure 7-18 You can create any icon you want, and then just put it into the ToolboxBitmap property.

Summary

In this chapter, you discovered how to work more efficiently by relying on the intelligent assistance of Wizards. First you learn how to create a custom property by hand. Then you learned how to make a contained control resize itself when a user resizes the container UserControl.

You also worked with two Wizards built into Visual Basic: the ActiveX Control Interface Wizard and the Property Page Wizard. These wizards can be of considerable assistance in helping you write code. Imagine trying to map two dozen properties *by hand* without the help of the ActiveX Control Interface Wizard!

Finally, you learned how to use Paint to help you create personalized icons to represent your UserControls on the VB Toolbox, or the Toolboxes of other applications and utilities, such as the ActiveX Control Pad.

CHAPTER EIGHT

INTERACTING ON THE INTERNET

IN THIS CHAPTER YOU LEARN THESE KEY SKILLS

MAKING AN ANIMATED CONTROL   PAGE 153

USING VBSCRIPT TO COMMUNICATE WITH
   CUSTOM CONTROLS   PAGE 160

SUBCLASSING ON YOUR OWN   PAGE 161

INTEGRATING ACTIVEX, VBSCRIPT, AND HTML
   PAGE 164

INCLUDING OPTIONAL ERROR CHECKING WITHIN AN
   ACTIVEX CONTROL   PAGE 169

I n this chapter you learn how to subclass a Timer control and use it with a subclassed PictureBox to create an animated object that repeatedly changes color, graphic, or size. You also try subclassing on your own, with only the final source code displayed in this book to compare to the source code you generate (with the Wizard's help). You learn how to communicate between HTML, VBScript, HTML controls, and ActiveX controls. You put an HTML button control into a Web page, along with an ActiveX TextBox control on an ActiveX Layout. Then you discover how to communicate between these objects. Finally, you learn where you, or a developer, can program error-checking code.

Creating a Control for Animation

A fter the examples you worked through in Chapter 7, you should now feel comfortable creating a subclassed ActiveX control. To deepen your understanding of subclassing, try building a control called *Flash* that will add animation to your applications or Web pages. The control can also behave like a CommandButton — displaying a graphic (or text saved as a graphic file) and then taking action if the user clicks it.

Building this control will also illustrate a flaw in the ActiveX Control Pad. The Picture property works fine when you use the Flash control within Word or Visual Basic or any other ActiveX-capable application. But the ActiveX Control Pad disables the Picture property, requiring, instead, a PicturePath property.

To begin building this control, follow these steps:

1. Start VBCCE.

2. Place a Timer control and a PictureBox onto UserControl1.

3. In the Properties window, change the Name property of UserControl1 to **Flash**. Then change the UserControl's BackStyle to **Transparent**.

4. Size the UserControl so that it's just a little larger than the PictureBox. Don't worry if the Timer disappears — it's still there and will never be made visible to users anyway.

5. Double-click the UserControl to bring up the code window.

6. In the UserControl's Resize event, type the following code to enable the developer to resize the PictureBox by dragging it:

```
Private Sub UserControl_Resize()
Picture1.Width = Width - 160
Picture1.Height = Height - 160
End Sub
```

Map Six Properties

Now select ActiveX Control Interface Wizard from the Add-Ins menu. Click Next, select all the members in the list on the right, and then click the back-arrow button to remove all of them (and return them to the left list). Then, in the left list, hold down the Ctrl key while you select BackColor, Click, DblClick, Interval, Picture, and Timer. Click the right-arrow button to send them all into the Selected Names list on the right. Click Next twice.

Now you can map the six members you've selected. Hold down the Ctrl key while you select BackColor, Click, DblClick, and Picture in the Public Name list. Click Picture1 in the Maps to. . .Control list. Map the Interval property and Timer event to the Timer control. Click Next and then click Finish.

Check the Source Code

As you saw in the previous chapter, you always want to read through the source code generated by a Wizard. You want to see if the Wizard's done anything wrong, so double-click the UserControl to get to the code window. Your source code should look like the following:

```
'Event Declarations:
Event Timer() 'MappingInfo=Timer1,Timer1,-1,Timer
Event DblClick() 'MappingInfo=Picture1,Picture1,-1,DblClick
Event Click() 'MappingInfo=Picture1,Picture1,-1,Click


Private Sub Picture1_Click()

End Sub


Private Sub UserControl_Initialize()

End Sub


Private Sub UserControl_Resize()
Picture1.Width = Width - 160
Picture1.Height = Height - 160
End Sub


Private Sub Timer1_Timer()
  RaiseEvent Timer
End Sub


'WARNING! DO NOT REMOVE OR MODIFY THE FOLLOWING COMMENTED LINES!
'MappingInfo=Picture1,Picture1,-1,Picture
Public Property Get Picture() As Picture
  Set Picture = Picture1.Picture
End Property


Public Property Set Picture(ByVal New_Picture As Picture)
  Set Picture1.Picture = New_Picture
  PropertyChanged "Picture"
End Property


'WARNING! DO NOT REMOVE OR MODIFY THE FOLLOWING COMMENTED LINES!
'MappingInfo=Timer1,Timer1,-1,Interval
Public Property Get Interval() As Long
  Interval = Timer1.Interval
End Property


Public Property Let Interval(ByVal New_Interval As Long)
  Timer1.Interval() = New_Interval
  PropertyChanged "Interval"
End Property
```

```
Private Sub Picture1_DblClick()
  RaiseEvent DblClick
End Sub

Private Sub Picture1_Click()
  RaiseEvent Click
End Sub

'WARNING! DO NOT REMOVE OR MODIFY THE FOLLOWING COMMENTED LINES!
'MappingInfo=Picture1,Picture1,-1,BackColor
Public Property Get BackColor() As OLE_COLOR
  BackColor = Picture1.BackColor
End Property

Public Property Let BackColor(ByVal New_BackColor As OLE_COLOR)
  Picture1.BackColor() = New_BackColor
  PropertyChanged "BackColor"
End Property

'Load property values from storage
Private Sub UserControl_ReadProperties(PropBag As PropertyBag)

  Set Picture = PropBag.ReadProperty("Picture", Nothing)
  Timer1.Interval = PropBag.ReadProperty("Interval", 0)
  Picture1.BackColor = PropBag.ReadProperty("BackColor", _
  &H8000000F)
End Sub

'Write property values to storage
Private Sub UserControl_WriteProperties(PropBag As PropertyBag)

  Call PropBag.WriteProperty("Picture", Picture, Nothing)
  Call PropBag.WriteProperty("Interval", Timer1.Interval, 0)
  Call PropBag.WriteProperty("BackColor", Picture1.BackColor, _
  &H8000000F)
End Sub
```

This code doesn't seem to need any modification. It looks fine at first glance. The Wizard didn't comment out the programming in the Resize event and has added all the necessary code to accomplish the requested mapping. But, as always, you'll want to test the control within VBCCE before sending it out into the real world.

Watch for Errors

Close the UserControl's code and design windows, thereby activating the UserControl on the Toolbox. Choose Add Project from the File menu and add a Standard EXE project. Double-click the UserControl in the Toolbox to put it onto the Form1.

Uh-oh, an error message. What's the reason for the error dialog box shown in Figure 8-1? The Wizard did it.

Figure 8-1   The Wizard made a mistake.

The message, Ambiguous name detected, is itself ambiguous. But if you take a look at the source code again, you'll notice that the Wizard inserted an empty Picture Click event near the top. You can't have two event procedures with the same name within the same Form or Module. How would Visual Basic know which one to run and which one was bogus? Close the Error dialog box, and, in the code window, remove the empty Picture1_Click procedure near the top of the code. (If you didn't get this error message, good for you. That means the Wizard has gotten smarter since this book was written.)

Now double-click the UserControl's icon again to put it on the Toolbox, and all should be well. Try changing the BackColor and loading a graphics file into the Picture property. Test the Timer's effects by setting the Interval property to **400**. Then double-click the UserControl to bring up the code window, and type the following code into the UserControl's Timer event:

```
Private Sub Flash1_Timer()

Static toggle As Boolean
toggle = Not toggle

If toggle Then
Flash1.Visible = False
Else
Flash1.Visible = True
End If

End Sub
```

And type this code into Flash1's Click event:

```
Private Sub Flash1_Click()
Flash1.Interval = 100
End Sub
```

Press F5 to run the project. You'll see something similar to Figure 8-2, flashing on and off. Then, when you click the picture, it really picks up speed.

Figure 8-2 This ActiveX control draws attention to itself.

Next, compile it into an .OCX file by selecting Flash (Flash.ctl) in the Project Explorer and then choosing Make .OCX in the File menu. In the Make Project dialog box, name the .OCX file **Flash** and click OK. Flash should now be registered as a valid ActiveX object in your computer.

To find out more about all the options available to you when you compile a project in VB, see the "Bonus" section of Chapter 14.

Finally, be sure to save this project by using the name **SSInput**. You'll make some modifications to this project at the end of this chapter. Now close VBCCE.

Testing a UserControl in a Web Browser

Now it's time to give your control a real-world trial run. You can put it into Internet Explorer and test it there. Open the ActiveX Control Pad.

To insert the Flash control into a Web page, follow these steps:

1. Click Edit → Insert HTML Layout .

2. Name the Layout **FL**.

3. Click the icon next to <OBJECT to open the Layout.

4. If the Toolbox isn't visible, select it in the View menu.

5. Right-click the Toolbox and choose Additional Controls.

6. Select Project1.Flash, as shown in Figure 8-3.

7. Close the Additional Controls dialog box, and then add a Flash control to the Layout.

8. Double-click the Flash control to bring up its Properties window.

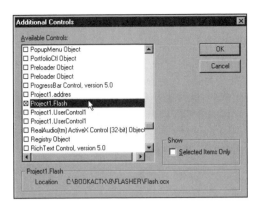

Figure 8-3 There it is, your Flash control ready to be added to a Toolbox.

9. Double-click the BackColor property and change the color to a color you like.

10. Try clicking the Picture property.

The Picture Property Fails

Alas, the Picture property of the ActiveX Flash control doesn't work in the Control Pad. It's disabled. Internet browsers expect an address from which they can download a graphic. As a result, the ActiveX Control Pad's Image control has a PicturePath property instead of a Picture property. The Flash control's Picture property works fine in Office97 applications and in Visual Basic applications, but it doesn't translate to the ActiveX Control Pad.

However, you can still achieve worthwhile animation effects on a Web page with the Flash control and its built-in Timer. Try the next example in which you create a subtle effect by flashing a button next to a Label control. The flashing is the subtle part: If you choose two similar colors, the effect is a gentle pulsation rather than a harsh flashing. Add a Label control to the Layout, and then change its SpecialEffect property to **Raised** and change the Caption property. Size and position the controls, as shown in Figure 8-4.

Figure 8-4 You can use the Flash control to call attention to a button the user can click.

This Wizard Is Feeble

Right-click the Layout control and choose Script Wizard. You can just use the Wizard as a way of inserting a VBScript template into the source code for this Layout control. Recall that this Wizard is relatively feeble and can't do many of the things you want VBScript to do. Nevertheless, in the Select an Event list, select Flash1 and then choose the Click event. In the Insert Actions list, select Flash1 and then double-click the Interval Property. Enter **0** and click OK twice to close the Wizard. Right-click the Layout and choose View Source Code. Answer Yes, and your source code appears in a Notepad window. At this point, your script will look quite simple:

```
<SCRIPT LANGUAGE="VBScript">
<! —
Sub Flash1_Click()
Flash1.Interval = 0
end sub
 — >
</SCRIPT>
```

All this code does is turn off the Timer if the user clicks the Flash control. Add the following code to create the pulsing light effect:

```
<SCRIPT LANGUAGE="VBScript">
<! —
dim toggle

Flash1.BackColor = &H00ff8000
Flash1.Interval = 1000


Sub Flash1_Timer()
toggle = not toggle
if toggle then
   Flash1.BackColor = &H00ff7000
else
   Flash1.BackColor = &H00ff8000
end if
end sub

Sub Flash1_Click()
Flash1.Interval = 0
end sub

Sub Label1_Click()
```

```
Flash1.Interval = 0
end sub

  - >
</SCRIPT>
```

No Static or Dimming Variable Types

TIP Unlike VB, VBScript does not have a Static command that enables you to preserve the status of a local (within a procedure) variable. Therefore, you can't use the code `Static Toggle` inside the Flash1_ Timer event. Instead, you must define the variable outside in the general section of the code. Variables defined like that will retain their value (contents) as long as the Web page is active within its browser.

Also, VB does not permit code such as the following: `Dim MyVar As String`. You can only declare Variant data types in VBScript. If you really need to specify a variable type, use one of the coercion commands to force the Variant to become the needed type: cBool, cByte, cDate, cDbl, cInt, cLng, cSng, cStr, or cVerr.

Notice also that the BackColor and Interval properties are defined outside a procedure. This causes them to take effect when the browser first loads this document and encounters the VBScript. By contrast, the code within a procedure will not be carried out until (or if) the event is triggered. Because the Interval property is set to 1,000, the Timer event will be triggered every second. However, the Flash control will keep pulsing at one-second intervals unless the user clicks the Flash or the Label, thereby turning off the Timer because it will then have a zero Interval.

It's usually a good idea to provide code in the Click event of a Label. Users will frequently click the Label rather than an associated button or other graphic.

Subclassing on Your Own

When users enter information (such as their social security number) into a TextBox or other input control, a developer or programmer must often test the user's input. This act of validating data can be left up to a developer. After your ActiveX control passes the data to the developer's programming, the developer can then validate it and decide when and how to notify the user of a problem and request that the user fix any errors.

Or, you (the creator of an ActiveX control) can build validation into your control. This way, the control won't pass invalid data to the developer. The developer can accept the data from your control without further testing.

Try Both Approaches

To see the benefits of both approaches to input validation, try subclassing a single-line TextBox that's dedicated to accepting social security numbers. First, create this SSInput control with no data validation. This example will also demonstrate how to use an ActiveX control and VBScript in concert with an HTML button control and some HTML scripting.

Start the VBCCE and, with the ActiveX Control Interface Wizard, subclass a TextBox control. You're more or less on your own this time, but you can check your source code against the complete source code that follows.

The following is a list of the qualities and members you'll want to map or program for this new SSInput control:

* Its Name property should be SSInput.
* The BackStyle property of the UserControl should be set to Transparent and the UserControl should be only slightly larger than the TextBox.
* It should map the following properties: BackColor, ForeColor, Font, and Text.
* It should map the Change event.
* The developer should be able to resize it, so you'll have to write that programming into the UserControl's Resize event. (Refer to the code in the following section if you've forgotten how to do this.)

After you create the SSInput control, test it by adding a Standard EXE project (as described in Chapter 7). You might have to remove an extraneous, duplicate Change procedure from the source code before the SSInput control will run on the Standard EXE Form1.

Check Your Source Code

When you're satisfied things are working as they should, double-click SSInput in the Project Explorer to bring up its design window. Then double-click the control in its design window to get down to the code window. Your source code should look like the following:

```
'Event Declarations:
Event Change() 'MappingInfo=Text1,Text1,-1,Change
'WARNING! DO NOT REMOVE OR MODIFY THE FOLLOWING COMMENTED LINES!
'MappingInfo=Text1,Text1,-1,Text
Public Property Get Text() As String
  Text = Text1.Text
End Property

Public Property Let Text(ByVal New_Text As String)
  Text1.Text() = New_Text
```

```
    PropertyChanged "Text"
End Property


'WARNING! DO NOT REMOVE OR MODIFY THE FOLLOWING COMMENTED LINES!
'MappingInfo=Text1,Text1,-1,ForeColor
Public Property Get ForeColor() As OLE_COLOR
    ForeColor = Text1.ForeColor
End Property


Public Property Let ForeColor(ByVal New_ForeColor As OLE_COLOR)
    Text1.ForeColor() = New_ForeColor
    PropertyChanged "ForeColor"
End Property


'WARNING! DO NOT REMOVE OR MODIFY THE FOLLOWING COMMENTED LINES!
'MappingInfo=Text1,Text1,-1,Font
Public Property Get Font() As Font
    Set Font = Text1.Font
End Property


Public Property Set Font(ByVal New_Font As Font)
    Set Text1.Font = New_Font
    PropertyChanged "Font"
End Property


Private Sub Text1_Change()
    RaiseEvent Change
End Sub


'WARNING! DO NOT REMOVE OR MODIFY THE FOLLOWING COMMENTED LINES!
'MappingInfo=Text1,Text1,-1,BackColor
Public Property Get BackColor() As OLE_COLOR
    BackColor = Text1.BackColor
End Property


Public Property Let BackColor(ByVal New_BackColor As OLE_COLOR)
    Text1.BackColor() = New_BackColor
    PropertyChanged "BackColor"
End Property


'Load property values from storage
Private Sub UserControl_ReadProperties(PropBag As PropertyBag)

    Text1.Text = PropBag.ReadProperty("Text", "Text1")
```

```
Text1.ForeColor = PropBag.ReadProperty("ForeColor", &H80000008)
Set Font = PropBag.ReadProperty("Font", Ambient.Font)
Text1.BackColor = PropBag.ReadProperty("BackColor", &H80000005)
End Sub

Private Sub UserControl_Resize()
Text1.Height = Height - 100
Text1.Width = Width - 100
End Sub

'Write property values to storage
Private Sub UserControl_WriteProperties(PropBag As PropertyBag)

Call PropBag.WriteProperty("Text", Text1.Text, "Text1")
Call PropBag.WriteProperty("ForeColor", Text1.ForeColor,
&H80000008)
Call PropBag.WriteProperty("Font", Font, Ambient.Font)
Call PropBag.WriteProperty("BackColor", Text1.BackColor,
&H80000005)
End Sub
```

Notice that the Font property, like the Picture property, is an *object*. Therefore, the Property Set procedure is used instead of the Property Let procedure (used with most properties). Likewise, when the Font object is queried or changed, the Set command is used in the code, like this:

```
Set Font = Text1.Font
```

Rather than the usual syntax for changing a property:

```
Font = Text1.Font
```

Now, after you've tested your SSInput control and checked it against the preceding source code, compile it to an .OCX file. Select SSInput in the Project Explorer, and then, from the File menu, choose Make Project1.ocx. Change the name to **SSInput.ocx** and click OK to begin the compilation.

Integrating ActiveX, VBScript, and HTML

At this point you can test the SSInput control in a Web page. The goal is to integrate one of your ActiveX controls with a traditional HTML control, such as a Button. You want to create HTML script that displays a Button control and gives the control a name. You'll then write VBScript code that reacts when the Button is clicked. This reaction is an event, but the event responds to an HTML control. Then, within that event, you change a property of a custom ActiveX control (the SSInput) while it's on a Layout. By trying this example, you'll find out how to communicate between the outer HTML document page, the Layout control, and VBScript.

Follow these steps to integrate HTML, an ActiveX control, and VBScript:

1. Close the VBCCE and start the ActiveX Control Pad.

2. Click Edit → Insert HTML Layout and name it **S**, which the Control Pad will modify to *S.ALX*.

3. Click the icon next to the <OBJECT tag.

4. Right-click the Layout's Toolbox and choose Additional Controls.

5. Select Project1.SSInput to place your newly compiled ActiveX control onto the Toolbox.

6. Click OK to close the dialog box.

7. Click the SSInput control and place it on the Layout.

8. Resize the Layout around the SSInput control, as shown in Figure 8-5.

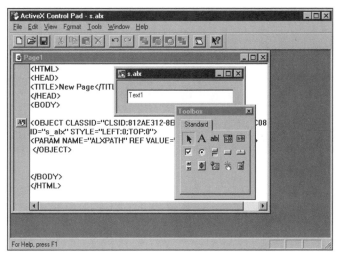

Figure 8-5   In this example you communicate between an
HTML Button control and this UserControl.

9. Close the Toolbox and the Layout control. If you get an error message, ignore it.

Some Mapped Properties Are Broken

 Recall that at the time of this writing, the ActiveX Control Pad and other Web page editors (such as Internet Explorer 4.0's FrontPad) do not correctly handle all mapped properties (such as BackColor). The SSInput will, nonetheless, operate correctly by using its default properties when loaded into Internet Explorer. (Doubtless, Microsoft is working hard to fix this problem.) Subclassed ActiveX controls work quite well when placed into Microsoft Office applications or Visual Basic applications.

Now, just under the <BODY> tag in the HTML document, type in the HTML code that displays what in VB would be called a command button:

```
<INPUT TYPE=BUTTON VALUE="Type your SS, then Click here."
  NAME="bttn">
```

Then, type in the following VBScript code that creates an event for the HTML Button control:

```
<SCRIPT LANGUAGE="VBScript">
<! —

Sub bttn_OnClick()
Answer = s_alx.SSInput1.Text
For I = 1 to Len(Answer)
Char = mid(Answer, I, 1)
If Not IsNumeric(Char) then
If Char <> " " And Char <> "-" Then
MsgBox "You have typed the non-numeric character:" & Char & ".
  Please try again."
Exit For
End If
End If
Next
end sub
 — >
</SCRIPT>
```

The entire HTML and VBScript combined should look like this:

```
<HTML>
<HEAD>
<TITLE>New Page</TITLE>
</HEAD>

<BODY>
```

```
<INPUT TYPE=BUTTON VALUE="Type your SS, then Click here."
  NAME="bttn">


<OBJECT CLASSID="CLSID:812AE312-8B8E-11CF-93C8-00AA00C08FDF"
ID="s_alx" STYLE="LEFT:0;TOP:0">
<PARAM NAME="ALXPATH" REF VALUE="file:C:\Contlpad\s.alx">
</OBJECT>

<SCRIPT LANGUAGE="VBScript">
<! —

Sub bttn_OnClick()
Answer = s_alx.SSInput1.Text
For I = 1 to Len(Answer)
Char = mid(Answer, I, 1)
If Not IsNumeric(Char) then
If Char <> " " And Char <> "-" Then
MsgBox "You have typed the non-numeric character:" & Char & ".
  Please try again."
Exit For
End If
End If
Next
end sub


 — >
</SCRIPT>

</BODY>
</HTML>
```

Notice that your event that responds to the BUTTON click uses the button's NAME *bttn*. Notice also that it uses the peculiar term *OnClick* rather than the more typical *Click*. In any case, the OnClick event responds whenever an Internet user clicks the Button control.

The first thing you do in this event is get the contents of the SSInput control located on the Layout:

```
Answer = s_alx.SSInput1.Text
```

It's important to remember that to contact a Layout control, you must use its ID (its name, in effect) exactly as defined within the <OBJECT> HTML code:

```
ID="s_alx"
```

How to Reference an ActiveX Control

When you reference a control in Visual Basic, usually you can simply provide its name: Text1.Text or Picture4.BackColor or List3.ForeColor. However, if the control is on a different Form, you must attach the Form's name to the control's name, separated by a period: Form3.Text1.Text or Form2.Picture4.BackColor.

Likewise, if you reference an ActiveX control on a Layout, you must add the Layout's name (not its filename) to the beginning of the control's name. You use this syntax as you would in Visual Basic to query or assign value to a property. For example, here's how you would remove all text from the SSInput control and make it blank:

```
s_alx.SSInput1.Text = ""
```

Notice that in the VBScript for the OnClick event in the preceding example, you use the InStr command to go through and look at each character the user typed in. If any character is nonnumeric (except for spaces and hyphens), the user is asked to try again. No alphabetic characters are permitted.

Test your HTML/VBScript/Layout/ActiveX Web page by selecting Save As from the ActiveX Control Pad's File menu. Then run Internet Explorer and choose Open from its File menu. Load your .HTM file. If you've left Internet Explorer's security options set to their defaults, Explorer will warn you of a potentially harmful ActiveX control, as shown in Figure 8-6.

Figure 8-6 This warning appears if an unauthenticated ActiveX control is about to be loaded.

There's little possibility, though, that you've created a virus in your SSInput control or the VBScript and HTML that accompanies it on this .HTM document. So, unless you're a multiple personality and you think one of your other selves might have written some rogue code and buried it in the SSInput, go ahead and click the Yes button. You should see the HTML button along with your SSInput control, as shown in Figure 8-7.

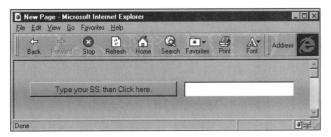

Figure 8-7 The HTML control on the left interacts with the ActiveX control on the right.

If when you load your .HTM file into Internet Explorer, you see the text *Text1* by default inside the SSInput control, you neglected to delete it when constructing the UserControl. The solution is to reload the source code for your SSInput control into VBCCE. Then, with the SSInput control selected in its design window, look for the Text property in the Properties window. Select *Text1* and press the Del key to delete it. Now recompile by using the Compile option on the VBCCE file menu. Note that you can also, at any time, rerun the ActiveX Control Interface Wizard to make additional changes to your UserControl.

BONUS

Enclosing Error Checking Within a UserControl

In the preceding example in this chapter, you validated the user-input *outside* the SSInput control by writing some VBScript code. You can, however, include error checking within an ActiveX control itself, which is the goal of this next example.

It's generally considered good programming practice to validate arguments and trap other kinds of errors *within* a server component's procedure (your UserControl is a server). This way, you can reject erroneous input and provide understandable, highly precise error messages back to the source of the error. What's more, you can prevent VB from shutting down the client. (Recall that when an ActiveX component is used by an outside application, the component is referred to as the *server* — servicing the needs of the *client*, the outside application.)

Consider the following example:

```
Public Function dByzero(n As Variant)
dByzero = 8 / n
End Function
```

You'll Collapse Both Client and Server

If this function is a method of an ActiveX UserControl or other server, when the client application passes a number, the *type* is checked by the *As Variant* command. If, however, instead of Variant, you specify a particular variable type (such as Long or String), the calling client must pass that same type of variable or VB will display a Type Mismatch error and shut down the client (simultaneously collapsing the instance of your ActiveX component too).

Similarly, any kind of error that occurs within a server will collapse the server and the client, shutting them both down. Assume that a client passes a zero to the preceding dByzero method listed in the previous code, as shown by the following call to dByzero:

```
Private Sub Form_Load()
z = 0
UserControl1.dByzero z
End Sub
```

When this program runs, a zero is sent to the server's method and the server attempts to divide eight by zero, an impossibility. The server displays a Division by Zero error message and shuts down both the server and the client.

As all experienced VB programmers know, you can prevent this abrupt shutdown-on-error by merely inserting On Error Resume Next. You can do it in either the server or client as shown in the following code:

```
Private Sub Form_Load()
On Error Resume Next
n = UserControl1.dByzero(0)
If Err then MsgBox Error(Err)
End Sub
```

or

```
Public Function dbyZero(n As Variant) As Variant
On Error Resume Next
dbyZero = 8 / n
If Err then MsgBox Error(Err)
End Function
```

Use On Error Resume Next

In the interest of conserving space, *On Error Resume Next* has not been included in the source code in the examples in this book. However, you should use it in many of your subs and functions (methods), as well as in other procedures such as Property Let and Property Get. Use it whenever there's a possibility that user- or developer-supplied information might generate an error. You should always use error trapping within a ReadProperties procedure. Perhaps the PropertyBag is missing, corrupt, or its data is otherwise incorrect.

In addition to On Error Resume Next, you should also use the companion line that alerts the developer or user that there was a problem: If Err then MsgBox Error(Err).

Now you can try improving the SSInput example by incorporating error trapping into the server ActiveX component. Start the VBCCE and load the SSInput project. If you didn't save it, you can get the code from the CD-ROM that accompanies this book. Add a CommandButton to the SSInput control, and change its Caption property to "Click when finished," as shown in Figure 8-8.

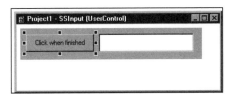

Figure 8-8 Add a VB CommandButton to the SSInput control.

Double-click the CommandButton and type the following code into its Click event:

```
Private Sub Command1_Click()
Answer = Text1.Text
For I = 1 To Len(Answer)
Char = Mid(Answer, I, 1)
If Not IsNumeric(Char) Then
If Char <> " " And Char <> "-" Then
MsgBox "You have typed the non-numeric character:" & Char & ".
  Please try again."
Exit For
End If
End If
Next
End Sub
```

The only change we had to make from the VBScript example earlier in this chapter was to substitute *Text1.Text* for *s_alx.SSInput1.Text*.

You'll want to let the developer have the option of changing the CommandButton's Caption property, so follow these steps to map it:

1. Run the ActiveX Control Interface Wizard from the VBCCE Add-Ins menu.

2. Click Next.

3. In the Select Interface Members dialog box, double-click Caption (found in the Available Names list) to move it to the Selected Names list.

4. Click Next twice.

5. In the Set Mapping window, click Caption and then choose Command1 as the Maps to. . .Control.

6. Click Next and then click Finish. The Wizard has added the Caption property to the ReadProperties and WriteProperties procedures. It has also created the Property Get and Let procedures for it.

Now recompile. Click SSInput to select it from the Project Explorer. Then choose Make SSInput.ocx from the File menu. Click OK. When asked if you want to replace the existing file, click Yes.

To test the new control, run the ActiveX Control Pad. From the Edit menu, choose Insert HTML Layout. Click the icon next to the <OBJECT tag and you'll see something odd. The icon for the SSInput control on the Layout's Toolbox has been crosshatched, as shown in Figure 8-9.

Figure 8-9 Something has happened to your ActiveX SSInput control.

If you try to place the SSInput control onto the Layout control, you'll see a message box claiming there's an invalid-argument problem. The Layout control will refuse to accept the SSInput. The solution: Right-click the SSInput control on the Toolbox, and then choose Delete SSInput to get rid of it. Then right-click the Toolbox itself and choose Additional Controls. In the list that appears, locate and click Project1.SSInput, and then click OK. This will put the newly compiled version of your SSInput control on the Toolbox, and you can now add it to the Layout with no problems.

Problems with Some Properties

If you want to change the Caption property, you'll run into no problems with this mapped property. Double-click the SSInput control and change the Caption in the Properties window. As you can see, some properties of some subclassed controls make it through to the ActiveX Control Pad. You can indeed change the Caption (though the change won't be retained when you display this document in Internet Explorer), but other properties (such as the BackColor of a TextBox) can't be changed in the Control Pad. All these problems should be fixed shortly, though, so you will be able to expect that mapped Picture properties or ForeColor properties will work as expected when you use ActiveX for Internet documents. The fact that they work perfectly in Visual Basic or Office applications isn't, of course, any excuse for their failure to work when ActiveX controls are placed into Internet documents.

Now test the newly compiled control. Close the Layout and Toolbox. From the ActiveX Control Pad's File menu, save this .HTM file. Run Internet Explorer, and, from its File menu, choose Open to load the .HTM file. Try typing **12aa233** or some other impossible social security number to test the ActiveX control's interior error-trapping facility. The error message box appears, as shown in Figure 8-10.

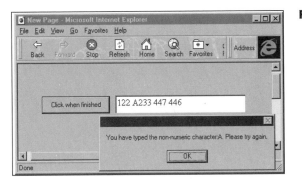

Figure 8-10 This error message comes from within the ActiveX control itself.

Always Think of the Developer

As usual, you, the creator of an ActiveX control, should try to make your control as flexible and customizable as possible. Developers have many varying needs and might deploy your control in many different contexts. Therefore, it's always good to let developers have the option of adjusting properties and other elements of your creation. For instance, what if they would prefer to provide their own error trapping and bypass the internal message box you've installed? This calls for a custom (not a mapped) property.

Follow these steps to make internal error trapping optional:

1. Fire up the VBCCE.

2. Using the ActiveX Control Interface Wizard, add a property called *ErrorMessage*.

3. When you get to the Wizard's Create Custom Interface Members dialog box, click New.

4. Name it **ErrorMessage**.

5. Click OK, and then click Next a couple of times until you get to the Set Attributes dialog box.

6. Define the Data Type as Boolean (True or False).

7. Type the following text into the Description field: **If the user enters anything other than a digit, an error message is displayed.**

8. Click Finish to close the Wizard.

9. Open the SSInput code window and add this new line at the start of the CommandButton's Click event:

```
Private Sub Command1_Click()
If m_ErrorMessage = False Then Exit Sub
Answer = Text1.Text
For I = 1 To Len(Answer)
Char = Mid(Answer, I, 1)
If Not IsNumeric(Char) Then
If Char <> " " And Char <> "-" Then
MsgBox "You have typed the non-numeric character:" & Char & ".
Please try again."
Exit For
End If
End If
Next
End Sub
```

10. From the VBCCE's File menu, recompile by selecting Make SSInput.ocx.

Summary

I n this chapter, you learned how to create an animated control and how to use a subclassed Timer control. You then tried subclassing all on your own, with a little help from the Wizard. Next, you found out how to write VBScript code that enables you to communicate between ActiveX controls, the ActiveX layout control, and controls, such as BUTTON, that are built into the HTML language. Finally, you tested several approaches to error checking.

In the first eight chapters of this book you worked on a variety of examples. Most of these examples involved principles of object-oriented programming (OOP). Now it's time to lift the curtain and look at the various techniques and concepts that, collectively, make up the practice of OOP, which is the subject of Chapter 9. If you've been hesitant to make the switch from traditional, procedure-oriented programming, you might discover that OOP is less alien and less difficult to understand than you thought.

CLASSES AND OBJECTS

This third section of the book delves more deeply into the world of objects, developing your understanding of the principles of object-oriented programming (OOP) and its implementation in Visual Basic. You'll try writing a program using the traditional, procedure-oriented technique, and then write the same program in OOP. You'll create a sophisticated elapsed-time ActiveX control, illustrating how to design and code more advanced ActiveX components.

*B*yte is a premier magazine source of technical information about computers for the general public. *Byte*'s reporting tackles complex and advanced topics and renders them understandable to the average intelligent reader. Tom Halfhill, *Byte* magazine's senior editor, joined *Byte* in 1992. The following is an excerpt from an interview with Halfhill in which he discusses his views on the future of both OOP and the Internet.

RM: Do you think OOP is an important programming technique?

TH: Yes, especially for commercial and corporate developers who can probably benefit the most from reusable objects in multiple projects. If you're trying to find a hardware analogy to OOP, it would be the concept of building things out of standardized parts. For example, there is a great variety of devices you can make with common electronic components. You don't have to create line filters, high-gain antennae, lightning protectors, backup batteries or other accessories from scratch. They're standardized parts that can be used to enhance a variety of electronic devices.

RM: In your own programming, how do you make use of OOP techniques?

TH: The primary object-oriented language I use is Java, which is a new language built with objects from the ground up. Everything in Java is an object, except for a few primitive data types (integers, characters, and so on). I've used Java to write my own objects (such as a custom "alert box" or "message box") that I've reused in different projects. If a particular project needs a slightly different form of the object, I can inherit most of the object's code and override the methods I need to change. However, the thoroughly object-oriented nature of Java requires a developer to have an equally thorough understanding of object-oriented programming, and the learning curve may be steep for people who are accustomed to procedural programming.

RM: What's your best guess about the future of the Internet?

TH: The Internet is fast becoming the most popular and most important computer "platform." From now on, developers should think twice about what kind of application they're creating. If it's an application that makes sense to deploy on a network — now or in the future — they should consider developing it for the "Internet platform," not just for one particular CPU or operating system. Machine-specific platforms come and go, but some form of the Internet will exist as long as there are computers.

HOW TO WRITE OBJECT-ORIENTED PROGRAMS

IN THIS CHAPTER YOU LEARN THESE KEY SKILLS

This chapter is all about objects — how to find them and use them in your programs. You learn the differences between traditional task-oriented programming and object-oriented programming (OOP). You also learn the meaning of the three primary elements of OOP: encapsulation, inheritance, and polymorphism. You find out what these elements mean in practical terms and how they're implemented in Visual Basic. Finally, you discover how to use the Ambient and Extender objects.

In Theory

So far you've learned several concepts that relate to object-oriented programming:

* The relationship between classes and their offspring, objects
* How to use subclassing to build new objects out of existing classes
* How to expose Public procedures to enable other programmers and developers to use the members of your object (its properties, methods, and events)
* How to hide Private procedures and variables, so outsiders can't get to unauthorized areas of your objects

But there's more to OOP than these maneuvers; OOP is a complete theory of programming. Learning OOP doesn't mean you must abandon techniques you've used in the past. After all, most people agree that classic *procedure-oriented* programming works very well for small projects, particularly if you're writing the project all by yourself. But OOP techniques have notable advantages when you're working on larger projects or programming as part of a team.

VB's Move Toward Full OOP

In its past three versions — Visual Basic 3, 4, and now 5 — the language has been moving closer to conformity with the standards and features of OOP. VB still can't boast as rigorous or as complete an implementation of OOP as purists might wish, but with VB 5, the language is pretty far along toward becoming a complete OOP environment.

Procedure-Based Versus OOP Programming

If you've been programming for a few years, you're undoubtedly familiar with the traditional, *procedure-based* approach to programming. Instead of just jumping in and writing long, complicated segments of programming code, you break down your overall task into smaller subtasks. You can test these sub-tasks more easily because they are small and self-contained. You define what goes into a subtask and what is expected to come out. These subtasks are called *procedures* (subroutines and functions).

Recently, though, new ideas have become popular under the general title of *object-oriented* programming (as opposed to procedure-based programming). To create ActiveX objects, you'll want to acquaint yourself with at least the basics of OOP.

Locating Objects

Many programmers have a hard time switching from traditional programming to OOP. It's not the actual programming that's so difficult. After all, the programming techniques that result in an OOP project — encapsulation, inheritance, and polymorphism — aren't that difficult or unfamiliar. After you've figured out what objects you should include in a project, the actual programming of those objects is relatively straightforward.

What bothers most people migrating to OOP is the *planning* stage — the time before you write any code. The troubling question in particular is, *How do you break a programming task down into objects?*

Most books about OOP either ignore this planning problem, or fog it up with unnecessary jargon and convoluted abstraction. The issue is simply this: Programmers used to traditional procedure-based programming think in terms of the jobs that have to be done. In fact, this is the way most people plan *anything*. It's more or less intuitive to subdivide a large task into a list of smaller tasks. However, OOP requires that you take a different approach, as you'll soon see. But first, consider the nature of the time-honored task-oriented approach.

Back when the first wooden bridge was built over a creek, the engineer of that bridge likely made a mental list of the smaller tasks that, taken together, would result in a bridge. That list might include the following tasks:

1. Use dead, dry trees.

2. Cut trees into logs, flat on two sides.

3. Cut trees into pegs.

4. Use dried hemp for ropes.

5. Weave ropes 1" thick, for fastening the logs.

6. Drag logs and ropes to creek.

7. Tie logs together using ropes.

8. Sling the whole thing across the creek and fasten it to pegs.

This is precisely the kind of break-it-down-into-smaller-tasks methodology that traditional procedure-oriented programming demands.

Computers Are Fundamentally Different

Computers, however, are fundamentally different from any tools we've had before, and object-oriented programming takes advantage of those differences.

For example, with a computer you can create objects at will — you can make *virtual* things that pop in and out of existence as often as needed. When building a bridge, you can't create logs at will.

And with a computer you can make as many virtual objects as you want — dropping them off the end of your assembly line with no additional cost. Five hundred computer objects cost precisely the same as only one object in energy (electricity) and man-years (your programming time). After you've written the class that contains all the programming to replicate the objects, producing hundreds of them at run time is free. And, indeed, a large application may have *thousands* of active objects at any given time.

Another major difference between the work a computer can accomplish and the work traditional building tools can accomplish is that computer objects can contain intelligence. They can understand methods (to accomplish tasks), react to outside stimuli (such as the Click event), and embody qualities (properties and data). In this way, computer objects differ from conventional tools. A hammer doesn't know how to hit a nail; a library card file doesn't know how to locate a book.

Computer objects can move themselves, change color, grow larger, or display messages on command. A computer object is much more like a robot than a traditional, real-world object like a hammer.

Diagram Tasks to Find the Nouns

When you've decided to create a program by using the OOP approach, start out as you would if you were taking a procedure-based approach: list the tasks. But take it one step further. Divide the tasks into three categories: nouns, verbs, and adjectives.

The nouns will be your objects. Then put the verbs (methods) and adjectives (properties) into the objects. To try it with the bridge example, see Table 9-1, which diagrams the tasks.

TABLE 9-1   The Elements of Building a Bridge

Nouns	Verbs	Adjectives
Tree		Dead, Dry
Log	Cut	Flat on two sides
Peg		
Hemp, Rope		Dried
Rope	Weave	1" thick
Log, Rope	Drag	
Log, Rope	Tie	
Log, Rope, Peg	Sling, Fasten	

You now have to make a mental leap from real-world objects (such as trees) to the virtual objects inside a computer. Computer objects can self-modify their qualities (such as their Color property) and carry out tasks (such as moving themselves with their Move method).

So, as you mentally collapse the bridge-building project into computer-type objects, remember that the objects — the Tree and Hemp — can do things to themselves.

Now simplify things by deciding which properties and methods should be located within which objects. Trees produce logs and pegs, so you can consider Logs and Pegs methods of a Tree object, along with Cut and Drag. Likewise, for the same reason, the Hemp object has a Rope method, along with Weave, Tie, Sling, and Fasten.

Now you have only two objects: Tree and Hemp. They can produce other objects and carry out various other jobs leading to the production of bridges. The Tree and Hemp objects know how to do things; they have methods built into them.

Now for the properties. A Tree has Dead, Dryness, and Flatness properties. Hemp has Thickness and Dryness properties. You can reconstruct your table to account for these properties, as in Table 9-2.

TABLE 9-2 The Methods and Properties of Two Objects

	Tree Object	**Hemp Object**
Methods	Logs, Pegs, Cut, Drag	Rope, Weave, Tie, Sling, Fasten
Properties	Dead, Dryness	Thickness, Dryness

In Table 9-2, you've organized the job as an OOP project and can now fire up VB's Class Builder or ActiveX Control Interface Wizard and specify the methods and properties of your objects.

The next time you start a programming project, try writing out the tasks as sentences, and then "diagram" the sentences to extract the nouns, verbs, and adjectives.

Now, what about *events*? Many objects don't need events because clients are merely going to make use of the objects' services (their methods), without expecting the object to react to a stimulus — such as a click — from the client application's user. UserControls, though, are the exception. Often you'll want a UserControl object to respond to keypresses and other user stimuli.

Add events where it seems necessary, but you generally don't need to consider events while diagramming your objects. You'll quickly know what stimuli your object needs if it has a visible, public user interface.

The main problem when designing an OOP project is figuring out what objects your project needs. And the process of diagramming a to-do list, as described previously, will help you locate the objects lurking in a new programming project.

The Special Qualities of Objects

I f you're authoring software for a small grocery store, the objects are probably these: the inventory list (a collection object), each customer's total bill, the deposit slips you give the bank, and each reorder form you give to suppliers. In other words, objects are essentially *things* as opposed to actions (tasks or verbs).

Another word for tasks is *procedures.* In the grocery store, the procedures are: counting the various items in the store, keeping a running total while checking a customer out, figuring a customer's tax, adding up the day's receipts, and deciding what to reorder. You must remember this: Objects are *things;* procedures are *tasks.*

Remember, too, that one major benefit objects give you that procedures don't is that objects can be freely *generated.* A class is like a little factory that can drop off objects as often as a programmer or developer wants them. If you have an ActiveX object (such as the Flash object you built in Chapter 8) for example, you can drop as many Flash objects into an Internet page as you want. In OOP terminology, bringing an object into existence — such as by dropping it into an Internet page or creating a new deposit slip object in a grocery application — is called *instantiating* the object. And if you put five Flash objects on an Internet document, you are said to then have five *instances* of the Flash class. You can't instantiate *procedures* (subs or functions), however; you must program them by hand, individually.

The Cookie Cutter

When you write a *class,* you write programming that creates qualities, behaviors, and sensitivities. Taken together, these *members* make up an object. As you've seen in earlier chapters, you can *map* the properties, methods, or events of existing controls. Or you can write the code to make unique, new properties, methods, or events of your own, such as the Percentage property you wrote for the FFrame control in Chapter 7.

In any case, once a class is programmed, it can be used repeatedly whenever objects from it are desired. That's why a class is sometimes compared to a cookie cutter: after the design has been figured out, you can stamp out identical *objects* from that design as often as you wish.

Going In and Out of Existence

Another aspect of objects is that they pop into existence (are instantiated), do their job, and then go out of existence (no instance of the object exists anymore). In fact, this "live fast and die" behavior happens regularly and sometimes quite often while a program is running or even while it is being designed.

When you place a TextBox onto a Form, you're *instantiating* that TextBox. When you close the Form in Design mode by clicking the *x* icon in the upper-right corner, you're destroying the Form object and any objects (such as the TextBox) that it contains. Similarly, during run time, your program can cause objects to be instantiated or destroyed, sometimes repeatedly and rapidly.

The Big Three: Encapsulation, Inheritance, and Polymorphism

OOP consists of three fundamental qualities: encapsulation, inheritance, and polymorphism.

Encapsulation

Encapsulation means hiding things, keeping them private. Unless you *expose* members of your class (its properties, methods, or events), they remain private to your object and cannot be fiddled with by outside applications or programmers or developers who later use your object. These class members are sealed within your object. The source code that contains all the details of your object is not given to developers. All they get is the functioning, compiled object, along with instructions you provide telling them which members of the object they can send messages to.

Recall that you used Private variables to hold the current status of properties in the ActiveX objects you created in earlier chapters. This means that nobody can directly change the value in those properties. Instead, developers must go through your Property Let (or Set) procedures where you can, among other things, check that the correct variable type is being used and take any other measures you deem appropriate. No outsiders are allowed access to the Private variable itself, or to the PropertyBag (the WriteProperties and InitProperties procedures are also private).

ALL THIS PARANOIA

All this paranoia prevents outsiders from manipulating the data or programming within your object. You design it, build it, and test it. Then you present (expose) only certain elements (the object's interface) to the outside world.

Think of a radio. Inside many older radios are small dials called variable capacitors. You can adjust them if you take the radio's cover off and twist the capacitors with a screwdriver. The problem is that the capacitors are supposed to be adjusted only at the factory when the radio is tested before shipping, or by a repairperson who has the right equipment to know where they're best set.

Newer radios have variable capacitors of a sort, but once twisted to the optimum setting, hot plastic is poured over the innards of the radio — forever sealing it from prying outsiders. This procedure guarantees that when the user twists the *exposed* dials (such as the volume or station dials), something predictable will happen. The factory-settings inside have been sealed off and cannot be disturbed. Even when you take in a modern radio or TV to a repair shop, more often than not the technicians simply pull out and replace a module.

Encapsulation is a form of abstraction. It removes developers from the innards of your ActiveX control and provides them only with a set of members they have permission to access — that is, encapsulation distances one object from another. Objects are supposed to pass messages back and forth, but never directly manipulate the data — the properties or other data — within another object. To accomplish this, an object exposes some methods and properties to the outside, but keeps other methods and properties private, encapsulated within itself.

A main rule of encapsulation is that you should never use Public variables within an object. Outsiders are permitted to work only with the interface you've provided — they remain ignorant of how the data is manipulated within your object. All outsiders need know is what members are exposed and how those members are to be used.

TIP **Let's face it. Object-oriented programming isn't entirely new. Its goals (clarity, simplicity, ease of revision, reducing bugs, reducing programming time, coordinating group programming efforts, reusability) are hardly new to programmers or, indeed, new to people who build dams, run schools, or design airplanes.**

The ideas that animate OOP are as old as human work. What is new are some of the techniques and processes that attempt to achieve these ancient goals. And often, what's new is merely a matter of emphasis. For example, programmers have long been cautioned to make their programming *modular,* to subdivide the larger tasks into smaller, more easily tested and maintained tasks. OOP, though, takes this idea further by concealing variables, some procedures, and other source code in the modules (the objects) from other programmers.

DATA COMBINED WITH PROCESSING

Encapsulation is probably the single most valuable OOP concept, as well as the concept most fully realized in VB to date. Unlike traditional procedures, objects combine data with processing. In traditional data processing, the data resided in a separate virtual location from the processing. You might have a Public variable at the very top of your program, and a subroutine near the bottom of your program that processes (acts upon or manipulates) that data. Any other sub or function in your program could also directly manipulate the data in the Public variable. This approach to programming, it was discovered, caused all kinds of bugs. It's particularly dangerous when several people work on the same program, or, when you come back in the future to modify a program you wrote but the details of which you have since forgotten.

Encapsulation refuses to give outsiders — or even *you* later on, or other objects in your own program — access to the Private variables within your object. This tactic, sometimes called *data hiding*, can decrease the number of bugs and increase the modularity of an object. *Modularity* means not only subdivision, but also the reusability of an object. If it's sufficiently modular, you or others should be able to easily plug the object into other client programs, with no unexpected side-effects.

A PRACTICAL EXAMPLE

To illustrate the programming technique of encapsulation, assume that you've written a program that is used in a small store to provide a total bill to each customer. The total bill is your object. Now think about the various tasks and qualities (methods and properties) that would make such an object work.

People come up and either buy food, which doesn't require that you add sales tax, or nonfood items, which does require that you add sales tax. Your object has to maintain a running total of the buyer's purchases — correctly adding or ignoring tax, as each item requires. To put this job into an object, you must first program the class that creates this kind of object. Then, probably in the Form Load event, when your project starts running, you'll *instantiate* your object.

To instantiate this total bill object, follow these steps:

1. Start the VBCCE.

2. Press Ctrl+N to start a new project and select Standard EXE. Use a Standard EXE because with it you can test your object's behaviors directly by pressing F5. As you may recall from earlier chapters, you cannot directly test an ActiveX UserControl project this way.

3. Choose Add Class Module from the Project menu.

4. In the Properties window, change its name from *Class1* to **Rtotal**.

5. You'll want two private variables: one to hold the sales tax and one to hold the running total. The sales tax can change, so you'll want to let the outside program tell your object the current sales tax. And, if a developer fails to tell your object this, your object will post an error message reminding them that the tax is necessary information, before the object can correctly function.

Here's how to define the two private variables that will only be available to your object, not to the outside program:

```
Private m_STax 'the current sales tax
Private rtotal 'the running total
```

6. Next, create a private method (a function) that will accept the price of an item and, based on that, return the sales tax for that item:

```
'Private Method to calculate the sales tax
'In: a dollar & cents amount (Variant)
'Out: the dollar & cents (rounded) of tax
Private Function figuretax(n)
If m_STax = 0 Then
   MsgBox "No sales tax has been defined."
   Exit Function
End If
t = m_STax / 100
figuretax = n * t
End Function
```

7. It's possible that the sales tax might result in a decimal number beyond the two places appropriate for dollars and cents, so type in the following private method, called *RoundOff*, which accepts a number and rounds it to two decimal places:

```
'round to two decimal places
Private Function RoundOff(n)
RoundOff = (Fix(n * 100)) / 100
End Function
```

So far, everything you've programmed into this class has been Private. In other words, most of the contents of your object are encapsulated.

8. What about the public interface that developers can send messages to? You are requiring that a developer using your object provide the sales tax, so create a pair of Property procedures enabling outsiders to provide or query the sales tax property of the object. Note that you include a verification of the tax. Your object doesn't want the tax expressed as a fraction such as .07, so you reject that kind of argument and put up a message box if they try to provide bad data to your sales tax property, as accomplished in the following code:

```
Public Property Get STax()
   STax = m_STax
End Property
```

```
Public Property Let STax(ByVal New_STax)
  If New_STax < 1 Or New_STax > 99 Then
  MsgBox "ERROR: The sales tax should be greater than 1 and
less than 99"
  End If
  m_STax = New_STax
End Property
```

9. Finally, type in the following Public method — the main contact point between your object and the outside world. An outsider sends in a message containing the price of an item and whether or not the item is taxable. Your object returns the running total of the purchases.

```
'the public method that takes in the price
'of an item and the boolean value TXbl which
'if true, causes a tax to be added to the
'running total along with the actual price
'In: the price & if taxable.
'Out: the running total

Public Function doRTotal(price, TXbl As Boolean)
If Not IsNumeric(price) Then
MsgBox "The price you're passing to this object is not numeric"
Exit Function
End If
If price = 0 Then
MsgBox "The price you specified is zero."
Exit Function
End If
If TXbl = False Then
rtotal = rtotal + price
Else
t = figuretax(price)
rtotal = rtotal + price + t
End If
rtotal = RoundOff(rtotal)
doRTotal = rtotal
End Function
```

Notice that this doRTotal method checks the validity of the outsider-provided price in two ways before going any further. Is the data nonnumeric? Is the price zero?

If the data appears sound, the price is then added to the running total, and then rounded off and passed back to the caller outside the object. If necessary, the figuretax method is invoked to return the tax on taxable items.

With all this encapsulation and the associated error checking, data validation, and other precautions, you've poured quite a bit of black plastic over this little running-total object. Outsiders had better observe the rules or they can forget about using this object.

Notice too that the object handles its own needs — rounding, calculating tax. It doesn't go to procedures outside its own box to accomplish those jobs. After being verified, the tax-rate data is kept inside the box along with the methods (the processing) of that data.

To test this object, you'll want to instantiate it and then feed it the prices of various taxable and nontaxable items. Put two CommandButtons, a TextBox, and a Label on Form1, as shown in Figure 9-1.

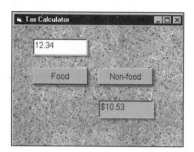

Figure 9-1 Your RunningTotal object can easily handle the needs of these controls.

Then, in Form1's code window, type the following:

```
Dim GetTotal As New rtotal

Private Sub Form_Load()
'specify the current sales tax
GetTotal.STax = 7
End Sub

Private Sub Command1_Click()
Label1 = "$" & GetTotal.doRTotal(Text1, False)
Text1 = ""
Text1.SetFocus
End Sub

Private Sub Command2_Click()
Label1 = "$" & GetTotal.doRTotal(Text1, True)
Text1 = ""
Text1.SetFocus
End Sub
```

When this Form is loaded, you bring your object into existence with the New command. There is an alternative syntax to the Dim. . .New syntax used in the preceding code. The following code will work just as well. Perhaps you'll find that this two-step syntax makes it clearer that you're creating an *object variable of the rtotal class type* and then assigning a new instance of that object to the word *GetTotal* so it can be used in the rest of the programming in this Form to reference the object:

```
Dim GetTotal As rtotal
Set GetTotal As New rtotal
```

In any case, once you've instantiated your new GetTotal object, you can then assign the current sales tax to the GetTotal.Stax property. When the user clicks the Food CommandButton, the GetTotal.doRTotal method (the one Public method in this object) is asked to do its job and provide the correct running total, which is then displayed in the Label. Users of your object don't know about the rounding, the validations, or any of the rest of the activity inside your object; that's all encapsulated. All users need to know is that they must initially provide the current sales tax, and then, thereafter, they can send into your object prices for taxable and nontaxable items. They'll get back a correct running total. The calculations, the computing, and processing of the data is hidden from a developer who's using your object.

To summarize, encapsulation helps you do the following:

* Simplify the debugging process
* Prevent other parts of a program or an outside application from causing unexpected side-effects
* Verify the validity of data passed into an object
* Make it easier to reuse the object because it is a stable, tested, reliable little virtual machine doing a simple job
* Provide a high-level tool to other programmers and developers who don't have to worry about the low-level coding within your object

Inheritance

The second primary quality of OOP is inheritance. You've already seen inheritance in action because *subclassing* is a type of inheritance, and you've subclassed several existing ActiveX controls in previous chapters.

In general, *inheritance* means you can use one class as the basis for creating another class. You usually transform a more general-purpose object into a more specific object, such as subclassing a generic TextBox control into a TextBox that specializes in accepting only social security numbers.

CHILDREN OR DERIVED CLASSES

Subclassed objects are also sometimes called *children* or *derived* classes. A subclass can choose to use the methods, properties, or events of the parent class. (Recall the mapping you did in previous chapters to borrow functionality from existing controls.) A subclass can also choose to ignore any members it wishes to ignore in the parent class; it can also define its own, unique members. (Recall the Percentage property you created for the FFrame object in Chapter 7. It was subclassed out of existing PictureBox and CommandButton controls.)

Visual Basic doesn't implement inheritance in the classic way. When you subclass a TextBox to create a child Social Security SSInput control (the surface), the interface looks and behaves as if true inheritance has taken place. However, the relationship between these two classes isn't a true OOP parent-child relationship. VB's designers blocked this traditional relationship because classic inheritance damages encapsulation.

ENCAPSULATION IS STRONG BECAUSE INHERITANCE ISN'T

VB's encapsulation features are quite strong, partly because the designers didn't implement classic OOP inheritance. In traditional OOP subclassing, when a child inherits the properties of the parent class, any changes later made to the parent can cause problems — unintended side-effects — in the child. It is precisely this kind of unwanted and hard-to-detect interaction between zones of a program that encapsulation is designed to eliminate.

In practical terms, all versions of VB keep the parent partitioned off from the child after subclassing occurs. You can still effectively subclass, however. The only real drawback to VB's approach to inheritance is that more programming code is required than in traditional OOP inheritance. But, so what? It's not that much more code, and VB's Wizards write most of the code for you anyway.

To summarize, inheritance helps you do the following:

✳ Save time by borrowing (mapping) properties and methods that have already been programmed in a parent class. You can stand on the shoulders of the people who spend countless programming hours writing the code that make TextBoxes, PictureBoxes, and other controls do all the things they do.

✳ Decrease the size of .EXE, .DLL, or other files because functionality isn't programmed redundantly.

Polymorphism

The last of the three elemental characteristics of OOP is called polymorphism, as in *polymorphous perverse*, one of Freud's more antic concepts. Literally, *polymorphous* means many forms, like a shape shifter.

But alas, as the word is used in computer programming, polymorphism is a more difficult idea to grasp than encapsulation or inheritance.

Consider Mom saying, "Everyone sit down for dinner, now." The command to *sit* is a single command; yet in practice, the various people do somewhat different things when they hear it. The family members go to their various chairs around the table. In OOP terms, several objects can be given the same command, but each object carries out that command in a way appropriate to it.

It's safe to assume that each family member is derived from the People class and each member has inherited many behaviors from the original class. However, each has modified some of those behaviors as necessary because each person is a *particular* object, a member of the BrotherBilly class or SisterSue class or DaddyJoe class. Each person has different chairs to go to when getting the message to *sit*.

The ultimate benefit of this individualized polymorphic reaction to a single command (method) is that Mom doesn't have to know what class each family member belongs to when making a request. Translated into the idea of polymorphism in the programming world, a developer who uses your objects doesn't have to know each object's particular class to send a polymorphic command (message) to the object. The object has the built-in sense to interpret the message correctly, freeing the developer from worrying about it.

For example, the VB property BackColor is polymorphic. A developer might change the BackColor of a Label and a PictureBox to pink. The Label changes colors immediately, but the PictureBox behaves differently. It first looks at its Picture property. If a graphic is being displayed by the PictureBox, the Box won't turn pink and cover up the graphic. A graphic overrides any BackColor. So the PictureBox interprets a change in BackColor differently than a Label. But the command from a developer, in both cases, is identical. The developer doesn't have to worry about how each object will end up implementing the command.

Likewise, the Cls method is supposed to erase any printed or drawn items on a Form, PictureBox, PropertyPage, or UserControl. You can just go ahead and use this command without worrying about exactly how, at a low level, each object will carry out this job. The Cls method, therefore, is polymorphic too.

Recall that Visual Basic, though, doesn't support formal, official OOP inheritance. And formal polymorphism depends on formal inheritance. So the VB implementation of polymorphism differs somewhat from strict OOP language definition. Nevertheless, the VB version of polymorphism does the job you want done. It enables you to create objects that have commands in common, but the objects carry out those commands in ways appropriate to themselves. The developer need not know the details of how the commands are fulfilled, only that they are.

To summarize, polymorphism helps you do the following:

* Work with objects more efficiently because you don't have to worry about the details of how each different object will interpret a command. Instead, you can just pass the command to the object and trust that your wishes will be carried out (because the creator of the object did the necessary low-level coding and testing to ensure that the job gets done). A developer using objects remains at an abstract, distant level from the minutiae.

* Upgrade or revise existing programming more easily.

* Create more effective interfaces (the members of an object — properties, methods, and events) because polymorphism helps reduce the number of members.

Identifying Classes

Because *objects* are difficult to identify and such a counter-intuitive way to break a job down into constituent parts, you might want to read the next few paragraphs. Here, you go through a brief review of the differences between OOP and traditional programming. If you feel confident that you can spot the objects hidden in a programming task, skip ahead to the "Bonus" section at the end of this chapter.

Divide the Overall Job Into Classes

When you approach a programming job using OOP techniques, you must learn to divide a project into classes, as opposed to dividing it into subtasks (subs or functions), as is done in traditional, procedure-based programming. In procedure-based programming, you subdivide the job into actions to be taken: keep a running total, round off numbers to two decimal places so they'll be dollars and cents, calculate a tax. Then you write the appropriate programming, subroutines, and functions, to accomplish these various behaviors.

When using the OOP technique, you divide the project into classes. Classes are not behaviors. Classes *contain* behaviors (called the *methods* of an object). Methods are sometimes compared to *verbs* while classes are similar to *nouns*. In the sentence *John is a 50-year-old doctor who has gray hair and performs three surgeries per day*, his age and hair color are adjectives (properties); *performs surgery* is the behavior (method); and *John* is the noun, the class.

Locate the Things — the Objects

If you are supposed to design a program that will handle the inventory, payroll, employee records, and tax payments for a small retail store, you must break the task down into nouns, not verbs. Encapsulate the verbs as methods of the classes you create. You must organize the project into classes. To do this, figure out the classes (the nouns) in this job. What are the things that are involved here? Don't look for behaviors or actions, look for *things*. The things in this little retail management job include the following:

* The Inventory Report that's printed each month
* The payroll summary that's sent to various banks for automatic crediting into your employee's accounts
* The database that maintains all the details about the employees (such

as their deductions, phone number, and address) and the latest description of their attitude toward work or whatever other information is kept about each person working here (you can make each employee an object)

* The tax form that's sent quarterly to the state
* The tax form that's sent quarterly to the federal government

These "things" are the objects. If you want this program to be object-oriented, you must subdivide it into these objects. Only after you've identified the objects can you then, for each object, begin to identify the tasks that that object must accomplish, and the qualities of that object you'll want developers or other users of your object to be able to manipulate. In procedure-oriented programming, you create a set of free-floating subs and functions. In object-oriented programming, you put the subs and functions (the methods) *inside* each object as appropriate.

BONUS

Using Ambient Properties and the Extender Object

Some interesting relationships exist between a UserControl and its container (such as a VB Form in a Standard EXE program). For instance, what if you want your UserControl's font to always match the font used by the container it is put into by a developer? And just how do the Left and Top properties of your UserControl get calculated, given that they're relative to the left and top positions of the container? To assist with these and other interactions between an ActiveX object and its container, you can use the Ambient and Extender objects, which are similar to the VB Parent property, but go much further.

When you create an ActiveX UserControl, you can't know precisely what kind of container a developer will place it into. Recall that you can use the Resize event when you want a UserControl to stretch or shrink itself when its container (such as a Form) is resized by the user. However, there are other qualities beside Height and Width that you might want to harmonize between your UserControl and its container. For example, when the BackColor property of a container is changed, the BackColor of a Label should also change.

AmbientChanged Triggers When the Container Changes

Ambient properties to the rescue! To free ActiveX controls from having to know the details of the particular type of container they've been placed into, the container provides a set of Ambient properties. Also, any time an Ambient property is changed in the container, the AmbientChanged event is triggered in the ActiveX UserControl.

The AmbientChanged event contains an argument (named PropertyName) that specifies which property of the container has changed. To see how this works, start a new VB project and make it a UserControl. In the UserControl's AmbientChanged event, type the following code:

```
Private Sub UserControl_AmbientChanged(PropertyName As String)
MsgBox "Changed " & PropertyName
End Sub
```

Select Add Project from the File menu and choose Standard EXE. Close the UserControl's design and code windows so the UserControl appears on the Toolbox. Then put a UserControl onto the Form. Now, in the Properties window, change the Form's BackColor. All of a sudden, the message box appears, even during design time. It can also respond during run time. Try putting the following code into Form1's Load event, and then press F5 to run the program:

```
Private Sub Form_Load()
BackColor = vbBlue
End Sub
```

The message box appears during run time, too. If you want to synchronize the BackColor of the UserControl to any changes made (run time and design time) to the container, make this change to the previous code:

```
Private Sub UserControl_AmbientChanged(PropertyName As String)
MsgBox "Changed " & PropertyName & " to " & Ambient.BackColor
x = Ambient.BackColor
BackColor = x
End Sub
```

You could use the Parent property to query the BackColor, like this:

```
Private Sub UserControl_AmbientChanged(PropertyName As String)
MsgBox "Changed " & PropertyName
x = Parent.BackColor
BackColor = x
End Sub
```

There is an AmbientProperties object that contains a set of read-only properties. You'll find this object referred to frequently in VB's Help feature. However, if you try using the command, AmbientProperties, in programming, VB doesn't recognize that name. Instead, you must use the Ambient command, as illustrated by the following line:

```
x = Ambient.BackColor
```

From here on, this object will be referred to as the Ambient object. You can access the properties of the Ambient object to find out the current status of a particular property of the container. However, the complete absence of programming examples for the Ambient object in VB5's Help feature or Books Online suggest that the property isn't yet fully functional. Perhaps it will be by the time you're reading this. The examples provided in this book have been tested, though, and do work.

Note too that you can never use the Ambient object in the Initialize event, but Ambient does become available by the time the InitProperties and ReadProperties events are triggered. And it is available at design time as well.

When writing an ActiveX UserControl, you can safely ignore the following properties of the Ambient object: MessageReflect, ScaleUnits, ShowGrabHandles, ShowHatching, SupportsMnemonics, and UIDead. They don't apply to an ActiveX component.

The UserMode Property Is Helpful

There are other Ambient object properties you can make use of. UserMode is one of the most useful properties; it tells your ActiveX control whether the control is currently executing at design time or at run time. If False, it is executing during design time. You can test this by adding a single line to the AmbientChanged event in the preceding UserControl example:

```
Private Sub UserControl_AmbientChanged(PropertyName As String)
MsgBox "Changed " & PropertyName & " to " & Ambient.BackColor
x = Ambient.BackColor
BackColor = x

If Ambient.UserMode then
Msgbox "It's run-time now."
Else
Msgbox "It's design-time now."
End If
End Sub
```

Now repeat the experiment you tried earlier. Shut down the UserControl code and design windows. With Form1 showing, try changing its BackColor in the Properties window. Then press F5 to run Form1 and activate its Form_Load event with the BackColor changed to vbBlue at run time. You'll see different messages depending on whether the property is being changed by a developer in the Properties windows while designing the container, or its being changed during run time.

What's the value of this UserMode run-time versus design-time test? As you know from programming Visual Basic, some properties can only be changed during design time, but never at run time, and vice versa. For example, the BorderStyle property of a Form is read-only at run time, but can be changed during design time. UserMode is the way that you can prevent changes being made at the wrong time to properties that you've created for an object.

How to Hide a Property

If you have a property that you want changed only during run time (in programming) rather than during design time (via the Properties window), you can prevent it from being displayed in the Properties window.

First, using the ActiveX Control Interface Wizard, you can select Not Available at Design-Time on the Set Attributes page of the Wizard. The Set Attributes page appears if you've defined a custom property (one you created) rather than merely mapped some properties. The Wizard then creates the following Property Let procedure:

```
Public Property Let Vaar(ByVal New_Vaar As Variant)
   If Ambient.UserMode = False Then Err.Raise 382
   m_Vaar = New_Vaar
   PropertyChanged "Vaar"
End Property
```

The Wizard also thoughtfully checks the Don't Show in Property Browser option on the Procedure Attributes dialog box, as shown in Figure 9-2.

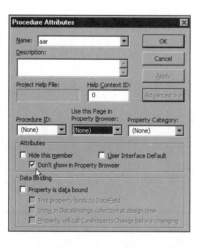

Figure 9-2 When the Don't Show in Property Browser option is selected, a property won't be displayed in the Properties window.

You can change this manually, without using the Wizard, by selecting Procedure Attributes from the Tools menu, and then clicking the Advanced button. (If Procedure Attributes is disabled on the menu, select your UserControl in the design window by clicking the UserControl.)

If this Don't Show. . . option isn't selected, any attempt by the developer to change the property value in the Properties window will display the cryptic and completely inaccurate error message shown in Figure 9-3.

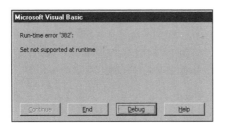

Figure 9-3 This baffling error message should say, "Property can only be changed during program execution, via programming. You cannot change it in the Properties Window."

The Wizard provides error number 382, and that's the wrong error.

Other Useful Ambient Properties

LocaleID and DisplayAsDefault are examples of two other useful ambient properties to enhance your ActiveX controls' functionality.

LocaleID

Ambient.LocaleID identifies the country and language of your ActiveX UserControl container. You're given a long integer variable type. The code for American English is 1033. Try putting this code in a UserControl's Show event to see the code for your language and country:

```
Private Sub UserControl_Show()
MsgBox Ambient.LocaleID
End Sub
```

You can edit the preceding Show event example to display a message box that shows the following Ambient properties:

Ambient.**DisplayName**

Ambient.**BackColor**

Ambient.**ForeColor**

Ambient.**Font**

Ambient.**TextAlign**

Each of these properties enable you to harmonize your UserControl with the prevailing colors or text qualities of its container. Use the InitProperties event of the UserControl, if you wish, to make the adjustment. InitProperties triggers when your UserControl is first placed onto a container by a developer (or dragged onto it by a user).

Or use the AmbientChanged event to permit users or developers to ensure that a UserControl's typeface (font) remains the same as the font used by the container. When the container's font is changed, the AmbientChanged event is triggered. If you've provided a custom property (such as SyncFonts), you could check in the AmbientChanged event to see if the user or developer has set the SyncFonts property to True. If so, you can assume that they want the UserControl font to be kept the same as the container, as shown in the following code:

```
Private Sub UserControl_AmbientChanged(PropertyName As String)
If PropertyName = "Font" Then
If SyncFont Then
UserControl1.Font = Ambient.Font
End If
End If
End Sub
```

Ambient.DisplayName is supposed to provide the Name of your UserControl. Note that it attaches a _1_ to the Name. UserControl1 becomes UserControl11. (See the Caution in Chapter 7 that describes this issue.) The DisplayName can be used in error messages to let a developer know which control — of possibly several in a given container — is generating the error.

DisplayAsDefault

Ambient.DisplayAsDefault can come in handy if you design the appearance of a UserControl yourself. So far, you've subclassed existing controls (such as TextBoxes) when creating a UserControl. In Chapter 16, however, you'll learn how to create a UserControl's appearance by using VB's drawing commands. Such UserControls are called _user-drawn_. If you've created a UserControl that is intended to be used like a CommandButton, you might want to provide the extra-thick border shown in Figure 9-4.

Figure 9-4 A hefty border around a CommandButton indicates that it is the *default* button on the Form.

If a Form contains several CommandButtons, the one with its Default property set to True will have a thick dark border around it. This border lets the user know that pressing the Enter key will trigger that button. Use the DisplayAsDefault property to make your user-drawn button have the appearance of a default button. DisplayAsDefault can be set to True or False. Note that a Font object includes several objects of its own that you can query or manipulate: Ambient.Font.Size, Ambient.Font.Bold, and so on. VB supplies MS Sans Serif 8 as the default Font if the container doesn't support a Font property.

The Extender Object Provides Default Properties

Similar to the Ambient object, the Extender Object is responsible for providing a default set of properties for a UserControl. Put another way, when you create a UserControl, recall that you can *map* properties from the controls you place onto the UserControl. You can also write custom properties from scratch, such as the Percentage property you added to your Frame UserControl in Chapter 7.

But when you place your UserControl onto a container such as a VB Form in a Standard EXE project, you'll see that a set of *extender properties* have been automatically added to the mapped or custom properties you gave to the UserControl. Put a UserControl onto a Form and look at the Properties window. There they are, automatically added to the Properties window for you: Name, DragIcon, DragMode, Height, HelpContextID, Index, Left, TabIndex, TabStop, Tag, ToolTipText, Top, Visible, WhatsThisHelpID, and Width. They're mixed right in there with any mapped or custom properties that you defined for the UserControl.

Let the Developer Decide the Values

For the most part, you should let the developer specify the values for the extender properties. It's the developer's decision what the UserControl's DragIcon should look like, or what ToolTipText is wanted. Certainly the Top and Left positions of the UserControl relative to the container is none of your business. You (the creator of the UserControl) shouldn't presume to define the Top property of the UserControl by writing code that specifies it.

However, there are times when you (the creator) may want to query the container about its properties or status. You can get necessary information from your queries, as shown in the following example:

```
Private Sub UserControl_Click()
On Error Resume Next
MsgBox Extender.Container.ScaleMode
End Sub
```

Not all containers will have the same extender properties. The Microsoft specifications urge that all containers include at least Name, Visible, and Parent properties (and for use with CommandButtons or other kinds of buttons, a Default and Cancel property). Beyond that, it's up to the designer of the container.

Because you can't usually know when designing your UserControl what kind of container it will be placed on, you should make no assumptions about what extender properties will be offered by the container. For this reason, always use On Error Resume Next **if you write code that accesses the extender object. That way, if the property you're trying to contact is in fact missing, at least the program won't shut down.**

It is strongly suggested that if you want to make your UserControl invisible during run time (like a VB Timer), you should set your control's InvisibleAtRuntime property to True rather than use the extender object's Visible property for this purpose.

VB Automatically Provides Methods and Events

Note that the extender object for a VB Form also automatically provides four methods (Drag, Move, SetFocus, and ZOrder) and four Events (DragDrop, DragOver, GotFocus, and LostFocus). Like the extender properties, these methods and events are automatically added to any methods or events that you (the creator) have given to your UserControl. You can access the methods like this:

```
Extender.Move 44, 155
```

And you'll find the four Events available in the UserControl's code window after you've placed the UserControl onto a container, such as a Form in a Standard EXE project.

Summary

In this chapter, you learned to distinguish your old programming habits — dividing a job into smaller, constituent jobs — from object-oriented programming (OOP) — dividing a job into *things*. Then you explored OOP more deeply, finding out the meaning of its three fundamental principles (encapsulation, inheritance, and polymorphism) and how each is implemented in Visual Basic. In the "Bonus" section, you learned how to employ the Ambient and Extender objects to manage the relationship between a UserControl and its container.

Now it's time to turn your attention from UserControls to objects *qua* objects. In Chapter 10 you find out how to create objects that have no visible user interface. These objects are more typical of what some OOP theorists consider objects, properly-so-called.

CHAPTER TEN

WORKING WITH CLASS MODULES

IN THIS CHAPTER YOU LEARN THESE KEY SKILLS

I t's time now to turn away from UserControls — ActiveX components with visual interfaces such as Frames and TextBoxes. In this chapter you learn how to create objects that don't display themselves to users, but nevertheless do important work under the hood. You find out how to create dynamic link libraries (DLLs) — objects that appear when you need such things as an answer to a tax question or specify the days between dates. You learn the uses of the six kinds of instancing — the Instancing property of an object is quite flexible. Then you create a real-world DLL, edit it, compile it, and test it. Finally, you see how collection classes can assist a developer in managing and keeping track of a set of related objects.

Using the VB Class Builder Utility

U ntil now, you've been learning how to create objects with faces — objects that display something a user can see, such as a flashing, colored button or a framed picture. However, most programming goes on behind the scenes, using objects that have no visible user interface.

At this point in the book, you turn your attention from UserControls and start working with objects that don't include controls or any visible surface. As a result, you'll want to switch from the VBCCE, which specializes in UserControls, to a commercial version of Visual Basic.

There are important aspects of OOP and ActiveX programming that are not available in the VBCCE. Many of the concepts and some of the examples in the rest of the book can be tried out using the free VBCCE, but others cannot.

Deciding Which Version to Buy

Which commercial version of Visual Basic should you purchase? Currently you can choose from three versions: Learning, Professional, and Enterprise. The latter two include all the features that are covered in the remainder of this book. Unfortunately, the Learning version, though less expensive, is missing the following features that you get with the Professional and Enterprise versions: the capability of creating ActiveX Controls and of using the ActiveX Control Interface Wizard (though the VBCCE has these features, as you've seen); the capability of creating ActiveX Documents (more about this critter later); several specialized Wizards; and the Setup Wizard's enhanced features (specifically designed to assist in distributing objects over the Internet).

It's VB From Now On

From here to the end of the book, when you see *start VB*, you'll know that the text is referring to the Professional (or Enterprise) Edition of the commercial version of VB 5. To better understand the idea of classes as you use VB, try building a small library of objects that ActiveX-capable applications can access.

You'll use VB's Class Builder Utility to build your library of objects. It's similar to VBCCE's ActiveX Control Interface Wizard in that it helps you by automatically generating programming code based on your specifications concerning the members you want to include in an object — its properties, methods, and events. However, the Class Builder has no *mapping* feature; in this case, you're creating a class from scratch, as opposed to *subclassing* existing controls (as you would do to create a UserControl).

The ActiveX DLL Component

By following the examples in this book, you've built a variety of UserControls (.OCX files). The commercial version of VB can also build UserControls just like those you've been working with in the VBCCE; however, VB calls them ActiveX Controls (simply another name for a UserControl).

VB can therefore produce .OCX files too, and VB, like the VBCCE, includes an ActiveX Control Interface Wizard to help you subclass existing controls and construct unique controls of your own.

The Six Classes in VB

The commercial version of VB can produce several additional object types — kinds of objects that the VBCCE cannot make. Both VB and VBCCE can produce UserControls. But VB can also produce the following additional project types: ActiveX.EXE, ActiveX.DLL, ActiveX.Document DLL, ActiveX.Document EXE, and Add-Ins. You'll explore the various uses for these different flavors of ActiveX components in future chapters. For now, focus on one of these new kinds of objects — the *ActiveX DLL* component.

The Differences Between DLLs and Other Objects

An ActiveX DLL component has several qualities that distinguish it from the other ActiveX project types available in VB. For one thing, an ActiveX DLL component is always *in-process,* which means it always resides within the address space and stack space of a client that's using it. A DLL component therefore loads fast compared to an ActiveX EXE component (which is always out-of-process). The DLL doesn't have the overhead of causing run-time DLL's to be loaded. In addition, messaging is faster. Procedures (methods) in a DLL can run as much as ten times faster than they would were they located in an ActiveX EXE-type project. This is one reason why you should almost always choose DLL as your project type.

TIP   **The term *out-of-process* means that a component is not running in the same address space or sharing a stack with its client application. UserControls and DLL-type components run in-process, simplifying and speeding up the process when the client manipulates properties and methods in the server. See Chapter 13 for more information on in-process and out-of-process options.**

A DLL (dynamic link library) is usually composed of a set of functions but contains no visible user interface. If you find yourself frequently needing to calculate the number of days between two dates and other date/time computations, you can collect several such procedures (the VB language includes them) into a single DLL. These procedures can be either those built into VB or new procedures you write yourself. The point is to collect them in a convenient library where client applications can easily reuse them.

When you create an ActiveX DLL component, keep the following points in mind:

* An ActiveX DLL object cannot be run across a network — the DLL must run in the same computer as the client application that instantiates it.

* An ActiveX DLL object will run only on a 32-bit Windows operating system.

* The End command cannot be used within the DLL's programming.

* The DLL must include at least one ClassModule, and the Instancing property of at least one of its ClassModules must be set to either MultiProcess or GlobalMultiProcess. Read on.

The Instancing Property

Now try building a small library of date/time functions, to see how a DLL is created and then later used by clients. Start VB. If a default project type automatically appears, select New Project from the File menu and choose ActiveX DLL. If the Property window isn't visible, press F4. An ActiveX DLL has only two properties. Change the Name property to **DateCalc**. Leave the Instancing property set to its default: MultiUse. Before you continue, you need to know the meaning of the various kinds of *Instancing* VB makes available to you.

How a Client Interacts with Your Component

The Instancing property defines how client applications interact with your component. Can a client even instantiate (create) an object from this class? And if objects can be instantiated, will they be out-of-process servers or in-process servers? Recall that the terms *client* and *server* are used to illustrate the relationship between an application such as Word (the client) when it's using the services of an ActiveX component (the server).

Setting the Instancing property to SingleUse means that each time a client instantiates your component, a separate component is created. This process is similar to what happens when you put five TextBoxes onto a Form — each TextBox is a *separate, independent* instance of the TextBox class.

This kind of multiple-component creation is often necessary, but it does consume memory. However, you can prevent this memory use by setting the Instancing property to MultiUse. That way, only one instance of the component is created, no matter how many instances the client requests. For example, say that your component calculates the days between dates. Obviously, only one instance of such an object is necessary, and it can service any number of requests. There's no reason for multiple objects of this kind; having several such calculators sitting around would be redundant. Notice that a DLL-type component is not even allowed to use the two SingleUse Instancing settings, so it's impossible for a client to create multiple instances of a DLL.

The Six Settings

Table 10-1 shows you which Instancing property settings can be used with each of the three primary kinds of ActiveX components.

TABLE 10-1 Settings for the Instancing Property

Instancing	ActiveX EXE	ActiveX DLL	ActiveX Control
Private	X	X	X
PublicNotCreatable	X	X	X
MultiUse	X	X	
GlobalMultiUse	X	X	
SingleUse	X		
GlobalSingleUse	X		

Setting the Instancing property to *Private* means that the objects can only be used within the DLL project. No clients can create objects from this class. (Remember that there can be several ClassModules in a given DLL project, but at least one of them must be MultiUse or GlobalMultiUse.) You would use the Private setting when a class provides procedures only for use within the server project itself. The *PublicNotCreatable* setting also prevents clients from creating objects. However, once your DLL project itself has instantiated an object, clients can then access any members that are declared Public. For example, if in your ClassModule set to PublicNotCreatable you have a method that is defined similar to the following:

```
Public Function MyMethod()
End Function
```

clients can use this Method if your project instantiates that ClassModule. The restriction is that the client cannot itself instantiate the ClassModule.

Setting the Instancing property to *SingleUse* means that every time a client instantiates this class, a new, independent object is created (as previously described). *GlobalSingleUse* is the same as SingleUse except that a client can use a simplified syntax when accessing the members of the class.

If an object's Name is WeatherObj and it has a Rainfall property, a client would normally access this property using the following syntax:

```
WeatherObj.Rainfall = 3
```

However, if the class has been defined as GlobalSingleUse, a client need not prepend the class name when reading or writing to a member. Clients can, in this example, leave off the *WeatherObj*. Clients can access it in the following two simplified ways:

```
Rainfall = 3
```

or

```
Inches = Rainfall
```

MultiUse is the default setting for the Instancing property. When a client attempts to create more than one instance of a class, new instances are not produced. Once an object exists, that same, single object can be used by more than a single client. UserControls (such as a TextBox) obviously cannot be set to MultiUse.

If you *can* use MultiUse, though, remember its advantage: You'll conserve memory. A single server object exists but can serve several clients at the same time. However, if your object is doing a complex, time- or processor-intensive job, choose SingleUse so that separate servers will be created for each client. In that situation, SingleUse is, in fact, the more efficient choice.

Creating an ActiveX DLL

Now that you understand the Instancing property options, it's time to build the working ActiveX DLL. You can call on the services of the Class Builder Utility, a Wizard by another name.

Using the Class Builder Utility

Choose Class Builder Utility from the Add-Ins menu. You'll see the Warning dialog box, as shown in Figure 10-1.

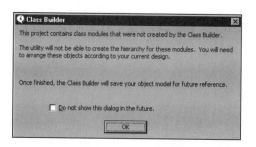

Figure 10-1 This warning tells you that you're responsible for arranging the modules in this project.

That warning can generally be ignored because the *object model* concept that the Class Builder is talking about is primarily of value in helping organize large projects with many classes. It has little value to you in the brief example utilities that you'll create in this book.

The object model hierarchy appears to be a step toward moving VB toward true inheritance where relationships between classes can be made hierarchical. Such a class hierarchy might, at some point in the future, lead to formal OOP inheritance, but right now it doesn't. In true OOP inheritance, a subclassed object inherits the members of the class from which it was derived. By contrast, VB5's *object model* creates code for a relationship that VB defines as *containment*.

Understanding Containment

When you create more than one ClassModule (another name for *class*) in a VB project, you can use the Class Builder to arrange them. Or you can just drag and drop them. For example, drag Class1 and drop it onto Class2 to make it *contained* by Class2. Or drag Class1 onto Project1 to make it equal to Class2 (neither one contains the other). All this is similar to the way you structure menus. You can make some items subordinate to others, if you wish. Or, you can make them equivalent.

Some people feel that creating a hierarchy like this helps them organize their programs, especially large projects. However, note that members, even Public members *within a contained class*, cannot be accessed directly by clients. To get to a method of a contained class, you have to "go through" the container class. This path leads to two unhappy penalties: The syntax can get pretty confusing, and all this abstraction can slow down execution. Moral: Avoid using the containment feature and wait until VB supports true OOP inheritance, unless you feel that your project is so complicated that creating a hierarchy would simplify things for you.

 For a more detailed discussion of the object model concept, see the "Bonus" section at the end of Chapter 13.

So, on with the DLL you're building. Ignore the warning screen shown in Figure 10-1. Click the OK button and you'll see the dialog box shown in Figure 10-2.

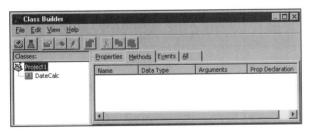

Figure 10-2 Add, delete, or edit classes or classes' members in this dialog box.

You want to provide the clients with two of VB's date calculation functions. Look up the DateAdd and WeekDay functions by pressing F2 and locating them in the VBA library's Date/Time classes. The following is the information you'll find:

＊ `Function DateAdd(Interval As String, Number As Double, Date)`

Returns a Variant containing a date to which a specified time interval has been added

✳ `Function WeekDay(Date)`

Returns a whole number representing the day of the week

Exposing Two Methods

You want your DateCalc object to expose two methods to a client: WeekDayCalc and DatePlusCalc. You also want to provide useful error messages if these methods fail to work when a client accesses them.

Click DateCalc to select it in the Class Builder Utility. Then click the Add New Method to Current Class button (the fourth button from the left on the toolbar, the one that looks like a flying green eraser). The Method Builder window appears, as shown in Figure 10-3.

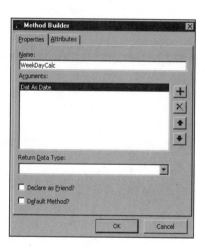

Figure 10-3 Add a new method to your class by filling in this dialog box.

Type in the name **WeekDayCalc**, and then click the + button to add an argument. Type in the name **Dat** and choose Date as the variable type, as shown in Figure 10-4.

Figure 10-4 Define an argument and its variable type here.

Click OK to close the Add Argument dialog box. You don't have to define this function's return argument type. Just leave it set to the default Variant type (that's what the DateAdd function will provide you with). You also want these to be Public, *exposed* methods. You want clients to be able to get at these procedures.

If you declare a method (or property) as the default, the client need not use the method or property's name when accessing it. For example, Text is the default property of a TextBox, so you can optionally invoke it this way:

```
Text1 = "Homestead"
```

Rather than having to specify the property name:

```
Text1.Text = "Homestead"
```

Don't bother to make anything the default (property or method). It seems dangerous to enable clients to take shortcuts (such as leaving off the names of properties or methods) by using this default trick. Likewise, it seems equally dangerous to let clients leave off class names (by using the GlobalSingleUse or GlobalMultiUse settings in the Instancing property of the class, as described in "The Instancing Property" section). Leaving out property, method, or class names makes the programming harder to read and understand, harder for others to figure out, and harder to maintain if the client's code needs editing in the future.

Click OK to close the Method Builder, and you'll see that your WeekDayCalc method has been added to DateCalc.

Follow these steps to add a second method:

1. Click the Add New Method to Current Class button again.

2. Type in **DatePlusCalc** as its name.

3. Using the + button add three arguments: Interval As String, Number As Double, and FirstDate as Date. You can use the same names for your arguments as VB uses in its DateAdd function if you wish.

4. Close the Method Builder.

5. Close the Class Builder Utility.

6. When it asks whether you want to update the project with changes, answer *yes*.

Look now at the source code. The Class Builder created the following code for you:

```
Public Sub DatePlusCalc(Interval As String, Number As Double,
    FirstDate As Date)
```

```
End Sub


Public Sub WeekDayCalc(Dat As Date)
End Sub
```

You could easily have just typed in this source code for these methods your-self. But as you saw in previous chapters, methods are relatively straightforward, simple, classic procedures. A Wizard really shines when you're generating the more complicated code used for objects' *properties*.

You want to return information to the client that calls these methods, so change them from Subs to **Functions**. Then fill in the programming that makes the two methods work:

```
Public Function DatePlusCalc(Interval As String, Number As Double,
    FirstDate As Date)
DatePlusCalc = DateAdd(Interval, Number, FirstDate)
End Function


Public Function WeekDayCalc(Dat As Date)
WeekDayCalc = WeekDay(Dat)
End Function
```

Editing, Compiling, and Testing a DLL

Before compiling or even just testing this DLL, take a look at its properties, and change some of them if you wish. Select Project1 Properties from the Project menu. You'll see the dialog box shown in Figure 10-5.

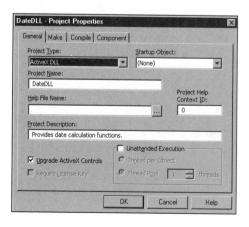

Figure 10-5 Set the properties for your DLL in this dialog box.

The Project Type should be ActiveX DLL. Leave the Startup Object set to None. Most of the time when you write a Standard EXE VB program, by default the first code executed is in the Form_Load event of Form1. However, a DLL has no Form, no visual interface. If a project has no Form, you can alternatively point VB to a Sub Main as the location of the first code it should execute. Sub Main is like *Autoexec.Bat* to DOS, or a macro named *Autoexec* to Word for Windows. However, you don't have a Sub Main in this DLL, so leave the Startup Object set to None.

Change the Project Name to **DateDLL**. This is the first of the two names that, combined, identify your object in the Windows registry. You've already named the one object in this project *DateCalc*, so the official name of the class will now be *DateDLL.DateCalc*. This is the identifier that will show up in the References dialog box, as you'll see shortly.

You can, if you wish, type in a description of what your DLL does. It will be displayed in the help features of client applications, such as object browsers or Properties dialog boxes. Leave the rest of the items in the dialog box set to their defaults and close the dialog box.

Testing a DLL

You can test a DLL more or less the same way you tested UserControls in previous chapters: Start a new project and instantiate your object. This time around, though, it's not quite as simple as taking a UserControl from the Toolbox and dropping it onto a Form. To instantiate an object with no visible interface, you use the As New or CreateObject commands to create the object during run-time.

Try it out now, with the DLL still loaded in the VB design environment. Choose Add Project from the File menu and select Standard.EXE. A new project will appear in the Project Explorer and it will have a default Form1.

You'll want to make the client (the project you just added to the existing DLL project) the startup project — the one that runs first. The client will contact and use the methods of your DLL server to test it. To make the client project the startup project, right-click Project2 in the Project Explorer, and then choose Set As Startup.

Setting the Reference

Before a project can use an object, you must first *reference* the object. Make sure the client project (not the DLL) is selected in the Project Explorer. You won't find your DLL object listed in the References dialog box if the DLL project itself remains the active project.

Select References from the Project menu. You'll see a list of the currently active references, as well as your DLL (DateDLL), as shown in Figure 10-6.

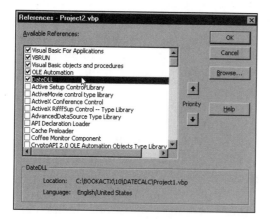

Figure 10-6 Click your DLL to make its object available to your client Standard EXE project.

Double-click Form1 in the Standard EXE test project, and then type the following code into its Form_Load event:

```
Private Sub Form_Load()
Dim i As String, n As Double, m As Date

Dim x As DateCalc
Set x = New DateCalc

i = "q"
n = 2
m = Now
z = x.DatePlusCalc(i, n, m)
MsgBox z
End Sub
```

In this programming you first define the file types of three variables, making sure they match the file types expected by the DatePlusCalc method of the DateCalc object. Then you define the variable *x* as of the DateCalc object type and instantiate a new DateCalc object by using the New command. Next, a value (the letter *q*) is assigned to the variable *i* that is used for Interval argument. The DateAdd command enables the following values for the Interval: *yyyy* for year, *q* for quarter, *m* for month, *y* for day of year, *d* for day, *w* for weekday, *ww* for week, *h* for hour, *n* for minute, and *s* for second.

Then you assign **2** to the number of Intervals and **Now** to the FirstDate argument. In other words, your various arguments translate: Tell me the date that is two quarters from today. Then you call the DatePlusCalc method of the object you've named *x* and display the results in a message box. Press F5 to see the result, or press F8 to step through the process of creating the object and then accessing its method.

Alternatively you can use the CreateObject syntax by changing two lines in the previous programming to the following:

```
Dim x As Object
Set x = CreateObject("Datedll.datecalc")
```

Note that all the usual scoping rules apply when you create an object programmatically. If you want to be able to create this object throughout the entire Form, put the Dim command at the top of the Form's code window, in the General Declarations section. Use the Public command (rather than Dim, which is the equivalent of Private) if you want to be able to instantiate the object from anywhere within the entire project (from any form or module). If the object was declared Public in the General Declarations section of Form1, you can then instantiate it, for example, from within Form4 by prepending Form1's name, as follows:

```
Set Form1.x = New DateCalc
```

Compiling the DLL

It's now time to make the DLL available to clients. To do that, you have to compile it and register it.

To register the DLL so it can be used by Office97 applications or other VB applications, follow these steps:

1. Right-click DateDLL in the Project Explorer and choose DateDLL Properties.

2. Click the Make tab and change the title to **DateDLL**. This is the same name you gave the project when filling in information in the General tab of this Properties dialog. (Why there is a separate Project Name and Application Title is beyond me!)

3. Click OK to close the dialog box.

4. Click `File` → `Make Project1.DLL` .

5. Change its name to **Date.DLL**.

6. Click OK to start the compilation process. Now the .DLL file has been created. It has also been registered in the Windows Registry for use by other clients. If you run the Windows Regedit program and search the Registry, you'll find DateCalc in several locations.

7. Close Visual Basic and start it up again.

8. If you don't have a Standard EXE project by default, click $\boxed{\text{File}} \rightarrow$ $\boxed{\text{New Project}}$ and make it Standard EXE.

9. Select References from the Project menu and look for the name or description of your DLL. If you don't see it, click the Browse button and find the .DLL file on your hard drive.

10. Once the DLL is listed and checked (selected) in the References list, click OK to close the dialog box.

11. Press F2 and switch to the DateDLL library. A list of your class and its methods appears in the Object Browser, as shown in Figure 10-7.

Figure 10-7 Your new DLL and the members of its class are now listed in the Object Browser.

Close the Object Browser, and then type the following into Form1's Load event to test the DLL now that it's on the hard drive and not part of a Project Group within the VB editor:

```
Private Sub Form_Load()
Dim d As Date

Dim x As DateCalc
Set x = New DateCalc

d = Now
MsgBox "Today is day " & x.WeekDayCalc(d) & " of this week."

End Sub
```

This programming is functionally identical to the programming you used previously to test the DLL from a client Standard EXE program while the DLL resided within the same Program Group. The only difference is that now you're trying out the WeekDayCalc method rather than the DatePlusCalc method.

BONUS

How to Use Collections

You may have noticed when you used the Class Builder Utility in this chapter that it featured two buttons on the far left of its Toolbar. The first button is what you'd expect to find: Add New Class . This is, after all, a *Class Builder* utility.

But the second button might seem mysterious. It's identified as an button Add New Collection . What's that doing here in a Class Builder dialog box?

VB has, as a feature of the language, a collection command. A *collection* is an object. It's like an array but has features that can make it easier to work with than classic arrays. You can create a collection during run-time within your programming code, like the following statement found in the General Declarations section of a Form:

```
Dim Teachers As New Collection
```

Then you can use the Item, Add, and Remove methods to manipulate the collection:

```
Private Sub Form_Load()
Teachers.Add "Murphy"
Teachers.Add "Jones"
MsgBox Teachers.Item(1)
End Sub
```

 TIP With this programming, a message box displays the word *Murphy*. Collections begin with item 1 (arrays default to a zeroth item as the first in the list). Therefore, Item(1) displays Murphy in this example.

For certain kinds of data manipulation, a collection is an improvement over the traditional array. With a collection, you don't have to know in advance the number of items in the collection to manipulate them as you would in a For. . .Next loop. You can just use the For. . .Each command and let VB worry about the number of items in the collection.

Collections Are Superior to Arrays

Whenever you're planning to work with a group of simple objects (that would, in traditional programming, be put into an array for easier manipulation), consider building a collection instead.

Assume you are given the job of organizing a university's collection of classic films. The school wants you to computerize the collection so students and faculty can search quickly for combinations of stars, directors, or other criteria. A procedure-oriented approach would focus on writing the search function and other data-management tasks involved in this job. But an object-oriented approach would think in terms of *film objects,* one for each movie. The problem is that each object, as objects do, can include data (properties) and processing techniques (methods) to act on that data.

Because there are going to be many instances of the film object, you'll want a way to manage this set of objects collectively, perhaps to give each a serial number (ID), or to find out the total number of objects (the collection's Count property tells you), and other collective chores. Solution: Put all the film objects into a collection.

Encapsulate a Collection, to Protect Its Data

But you also want to prevent accidental damage to this collection, such as someone adding the wrong kind of data to the collection. A collection, by nature, will accept *any kind of variable,* and yet you want this to be a collection of film objects and only film objects.

To be able to guarantee precisely how this collection will be used, you must encapsulate it — insulating it from the outside world. To do that, you can create a *collection class* that will produce collection objects — with specific ways that a new object can be added to the collection (nothing but film objects allowed).

Like any other class, a collection class acts like a factory that builds new objects (in this case new collections) on demand. However, the purpose of a collection class is to encapsulate a collection (or several).

In the following example, you see how to use the Class Builder Utility to create a collection class. You can imagine how useful this kind of collection class would be in encapsulating data objects. If you can't, investigate this next example.

To create a collection class, follow these steps:

1. Start VB. You should have a Standard EXE project with the default name Project1 and a Form1.

2. Run the Class Builder Utility.

3. Click File → New → Collection.

4. Select the New Class option button, as shown in Figure 10-8.

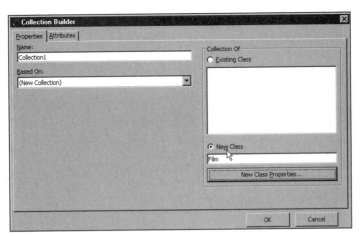

Figure 10-8 Defining this class as a collection causes the Class Builder
to add a *wrapper* to it.

5. Click the New Class Properties button and name it **Film**.

6. Change the name of the collection itself to **Films** (type this name into
   the TextBox just above the Label *Based On* in the Properties tab of the
   Collection Builder dialog box shown in Figure 10-8).

7. Click OK to close the dialog box.

8. Close the Class Builder Utility.

9. When it asks whether you want to update the project with changes,
   answer yes.

Now look at the methods the Class Builder has added to your Films collection class. Your project should now have three modules listed in the Project
Explorer: Form1, Film, and Films. Film is the class for each film object and Films
generates the collection of these film objects. Double-click Films in the Project
Explorer, and you should see the following source code:

```
'local variable to hold collection
Private mCol As Collection

Public Function Add(Key As String, Optional sKey As String) As
   Film
   'create a new object
   Dim objNewMember As Film
   Set objNewMember = New Film


   'set the properties passed into the method
   objNewMember.Key = Key
```

```vb
    If Len(sKey) = 0 Then
      mCol.Add objNewMember
    Else
      mCol.Add objNewMember, sKey
    End If


    'return the object created
    Set Add = objNewMember
    Set objNewMember = Nothing
End Function

Public Property Get Item(vntIndexKey As Variant) As Film
    'used when referencing an element in the collection
    'vntIndexKey contains either the Index or Key to the collection,
    'this is why it is declared as a Variant
    'Syntax: Set foo = x.Item(xyz) or Set foo = x.Item(5)
  Set Item = mCol(vntIndexKey)
End Property


Public Property Get Count() As Long
    'used when retrieving the number of elements in the
    'collection. Syntax: Debug.Print x.Count
    Count = mCol.Count
End Property


Public Sub Remove(vntIndexKey As Variant)
    'used when removing an element from the collection
    'vntIndexKey contains either the Index or Key, which is why
    'it is declared as a Variant
    'Syntax: x.Remove(xyz)


    mCol.Remove vntIndexKey
End Sub


Public Property Get NewEnum() As IUnknown
    'this property allows you to enumerate
    'this collection with the For...Each syntax
    Set NewEnum = mCol.[_NewEnum]
```

```
End Property


Private Sub Class_Initialize()
  'creates the collection when this class is created
  Set mCol = New Collection
End Sub


Private Sub Class_Terminate()
  'destroys collection when this class is terminated
  Set mCol = Nothing
End Sub
```

The only change you should make to the preceding VB-generated code is to change one line in the Add method from

```
objNewMember.Key = Key
```

to

```
objNewMember.FName = Key
```

because you're soon going to create an FName property for Film class. Every time a new Film object is added to the collection, the FName (film name) must be passed to the Add method.

You can see that the Class Builder constructed Add, Remove, Initialize, and Terminate methods for this collection, as well as two properties: Item and Count. Note that these properties are read-only; outside programming cannot change them (there is no Let or Set procedure). These properties are managed by the collection itself.

The Mysterious NewEnum Property

The mysterious NewEnum property is VB's way of enabling outside programming to use the For. . .Each command to go through the collection (it's faster than using the For. . .Next command, plus you don't have to know the total number of items in the collection).

The methods added by the Class Builder are called *wrappers* because they simply enclose already existing functionality, in this case, several features (Add, Remove, and so on) built into a collection object. Now you have a working collection class. The actual Film object itself doesn't yet have any properties, methods, or events, but the collection, *Films,* is functional.

Now add an FName property to the Film class. Start the Class Builder Utility and click Film to select that class. A bug might keep the Toolbar buttons disabled. If so, click the Films class, then click the Film class. That should enable the buttons. Click the Add New Property button and name it **FName**. Click OK and close the Class Builder. The utility will have added the following code to your Film class (in addition to the existing Key property):

```
'local variable(s) to hold property value(s)
Private mvarFName As Variant 'local copy

Public Property Let FName(ByVal vData As Variant)
'used when assigning a value to the property, on the left side of
    an
'assignment. Syntax: X.FName = 5
    mvarFName = vData
End Property


Public Property Set FName(ByVal vData As Object)
'used when assigning an Object to the property, on the left side
    of
'a Set statement. Syntax: Set x.FName = Form1
    Set mvarFName = vData
End Property


Public Property Get FName() As Variant
'used when retrieving value of a property, on the right side of an
'assignment. Syntax: Debug.Print X.FName
    If IsObject(mvarFName) Then
        Set FName = mvarFName
    Else
        FName = mvarFName
    End If
End Property
```

This property accepts a Variant, so, covering all bases, the Class Builder has included both a Let and a Set procedure. Set will be needed if a developer assigns an *object* to this property.

How to Test the Collection Class

Now you're ready to test the collection class. Select Form1 in the Project Explorer and put a CommandButton, TextBox, and ListBox on Form1. Type the following into the General Declarations section of Form1:

```
Public m_F As New Films
```

Then type the following into the CommandButton's Click event:

```
Private Sub Command1_Click()

m_F.Add Text1

List1.Clear

f = m_F.Count

For i = 1 To f
List1.AddItem m_F.Item(i).FName
Next


End Sub
```

This is simple enough. You create a new collection object named m_F, then whenever the CommandButton is clicked, the collection's Add method is triggered and the contents of Text1 are put into a new Film object. Next, the ListBox is cleared and the Count (the total items) in the Films collection is put into the variable f. Finally, the Name property of each of the items in the collection class is placed into the ListBox.

If you prefer to use the For. . .Each structure, replace the following:

```
f = m_F.Count

For i = 1 To f
List1.AddItem m_F.Item(i).FName
Next
```

with this

```
Dim f As New Film

For Each f In m_F
List1.AddItem f.FName
Next
```

Of course, to complete this example you'd want to add more properties to the Film class, such as Director, Stars, Year made, and so on. You'd also want to add methods that would save and load the collection to and from the hard drive.

X-REF You'll find out how to make a collection class save and load its data in Chapter 11.

Why Use Collection Classes?

In the preceding example, you could have just used a straight collection without going to the trouble of creating a collection class. After all, it's something of an abstraction. What's the point?

The VB Books Online Help feature points out that there are three ways you could implement a collection of objects, but there's only one good way (make a collection class). To judge for yourself, consider the other two approaches:

1. Create a collection within an object. In the preceding example, you would just create a simple collection and make it public so clients of the Film object could access the collection. In the Film object's General Declarations section, you would type the following line:

   ```
   Public Films As New Collection
   ```

   Then, to add items to this collection, in the client's General Declarations you would type:

   ```
   Dim Nork As New Film
   ```

   And, to add or retrieve items from the collection, you could type this into the client's Form_Click event:

   ```
   Private Sub Form_Click()

   Nork.Films.Add Text1

   For Each n In Nork.Films
   Print n
   Next n

   End Sub
   ```

   However there's a big drawback to this Public declaration of a collection: It's not encapsulated. That's just as bad as using a Public variable to hold a property, instead of using Property Let, Get, and Set to protect that property from direct outside access. So avoid making collections within objects Public.

2. The second alternative to creating a collection class is to make an object's collection Private, thereby encapsulating that collection within the object. This avoids the problems just described when a collection is made Public. However, if you make it Private, you'll have to create some methods for the Film object that enable clients to Add, Remove, and otherwise manipulate the collection. And you lose the ability to use For Each . . . Next. You can make a private collection within the Film object as follows:

   ```
   Private Films As New Collection
   ```

Moral: Whenever you want to manipulate a group of objects as a collection — and that's often — create a collection class. The Class Builder Utility does most of the work for you anyway.

Summary

n this chapter you turned your attention to objects under the hood — dynamic link libraries that don't display anything to the user but can be used by a developer to provide services to a client application. You found out how to build DLLs, how to set the Instancing property of an object, and how to edit, compile, and test an ActiveX DLL component. In the Bonus section, you saw how collection classes can be used to track a set of objects, collectively. In the next chapter your understanding of OOP is reinforced as the OOP programming principles explored so far, particularly in Chapter 9, are reviewed via example. You create a project employing traditional, familiar procedure-oriented programming techniques. Then you create the same project again, but this time using OOP techniques.

PROCEDURAL VERSUS OBJECT-ORIENTED PROGRAMMING

IN THIS CHAPTER YOU LEARN THESE KEY SKILLS

This chapter is an extended exercise in object-oriented programming. By combining some new OOP concepts with those you've learned in previous chapters, you'll build a moderately large project — a specialized calculator for real estate agents. The calculator will figure monthly mortgage payments, as well as provide the maximum monthly payment a buyer can afford based on income. Because the various kinds of ActiveX components (DLL, Document, EXE, UserControl) are all *objects*, it's important to get a solid feel for OOP and to become comfortable designing a project by focusing on creating classes rather than procedures.

First, you'll build the Real Estate Calculator the traditional procedure-oriented way. Then you'll build the calculator a second time, using the techniques described in Chapter 9 to subdivide the job into separate objects. You'll create collection classes to encapsulate collections of objects in the project. Finally, you'll see how to make the data contained within an object *persistent*: You'll learn a technique that saves a collection to disk and reads it back.

Procedural Programming

On the subject of your programming style, there are two possibilities:

* You feel comfortable using traditional procedure-based programming.
* You learned to program recently and, as a result, were taught OOP from the start.

If you fall into the first category of programmers, this chapter is for you. You'll expand and deepen your feel for OOP by creating a larger example project than those in Chapter 9. First, you'll write the project in the traditional way, and then you'll write it a second time, in OOP style.

If, however, you're at ease with OOP, you might want to skip to the end of this chapter and just take a look at the Bonus section. For most programmers, though, this chapter will likely be illuminating. You'll create the same project in two ways, using procedure-based and then object-oriented techniques.

Breaking Tasks Down

The first thing you do when designing a large application is break it down into its components — the various tasks the application must be able to accomplish. For example, a real estate agency has asked you to create a program that will perform the following jobs:

* Calculate depreciation
* Display comps (property recently sold that's comparable to homes currently on the market)
* Calculate monthly mortgage payments
* Provide a prospect with an affordability estimate that shows how much house they can afford to buy, based on their salary
* Keep track of commissions

For this example, you'll create a program that will perform the final three features: calculate mortgage payments, estimate affordability, and track commissions. This example will serve to illustrate the differences between procedural and object-oriented programming. Adding the other two features merely makes the project larger, not structurally or fundamentally different.

Programming by Task

Now that you've listed the tasks that have to be done, you can start procedural programming. Most Visual Basic programmers begin with the visual, user-interface, and then create the procedures underneath it. This has been a fairly efficient approach: The visual interface serves as a kind of outline of the entire application. It reminds you of what jobs have to be done, what the user puts into the project, and what the project returns back to the user.

Start VB and choose the Standard EXE project. Put a Label and five CommandButtons on a Form, as shown in Figure 11-1.

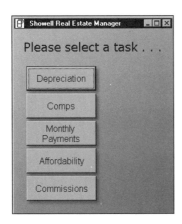

Figure 11-1 The first dialog box for the Real Estate Calculator project.

Form1 is merely a menu. The only programming required is to display a different Form, depending on which CommandButton the user clicks. Type the following into the buttons captioned Monthly Payments, Affordability, and Commissions:

```
Private Sub Command3_Click() 'Monthly Payments
Form2.Show
End Sub
Private Sub Command4_Click() 'Affordability
Form3.Show
End Sub
Private Sub Command5_Click() 'Commissions
Form4.Show
End Sub
```

However, you need a couple of public variables to hold the commissions. You can't put a public array in a Form, so choose Add Module from the Project menu. Then type the following into the Module:

```
Public totalcommis As Integer 'holds total number of commissions
Public commis(1 To 100) 'holds array of commissions
```

Avoid Hard Coding

The variable *totalcommis* holds the current number of items within the array named *commis*. That array holds the actual value of each commission. When recreating this project using OOP techniques later in this chapter, you'll see how to replace this array with a collection class.

One of the advantages of using a collection instead of an array is that you don't need a variable such as *totalcommis* because every collection includes a Count property. What's more, a collection isn't limited to a certain number of items, as is an array. You defined the array in the preceding code snippet as having 100 elements, but a collection can expand indefinitely. This is one of the significant advantages of OOP: You can often avoid the limitations of *hard coding*; for example, you can set an upper limit of 100 on a group of items. OOP is more relativistic than classic programming.

You can see this trend toward relativity in Internet programming. When you describe a fontsize in HTML, you use commands that are not specific. The HTML commands essentially say: big, bigger, biggest, rather than specifying a particular, precise point size.

How do you (the programmer) know, in advance, the size of the user's screen or browser? You don't. So you specify that this piece of text is just *bigger* than that piece, but what "bigger" actually means (in absolute measurements) depends on local conditions in the user's system and the settings the user has chosen for his browser's text-display preferences.

CALCULATING MONTHLY PAYMENTS

To make your program calculate monthly mortgage payments, select Add Form from the Project menu and place five Labels, five TextBoxes, and one CommandButton on Form2, as shown in Figure 11-2.

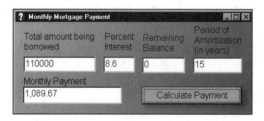

Figure 11-2 This is where the user calculates monthly mortgage payments.

For convenience, you can name each TextBox after the job it does. From left to right, change the names of the TextBoxes to: **Amount**, **Percent**, **Balance**, **Period**, and **Payment**.

Because this programming is procedure-driven, just put the code right into the Click event of each CommandButton. Events are, after all, subs. And that's another name for *procedure*. The following is the programming that calculates monthly payments:

```
Private Sub Command1_Click()
Dim Formt, A, B, P, Per
Formt = "$###,###,##0.00"

B = Balance   ' (What's left when paid, normally 0)
A = Amount

P = Percent
If P < 1 Then
MsgBox "Please change the Percent Interest to a whole amount, such
   as " & P * 100
Percent = P * 100
Exit Sub
End If
P = P / 100

Per = Period * 12 'number of monthly payments

Payment = Format(Pmt(P / 12, Per, -A, 0, 0), Formt)

End Sub
```

This procedure is fairly straightforward. The four variables — *B, A, P,* and *Per* — are filled with the values from the first four TextBoxes. A little error-checking is done to make sure the user has not typed in the percentage as a fraction. Then the VB Pmt command performs the actual calculation.

ESTIMATING AFFORDABILITY

The second procedure you're creating — Affordability — is simpler. You ask the buyer how much they make per month and multiply it by an affordability factor, traditionally .28 or .30 (but if there's a depression, all bets are off). This calculation results in the monthly mortgage the user can, according to most lenders, afford to carry without personal fiscal implosion.

Follow these steps to create a mortgage calculation routine:

1. Choose Add Form from the Project menu and, onto Form3, put two TextBoxes, a Label, and a CommandButton, as shown in Figure 11-3.

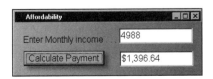

Figure 11-3 This procedure tells the realtor how much monthly mortgage a person can afford.

2. In Form3's code window, in its General Declarations section, type the following:

```
Const factor = 0.28
```

3. Name the two TextBoxes **Amount** and **Payment**. In the Click event of the CommandButton, type the following:

```
Private Sub Command1_Click()
Formt = "$###,###,##0.00"
Payment = Format(Amount * factor, Formt)
End Sub
```

TRACKING COMMISSIONS

The third procedure enables the user to review all existing commissions by seeing the total money earned, or to add a new commission to the list. Choose Add Form from the Project menu. Then, onto Form4, put a TextBox, a CommandButton, two Labels, and a ListBox on the Form, as shown in Figure 11-4.

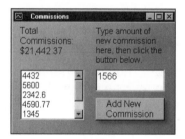

Figure 11-4 The final dialog, where an agent can review commissions earned.

The only job in this Form is triggered — as is so often the case — when the CommandButton is clicked. Type the following into its Click event:

```
Private Sub Command1_Click() 'add to commissions
cr = Chr(13)
Formt = "$###,###,##0.00"
totalcommis = totalcommis + 1 'raise counter
List1.Clear
commis(totalcommis) = Text1
For i = 1 To totalcommis
t = t + CCur(commis(i))
List1.AddItem commis(i)
Next i
Label2 = "Total Commissions:" & cr & Format(t, Formt)
End Sub
```

Notice that you first must raise the public variable *totalcommis* to keep track of how many items are in the *commis* array. Then you add the new item to the array and also add it to the ListBox. Of course, to complete this project you would create facilities for reading and writing data to the hard drive. As it stands, the information on commissions is not persistent. When the project shuts down, the array evaporates. However, this will serve to illustrate the traditional, procedure-oriented approach to project design.

The OOP Version

Now that you've built the project by viewing it as a set of tasks, it's time to break it down into a group of objects instead of tasks. You may recall that you can usually locate objects by finding the nouns within the task list as illustrated by the following list:

* Calculate monthly mortgage *payments* for a *client*.
* Provide a prospect with an affordability *estimate* that shows how much house a *client* can afford to buy, based on their salary.
* Keep track of *commissions* for a *broker*.

Not All Objects Are Created Equal

The five italicized words in the previous list are your five objects: payments, client, estimate, commissions, and broker. But note that often all objects aren't created equal. In this project there are two "higher" objects — Client and Broker — that can contain the "lower" objects. For example, you can enclose the payment and estimate objects within the Client object. You can put the Commissions object within the Broker object.

In fact, why not make payments and estimate methods of a Client class and make commissions a method of a Broker class? This way, you can easily add as many clients and brokers to this project as you want. You won't have to change any of the programming within the Client or Broker classes to add new clients or brokers to this project.

Start the OOP version of this project by following these steps:

1. Click File → New Project

2. Choose Standard EXE.

3. Click Add-Ins → Class Builder Utility

4. Click the Add New Class button on the left.

5. Type **Client** and click OK.

6. Click the Add New Class button again.

7. Type **Broker** and make sure to select the This class is a Top Level Object checkbox. Click OK.

8. Select Broker and add a new method by clicking the fourth button from the left.

9. Name this method **Commissions**. Make its return data type Currency.

10. Click the + button and add an argument named **col_AllCommissions**. Make its data type Object (a collection is an object and you're going to pass a collection as this argument). Click OK.

11. Now add two methods to the Client object. Click Client to select it, and then add a method to it named **Payments**. This method tells you the monthly payments that a mortgage will require. Make the return data type Currency.

12. Add three arguments: **Amount** (make it Currency type); **Interest** (make it Variant); and **Period** (Variant).

13. Add a second method named **Estimate** and make the return data type Currency. This method tells you how much a client can afford to pay for shelter per month, based on his or her salary. Add two arguments: **Factor** (make it a Variant type) and **Salary** (make it Currency).

14. Close the Class Builder and answer yes, you do want to update the project with the Class Builder's source code.

The Code for Methods Is Simple

The source code generated for methods is quite simple. Here's what the Class Builder created for the Broker class:

```
Public Function Commissions(col_AllCommissions As Object) As
    Currency
End Function
```

And here's what it generated for the Client class:

```
Public Function Estimate(Factor As Variant, Salary As Currency) As
    Currency
End Function


Public Function Payments(Amount As Currency, Interest As Variant,
    Period As Variant) As Currency
End Function
```

These are just some empty functions. It's up to you to add the programming that makes these methods work. The following is what to add to the Estimate method:

```
Public Function Estimate(factor As Variant, salary As Currency) As
    Currency
```

```
If factor < 1 Then
MsgBox "You must provide a Factor as a whole number, like 28.
   (Client Object)."
Exit Function
End If


factor = factor / 100
Estimate = salary * factor
Estimate = Estimate / 12 'provide it as a monthly figure
End Function
```

Test it by typing the following into Form1's Load event:

```
Private Sub Form_Load()
Dim ClientObj As Client
Set ClientObj = New Client

Dim factor, salary As Currency

factor = 28
salary = 65000
z = ClientObj.Estimate(factor, salary)
MsgBox z

End Sub
```

Press F5 to run the project and you'll find that it displays the correct answer: 1516.6667.

Flush out the Payments method by typing this:

```
Public Function Payments(amount As Currency, interest As Variant,
   period As Variant) As Currency

If amount = 0 Then
MsgBox "Please specify the total amount of the loan (Client
   object)"
Exit Function
End If


If interest < 1 Then
MsgBox "Please specify the interest on the loan (Client object)"
Exit Function
End If


If period = 0 Then
```

```
MsgBox "Please specify the number of years of the loan(Client
    object)"
Exit Function
End If


interest = interest / 100
period = period * 12


Payments = Pmt(interest / 12, period, -amount, 0, 0)


End Function
```

Then test this method by typing the following into the Form_Load event:

```
Private Sub Form_Load()
Dim ClientObj As Client
Set ClientObj = New Client
Dim amount As Currency, interest, period


amount = 100000
interest = 8.4
period = 15


z = ClientObj.Payments(amount, interest, period)
MsgBox z
End Sub
```

Press F5 to run the project and again it will display the answer you're looking for: 978.8866.

Okay, you've got the Client object working pretty well. It answers questions correctly about the client's ability to pay, and how much the mortgage they're considering will require that they pay.

Now on to the Broker class. It has only one method, Commissions. When you provide this method with the collection containing a list of all the commissions that a particular broker has earned, it gives back a total. The following is the code that calculates the total:

```
Public Function Commissions(col_AllCommissions As Object) As
    Currency


Dim m_obj                'create an object variable
Set m_obj = col_AllCommissions        'make it the right type


Dim t As Currency
```

```
For Each x In m_obj               'add up the total
t = t + x                         'calculate total commissions
Next x


Commissions = t 'return the result


End Function
```

You can test this method by creating a collection and filling it with data:

```
Private Sub Form_Load()
Dim BrokerObj As New Broker

Dim col_comms As New Collection

For i = 1 To 10
col_comms.Add 1200
Next i


z = BrokerObj.Commissions(col_comms)
MsgBox z
End Sub
```

Press F5 to test this and, yes, it tells you that if a broker earns 10 commissions of $1,200, that broker will have earned a total of $12,000.

Now you have two objects: the Client object and the Broker object. The Client object has an Estimate method, which requires two arguments: a Factor argument (the percentage of salary that should be devoted to paying for shelter) and a second argument: the actual Salary. The Estimate method gives back what the client can afford to pay.

The Client object can also answer the question: *How much is the monthly payment on a mortgage?* To answer this question, the Client object requires three arguments: duration, interest, and amount.

The Broker object can tell you the total earned commissions of a particular broker at this real estate agency.

They're Easily Augmented

These objects can easily be expanded to include data. You can add properties to the Client object, such as a phone number, desired location, number of bedrooms, and bathrooms needed, client's salary, and so on.

You can also add various properties to the Broker object including social security number and all the usual personal information required.

X-REF Then, to manage the group of Clients, you can put them into a collection class, as described in the Bonus section in Chapter 10. You'll review creating collection classes at the end of this chapter, too. You should also create a collection of Brokers. And, finally, save these collections to the hard drive to make the objects persistent.

One reason people find OOP superior to the traditional procedure-oriented approach is illustrated in this example: You can create as many clients or brokers as you want, without changing a single line of code within those objects. Replicants, agents, stamped-out cookies, call them what you will — it's nice to be able to bring functioning objects into existence with a simple As New Object command anytime you want.

How to Visualize Objects

You can feed the Client and Broker objects the information they need. They'll react with no side effects. You've encapsulated (cordoned off) their behaviors. You can now predict what will happen when you ask them a particular question such as *What monthly payments can this dude afford?* These objects have no other or hidden relationships to the Client program — the outside. They always do the same thing when you give them a job. They're dependable.

You've created reliable *things*. Once they've been tested, objects have qualities and behaviors that you can trust; they won't sabotage any other parts of your project. You can set them loose (instantiate them) and they will not harm your project. They will merely, like automatons, run around doing their personal job, and they won't bother other elements of your project.

Think of Robots or Agents

Understand objects like this: You are defining little robots when you create a class. After they're instantiated, they take on a life of their own and wander about your project doing jobs (methods) they've been trained to do and having the qualities (properties) you or a developer or a user specified for them.

Thousands of objects can exist comfortably and simultaneously in the same computer. Billions of them can concurrently roam the Internet. They have a kind of *independence* from the rest of your project (the client aspect) and from each other.

Objects Are Self-Contained and Infinitely Reproducible

Remember in 1991 when Visual Basic first appeared? Writing programs for the Windows operating system suddenly became much easier. You could drag a TextBox onto a Form and that TextBox had all kinds of abilities you didn't have to program into it.

OOP is similar — you make robots that are infinitely reproducible. You can generate as many of them as you want. And these robots have self-contained abilities — they know how to do things for you. When you define a class, you are drawing the blueprint that produces a particular kind of robot. And once the blueprint is tested and trustworthy, it can produce countless objects that are equally dependable. Then, whenever your program needs another one of these robots, you just add the following code:

```
Dim ClientObj As New Client
```

And there it is, ready to do your bidding. Do you want a second one? Add this:

```
Dim ClientObj2 As New Client
```

These Client objects are independent robots, no cross-interference, no buggy harmonics. Just address each one by its name and it does its thing without affecting the other, or your project in general.

Completing the Project

To finish mentally integrating the concepts of objects, properties, methods, and collections, you can now flush out the Real Estate Calculator. First, add a Salary property to the Client object, and then create two collection classes to encapsulate the collections of Broker and Client objects.

Start the Class Builder Utility and double-click Client. Add a new property named **pSalary** and make it a Public property and a Currency type. Close the Class Builder, agreeing to update the project.

You should now change the Estimate method of the Client class, as shown in the following code (it no longer needs Salary as an argument because the client's salary is now a property):

```
Public Function Estimate(factor As Variant) As Currency
If factor < 1 Then
MsgBox "You must provide a Factor as a whole number, like 28.
   (Client Object)."
Exit Function
End If


If pSalary = 0 Then
MsgBox "You must provide a Salary, by setting the cSalary property
   of the Client object."
Exit Function
End If


factor = factor / 100
```

```
Estimate = pSalary * factor
Estimate = Estimate / 12 'provide it as a monthly figure
End Function
```

The Class Builder added the following code to handle the pSalary property:

```
Private mvarpSalary As Currency 'local copy
Public Property Let pSalary(ByVal vData As Currency)
  mvarpSalary = vData
End Property


Public Property Get pSalary() As Currency
  pSalary = mvarpSalary
End Property
```

You can test the Client object with this code:

```
Private Sub Form_Load()
Dim ClientObj As New Client

ClientObj.pSalary = 53000

factor = 28
z = ClientObj.Estimate(factor)
MsgBox z

End Sub
```

Make a Collection Class

Now it's time to create our new-style "array" (a collection class), to manage the Client objects.

Follow these steps to create the collection class that will encapsulate the collection of Client objects:

1. Start the Class Builder.

2. Click the second button from the left, Add New Collection. The dialog box in Figure 11-5 appears.

3. Select Client in the Collection Of. . . list.

4. Name the new collection *m_colClients*.

5. Click OK and close the Class Builder.

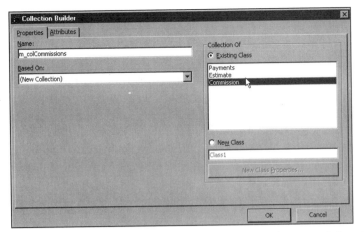

Figure 11-5 You can create a collection class based on an existing class.

 Note that at the time of this writing, the Class Builder has a slight problem with the following line in the source code:

```
Public Function Add(, Optional sKey As String) As Client
```

Therefore, change it to:

```
Public Function Add(Key As String, Optional sKey As String) As
    Client
```

However, you'll want to customize this Add method of the collection class so that missing argument doesn't really matter. Change the Add method to the following:

```
Public Function Add(Salary As Currency) As Client

    'create a new object
    Dim objNewMember As Client
    Set objNewMember = New Client


    'set the properties passed into the method
    With objNewMember
    .pSalary = Salary
    End With

    mCol.Add objNewMember

    'return the object created
    Set Add = objNewMember
```

```
      Set objNewMember = Nothing
End Function
```

Pause a minute to consider what this Add method does. First, it instantiates a Client object. Then, it takes the Salary argument and assigns it to the object's pSalary property. You can permit the client to send arguments that contain every property of the object, but the Client object has only a single property in this example. Or, you can let the client first populate the collection, and then later add properties to each member of the collection. There are even ways to send whole clusters of data to a method (see the Paramarray command in VB).

Next, add the line:

```
mCol.Add objNewMember
```

which does the actual job of adding this new Client object to the mCol collection. mCol is a Private collection contained within the m_ColClients object. mCol is defined in the General Declarations section of the m_ColClients class:

```
Private mCol As Collection
```

Finally, it's customary to use Set Add = objNewMember to return the object to wherever in the client this Add method was invoked. However, you'll make no use of this returned object; it's been stored into the collection, and that's where you want it. Finally, the objNewMember object is destroyed by being set to Nothing. (Your object has already been safely added to the mCol collection remember.)

Test the Stored Objects

Here's how to test that the Client objects are being stored into the collection. Add a ListBox, a CommandButton, and a TextBox to Form1, as shown in Figure 11-6.

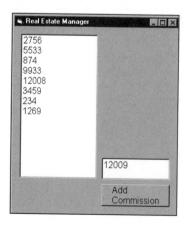

Figure 11-6 Use this form to test the collection of Client objects.

Type the following into the General Declarations section of Form1:

```
Public m_Client As New m_colClients
```

Then, in the CommandButton's Click event, add:

```
Private Sub Command1_Click()

m_Client.Add CCur(Text1)

List1.Clear

f = m_Client.Count

For i = 1 To f
sal = m_Client(i).pSalary
est = m_Client(i).Estimate(28)

List1.AddItem "Client #" & i & ": Salary = $" & sal & "  Can
    afford $" & est

Next

End Sub
```

In this test, you create a Collection object named m_Client (by using the m_colClients class). Then you add the contents of Text1 (the client's annual salary). The ListBox is cleared and you find out how many Client objects currently exist in the collection (the Count). Then you find out the Salary property of each object and use its Estimate method to figure out how much of a monthly mortgage this client can afford. Both of these pieces of data are then displayed in the ListBox, as shown in Figure 11-7.

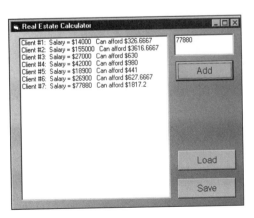

Figure 11-7 Two kinds of data are combined, and then displayed in this ListBox.

BONUS

Making Them Save Themselves

You can give a collection the capability of saving itself to disk. So far, the Client object's data (the Salary property) has not been persistent. As soon as the project is shut down, all the objects evaporate. Try adding a Load method and a Save method; they will be methods of the m_colClients collection class. You'll save the salary as a string variable, with an integer variable at the start that tells you how long the string variable is.

Methods Don't Require a Wizard

Because methods are so elementary (merely subs or functions), you don't need to run the Class Builder if you don't want to. There's no particular reason to fire up that Wizard with something so simple. Here's what to type in for a cSave method that stores a collection on the hard drive:

```
Public Function cSave(Optional fName As Variant) As Variant
Dim intg As Integer, str As String
On Error Resume Next

If IsMissing(fName) Then 'client didn't pass path so provide
  default

 fName = App.Path & "\clients.bin"
End If


Kill fName 'eliminate existing file


fnumber = FreeFile


Open fName For Binary Access Write As #fnumber
If Err Then
 If Err <> 53 Then ' Ignore "file not found" errors
MsgBox Error(Err): Close: Exit Function
 End If
End If


c = mCol.Count 'how many objects?
```

```
For i = 1 To c
 str = mCol(i).pSalary
 intg = Len(str)
 Put #fnumber, , intg
 Put #fnumber, , str
Next i

Close #fnumber
End Function
```

This is mostly straightforward, standard VB file-saving code. The client can optionally pass a path and filename argument, or if they don't, the method generates a path\filename based on the location of the .EXE file of this project (App.Path). You kill (delete) the existing file, if any, and then find out how many objects the collection of Client objects (mCol) currently holds. Then you save each one's data in turn, first saving the length of the string (the salary is the only property here, but in a real project you'd have many more properties). After the length is stored, you then save the actual data as text.

Reading Is Similar to Saving

The file-reading method is quite similar to the file-saving method. The primary difference is that you keep testing for End of File (EOF) as you draw in the data. The number of items of data determine how many objects will be created using Add CCur(str). You may recall that the following collection's Add method accepts a single argument, the Salary of the client:

```
Public Function cLoad(Optional fName As Variant) As Variant
Dim intg As Integer, str As String
On Error Resume Next
fnumber = FreeFile

If IsMissing(fName) Then 'client didn't pass path
 fName = App.Path & "\clients.bin"
End If

Open fName For Binary Access Read As #fnumber

Do While Not EOF(fnumber)
 Get #fnumber, , intg

 If Not EOF(fnumber) Then
  str = String(intg, " ")
  Get #fnumber, , str
  Add CCur(str) 'create an object in the collection
```

```
      End If
Loop

Close #fnumber
End Function
```

To test these new methods, put two new CommandButtons on the Form and label them *Save* and *Load*. In the Load CommandButton's Click event, type the following code to bring in a saved collection from disk:

```
Private Sub Command3_Click()

m_Client.cLoad

f = m_Client.Count

For i = 1 To f
sal = m_Client(i).pSalary
est = m_Client(i).Estimate(28)

List1.AddItem "Client #" & i & ": Salary = $" & sal & "  Can
  afford $" & est

Next

End Sub
```

This code simply invokes the cLoad method of the Collection object. Remember that an instance of the Collection object, m_Client, is instantiated in the General Declarations section of this Form (Public m_Client As New m_colClients). Then, after the cLoad method brings in the data and creates all the new Client objects in the collection, the ListBox is filled with the just-loaded data so you can see it.

Clicking the CommandButton that was labeled *Save* only requires a simple call to the cSave method:

```
Private Sub Command2_Click()
m_Client.cSave
End Sub
```

However, you may want to add more error-trapping within the cSave and cLoad methods. Error-trapping is important whenever contacting the user's disk.

Summary

In this chapter, you created a project the old, traditional, procedure-oriented way, and then built the same project a second time using object-oriented programming techniques. You learned why it is better not to hard-code data and ways to think of objects when you're designing an OOP-style project. Then you further explored the uses of collection classes as a way of encapsulating and managing array-like data within a component. Finally, you experimented with a way to store data to the hard drive and retrieve it the next time the component needs it. In the next chapter, you'll continue to refine your grasp of object-oriented programming by building a useful, fully realized ActiveX component.

POLISHING CONTROLS

This chapter demonstrates how to build and modify a useful timer component, the most sophisticated project you've yet to tackle in this book. Along the way you'll also see how to improve components. You'll learn to send messages from the server to a client (that is otherwise occupied). You'll also discover ways to modify source code generated by a Wizard and a way to test a client that contains a WithEvents command. Finally, you'll see how to make it easy for a developer to *bind* (connect) one of your ActiveX components to a database.

So far in this book you've worked exclusively with methods and properties. And the messages have gone pretty much in one direction: from the client to the server. The client (an application the developer writes) contacts the server (your ActiveX component) and changes one of the server's properties or requests that some task be accomplished by invoking one of the server's methods.

All this makes sense. The server is, after all, the one that's providing services for the client. Therefore, the server quite naturally takes instructions from the client — just as in a restaurant a server takes orders from a client.

Server-to-Client Communications

Although the conversation is nearly always one-sided from the client to the server, there are times when the server needs to send a message to the client. The message from the server will usually be something to the effect of "I'm finished with the job you gave me." This server-to-client messaging can be necessary in two situations: the client requested a time-consuming job (such as downloading a graphics file) and wants to know when the job is finished. Or, the client wants to be told when a certain amount of time has elapsed (the server acts as an alarm clock).

You know how to instantiate a server object, then send messages to it that change its properties or invoke its methods. But how do you send a message back to the client from the server? You might argue that a Function-style method in the server sends something (a return value) back to the client. True enough, but this kind of messaging is still instigated by the client. The client is requesting the services of the server and the server responds. But what if the server itself must generate a message?

In this chapter, you'll construct a Time Manager named TimeMinder that enables a client application to start a Timer countdown (or several of them). Then, when the time has elapsed, the client is notified. When the client starts a countdown, the client can optionally send a text reminder, such as "Time to call Elizabeth." When the client is notified that the countdown has concluded, the text reminder is also passed back from the server.

Servers sometimes need to notify a client that it has finished a job. For example, if a server is downloading a large graphics file from the Internet, the server should have a mechanism that lets the client know when the file transfer is complete. Interval-sensitive jobs, such as building the TimeMinder, fit into another category where servers must contact their clients. Perhaps a server is assigned to check for e-mail every ten minutes; if so, let the client know if any has arrived.

VB and VBA Clients Are Simplest

If the client's language is Visual Basic or Visual Basic for Applications, sending a server-to-client message is easy. You can use the WithEvents command in the client, which adds an event to the client. The event will trigger whenever the server wants to trigger it. (Technically, the event is actually an attribute of the instantiated object, as you will see.)

So if both client and server languages are VB or VBA, you notify a client from a server by raising an event in the server. That event will appear in the client's list of events, along with Form Load and all the usual events.

ActiveX UserControl (.OCX files, when compiled) components are the simplest of all to program when you want to communicate server-to-client because you don't even need to use the WithEvents command. The next section gives you an example.

You Can Put an Event into the Client

Follow these steps to raise an event:

1. Start VB and choose ActiveX Control (UserControl) as the project type. If you've changed VB's options so when it starts running it doesn't display the dialog box showing the various kinds of projects, press Ctrl+N. Then choose ActiveX Control.

2. Put a CommandButton and a Timer control on the UserControl's Form.

3. Type the following into the UserControl's General Declarations section:

```
Event timeup()
```

4. Then type this into the Timer's Timer Event:

```
Private Sub Timer1_Timer()
RaiseEvent timeup
End Sub
```

This RaiseEvent command means that when the Timer has counted down to zero, the *timeup* event will trigger.

5. Finally, in the CommandButton's Click event, type the following:

```
Private Sub Command1_Click()
Timer1.Interval = 20000
End Sub
```

6. Now close both the design and code windows of this UserControl, thereby making its icon appear on the Toolbox.

7. Click File → AddProject and choose Standard EXE.

8. Double-click the UserControl icon in the Toolbox to place an instance of it on Form1. Remember the kink in VB that occurs when you're testing: Make sure that in the Properties window you change the name of the UserControl to **UserControl1** (not *UserControl11* as VB, at the present time, automatically renames it).

9. Double-click Form1 to bring up its code window and look for the UserControl1_timeup event. If it says UserControl11, change it to **UserControl1** too. (This UserControl11 issue is discussed in a Caution in Chapter 7.)

10. Type the following into the UserControl1_timeup event:

```
Private Sub UserControl1_timeup()
MsgBox "TIME'S UP, TURKEY BOY!!"
End Sub
```

11. Now press F5 to run the project and click the CommandButton to trigger the countdown. After 20 seconds you'll see the message appear.

Simple, eh? But if an ActiveX component is working for a client that doesn't use VB or VBA, the job of notifying the client becomes somewhat less simple. If you intend for your ActiveX server to work with all kinds of client languages, you'll have to be a bit indirect.

Generic Server-Client Communication

There are two primary ways you can accomplish server-to-client communication when the client doesn't support the WithEvents command:

* **Polling.** The client regularly checks a property in the ActiveX server. For example, give the server a property named Done that is, by default, set to False. When a lengthy job begins, the Done property is set to False. The client, using a Timer control, regularly queries the server's Done property. Eventually the server is finished and, at that time, sets its Done property to True. The next time the client checks in, it detects that the property has become True. This technique, of course, puts the burden on the client and uses system resources for the continual polling. The server doesn't really, actively notify the client.

* **Callback.** Using this technique, the ActiveX server does actively notify the client when the server's job is finished. You can pass information from an out-of-process server to a client in several indirect ways (when WithEvents isn't available). The easiest way may be to trigger a Change event in one of the controls in the client. You'll soon see how to use this approach when you build the TimeMinder server in this chapter. Triggering a Change event in the client is, admittedly, a bit sly and roundabout, but it's easy enough to program and works well.

 See Chapter 13 for more information on in-process and out-of-process options.

Use a Change Event with the Callback Technique

The callback technique requires the client to have a control that has a Change event. In VB, several controls have a Change event: the various ListBox-type controls, ScrollBars, Labels, PictureBoxes, and TextBoxes. Of these, Labels and ScrollBars use up the fewest resources. You'll use a Label or TextBox in the client to test the TimeMinder server example in this chapter.

Here's how the callback technique works: The client puts a Label onto a Form, and then sets the Label's Visible property to False. The user need not see this control, it's just there to enable one of its events to be triggered by the server. You can trigger a Label's Change event by changing its Caption property: Label1 = "new text". Then, in the Label's Change event, developers can write whatever code they want to react to the fact that the server has notified them that the server's job has finished.

Developers could at this point query the server's properties, activate a method in the server, or just terminate the server, whatever is appropriate. When you use the callback technique, the client is free to ignore the server — no polling is necessary. When the server is ready, it will notify the client.

Pass an Object Reference

Wait a minute. All this sounds good, but it begs the question: *How can the server change a property in the client?* To make this possible, it's necessary for the client to *pass a reference* to the invisible Label or whatever object in the client is being used as the trigger. When you write the server, you'll make this object reference a required argument of one of your server's methods. In the example in this chapter, the client will have to pass this object reference to the method that starts the TimeMinder running.

Here's how it works. The TimeMinder server has a method named StartOne that requires an object, the Label in this example, be passed as an argument:

```
Private ClientObj As Object ' this variable stores the Client's
    object reference

Public Function StartOne(Client As Object)
Set ClientObject = Client
```

Notice the Private ClientObj variable. This variable holds (remembers) the object reference (a Label control) passed by the client. When your server is ready later to report back by changing a property of that Label, the server will use that ClientObj object variable.

The client starts a new countdown by invoking the StartOne method in the server. First, an object variable in the client is created, representing an object in the server (a method named *contact*). This is accomplished in the client's Form1 General Declarations section:

```
Dim WithEvents c As TimeMinder.contact
```

Next, you instantiate the c object within the client's Form_Load event:

```
Private Sub Form_Load()
Set c = New TimeMinder.contact
End Sub
```

Then, when a TimeMinder object has finished its countdown and wants to notify the client, it triggers the Change event in the client with the following code:

```
ClientObj = items
```

items is just a text variable. The ClientObj is a Label, remember, so its default property is its Caption, requiring a text variable. By sending this text (string) variable to the Label, the Label's Change event is triggered. The client can react any way it wants to this trigger:

```
Private Sub Label1_Change()
Print "CONTACT FROM THE BEYOND!"
End Sub
```

The First Decision: What Kind of Component?

Your first job when creating an ActiveX component is to decide which kind to use — there are several flavors with different capabilities: ActiveX DLL? ActiveX Document EXE? ActiveX Document DLL? ActiveX EXE? ActiveX Control? (Hint: Usually you'll want to use the DLL rather than the EXE flavor.)

 You'll find an in-depth discussion of these alternative component types in Chapter 14.

The TimeMinder component you're going to build in this chapter is like a micro-PIM. It can't schedule your week, but it can help schedule your morning.

Leave the User Interface to the Client

Should the component have a user interface — a Form with provisions to accept reminders in a TextBox, a ScrollBar to set the delay, a CommandButton to start the countdown, and so on? Or should it be faceless, merely a set of methods and properties that a client can manipulate? In other words, should you leave the user interface up to the client? It's almost always a better idea to let the client design the user-interface. Most of the time, you'll want to make your servers as generic as possible. You'll want to let the client (the developer) decide how to deal with the user.

When you're creating classes, you usually try to keep them independent of any user interface. Developers might want to use your component within a browser or integrate your component into a larger PIM application. Sometimes developers already have a user-interface in mind, or they want a consistent look to the user interfaces in their applications. For these various reasons, as a rule it's best not to create a user interface for your components. (There are exceptions.)

With the TimeMinder, you'll let the client decide which controls should be used to get or give information. Some clients might prefer to use a Slider control and others might prefer a Horizontal ScrollBar as a way of setting the time delay for the TimeMinder.

Some clients might want to supply some information within the programming rather than letting the user make all the decisions. Maybe the developer wants to hide a property of your component from the user. That's not possible if you've hard-wired the user interface to display a CheckBox with a Label displaying `Please check this box if you want music as an alarm.`

Generally, then, you want to create classes that are not anchored to a particular visual user interface (a particular window with particular controls in particular positions). So, for the TimeMinder example in this chapter, you'll leave the user interface up to the client. Your server will merely provide services behind the scenes.

Choose Between In-Process or Out-of-Process

Now, should this be an in-process (DLL or UserControl) or out-of-process (EXE) component? An EXE ActiveX control can run as an independent utility under Windows, just like a VB Standard EXE project. An EXE-type component can run like any other Windows program — such as Notepad. It doesn't need to be instantiated by a client (though it can be).

Because you're leaving the user interface up to the client, there's no point in making this component capable of running independently. Nothing would happen. It would be running, but without a visible user interface, the .EXE-style component would just use up memory pointlessly.

Make the TimeMinder a .DLL-type server, requiring activation and manipulation by a client. Besides, in-process components (.DLLs) run faster.

TIP When you're writing a server, you can change an ActiveX .DLL-type component into an ActiveX .EXE-type component merely by choosing Properties from the Project menu, and then changing the project type. In the client nothing changes — a developer can still use WithEvents and instantiate the server the same way as if it were an in-process (.DLL) component.

The next step in creating the TimeMinder is to design it. What features should it have? What jobs should it do? After you develop a task list, you can then locate the verbs and nouns in the task list to isolate the objects within.

The TimeMinder utility should act like a group of kitchen timers: The user winds one of them to, say, 20 minutes and when that duration is up, that TimeMinder "rings." The user can set as many of these timers as the user wants. When one "rings," it displays a reminder message and, optionally, plays a .WAV file to make audible music or a sound effect.

List Your Project's Goals

Most likely, you'll want the TimeMinder to memorize as many individual *reminders* as the user requests.

Each reminder is a "package." It is composed of two items of data: the specific time of day when the package "rings" and the message that the client passed and wants back when the package rings. Whether or not an actual sound is heard when a package rings is left up to the client. You'll call this package a *TimeItem*.

The reminder/time packages, the *TimeItems*, are part of a *collection*. The server will contain a *Timer* object that will check the collection every 30 seconds to see if any of the packages are ready to ring.

The client is not allowed direct access to the collection. Instead, an object called the *Contact* is exposed to the client, and it is through this Public interface that the client must go in order to deal with the collection. That's because you decide that your server will manage the collection of reminders itself — checking it periodically to see if any of the reminders are ready to "ring," and removing or adding new reminders as necessary. The client will not have any access to the innards of your server; it must send messages to the Contact object.

It looks like one way to structure this project is to create three classes:

* A class named *TimeItem*. Each object created by this class will contain a single reminder package (a message and a time). This is the innermost object and the client cannot access it.

* A collection class named *m_colTimeItems* to encapsulate the TimeItems. This collection, too, is not made accessible to the client.

* An outermost class named *Contact* that does interact with the client. This class is the only *Public* class in the server. The other two classes are Private. Contact is the object that the client will instantiate; it is also the object with whose methods and properties the client will interact.

You can, of course, structure this server in other ways. However, because the server contains its own Timer control (to repeatedly check the set of TimeItems), it makes sense to remove this job from the client. The client has no reason to have direct access to the collection of TimeItems; the client will not *poll* the server. The server will, instead, notify the client when a TimeItem has elapsed.

Now you can go one level lower (you've now found the objects within the task list). Now you should describe the elements of each of the three objects that you found. Start with the lowest-level object, the TimeItem class.

Each TimeItem object is simple, just a piece of dual-data: Message and Time. It has no methods; it merely holds information. So give this object two properties named *Message* and *TimeUp*.

m_ColTimeItems is a typical collection class. The Class Builder Utility will create it for you, writing the code for all the usual collection wrappers: add, remove, item, count and so on. And, as is usual with collection classes generated by the Class Builder, all you'll have to do to make the collection class workable is modify its Add method. You'll customize it so it adds the TimeItem methods as each new TimeItem is generated.

Have Only One Class Interface with the Client

The outermost class, Contact, is the only complicated class. It interfaces with the client, and also handles the server's Timer control.

Contact should have a Public method named *StartOne* that creates a new TimeItem each time the client invokes that method. It should have a property named Message and another named TimeToRing that the client sets. The Message property is optional, but TimeToRing is not optional. If the client tries to invoke the StartOne method without having provided a TimeToRing, the StartOne method refuses to start a new TimeItem and displays an error message.

Also, the StartOne method starts the Timer control by setting its Interval property to 30,000 (30 seconds). It may be a good idea to let the client specify the precision here: how often the server should check to see if a TimeItem has elapsed. Making this a property of the Contact class is a good idea. Always consider whether it makes sense to provide an option to the client, rather than hardwiring something like this into your server's code. The client might require greater precision of timing than every 30 seconds. Leave it up to the client to determine the trade-off between precision and using up system resources by checking the time too often.

Contact should also have a Private method named *Report* that reports back to the client, announcing that a TimeItem has elapsed and passing back the reminder message associated with the TimeItem.

Finally, the Contact object should contain a Private method named *CheckEm* that goes through the collection of TimeItems to see if any of them are ready to "ring." If one of them has elapsed, the CheckEm method triggers the Report method to make contact with the client and inform the client that one of the TimeItems has finished. Also, if there are no additional TimeItems left in the collection, the CheckEm method should destroy the collection object (make CollectionObject = Nothing) and also shut down the Timer control (sets its Interval Property to 0).

Create the TimeMinder's Classes

Now that you have chosen the constituent members of the TimeMinder server, it's time to fire up the Class Builder Utility.

Follow these steps to create the TimeMinder's classes:

1. Start a new VB project by pressing Ctrl+N.

2. Select ActiveX DLL as the project type.

3. Click `Add-Ins` → `Class Builder Utility`. (If the Class Builder isn't listed, click the Add-In Manager and select Class Builder from the list you'll be shown.) The default Class1 will be visible in the Class Builder.

4. *Slowly* double-click the name Class1 and change it to **TimeItem**.

5. Right-click the name TimeItem and select Properties. Make this class Private so clients won't be able to see, or modify, its properties. Private makes the class available from anywhere within your server project, but hides it from outsiders (clients).

6. Click the Attributes tab and describe TimeItem as: **An object containing Message and TimeUp properties. When the server detects that Now is later than the TimeUp time, the server notifies the client and passes the Message to the client.**

7. Click OK to close the dialog box.

8. Click the third button from the left — the hand that's holding a letter icon — to add a Message property to the TimeItem class. Name the property **Message** and change the variable type to **String**. You can leave it Public if you want. It won't really be Public; because the entire TimeItem class has been set to Private Instancing, none of the members of the TimeItem class will override this class-wide Private setting.

9. Add a second property named **TimeUp** and make it a Date variable type.

10. Click Project1 to select it. If you leave the TimeItem class selected when you add a new class, that class will become a *child class* (a contained class) of TimeItem. That's not what you want, so make sure Project1 is highlighted. Then click the button on the far left of the Toolbar to add a new class.

11. Name this class **Contact** and leave it set to the default MultiUse Instancing, and also leave the default Based On New Class. Click the Attributes and describe Contact this way: **The Contact object is the only Public interface of the TimeMinder server. Define an object variable that points to the TimeMinder server this way: Dim WithEvents ObjectVariable As TimeMinder.contact. Then, in the client's Form_Load event, instantiate this object variable like this: Set ObjectVariable = New TimeMinder.contact. Finally, the client should look in its code window and drop down the list of events. Locate the Private Sub ObjectVariable_TellEm (Msg As String) event. This event will be triggered by the TimeMinder any time a countdown has been completed.**

The client can start as many timer countdowns as desired. When the client wants to start a new timer countdown, merely set the TimeMinder's TimeToRing property by providing a date variable sometime in the future (later than Now): ObjectVariable.TimeToRing = DateVariable. The client can optionally also pass a message associated with this countdown: ObjectVariable.Message = StringVariable. Then the countdown is started by invoking the TimeMinder's StartOne method and passing a reference to the ObjectVariable that the client instantiated in its Form_Load event earlier:

```
Result = ObjectVariable.StartOne(ObjectVariable)
```

12. Click OK to close the Class Module dialog box, and then add a property named **Message** to the Contact class. Make it a String variable type. Leave it Public and click the Attributes tab to describe the property this way, for the client to see: **Set the ObjectVariable.Message = "Time to wash the car" if you want a particular message associated with the next countdown you begin.** The Message property is optional. If you don't set the Message property, the default message `Time's Up` will be passed back to you when the countdown has been completed. Close the Property Builder dialog box.

13. Now add a property named **TimeToRing** to the Contact class. Make it a Date variable type. Leave it Public and click the Attributes tab to describe the property this way, for the client to see: **Set the ObjectVariable.TimeToRing = DateVariable.** Use the Visual Basic Date variable type to provide the end of the countdown. For example, the client has a Horizontal ScrollBar on a Form. Its Max property is set to 59, so the user can slide it to create a duration up to an hour. The client passes this duration to the TimeMinder like this: **ObjectVariable. TimeToRing = Now + TimeSerial(0, HScroll1, 0).** The TimeToRing property is not optional. If you don't set this property, the TimeMinder server will display an error message and will not start a countdown.

That takes care of the two properties of the Contact class. There are several methods you'll add to the Contact class, but methods are merely functions (or subs) so the only advantage of using the Class Builder Utility when creating methods is that you can add a description. A description is important for public members because it assists developers by telling them how to manipulate your ActiveX server. So, add one final member to the Contact class:

14. Add a method (click the flying green eraser icon) and name this method **StartOne**.

15. Click the + button in the Class Builder to add an argument. Name the argument **ClientCont** and make it an Object variable type. The return data type can be left set to the default Variant; the client won't be using the return variable because the server won't pass anything back.

16. Click the Attributes tab and describe StartOne this way for the client: **After you have set the TimeMinder's TimeToRing property, and optionally the Message property, you then start a countdown by invoking the TimeMinder's StartOne method, like this:**

```
Result = ObjectVariable.StartOne(ObjectVariable)
```

The TimeMinder immediately stores your TimeToRing/Message information and begins periodically checking to see if your TimeToRing is up.

Okay, that finishes the Class Builder's work building the Contact class. All that remains is to add the collection class that will encapsulate the TimeItem objects.

Follow these steps to hide the TimeItems within the collection class:

1. Click Project1 in the Classes list to select it, and then click the second button from the left to add a new collection.

2. Name the collection **m_colTimeItems.**

3. Make its instancing Private.

4. In the Collection Of. . .list click TimeItem to make this a collection of TimeItem objects.

5. Click OK.

6. Close the Class Builder and answer *yes* when asked if you want to update the program.

Fix the Project's General Properties

Next, right-click Project in the Project Explorer window and choose Project1.Properties. Under Project Name change it to **TimeMinder**. Change the Startup object to **Sub Main**. Click the Make tab and change the Title to **TimeMinder**. Click OK to close the dialog box.

It's generally considered good programming practice to provide a Module with a Sub Main when you create a DLL server. A traditional Standard EXE VB project has a Form that is the default Startup Object. However, ActiveX DLL servers often don't have any Forms, so you can get into the habit of using a Module as the Startup Object for a DLL-type project. You've already pointed the Startup object to Sub Main, so select Add Module from the Project menu. Type the following code into the Module's code window:

```
Public Col As New m_colTimeItems
Public Cont As New Contact
Sub Main()


End Sub
```

You're not going to need to use Sub Main, but you do want to create an instance of the collection class and the Contact object right off the bat when the server is first fired up by a client. These two object variables will be used as long as the server remains instantiated by the client.

Finally, to complete the major elements of the project, choose Add Form from the Project menu. Then double-click the Timer control in the Toolbox to place one on the Form. Double-click the Timer on the Form to open the code window and add this code:

```
Private Sub Timer1_Timer()
Cont.CheckEm
End Sub
```

All the Timer does is periodically invoke the CheckEm method of the Contact object (Cont). You'll write **CheckEm** shortly as you complete the programming for the TimeMinder.

Massaging the Code

The Class Builder Utility did a fine job, as usual, with the properties and other housekeeping chores involved in creating classes. In particular, the Class Builder dealt with the tiresome details required to provide wrappers for members of a collection class. But you need to do a little more to finish this project.

Fix the Add Method

The TimeItem class can be left as is. The Class Builder did everything necessary there. As usual, though, you have to customize the Add method a bit in the collection class. Double-click m_colTimeItems in the Project Explorer to open its code window. Essentially, you want to remove some items that the Class Builder has coded. Here's what the Class Builder did:

```
If Len(sKey) = 0 Then
    mCol.Add objNewMember
Else
    mCol.Add objNewMember, sKey
End If


    'return the object created
    Set Add = objNewMember
    Set objNewMember = Nothing
```

But you should delete some of the lines so it reads like this:

```
mCol.Add objNewMember

Set objNewMember = Nothing
```

You're not using a key (a unique ID), nor are you passing back the object after it's been added to the collection. So deleting those lines makes the programming more readable.

Also, you're not sending back a TimeItem object, so remove the *As TimeItem* from the Add function, and the Optional sKey argument too. It should look like this:

```
Public Function Add(Message As String, TimeUp As Date)
```

Create an Event

Finally, to complete the project, double-click Contact in the Project Explorer. Here you'll want to adjust several elements of the source code. First, establish the event that will be triggered in the client when a countdown has been completed. Type the following code into the General Declarations section of Form1:

```
Public Event TellEm(Msg As String)
```

Next, fill in the StartOne method of the Contact object, by typing in this code:

```
Public Function StartOne(ClientCont As Object)

If TimeToRing = 0 Then
MsgBox "You must first set the TimeToRing property before starting
   a countdown."
Exit Function
End If

If Message = "" Then Message = "Time's Up"

Set Cont = ClientCont 'store the client's instantiation of the
   Contact object

Form1.Timer1.Interval = 30000 ' check every 30 seconds

Result = Col.Add(Message, TimeToRing)

Message = "": TimeToRing = 0 'reset them

End Function
```

When the client invokes this StartOne method, the client passes its Contact object. This is necessary. Otherwise, when the server makes use of Contact, a different instance of Contact is generated. You don't want two instances of Contact. You want the client and the server both using the same Contact object. Otherwise, when the server tries to check the Col (the collection class) a new instance of the collection will be created. There will be no TimeItem objects in this new collection.

The StartOne method first checks to see if the client has set the TimeToRing property. If not, an error message is displayed and the function is exited. On the other hand, if the client provided no message, then the server provides a default message. *Cont*, the object instantiated in the server's Module, is set to the Contact object started by the client. This ensures that all future references to Cont in the server will be to the client's Contact object.

The Timer Goes Off Every 30 Seconds

Next, the Timer is set to go off every 30 seconds. Each time it goes off, it invokes the CheckEm method of the Contact object. (You'll create CheckEm in a moment.) Then the Message and TimeToRing are passed along as the collection class (Col) is asked to add a new TimeItem object. Following that, the Message and TimeToRing properties are emptied, ready for the client to request another countdown if the client so desires.

Now create the CheckEm method (for the Contact class). The CheckEm method is regularly invoked by the Timer. This method is not for the client's eyes, so use the Friend command to limit it to the server project (that way, CheckEm won't appear in the client's Object Browser):

```
Friend Function CheckEm()

'Go through the collection of TimeItems
'to see if any has a TimeUp property that
'is less than Now.

X = Col.Count

Do
  If Col(X).TimeUp <= Now Then
    'send message to client
    Report (Col(X).Message)
    Col.Remove X 'destroy this TimeItem
  End If

X = X - 1

Loop Until X = 0

' Now check to see if there are any TimeItems left

If Col.Count = 0 Then
  Set Col = Nothing 'destroy the collection object
  Form1.Timer1.Interval = 0 'shut down the timer
  Report ("") 'let the client know that there are no more
```

```
      TimeItems
   End If

   End Function
```

The variable *X* gets the total number of TimeItems. Then, within a Do Loop, each TimeItem is looked at to see if the countdown has elapsed and, if so, the client is notified and that TimeItem object is destroyed.

If all the TimeItems have been destroyed, Col.Count will equal zero after the looping has been completed. In that case, you destroy the collection, stop the Timer control, and send an empty string to the client to let the client know that every task has been completed.

Use the RaiseEvent Command

All you have to do now is add the brief method named Report (for the Contact class) that lets the client know that a TimeItem has elapsed by passing back a Message. Type the following code into the Contact class:

```
   Private Function Report(items As String)
   RaiseEvent TellEm(items)
   End Function
```

This method simply raises (triggers) the TellEm event in the client. The client can do what it wants to when its event is triggered. (Technically, the client has instantiated a TimeMinder.contact object WithEvents. Therefore, the TellEm event — though it resides in the client's code window — is, properly speaking, an event of the Contact object.)

That's it. You have now written a useful timer-reminder engine, an ActiveX DLL that can be invoked by clients for their purposes. Now it's time to test this DLL.

Testing the TimeMinder

You've given the client the freedom to decide how the user interface will look and work. To test the TimeMinder, select Add Project from the File menu. Choose Standard EXE as the project type. Put a TextBox, Label, CommandButton and a Slider control on the Form, as shown in Figure 12-1.

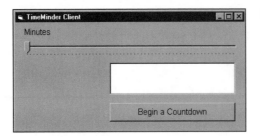

Figure 12-1 This client is going to request several countdowns of the server.

Right-click the ToolBox and choose Components. Then select Microsoft Windows Common Controls to get the Slider control. If you wish, just use a Horizontal ScrollBar instead. Set the Slider's Max property to 59 and make *Minutes* the Caption of the Label. Set the TextBox's MultiLine property to True.

To make the TimeMinder available to the client, select References from the Project menu. Click TimeMinder. It should be near the top of the list, as shown in Figure 12-2.

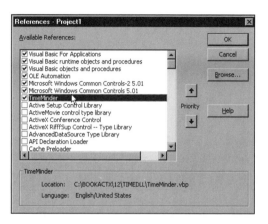

Figure 12-2 The TimeMinder server is ready to be put to the test.

The Client Uses the WithEvents Command

The programming for the client is relatively straightforward. Double-click Form1 to get to its code window. Then, in the General Declarations section of Form1, type the following to create an object variable:

```
Dim WithEvents objContact As TimeMinder.contact
```

In the Form_Load event, instantiate the Contact object:

```
Private Sub Form_Load()
Set objContact = New TimeMinder.contact
End Sub
```

Now locate the TellEm event that will trigger when a TimeItem has completed its countdown. Type in some reaction to this, such as changing the contents of Text1:

```
Private Sub objContact_TellEm(Msg As String)
Text1 = "From the server, this message: " & Msg
End Sub
```

Finally, in the Click event of the CommandButton, type the following code to start a TimeItem countdown:

```
Private Sub Command1_Click()
```

```
objContact.message = Text1
objContact.timetoring = Now + TimeSerial(0, Slider1, 0)

Result = objContact.startone(objContact)

End Sub
```

Now make the client the startup project by right-clicking Project1 (the default name given to this client Standard EXE project) in the Project Explorer. Choose Set as Start Up. Press F5.

How to Add Sound

TIP **The client might want to ring a bell or play some other sound when the TellEm event is triggered. In the General Declarations section of a Module, or Form1, type the following all on a single line (make sure you don't press the Enter key until you've typed the last word *Long*):**

```
Private Declare Function sndPlaySound Lib "winmm.dll" Alias
    "sndPlaySoundA" (ByVal l As String, ByVal u As Long) As Long
```

Then, in the TellEm event, refer to a .WAV file on your hard drive. In the following code, change *reminder.wav* to the name of a .WAV file on your machine:

```
x = sndPlaySound("c:\reminder.wav", 0)
```

Callback: Contacting a Client's Control

Earlier in this chapter you learned of a technique named *callback* that you can use if the WithEvents command isn't available in the client's language. Try it now. Put a second Label control onto the Form and set its Visible property to False. It will be named Label2 by default. In the client's CommandButton Click event, change the call to the StartOne method to the following (passing Label2 as a reference):

```
Result = objContact.startone(objContact, Label2)
```

The Change Event Is Triggered

Then, in Label2's Change Event, type the following:

```
Private Sub Label2_Change()
MsgBox "The Server Says..." & Label2.Caption
End Sub
```

Then open the server's code window for the Contact class and type the following into its General Declarations section:

```
Private ClientObj As Object
Private mvarMessage As String 'local copy
Private mvarTimeToRing As Date 'local copy
Public Event TellEm(Msg As String)
```

Pass an Object Reference

Now, in the server's StartOne Function, right above the line that assigns ClientCont, type this new line to store the passed reference to Label2:

```
set ClientObj = Client
Set Cont = ClientCont 'store the client's instantiation of the
    Contact object
```

Then adjust the Function definition itself, to add a second object as an argument:

```
Public Function StartOne(ClientCont As Object, Client As Object)
```

Finally, add this line in the server's (Contact object) Report Function to trigger the Change event in the client's Label2:

```
Private Function Report(items As String)
ClientObj = items
```

TIP **The ClientObj variable points to Label2 and Label2's default property is its Caption. Therefore you need not mention the Caption property in your code (you don't use ClientObj.Caption = items). Indeed, this approach is preferable because that way you allow the client the flexibility of passing a reference to a TextBox if the client so wishes. In fact, any control whose default property is a string variable can be used.**

Now press F5 and try running the client to see what happens. You should see the MessageBox displayed when the countdown is finished. Of course, the RaiseEvents and WithEvents commands are still in use as well, so you'll see both effects. Before you compile this .DLL to a finished ActiveX server, you should delete one of these two callback techniques.

BONUS

Making Controls Data-Aware

You can make some controls capable of displaying, and changing, information held in a database. Binding an ActiveX component to a database has obvious advantages over alternative ways of importing and editing large amounts of data.

Techniques That Don't Require a Database

You can store relatively small amounts of raw data within a program itself by using the Array command or by typing in the contents of constants or variables. But if there's any significant amount of data, this approach is inefficient; it bulks up the control and is time-consuming to program, though fast at run time.

Similarly, you could provide data in an ordinary file by using the old-fashioned technique of managing data with VB's Open command. However, VB's Data control offers a gateway into more efficient, dedicated database managers such as Microsoft's Jet Engine. VB now offers a complete data-manipulation language, built right into VB itself. So, when you want to offer users or developers a way to access databases, you'll need to provide *data binding* for your ActiveX control.

The VBCCE doesn't have any built-in support for database access, but Visual Basic does. Try creating a simple database viewing tool to see how this works. VB5 includes a sample database named *Biblio* with which you can use to practice.

Follow these steps to bind an ActiveX control to a database:

1. Start VB and choose ActiveX Control as the project type.

2. Put two TextBoxes on the UserControl, and also add a Data control, as shown in Figure 12-3.

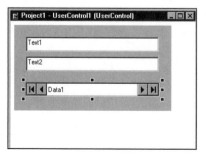

Figure 12-3 These TextBoxes can be bound to the Data control.

TIP There are four properties that must be set to display data from a database in a TextBox:

* DataBaseName (a property of the Data control)
* RecordSource (a property of the Data control)
* DataSource (a property of the TextBox; it's the name of the Data control)
* DataField (a property of the TextBox; provide the name of a field in the database)

3. Click the Data control to select it. Then, in its Properties window, make its DatabaseName property refer to BIBLIO.MDB, the sample database file that you should find in your VB5 directory. You have to provide the path in addition to the .MDB filename (for example, C:\VB5\BIBLIO.MDB), or whatever path points to the file on your system.

4. Then click the RecordSource Property in the Properties window and click the arrow symbol to display the various fields in the database.

5. Select Authors.

6. Click Text1 to select it, and in its Properties window, set its DataSource property to *Data1* (the Data control).

7. Set Text1's DataField property to *Au_ID*.

8. Follow these same steps to bind Text2 (set its DataSource property to Data1), except set its DataField property to *Author*.

9. Close the UserControl design window, click File → Add Project , and choose Standard EXE project.

10. From the ToolBox, put a UserControl onto Form1 of the Standard EXE project and press F5 to run the project.

Try clicking the various buttons on the Data control to move through the database, as shown in Figure 12-4.

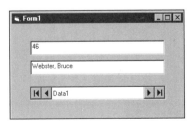

Figure 12-4 VB makes it easy to connect to a database, using the Data control and data-aware controls such as the TextBox.

Hard-Wired Code Limits a Component

This is all well and good, but unless you're providing the actual database along with this UserControl, the whole package won't be of much use to a developer. A developer might want to use your database viewer to see some other database, but you've hard-wired BIBLO.MDB into this UserControl.

To make a UserControl both data-aware and yet flexible for the developer, you can create some properties that developers can bind to a Data control of their own (on their Form, not within your UserControl).

To do this, you'll use a special Procedure Attributes dialog box, as you'll see in the following steps:

1. Press Ctrl+N to start a new project and choose ActiveX Control as the project type.

2. Put two TextBoxes on the UserControl.

3. Double-click the UserControl to get to its code window.

4. Type these two properties into the code window:

```
Public Property Get C() As String
  C = Text1
End Property

Public Property Let C(NewValue As String)
  If CanPropertyChange("C") Then
    ' Set the value.
    Text1 = NewValue
    ' Update the data source.
    PropertyChanged "C"
  End If
End Property

Public Property Get D() As String
  D = Text2
End Property

Public Property Let D(NewValue As String)
  If CanPropertyChange("D") Then
    ' Set the value.
    Text2 = NewValue
    ' Update the data source.
    PropertyChanged "D"
  End If
End Property
```

The CanPropertyChange function isn't currently working in VB. It always answers *yes* at the present time, no matter what. But you're asked to get into the habit of using this function because it will eventually be used by VB.

These property procedures are standard — they resemble most other property definitions. However, now you'll see the trick that binds a property to data.

5. Choose Procedure Attributes from the Tools menu.

6. Click the Advanced button and you'll see the dialog box shown in Figure 12-5.

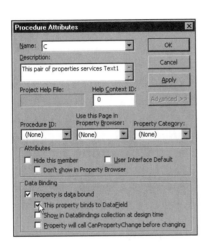

Figure 12-5 This dialog box is where you make properties bindable to a database.

For the property you named C, choose *Property is data bound* and then click *This property binds to DataField*. Only one property (in this example it is the one that services Text1, property C) in a UserControl can be bound to the DataField. All this means is that when a developer looks at the Properties window for your UserControl, the developer will find a DataField property. The developer can make this DataField point to a particular field in the database, such as AuthorAge or AuthorAddress.

Remember that a UserControl has only one Properties window — a developer won't find an individual Properties window for each control you've placed onto your UserControl. The UserControl is all one piece — it's just one object (with other objects *contained* inside it). Therefore, the developer can't set individual DataFields for each of the two contained TextBoxes. You can, though, let the DataField property of the entire UserControl point to *one* of the TextBoxes, which is precisely what you did when you selected: This property binds to DataField.

Well, what about property D, the one that services Text2? How are you going to let the developer specify a DataField for this TextBox and, indeed, for any additional data-bound controls you might want to put onto this UserControl?

There's a special device that you can make available to developers during their design-time; it's called the DataBindings collection. It will appear in the UserControl's Properties window during design time when the developer is working with your UserControl.

7. Click the Name list in the Procedure Attributes dialog box and change it to *D*.

8. Select *Property is data bound*, and then click *Show in DataBindings collection at design time*.

9. Click OK to close the dialog box.

10. Close the UserControl design window to place the UserControl on the Toolbox.

You might think, why even bother to attach only one of the data-aware controls to the DataField by selecting *This property binds to DataField*? Why not just select *Show in DataBindings collection at design time* for all the controls you want data-bound? The answer is that one of the controls *must* be bound to the DataField. If you don't do that, there will be no DataSource or DataField properties for the UserControl (when the UserControl is placed onto a client) in its Properties window.

11. Click `File` → `AddProject` and choose Standard EXE.

12. Place a UserControl on the Standard EXE's Form and also place a Data control on that Form.

13. Click Data1 (on Form1) to select it, and then display its Properties window.

14. Double-click DatabaseName in the Properties window and choose *BIBLIO.MDB* in your VB5 directory.

15. Click the RecordSource property and choose Authors.

Now follow these steps to bind your UserControl to the "developer's" Data control:

1. Click the UserControl on Form1 to select it.

2. Set the DataSource property to Data1 and set the DataField property to Au_ID. (This is the only DataField property that the UserControl has. You may recall that you pointed this property to Text1 when you clicked *This property binds to DataField* in the Procedure Attributes dialog box. You did this for the UserControl's property C, the one that services Text1.)

3. Now you must use the DataBindings (it's a collection) property of the UserControl to specify a database field to be displayed in Text2 (and any additional data-bound controls you add to the UserControl). Click DataBindings in the UserControl's Properties window.

4. Select property D in the Name list and bind it to the Author data field, as shown in Figure 12-6. Click OK to close the dialog box.

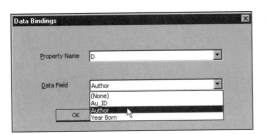

Figure 12-6 Choose the data field to display Text2 in this dialog box.

5. Press F5 to run the Standard EXE project, and you'll see that both TextBoxes have been bound to the Data control and are displaying their respective fields, as shown in Figure 12-7.

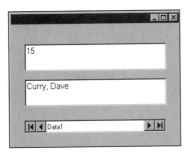

Figure 12-7 The TextBoxes are on a UserControl but are bound to the developer's Data control.

Of course, a 2,800-page book could be written about Visual Basic database management techniques. However, you now know the fundamental techniques to use if you want to provide ActiveX components with data-bound features.

Summary

n this chapter, you created the most complex component you've yet attempted in this book. In the process, you saw how to reverse the normal flow of messages and send information from a server to a client — even if the client is doing something else at the time. An object has three kinds of members — properties, methods, and events. But properties and methods are by far the most common. In this chapter, you found out how to trigger an event in a client when the server is doing something time-consuming and you don't want to burden the client with continually polling the server. You were reminded of the necessity to modify the collection class source code generated by the Class Builder Utility. And you tested the WithEvents command in a client. Finally, you learned how to make it easy for a developer to connect one of your ActiveX components to a database.

So far, the book has been focusing mainly on servers. In the next chapter, you'll consider issues from the client's point of view.

SPECIALIZED ACTIVEX

This final section extends your understanding of ActiveX technology in two ways. You'll take a second, deeper look at several important topics introduced in earlier chapters, such as polymorphism and encapsulation. Second, you'll learn several additional advanced ActiveX techniques. For instance, you'll learn how to create and test the new Document-style components as well as how to build User-drawn controls (you design their appearance as well as their behaviors). You'll also find out how to optimize compilation, and which setup and security options suit your project best. Finally, you'll experiment with several sophisticated OOP and ActiveX features, including tapping into the vast collection of functions in the Windows operating system, and discovering ways to apply containment techniques to your components.

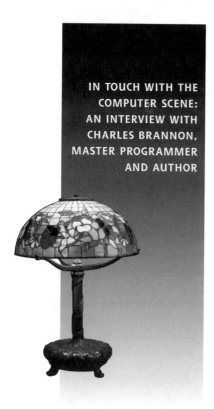

IN TOUCH WITH THE
COMPUTER SCENE:
AN INTERVIEW WITH
CHARLES BRANNON,
MASTER PROGRAMMER
AND AUTHOR

For several years, Charles Brannon was Program Editor for Compute Publications, where he developed numerous ground-breaking programs, including SpeedScript, the best-selling word processor for home computers. He has written hundreds of articles on computer-related topics, in addition to three books. He is currently a computer consultant, network administrator, and freelance author. The following is an excerpt from an interview with Brannon in which he shares some of his ideas about trends in the industry he knows so well.

RM: Do you think that Internet security issues can ever be truly solved?

CB: It's really a moot point. The expansion of Microsoft's role on the Internet makes it obvious what the future of Web browsing holds: a world united by Microsoft products, with the Internet being the critical "tie that binds."

RM: Are there issues relating to intranets in particular? That is, are there things to do for an intranet site that you don't have to do when setting up an Internet site? More maintenance? Heavier local traffic? More naïve users?

CB: Of course managers are concerned when it comes to putting together an intranet that itself is tied into the Internet. Security issues are well-enough understood that this should be no obstacle for anyone. Clearly there is much more maintenance if the job is handled in-house, but the most effective intranets are managed by third-party companies.

RM: What's the easiest way to design a Web site?

CB: There's no question that Microsoft FrontPage 97 is the best overall solution that is also the easiest to use.

RM: How long do you think it will be before the Internet bandwidth becomes sufficient to display movies in real time?

CB: If you were to suck up all the bandwidth and distribute it to fewer users, it wouldn't be a problem. Instead, we need to expand capacity in a reasonable time frame.

RM: What's the speed of the best Internet connection available today and what's its name?

CB: The best modem connection is probably K56Flex, but USR's X2 is rapidly gaining customer support. Both offer between 33.6K and 56K. The best alternative is ISDN. It offers either 64K or 128K, and is pure digital. Key ISP's provide affordable ISDN access, but what's really killing the market is the telco tariffs. ISDN service must be made as inexpensive as two "no frills" telephone accounts. Competition will drive the price down, and demand will go up. ISDN is not a long-term solution, but it has a lot of industry support.

FROM THE CLIENT SIDE

S o far you've been looking at things, for the most part, from the server's point of view. That's only natural; this is a book about ActiveX components, and they are, in general, intended to be used as servers.

However, there are several issues that you should consider from the client's point of view. First, why use servers at all? Why not just code the features of a server into the main application?

And how will the server be instantiated: using early-binding or late-binding? How will the client use your server? How does a developer integrate a server component into an application? How much documentation should you provide to a developer, and how should you provide it?

Finally, how much encapsulation should you employ? Put another way, how much access to your server component should you provide to a developer? This chapter endeavors to answer these questions.

The Server Advantage

First things first: Why even use servers? For many years applications were self-contained. They didn't rely on run-time support from dynamic link libraries (DLLs) or other kinds of servers. Servers come into the computer's memory while the client application is running, at the request of a client. Servers *dynamically* link to a client; they are not embedded within the client's executable file.

If we got along without OLE/ActiveX components for so long, why are they becoming so popular now? There are several efficiencies gained by using components. And there are compelling reasons to use components because everyone benefits: the creator of servers, developers who employ the servers in their own applications, and end users.

Disk and Memory Efficiency

For example, spell checking is a useful feature of an e-mail program. E-mail benefits as much from spell checking as does a word processor. Nevertheless, a user shouldn't have to take up space in memory or on the hard drive with two duplicate spelling checkers, or maintain duplicate custom dictionaries. And, a user shouldn't have to remember two different interfaces, customization schemes, and other redundancies caused by duplicate spell checking utilities.

Computer memory shouldn't be wasted by hosting two checkers, if both the e-mail and word processors are simultaneously running. Nor should memory be wasted by loading in all an application's features when the user never seems to use some of those features.

Ease of Upgrading

Perhaps most important of all, using ActiveX components makes it much easier to fix bugs and upgrade applications using *service packs*, as they're called. A developer doesn't have to replace an entire application, just a component or two (a DLL, for example).

You've seen how to encapsulate features within classes, and then selectively expose some members (some properties and methods) to the project in which the class resides. The members you expose are, collectively, called the *interface* of your class. Recall from Chapter 12 that you created a TimeItem class that you exposed to the TimeMinder utility. The TimeItem class is internal to the TimeMinder, not designed to be directly accessed by outside clients. Before the idea of dynamic components became popular, the features of an application were self-contained.

But say that you decide to improve a class and add new features, or perhaps after selling hundreds of copies of your application, you get back hundreds of letters pointing out a serious bug. In the past you'd have had to provide a new copy of the entire application to all your customers. Or, at least, you'd have had to send out special patch .EXE utilities that, when run, directly replaced sections of the application's binary code.

Then OOP came into the picture. But using classes, in itself, doesn't guarantee efficient upgrading. If all the classes in a project are internal, and if you're not using any components, to fix a bug you still have to replace all copies of the project with the fixed version.

An ActiveX server neatly solves this problem. An ActiveX component is a class or group of classes that is compiled into an .EXE, .DLL, or .OCX (UserControl) file. One or more of the class or classes within the server is Public. Client applications use the features of the server, but the client knows nothing about the actual source code within the server, nor does the client care. And, above all, if you, the creator of the server, need to make changes to the source code, you only have to change it in one place: within the server. Then you can provide the improved server to all your customers, not the entire application. What's more, many servers are quite compact. For example, when you create a compiled DLL of the TimeMinder server you created in Chapter 12, it is only 25,600 bytes large. That makes it easy to deploy the DLL on the Internet. Users would hardly notice or mind downloading a file that small. Graphics are often ten times larger. (Of course, this assumes that the user already has the support files needed by a DLL, but those support files are a one-time-only hit. See Chapter 15 for more on this issue.)

Many Are Confused

Many people have become confused about ActiveX and think that programming an OLE (now called ActiveX) component is devilishly difficult. In fact, before VB5 (with its programmer-friendly Basic language), the job was indeed tough. But VB5 offers its helpful Wizards and its many exceptional programming features — all the toolbars, toolboxes, debugging facilities, new object-oriented commands, and other efficiencies. So there's no reason not to learn OOP and not to create ActiveX components.

Another source of confusion is the notion that ActiveX is only useful when you're programming for the Internet. The truth is that you can use ActiveX technology for any kind of programming. You may recall that several of the components and classes you've experimented with in this book can just as easily be deployed into a Word macro as into a Web site. The TimeMinder could be used by a spreadsheet program or by any other program where the user might want to be reminded to do something. Servers are for clients, but many clients are not on the Internet. Indeed, Internet programming is, at this stage anyway, still only a minor aspect of ActiveX programming.

Worlds Within Worlds

Perhaps *server* isn't the best possible term to use — memorable and colorful though it is. In a sense, any time you write a class, you're creating a server (or, to be precise, you're designing a blueprint that can instantiate server objects).

Each class can generate objects that can be used by a client, even if the "client" is only another Module or Form within the same project. But it's common practice to reserve the word *server* for those entities — those files on the hard drive that result when you compile a class or a group of classes into an .EXE, .OCX, or .DLL file. However you want to use the term, remember that (at least abstractly) every class produces objects that are, in a real sense, servers to some client.

ActiveX Presupposes OOP

Similarly, you shouldn't think of ActiveX and OOP as separate ideas. The one presupposes the other. And don't think of ActiveX as only a way of creating server components. ActiveX, in its broadest definition, is the way to create *classes*, whether those classes are deployed onto a hard drive, a network, or sent over the Internet into the world. Remember that classes can exist within a project and never be deployed outside at all. They can just be used privately. At the most fundamental level, ActiveX simply means sharing objects.

Even the distinction between servers and clients can blur. Word can be a client to your TimeMinder component, but you can use objects within Word as servers to one of your components. This is why some people prefer to use the phrase *ActiveX components* rather than *ActiveX servers* or *ActiveX clients*.

If you have Word 97 on your system, try this. Start a new VB project. Make it a Standard EXE project for simplicity. (You could easily use a .DLL, .OCX, or an ActiveX .EXE-style project — in other words, an ActiveX component. If you want to try this example using a component, just add a Form to the component.)

As we all know, a component can be a server, but you'll make it a client in the following example.

To make a component a client, follow these steps:

1. Click Project → Add Form .

2. Put a TextBox and a CommandButton on the Form, as shown in Figure 13-1.

Figure 13-1   Word's spelling checker says there's an error in this TextBox.

3. Type the following into the CommandButton's Click event:

```
Private Sub Command1_Click()

Dim objWord As Object
Set objWord = CreateObject("Word.application")

n = objWord.CheckSpelling(Text1)

MsgBox n

Set objWord = Nothing

End Sub
```

4. Press F5 to try running this client/server pair.

5. Type something spelled wrong into the TextBox, and Word's spell checker will reply False.

6. Correct the spelling, and the server (Word) will then reply True.

This example uses the CreateObject command (causing late-binding). However, you can avoid that and early-bind if you prefer. Just make a reference to Word's object library. Make a reference to Word by selecting References in the Project menu and selecting Microsoft Word 8.0 Object Library, as shown in Figure 13-2.

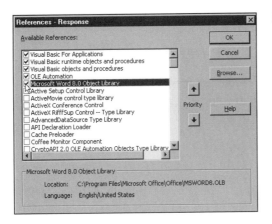

Figure 13-2 If you create a reference to Word, you can use early-binding.

Then replace the second line of code with this:

```
Set objWord = New Word.application
```

Aside from executing more rapidly, early-binding allows you to press F2 and use the Object Browser to see lists of all Word's objects, constants, methods, and properties.

That brings up the question, What is *binding,* and why is it early or late?

Early- Versus Late-Binding

You'll hear the terms *early-binding* and *late-binding*. These terms describe how a server is connected to a client when the server is first instantiated in the client.

When a client declares a new object, by naming it directly, that object is said to be early-bound (as opposed to using the generic command: *As Object*). In the previous example, after you create a reference to Word's object library, you can then use a line of programming like this to cause early-binding:

```
Set objWord = New Word.application
```

When run, you'll see the description `Client of Word`, as shown in Figure 13-3.

Figure 13-3   Look on the Windows taskbar to see a project described as a Client of Word.

In this next example, your project includes a class named *Client* so you can directly instantiate it by name (you don't have to set a reference):

```
Dim ClientObj As Client
Set ClientObj = New Client
```

How to Identify Late-Binding

What happens when a class you want to use isn't contained within your project or referenced by using the Reference option on the Project menu? Say that it's an ActiveX component that's registered in your Windows Registry, but you don't want to be bothered using the References option on the Project menu. In cases when a client uses the *As Object* and *CreateObject* commands, an object is said to be late-bound:

```
Dim New_Object As Object
Set New_Object = CreateObject("excel.application")
```

Late-binding occurs because, when a project is compiled (during *compile time*, as this process is called), VB cannot yet determine the members of the object to which your object variable points. References to members (such as New_Object.Text) must be checked later, during run time, when the object is finally bound to your component.

If your client can refer to objects using the early-bound technique, the server will perform more efficiently. The reason for this is that when VB compiles a project (when you select Make Project in the File menu) containing a late-bound object reference, VB cannot check to see if there are any incorrect members.

For example, it's safe to assume that Excel has no Rftpdq property, as shown in the code that follows:

```
Public ObjExcel As Object
Set ObjExcel = CreateObject("Excel.Application")
ObjExcell.Rftpdq = "Fury"
```

When VB compiles this code, no error will be generated. VB doesn't check and doesn't know that Excel doesn't have this Rftpdq property. VB does not check the object library of a late-bound object reference. This means that VB must add code in the compiled project's .EXE file that will have to check *during run time* for the validity of each reference to any members of the object. Clearly this retards the speed of execution. An early-bound reference, by contrast, simply and directly codes the pointer to the object's member, eliminating the necessity of having to check the validity of that reference during run time.

Early-Bound Objects Are Already Referenced

With early-binding, you define an object variable and make that variable point to a particular object that's already referenced in the current project. When this happens, VB can employ early-binding for all uses of that object variable everywhere it appears throughout your source code, whether to change or read properties, or to invoke methods.

TIP   **Late-binding is always employed when you declare an object variable As Control or As Form.**

If you have a class module in a project, any objects defined by classes within that module can obviously be early-bound because you can directly reference them by name. If an object's class exists on the system (it's registered in the Windows Registry), you can also implement early-binding for that class's objects by selecting that class in the References option on the Project menu.

But late-binding requires that during run time the actual details about this object's interface (its members, meaning its properties, methods, and events) be resolved — slowing things down. The advantage of early-binding is that, during run time, accessing the object's methods and properties is somewhat faster.

The main advantage of late-binding is that you don't have to set a reference to the object (in VB's References dialog box). If you ever try to test a project and get the "User-defined type not defined" error message, it means that you've not set a reference to the object you're trying to instantiate by using early-binding. (Or you've referenced the object by using the wrong syntax — you mistyped the name, for instance.)

Error-Checking Won't Work

Another price you pay for late-binding is that VB's usual error-checking won't work if the client uses the wrong syntax to call a member of the object, or passes the wrong data type to the object. The burden of performing this kind of error-trapping falls entirely on the server object. This is one good reason why you should include error-trapping in your object's members. How can you tell whether a developer will instantiate your ActiveX component using late- or early-binding? A few client languages don't even offer early-binding as an option. And, as mentioned, late-binding slows things up a bit at run time. If you're writing a client's code, you'll likely usually use early-binding. There are some arcane, advanced programming tricks you can try with late-binding, but just stick with early-binding whenever possible.

SIDE TRIP

Every Rule Has Its Exception

You should always use late-binding when making calls to the Internet Explorer scripting object model, or you'll face compatibility difficulties. IE's *scripting object model* allows you to contact and modify the qualities or behaviors of Microsoft's Internet Explorer browser. You insert VBScript (or JScript) into an HTML document that can contact the browser itself as if it were an object. This way you can change properties of the HTML page, such as its backcolor. One of the exposed members of an HTML page within the Internet Explorer scripting object model is *Document*. Therefore, if you want to display a message directly in the HTML page, you can do it within VBScript the following way:

```
<SCRIPT LANGUAGE="VBScript">
document.write("This isn't HTML. It comes from VBScript.")
</SCRIPT>
```

When using Internet Explorer 4.0's scripting model, you enjoy rather complete *programmatic* control over a Web page. You can use VBScript to manipulate most aspects of an HTML page: the tags, images, text, and other objects. For example, there are dozens of methods (Add, Blur, Clear, Focus, Navigate, Select, StartPainting, and many more).

WEB PATH For more information on the Internet Explorer scripting object model, see the following address on the Internet:

```
http://www.microsoft.com/Workshop/prog/inetsdk/docs/inet0474.htm
```

TIP The term *object model* refers to the hierarchy of a group of objects that work together. For example, the *object model* of the TimeMinder project you built in Chapter 12 can be described as a *root object* (the primary object, named Contact) with a subordinate collection object (m_colTimeItems) that contains a subordinate collection of TimeItem objects. A root object in a sense "contains" all the other objects in the object model. You'll find out much more about root objects at the end of this chapter in the Bonus section. Also, see the discussion of various kinds of containment in the Bonus section at the end of Chapter 16.

Both early-binding and in-process execution help speed up a component. A component running in-process (as do .DLL and UserControl .OCX-type components) with its client usually runs more efficiently. Every time the client accesses the members of the server, the client doesn't have to take extra steps to cross over into other processes and slow things down.

Consider the Client

A developer wants to use your component. You've created some useful tax-preparation functions and gathered them together into a DLL. Or you've written a fancy UserControl that displays a message and then dissolves the message like a TV wipe. Whatever you've done, it's good, and they want to use it. But how do they use it with their application?

Three Ways to Provide Documentation

It's your responsibility to provide developers with documentation. There are three primary ways to do this:

* You can build a Help file.
* You can provide information that they can read in an Object Browser (assuming their development environment — the editor they write source code in — features a browser).
* You can provide a README.TXT file they can look at (or provide the same documentation on paper).

Describing how to accomplish the first option, creating a standalone .HLP file, is beyond the scope of this book. But consider the second option, the Object Browser: It can provide substantial information for a developer. It lists all Public members in your component. If you've been conscientious, the Object Browser will also display a description of the syntax and purpose of each of these exposed members.

Two Ways to Document with the Object Browser

There are two ways to create descriptions that show up in the Object Browser. You can write them when using the Class Builder Utility. Or you can write them in the Object Browser itself.

If you're running the Class Builder, each time you add a new member, you'll see the dialog box shown in Figure 13-4.

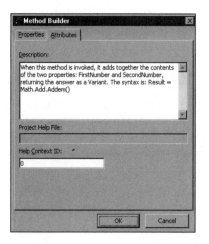

Figure 13-4 Under the Method Builder dialog box's Attribute tab, you should describe the purpose and syntax for a member.

If you're not in the Class Builder, you can press F2 to bring up the Object Browser. Then, in the list of Libraries, select your project. Right-click any class that you want to document, as shown in Figure 13-5.

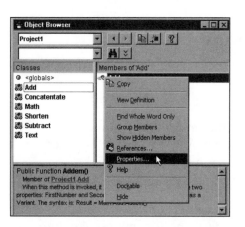

Figure 13-5 Right-click any class, and you can document it in its Properties dialog box.

When you choose Properties, the Procedure Attributes dialog box appears, as shown in Figure 13-6.

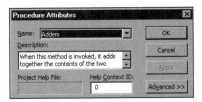

Figure 13-6 The Procedure Attributes dialog box is where you can type in a description in the Object Browser.

Encapsulation Revisited

Another decision you must make when considering the developer's use of your component is How much functionality should you expose? Put another way, which classes should you make Public, and within each Public class, which of its members should you make Public? (If you make the entire class Private, a client cannot access any of its members, whether or not you make those members Public.) Encapsulation is so significant a concept that it's worth a brief review, followed by some new thoughts about organizing a large set of classes and creating an object model.

What to Show, What to Hide

The essence of encapsulation is the question of what to show and what to hide. You may recall that encapsulation is considered the primary strength of OOP and that VB has implemented a particularly strong kind of encapsulation. By avoiding some of the elements of traditional OPP inheritance, VB allows you to firmly cordon off code. You'll have no worry at all that your encapsulated code will cause unintended side effects in the rest of the project (or in a client project). Nor need you worry that the rest of the project or a client will cause side effects within your encapsulated code.

This is the black-box idea. Remember the example in Chapter 9 of a radio's innards encapsulated by pouring hot plastic over them, sealing the variable capacitors off from prying hands? A developer might have no taste at all and consequently select a hideously unreadable and vulgar combination of text color and backcolor. There's nothing much you can do about bad taste. But at least if you've encapsulated the color properties, you've ensured that a ghastly color combination won't occur accidentally during run time because a global variable was inadvertently changed.

The Interface of a Class

When you encapsulate, you provide well-defended pathways through which a developer must go to get to properties or methods in your objects. These defended pathways are the members — properties (created with Property Let, Property Get, or Property Set procedures) and the methods (created with

Functions or Subs) — that collectively make up your class's *interface*. Taken together, the members of a class are called its interface. (If your class raises any events in the client, those events are also part of the class's interface.)

Within these procedures, you can provide error checking, display error messages, and take any other precautions you want before permitting a property to be changed or a method to be invoked. You can even refuse to make a change or invoke a method. Just use the Exit command and deny the developer the use of the rest of the code in your procedure until you get the right kind of variable, or if you're particular, a backcolor that you think is appropriate.

 TIP In general, it's considered preferable programming practice for a server to raise errors for the client, but not to display error messages to the user.

Data-Hiding

Technically, encapsulation is called *data-hiding*, which means that the data (such as the value of the current BackColor property) within an object is never directly made available to a client. The data in an object is manipulated only within that object. Clients never know how the data is stored (all the variables within a class are Private) nor do they know how the data is manipulated. All a client needs to know is which members of the class have been made available (or *exposed* as it's sometimes called), which parameters they require, and what information they return, if any.

Two Levels of Encapsulation

There are two levels of encapsulation: class-level and member-level. You can hide an entire class by setting its Instancing property in the Properties window to Private. When you do this, *none* of its members (its properties, methods, or events) will be available to an outside application (a client). It doesn't matter if the members are declared Public or not. They will not be listed in the developer's Object Browser, nor will the developer be able to make any use of them during run time. The members are firmly encapsulated.

CLASSES ARE EXPOSED BY DEFAULT

The default setting, however, for a class's Instancing property is MultiUse. By default, a class is exposed for use by outside applications.

Going down to the lower level, each property or method in a class can be exposed or hidden by using the Public, Private, or Friend declaration commands. You may recall that Public makes a member available to the entire project, and also to any outside client application (if the Instancing of the class in which the member resides isn't, itself, Private):

```
Public Property Get Bcolor ()
```

PRIVATE CAUSES MODULE-ONLY ACCESS

TIP The Private declaration makes a member available only to other code within its module. (Remember that there are three kinds of modules in VB: Forms, Plain Modules, and Class Modules. Plain Modules have no user interface like a Form. Plain Modules can be used to hold Subs or Functions and variable declarations that you want made available to the entire project. Class Modules hold class definitions.)

A method in the same class can access a Private property:

```
Private Property Get Bcolor()
```

Then, in a method in the same class, the following would work:

```
X = Bcolor
```

However, code found elsewhere in the project, in other modules or forms (not to mention outside client applications) cannot access a procedure that is declared Private.

THE FRIEND COMMAND IS A COMPROMISE

Between the two extremes of Public and Private is the new Friend declaration command. The Friend command makes a member available to all modules within its own project, but not available to outside client applications.

13

BONUS

Object Models and Roots

Remember the TimeMinder utility that you built in Chapter 12? A primary lesson you should take away from the experience of constructing that component is that the three classes that make up the component are on different "levels."

To provide a sense of the subtle ways in which classes can relate to each other hierarchically, an analogy between a project and the human brain might be of some use.

A Root Object Can Resemble Consciousness

In the TimeMinder, at the outermost level, is the Contact class. It interacts with the client and coordinates several behaviors of the other two classes. Clearly there's something special about the Contact class. It's a bit like the upper levels of the brain where consciousness resides. The Contact class interprets and routes messages coming in from the outside world (the client) and, to an extent, governs the behaviors of the lower parts of the project's "brain" — the more automatic, less complicated parts.

On the second level (with some limited, less varied behaviors) is the *m_colTimeItems* class, which is the collection class. This class, in turn, manages the simplest class of all, the TimeItem class. Each TimeItem is a single, simple little package of information: a time to notify the client wrapped together with an optional message to give to the client. In fact, as you become more experienced with OOP, you'll find that many of your projects break down into objects of these three kinds: the Contact-style public interface class, the collection class, and the things-collected class.

The Typical OOP Project Structure

A more complicated project might have a dozen collection/things-collected class pairs, but would still only have a single Contact-style class. In any event, most projects will evidence this kind of hierarchy. In fact, it's typical to find an OOP structure such as the one shown in Figure 13-7. As you can see in this figure, there are three collection/things-collected class pairs, but still only a single Contact class.

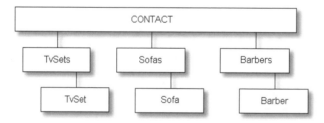

Figure 13-7   Like many object models, this one has several collections/things-collected class pairs, but only a single public class that manages them all.

Top-Level, Primary, and Root

What we've been calling the Contact-style class is, in formal OOP terminology, confusingly called several names: the *top-level class*, the *primary class*, or the *root class*. Seems that no one can decide whether this class should be visualized as residing at the top of the component or the bottom. Previously, I introduced the Contact class as "at the outermost level," which means more or less the same thing as top *or* bottom.

The class that interacts with the outside (and often has management responsibilities within the component as well) *is* furthest away from the *center* of the component — whether you want to think of this as top-level or root. To remain consistent with the terminology that Microsoft seems to prefer, the book will refer to this special class as the *root* class of a component.

The Meaning of Object Model

And, while we're defining terms, the hierarchical relationship between the objects in a project or component is called that project's *object model*. So, the book will use the term *object model* from now on as well. The diagram in Figure 13-7 is an object model. It shows all the classes, and their relationships to each other.

The root class of an object model typically *embraces* or, in a sense, *encloses* all the other classes in the model. And the root class is often the only creatable class in the model. (*Creatable* means that a client uses the CreateObject or New commands to instantiate an object. It means the class is exposed.) Recall that you made the Contact class Public in the TimeMinder object model, but made the other two classes, m_colTimeItems and TimeItem, Private. No client can instantiate those two classes.

One approach to hierarchical structures is to use the Class Builder Utility to make some classes explicitly subordinate to other classes. You did not take that approach in the TimeMinder. However, if you do take that approach, a client would usually be forced to use a compound form of address to manipulate properties or invoke methods:

```
TimeMinderObj.m_colObj(2).Message = "Wake up."
```

 X-REF You'll find out more about this kind of *containment* in the Bonus section of Chapter 16.

The TimeMinder component was built without this kind of subordination. Each time you add an extra layer of distance between the client and the job the client wants to do, you create unnecessary trouble. A long string of subordinated objects is hard for the client to handle. Clients make typos, they forget the relationships, and reverse the object references. It's much better for the client if they can type:

```
ContactObj.Message =
```

rather than:

```
ContactObj.InnerObj.TinyObj.Message =
```

It seems to me that this process somewhat shifts the burden of organization from you (the creator of the component) to the developer who has to use the component. Sure, it's easier for *you* to keep things straight while writing your project if you enclose classes within classes within classes in this way. But, as the TimeMinder illustrates, it's possible to create a hierarchical relationship, have a single root class, and keep things straight without rampant literal hierarchies that require complex syntax when a developer tries to use your component. Also, once you start nesting objects, you retard the execution speed of your component.

The root object's role can also be compared to a diplomat. It accepts messages from the outside, translates, modifies, and/or error checks them, and then passes them on into the interior of the object model for action by other, lessor classes. Often when an interior class is finished changing a property or carrying out a method, the interior class passes back some information or, at least, a message saying: *Okay, I did the job you asked.* The root object can then pass that response on to the outside client.

Worlds Within Worlds, Redux

Now you should see how the relationship between a root object and the object model as a whole (the entire project) is similar to the relationship between a single object's Public members and the interior, Private members of that object. It's worlds within worlds when you employ object-oriented-programming. After a little practice, though, you'll begin to think along these lines when designing your projects. It will all come to seem, if not entirely natural, at least logical.

TIP **What name should you give your root class? Many programmers have used the term *Application* for their root's name. For programs such as Word (which does have an Application object, but has many additional Public objects as well), the term *Application* seems appropriate.**

However, if you're writing a DLL or some other kind of component, it might be better to pick a name that best describes the service your component offers the client. Or just use *Contact* to remind yourself that this is the only Public interface in the component.

Summary

In this chapter you learned why component programming is the wave of the future, and how easy it now is to create components using Visual Basic. You found out that components are useful for most computer activities, not just for the Internet. Then you saw how components could easily become clients because (like the sometimes blurry distinction between properties and methods) the differences between client and server are not written in stone. You explored the difference between early- and late-binding and considered various ways to provide documentation to a developer who uses your component. Finally, you went deeper into the important issue of encapsulation and learned of ways to organize a project by using an object model.

DOCUMENT COMPONENTS

This chapter introduces a new kind of component, the *document*. Similar to a Word .DOC file, a document-style ActiveX component is designed to be contained within an Internet browser or any other container that is ActiveX-document capable. You'll practice building a document and then learn how it works within the Internet Explorer browser. You'll see how to use the Document Migration Wizard to transform existing Visual Basic Forms into UserDocuments (the UserDocument is to a Document-style ActiveX component what the UserControl is to an ActiveX Control-style component). Then you'll explore the techniques you can use to switch from one document to another. You'll also learn which to choose from among the various compilation options you see when you select Compile from VB's File menu.

How Documents Work

When you select New Project (Ctrl+N) in VB, you'll see a selection of various kinds of projects, like those shown in Figure 14-1.

Figure 14-1 VB features seven different kinds of projects.

So far you've experimented with ActiveX EXE and ActiveX DLL projects. This chapter introduces a specialized kind of project, the *Document*. You'll create an example of an ActiveX Document EXE and ActiveX Document DLL. This way you'll see the differences in how these two component-types behave, in how they are programmed, and in how they are deployed as servers. The two Document-style components offer exciting possibilities for use on the Internet or intranets.

You may recall that when you first decide to create an ActiveX component, your first question is Should I make this a DLL or EXE project? DLL's run faster because they share the address and stack space of their client (in-process servers). EXEs can be useful for two reasons: They can run as standalone programs (they don't require a client), and because they run out-of-process, it's easier to use them for applications that share resources (like a continually updating news-server). An EXE-style server won't freeze up its client if the server is working on a time-consuming task such as a batch file save. However, a Document-style EXE project cannot run as a standalone, it needs a container such as the Internet Explorer browser.

You'll Nearly Always Choose DLL

In practice you're likely to choose to build a DLL-style server most every time you create an ActiveX component — the speed advantage alone can be significant. What's more, if you're merely interested in creating a component that can run independently as a standalone application, just go ahead and create the old standby: a Standard EXE project.

An ActiveX Document is a disk file that contains an OLE link (or several). Once fired up, an ActiveX Document can manipulate data within its own file, or access other files.

An ActiveX Document works within an ActiveX Document container (the client) that is capable of hosting an ActiveX Document. This technology used to be called *Object Linking and Embedding* (OLE) in the past, and was seen as a move toward *docucentric* computing.

All of Microsoft's applications, such as Word and Excel, along with languages such as VB, are capable of acting as ActiveX Document containers. Many other software houses have also made their applications capable of hosting ActiveX Documents.

The fundamental difference, then, between an ordinary ActiveX DLL server and an ActiveX Document DLL is that the Document is a specialized kind of ActiveX component, designed to be activated within an Internet browser or another container application such as Word.

A Document Is Designed to Be Contained

Think of a classic document, a Word .DOC file. It has data (text) and some information about how it should look (italic, or whatever). When you load it into Word, the .DOC takes on a particular appearance — Word, the container, displays it. So you're dealing with two entities: the data file (.DOC) and the application that displays it (WORD.EXE). Similarly, when you create an ActiveX Document component, two files are deposited on the hard drive: a Visual Basic Document file (.VBD) and an associated .EXE or .DLL file.

An ActiveX Document is not an independent entity. Like all other ActiveX components except the ActiveX EXE, the ActiveX Document requires a client. With ActiveX Documents, the client is a *container* like the Internet Explorer browser. When an ActiveX Document is attached to a container, the process is called *siting*. Once the ActiveX Document has been sited, properties of the container (the Parent property, for example) then become available.

When you ask VB to create a Document component, VB displays a *UserDocument*. Try it now: Press Ctrl+N to start a new VB project and then choose ActiveX DLL Document. You'll see the new UserDocument in the Project Explorer, as shown in Figure 14-2.

Figure 14-2 A UserDocument is the basis for a Document component.

Special Qualities of User Documents

As you can see, a UserDocument is similar to the familiar VB Form. However, a UserDocument is in several ways dependent on its container. For example, the container determines when and how a UserDocument is displayed. Therefore, a

UserDocument has no Show, Hide, Load, or Unload methods of its own. You cannot write programming like this: UserDocument1.Hide.

Testing a UserDocument

And because of this intimate relationship between a Document-style server and its container, the easiest way to test a Document server is within Internet Explorer.

To see how to test a UserDocument, follow these steps:

1. Put two TextBoxes on the UserDocument.

2. In the Properties window, change both their MultiLine Properties to True.

3. Double-click TextBox1 to get to its code window and type the following into its Change event:

   ```
   Text2 = Text1
   ```

4. Now press F5 to run the UserDocument.

5. Start Internet Explorer running, or if it's already running, switch to it. (It's not necessary to actually connect to the Internet.)

6. Click [File] → [Open]

7. Type in the path to your VB directory. By default, the current UserDocument file is located in VB's directory, and the file you're looking for ends in .VBD (VB document). So type in a path something like this:

   ```
   c:\vb5\userdocument1.vbd
   ```

8. The document will be loaded into Internet Explorer, as shown in Figure 14-3.

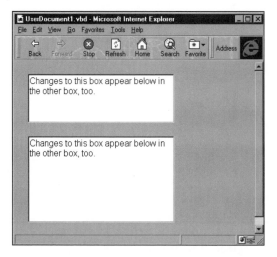

Figure 14-3 Test your UserDocuments in Internet Explorer.

If you're going to be cycling back and forth between VB and Internet Explorer to make changes, then test them; you might want to highlight c:\vb5\userdocument1.vbd and then press Ctrl+C to copy it. Once you've typed it into the Internet Explorer Open dialog box, you don't want to have to type it in over and over each time you go back to IE for another test. Why do you have to retype? Unfortunately, you have to shut down and restart Internet Explorer each time you start a new cycle of testing. If you stop the running VB UserDocument to make some adjustments, you'll see the warning shown in Figure 14-4.

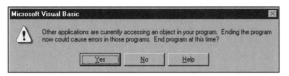

Figure 14-4 This means that by stopping VB from running your UserDocument, you'll also have to shut down and restart Internet Explorer.

Once you've stopped the running UserDocument, if you go back to IE and try to reload the UserDocument, it won't work. Neither will the Refresh, Back or Forward features of IE work. The only solution is to shut down IE and restart it, and then open your running .VBD UserDocument file from IE's File menu once again. UserDocuments in VB are in this way somewhat more difficult to test than are UserControls in VBCCE or the ActiveX Control Pad.

From the Container's Side

Normally IE displays HTML pages. HTML is largely a page description language with a few built-in controls (it has, for example, a BUTTON control <INPUT TYPE=BUTTON>). However, IE can also display ActiveX UserControls and other objects, as you learned earlier in this book. These objects are inserted into an existing HTML page by use of the HTML <OBJECT> tag, and they communicate by using VBScript <SCRIPT>.

However, the relationship between an ActiveX Document DLL component and IE is quite different from components that are merely embedded within HTML and must rely on VBScript.

ActiveX Documents Need Not Be in a Web Page

An ActiveX Document can be displayed in the IE browser *independently*, instead of within a Web page. In effect, when IE is displaying an ActiveX Document, it is hosting a *Visual Basic application* in the user's computer, with all the facilities and features available to any ordinary .EXE VB application. You may recall that VBScript, like JavaScript, is a stripped-down language. VBScript has no facilities for managing or even contacting the user's disk drive, and is missing a number of other features. Visual Basic, as you know, is not restricted in any way at all.

However, at the time of this writing, only IE and Microsoft Office Binder are ActiveX Document-capable containers. In the future, it's likely that additional browsers and other containers will be able to host Documents, perhaps even the NT or Windows operating systems themselves as they transition into Internet browsers/operating systems. To some extent, the eventual popularity of Document-capable containers depends on how well security issues can be addressed (see Chapter 15).

In any case, if you create ActiveX Documents, you should be aware that Netscape users won't be able to view or use these documents. If you're creating objects for a Windows- or NT-based Intranet, no problem. But don't expect to cast Documents out onto the Web at this time and make them available to everyone.

How to Determine the Container

Because containers can vary, you should have a way of detecting, within your Document's programming, what container the Document is currently in. Here's how:

```
MsgBox TypeName(UserDocument1.Parent)
```

If the ActiveX Document is in IE, this code will, according to Microsoft, result in the following:

```
IwebBrowserApp
```

However, on my system using IE, the result is:

```
IWebBrowser2
```

You might, however, prefer to use the following approach instead:

```
UserDocument.Parent.Name
```

This results in:

```
Microsoft Internet Explorer
```

Neither the TypeName nor the Name commands tell you the version of the container, but they can at least tell you if you're in IE or not. Using the TypeName or Name commands is similar to HTML code that is sometimes used to detect whether an HTML page is loaded in IE or Netscape's browser — and then different programming is invoked, based on the capabilities of the user's particular browser. Eventually, everyone hopes, standards will emerge and all this double-coding won't be necessary.

Use the Show Event for Initialization

Where should you write initialization code in a Document-style component? Unlike Standard EXE VB Forms, a Document has no Load event. You should use the Show event instead. Show is best because it is triggered when the Document is sited in the container. However, note that every time the Document is displayed (by clicking IE's Back button, for example) its Show event is triggered. You might be tempted to use the Initialize event, but don't; Initialize is triggered before a Document is sited. In general, though, at the present time you'll likely limit ActiveX Document components to intranet sites where you'll usually know in advance the container (IE) that is used to view them.

The Document Migration Wizard

You might have noticed on the VB Add-Ins menu the ActiveX Document Migration Wizard (if you don't see it, click Add-In Manager in the Add-Ins menu). The Document Migration Wizard can be useful if you have complex existing VB Forms that you want translated into Documents. It cannot translate an existing VB application into a Document-style application, it merely makes a Form into a Document-style object. The properties of the Form and its resident controls are preserved, including the Name properties. Your programming code is preserved, too, to the extent that it is usable in a Document. For example, events such as Load will be commented out, but won't be transported into the Document's Show event.

You can test the Wizard by creating a simple, ordinary Standard EXE VB Form, as shown in Figure 14-5.

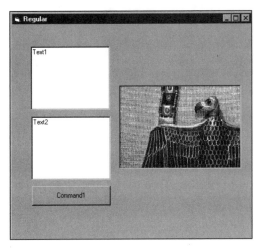

Figure 14-5 You can let the Wizard convert this ordinary VB Form into a Document component.

Then you can put some code in some of the events to see what the Wizard does to the code:

```
Private Sub Command1_Click()
MsgBox "HI"
End
End Sub


Private Sub Form_Load()
MsgBox "LOADING"
End Sub


Private Sub Text1_Change()
Text2 = Text1
End Sub
```

Start the Wizard and answer the questions that appear on the Wizard's third page, as shown in Figure 14-6.

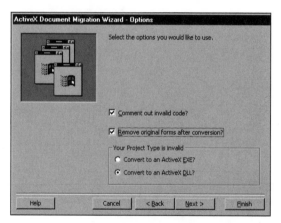

Figure 14-6   Tell the Wizard to check for code that's impossible in a Document (such as the End command).

The Code Has Changed

Keep clicking the Next button, and then finally click the Finish button to complete the Wizard's job. Your VB Form will have been mutated into a Document-style Form. It will still look the same as Figure 14-5 — same controls, same sizes, and positions. But the code will have changed to the following:

```
Private Sub UserDocument_Initialize()
 Call Form_Load
End Sub
```

```
Private Sub Command1_Click()
MsgBox "HI"
'[AXDW] The following line was commented out by the ActiveX
  Document Migration Wizard.
'End
End Sub


Private Sub Form_Load()
MsgBox "LOAD"
End Sub


Private Sub Text1_Change()
Text2 = Text1
End Sub
```

An ActiveX Document component has no Form_Load event, so the Wizard has called Form_Load from the Initialize event (it should probably have called the Show event instead). But for clarity, when you read the code in the future, you'll probably just want to move whatever programming is in this "Form_Load" procedure (it's not a real event, just a Sub with an odd name) to the Show or Initialized events and erase the Form_Load procedure entirely.

When the Wizard finishes, it tells you to search for AXDW within your programming to see the places where it made changes by commenting out impossible code. In the preceding example, the End command was commented out. A Document cannot end itself — that's the responsibility of its container.

Menus Are Preserved

If you have a menu on your Standard EXE Form before the Wizard translates it to a Document Form, the menu will be preserved — along with the programming in the menu's events. However, the menu won't appear at the top of the Document itself. Instead, it will be blended into the menus of the IE (or other container).

To see an example of this menu-blending feature, follow these steps:

1. Start a Standard EXE project.

2. Use the Menu Editor in the VB Tools menu to create a menu.

3. Caption it **DocMenu** and name it **dm**.

4. Close the Menu Editor.

5. Type the following into the dm_Click event, to react when the user selects this menu:

```
Private Sub dm_Click()
MsgBox "This is the Document's Menu, not the Browser's."
End Sub
```

6. Run the Wizard to change this into a Document Form and component. Notice that the Wizard leaves the Name of the new UserDocument set to its original *Form1* rather than translating it to UserDocument1.

7. Run this project by pressing **F5**.

8. Switch to IE and choose Open from IE's File menu.

9. Type in the following to load your new Document (or some variation, just remember you're loading Form1 now):

```
C:\VB5\FORM1.VBD
```

You'll see the IE menus change to accommodate the new menu item DocMenu, as shown in Figures 14-7 and 14-8.

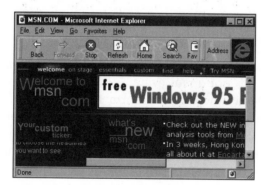

Figure 14-7 BEFORE: This is Internet Explorer's default collection of menus.

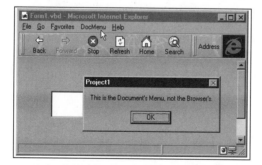

Figure 14-8 AFTER: When your UserDocument is loaded, the Edit and View menus are removed and your DocMenu is inserted.

Jumping Around

With ordinary VB Standard EXE applications, you can use simple Load or Show commands to hide or reveal the various Forms within your project. You can start other applications or utilities with the Shell command, or switch to other applications that are already running by using the AppActivate command.

Using Hyperlinks

In a browser, though, transferring focus to a different document requires somewhat different techniques. A person surfing the Internet often navigates by clicking Hyperlinks — jump-off points within a document that take them to a different Web site or a different area within the current Web site or even locally to a different zone within the currently displayed document. So, you won't be surprised to find out that a UserDocument component (an ActiveX Document DLL or EXE server) requires what's called a *Hyperlink object* to move to other ActiveX documents. The target of the Hyperlink object can be any URL (which stands for *universal resource locator*, but more commonly known as an Internet address).

Using the NavigateTo Method

The Hyperlink object has a NavigateTo method. You use that method to jump out somewhere on the Web.

Follow these steps to learn how to use the NavigateTo method and then test it:

1. Press Ctrl+N to start a new ActiveX Document DLL.

2. Double-click *User Documents* in the Project window.

3. Double-click UserDocument1 to display its design window.

4. Put a CommandButton on the Document.

5. Double-click the CommandButton to get to its code window.

6. Type the following into the code window:

   ```
   Private Sub Command1_Click()
   UserDocument.Hyperlink.NavigateTo "http://www.usatoday.com/"
   End Sub
   ```

7. Now test it by pressing F5 to run your Document component.

8. Start a new instance of IE running.

9. Click File → Open .

10. Type in: **C:\VB5\USERDOCUMENT1.VBD**. (Or use whatever path points to your copy of VB5, if your path isn't C:\VB5.)

11. Click the CommandButton, and you'll jump to the USA Today site.

You can also use the Hyperlink command to point to a .VBD file (another ActiveX Document DLL or EXE) or to a Word or Excel document. If you have a second .VBD file on your computer, try this:

```
UserDocument.Hyperlink.NavigateTo "file://c:\VB5\TestDoc.vbd"
```

Beyond that, you can back or forward through IE's cache of documents — as if the user had clicked the Back or Forward buttons on IE's toolbar. Note that the error-trapping is necessary in case you're at an end of the cache and no other document is available:

```
Private Sub Command1_Click()

    On Error GoTo Quit
    UserDocument.Hyperlink.GoForward
    Exit Sub

Quit:
    Resume Next
End Sub
```

BONUS

Compilation Options

After all your designing, coding, and testing, you've finally built an ActiveX component, and you're ready to send it out into the world. Generally you're not going to release your control as source code. One of the values of encapsulation is that developers, much less users, need not know the low-level details about how your component does its job. All a developer has to know is what members your component exposes (what properties, methods, and possibly events, it makes Public) and the required syntax to make use of these components (the arguments and the arguments' datatypes, and what information, if any, they return to the developer).

When you're ready to distribute a component, it's time to *compile* it. You select Make *NameOfYourProject* from the VB File menu, click Options, and then click the Compile tab. You should see the dialog box shown in Figure 14-9.

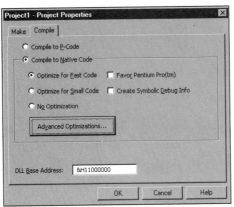

Figure 14-9 Before you compile a component, you have some decisions to make.

Use P-Code or Native Code?

A major decision you must make is whether to compile it in p-code or native code. P-code means *pseudo code*, and it isn't the elemental language of the computer. Instead, it must be interpreted at run time. P-code is far more efficient than would be a run-time attempt to interpret your VB source code. However, p-code can execute somewhat more slowly than native code, though native code tends to create larger executable files (the final .DLL, .EXE, or .OCX files).

It's the old trade-off. If you're worried about the size of your final component, always choose the p-code option. For example, a simple test .DLL component compiled to 9728 bytes in native code shrinks to 8192 bytes in p-code — about a 20 percent decrease in size.

If file size isn't significant, go for the speed efficiencies of native code. Again, however, the execution speed differences between the two modes of compilation can sometimes be slight, which is because an average VB program spends 95 percent of its time executing code *that's not in your executable*. Instead, the program is executing functions in the support libraries. Therefore, regarding speed, it matters little which compilation option you select.

The only time you always should take advantage of native code compilation is when your component is a processor hog. That is, you're doing something in your component that takes a long time — and consequently the component's run-time *will* be more than 5 percent of the time spent executing within your code. In that case, go for native code. My informal speed tests of computation-intensive ActiveX DLLs resulted in 60-80 percent faster execution times when the DLL was compiled into native code. It can make a difference.

Once you do decide to go with native code, you're offered a set of additional choices, as shown in Figure 14-9. The six options are as follows:

* **Optimize for Fast Code.** This means that the compiler will choose speed over file size whenever that tradeoff comes up during the compilation process. You should select this option in nearly all cases. Memory is cheap, but time is money.

* **Optimize for Small Code.** The opposite of Optimize for Fast Code, this produces the smallest possible executable file, at the expense of speed.

* **No Optimization.** You should avoid this choice, unless you want a compromise between the two previous optimizations.

* **Favor Pentium Pro.** If you're sure that your component will be used by only on a Pentium Pro machine, go ahead. Otherwise, you'll create a component that runs inefficiently on other computers — though it will still run.

* **Create Symbolic Debugging Info.** This option can be useful if you use Visual C++ or a debugger that can work with the .PDB files that are deposited on your hard drive if this option is selected. However, VB's IDE (integrated design environment) is world famous for its excellent debugging facilities.

* **DLL Base Address.** Normally you'll just leave this option set to the default. When your component is loaded into memory, Windows will try to insert it into the address specified. If Windows can't put it there, it will put it elsewhere in memory (this slows down the loading, and usually prevents the code in your component from being shared by different clients). If you're concerned about this issue and want to try to prevent memory conflicts between your components (they'll all, by default, be compiled to that same address), see the suggestions in VB's Books Online (on the Help menu).

Now click the Advanced Optimizations button on the Compile dialog box. Six more options appear, as shown in Figure 14-10.

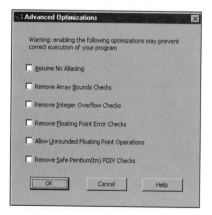

Figure 14-10 Selecting some of these options can speed up your ActiveX component.

Often the speed at which a component executes isn't an issue — it runs plenty fast. However, if you want to attempt to make your component run faster, you can select all these options and thereby turn off these various kinds of run-time error-checking.

Leave Error-Checking Active

Nevertheless, my informal tests revealed that when these options were selected, the DLL actually executed a little over 1 percent *slower*. Moral: If you want to try using these options, compile your component both with and without the options, and then decide which approach to use. In general it's best to leave error-checking active. The performance gain, if any, isn't usually significant, and without these run-time messages, bad data or bad user input can produce errors that are hard to figure out.

For example, consider the Remove Integer Overflow Checks option. Here is some code that adds two Integer variables together and tries to put the result into a third Integer variable. Integers can only hold numbers up to 32768, so the addition of 20000 to 20000 overflows the Integer variable type:

```
Private Sub Form_Load()
Dim z As Integer, r As Integer, a As Integer
z = 20000
r = 20000
a = r + z
MsgBox a
End Sub
```

When you run this code at design time, you get an error message (overflow) on the line a = r + z. However, if you compile this program and specify that Integer Overflow Checks should be removed from the compiled code, no error message will appear, but the result will be –25536. This kind of error can be beastly difficult to track down, because once your component is out in the world, how do you know what kinds of data will be presented to it for processing? The user might type in a large number. Or the user might have a large number in a database that is accessed by your component. Either of these situations could cause your code to stumble, but there would be no error message to help debug the problem.

Summary

In this chapter you learned the virtues and drawbacks of the Document-style ActiveX component. You found out how to create one, why and where to use one, and how they can be tested in Internet Explorer. You tried transforming an existing VB Form into a document and discovered how to navigate from one document to another using the NavigateTo command. Finally, you learned the comparative worth of the several VB compilation options — what settings you should select when you're ready to create the final, executable version of your ActiveX component.

In the next chapter, you'll find out how to package your ActiveX components for distribution. You'll also learn about the various security features built into browsers and how to use the Setup Wizard to simplify the process of creating foolproof installation packages.

This chapter is all about packaging your components for distribution. Once you've written a useful ActiveX component, you'll want to pass it around to friends, install it on a local intranet, or perhaps sell it. No matter how you plan to disburse a component, you'll want to first address users' justifiable fears about the possibility that it contains a virus, or is capable of invading their privacy.

In this chapter you'll discover the various security features that are offered by browsers to endeavor to protect a user from the dangers of downloading scripts and components from Internet sites. You'll also find out how to create two kinds of installation packages: one for distributing a component via diskette and the other for deploying a component on the Internet.

The Double Danger of Viruses

Although the chances of your computer system getting a virus are slim, if you *do* get one, the effects can be devastating. A vicious person can construct a deadly little executable — only a few lines of code are needed — that will erase or scramble the contents of your hard drive. Any documents not backed up can be lost forever. You'd have to reinstall all your applications, and then spend the time to customize them all over again by adjusting options, rerecording macros, and specifying any other preferences you've come to rely on. And there's a double danger: While a virus might attack your system, perhaps equally unsettling is the chance that a virus could cause private data from your hard drive to be uploaded and viewed and abused by a stranger.

Until the Internet and World Wide Web became so pervasive, the comfort level about avoiding viruses was fairly high. You bought software in shrink-wrapped boxes from well-known software manufactures. Sure, perhaps every now and then a disturbed employee would plant a virus in a commercial game or application, but this was rare. Unless you downloaded a lot of shareware from bulletin boards, the odds against suffering from a virus attack were quite small.

It Cuts Both Ways

The comfort level, however, has gone down now, because of the World Wide Web. When you surf the Internet you're often bouncing from one untested and unknown site to another. You can probably trust MSN and CNN and other large organizations, but what about all the millions of little sites out there? Is there any danger?

Often, the answer is no. HTML — the language used to construct many Internet sites — is harmless. HTML is merely a page-description language that tells your browser how big to make the text, or what color to make the background, or where to locate a picture to display. Pictures and text, by themselves, are merely *visual.* They cannot send commands to your operating system that will erase your hard drive. It's impossible for a picture of a fish to execute computer commands. These things are merely for display on the screen and have no programming component whatsoever.

Even Documents Are No Longer Safe

Until the introduction of Microsoft's Word 6.0, people unfamiliar with computers often felt safe from viruses after being told that *documents* (such as Word's .DOC files, or Notepad's .TXT files) contained pure *data* (strings of characters for display) and had no programming in them, thus no possibility of harboring viruses. A text document file could no more damage your hard drive than a cookbook could burn dinner.

But as you've seen in this book, objects blur the distinction between data and behavior (programming). Sure, an object has data (its properties), but it also contains executable programming (its methods) as well. This was made all too clear when, in 1996, people began experiencing viruses simply by displaying Word 6 *documents* on their screen. It turned out that Word 6 .DOC files — like good objects everywhere — also contained embedded executables (mini-programs in the form of macros). And some of these macros were designed to automatically run when the .DOC file was first loaded into the Word application. A letter from your aunt could contain autoexec methods.

This knowledge really shook things up. Many computer-naive people who'd been assured that merely reading a letter from Aunt Dorrie could never, ever introduce a virus into their system were suddenly shocked. Some of them still haven't calmed down.

Script Languages Add Computing Power

Now the Internet exposes your computer to perhaps dozens of Web pages a day — Web pages that were constructed by who-knows-whom?

If HTML is safe enough, what about scripting languages such as Java and VBScript? These languages can be embedded within HTML and are designed to extend the features of Internet documents. Until these script languages appeared on the scene, it was awkward to perform calculations or provide any real interactivity or multimedia effects. HTML was designed as a static *display* language. It has no facilities for adding 2 + 2 or playing the latest rock anthem.

Say you wanted to create a Web page with a little program that accepts the user's total savings and current interest and then calculates how much more interest the user would earn at your bank. (HTML can't calculate anything.) You would have to send the user's input back to your Web page server, do the calculations there, and then send the result back to be displayed to the user. Rather roundabout and, if the interactivity you were attempting required large amounts of data, the idea of remote (server) computation would begin to seem terribly inefficient. Why not compute at high speed by having an executable object downloaded right into the user's personal computer?

Safeguard Strategies

The Script languages were designed to compute locally. Then embedded objects — ActiveX controls for example — upped the stakes even further. An ActiveX control is a Visual Basic *program* that is downloaded into a user's system. It can do to the user's system whatever a Visual Basic .EXE program can do: pretty much anything it wants. No reputable software store, no shrink-wrapped box, no famous manufacturer — just a running program slipping silently into your system from who-knows-whom and who-knows-where on the Internet.

Step 1: Sandboxing

Various strategies have been introduced to protect the innocent. For one thing, VBScript and JavaScript are emasculated languages. They've been stripped of potentially harmful commands available in their parent languages (VB and Java). The script languages contain no disk reformatting or file deletion commands; they cannot directly contact any operating system features, such as the Windows Registry (just mucking that up can immobilize a computer); they cannot create objects.

Of course, the script languages cannot directly communicate with peripherals or the computer's memory. They can't even print a page to the printer. This neutering of these script languages to make them safe for Internet surfers is called *sandboxing,* though *sandbagging* might have been a more accurate term.

Step 2: Provide a Virtual Shrink-Wrapped Box

What if, Microsoft thought, we could authenticate downloadable objects (ActiveX controls) and assure the user that what was coming in over the Internet was, yes, an executable like any other application, but it's been verified as having no harmful viruses. In other words, run a virus-checker at the source rather than on the user's system.

This idea gave rise to the following three variations of authentication:

DIGITAL SIGNING

Add a *digital signature* that identifies the source of the control. Then, if the control does harm, somebody can be held responsible. A third-party company authorizes you (the control's creator) to "sign" your control (using VB's Setup Wizard to embed the signature, as described later in this chapter). This third-party maintains your name and address, so if anything goes wrong, everyone knows where to pin the blame: on you.

SAFE FOR SCRIPTING

Mark a control *safe for scripting.* When you select this option in the Setup Wizard, you are saying to users: Look, relax, I'm telling you that nothing in this control can be activated by a script language (some VBScript or JavaScript in the document you're downloading), triggering the control to do something damaging. This control is safe. Ha, ha, ha!

SAFE FOR INITIALIZATION

Mark a control *safe for initialization.* This Setup Wizard option tells users: Nothing in this control can harm your system if some malign individual tries to use HTML (<PARAM> tags) to send strange data when the control is being initialized in your browser. For example, allowing a <PARAM> command to change the color of your control is safe for initialization. Allowing a <PARAM> command to save something to the user's disk drive is not. So, when marked safe for initialization, the user can take it easy and just let this kind of "guaranteed" control into the browser. Ha, ha, ha!

The reason for these Ha, ha, ha's is that any deranged virus designer can buy a copy of Visual Basic and easily create ActiveX components. This book demonstrates just how easily. Then, using the Setup Wizard, it only takes a couple of mouse clicks to "mark" the nasty, deadly component as safe. What kind of protection is this? We might as well require that before entering a bank, everyone sign a card reading "I promise I don't have a gun. Honest."

But any shelter in a storm is good, I guess. Internet Explorer is by default set to warn the user of any incoming component that has not been marked "safe" for scripting and initialization. You'll still be notified if you choose "Medium," but at least the protection, shown in Figure 15-1, won't turn away all incoming executables. To set these levels, run Internet Explorer (IE) and then choose Options from the View menu. Click the Security tab and then click the Safety Level button.

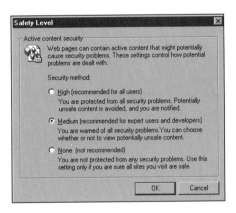

Figure 15-1 Unless you want to interrupt your navigation of the Internet, don't leave this option set to the default "High."

When Internet Explorer comes upon a Web page with an embedded ActiveX object, it checks to see if there are any <SCRIPT> or <PARAM> tags within the HTML that address the object. If not, IE lets the object become active and visible, whether or not it is marked safe for scripting or initialization. It's only if <SCRIPT> or <PARAM> tags address (work with) the object that it must be marked safe before IE will pass it. The reason for this is that if no <SCRIPT> refers to the object, any script that exists on the page can't cause the control to damage the user's system. Same thing with PARAM tags that don't reference the control in question. Of course, none of this does anything to protect the user against a rogue control that contains its own virus attack-code within. Remember, viruses aren't the only danger when you let a stranger into your machine. A second peril is *hyperspace peeping*; private information about you stored on your hard drive can be gathered and misused.

Safety Warnings the User Sees

To see how all this works from the user's point of view, create a simple ActiveX control and use the ActiveX Control Pad to embed it within an HTML file. Choose Open from IE's File menu and browse your hard drive for the .HTM file you just saved. It has not been digitally signed, nor marked safe for scripting or initialization. If you have the Safety Level settings (refer to Figure 15-1) on High, you'll see the warning shown in Figure 15-2.

Figure 15-2 When Safety is set to High in Internet Explorer, the browser refuses to even load a component.

However, if you set the Safety Level to Medium, you'll see the advisory displayed in Figure 15-3.

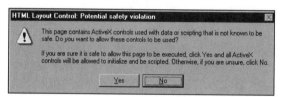

Figure 15-3 The Medium setting gives the user the option to reject a component or take the risk.

Assuming that you want to mark your ActiveX creations safe for scripting, how do you make sure they in fact are? Microsoft suggests that you make a list of all your control's public properties, methods, and events. And make a second list of any files, registry items, or API calls accessed. If data is transferred between items on these lists, or if there are any dependencies (one needs the services of the other) between items on the lists, chances are the control isn't safe for scripting.

To check if your component is safe for initialization, be sure that you're checking — in the object's exposed procedures — the validity of any data passed within your object's ReadProperties event.

The Problem in a Nutshell

Though they unquestionably greatly enrich the Internet, making the Internet both more alive and more efficient, scripting languages and embedding objects also raise serious concerns about security for everyone who visits Web pages.

VBScript, Java, JavaScript, and ActiveX all send executable content into a user's system. And executable content, like a knife, can work for good or ill.

The user has three basic options when dealing with executables that come knocking at his or her virtual door. The browser can be configured to reject all potential incoming dangers, as previously described. Or the user can make individual decisions by using IE's Medium setting, asking to be alerted and then admitting or rejecting executables on a case-by-case basis.

The third option is, in my mind, the only option that provides any actual measure of security, everyone's best efforts and protestations to the contrary notwithstanding. The third option is *digital signing*. Unfortunately it's not foolproof either. When an ActiveX control is digitally signed, that signature is registered with a credential registry (AT&T maintains one, and Verisign is a famous one). The creator of the control is therefore known and authenticated. So if the control introduces a virus or other problem into your system, you can complain to the actual author of the control, to the registrar, to your neighbors, and all who will listen. Exactly what happens when you complain isn't known. No ActiveX component has yet introduced a virus into anyone's system at the time of this writing. Of course, it will happen sooner or later.

However, the user can take some comfort in digital signing. Digital signing will certainly deflect controls authored by casual or simple-minded virus purveyors. "Marking safe" provides virtually no protection whatsoever. To benefit from digital signing, the user builds a list of known, trusted sources of executables (such as Microsoft) or can alternatively give blanket permission to accept any controls registered by a particular registration service such as Verisign.

The user is saying to the browser: If it definitely comes directly from Microsoft, you can let it in without alerting me. To see this list, Choose Options from IE's View menu, click the Security tab, and then click the Publishers button. You'll see the dialog box shown in Figure 15-4.

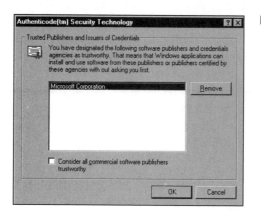

Figure 15-4 The IE user can build a list of trusted registrars of digital signatures and of individual publishers.

 WEB PATH If you create ActiveX controls that you want to sign, check with Verisign at http://www.verisign.com

Digital signing and marking safe are accomplished with the assistance of the VB Setup Wizard. The Setup Wizard is also the best way to distribute your ActiveX component, whether you're giving it to coworkers on an intranet in your office, or sending it out to developers around the world for deployment on the Internet, or their intranets. Both the commercial version of VB, and the free VBCCE include the Setup Wizard, though the Wizard in VBCCE can only create installation packages for UserControls. VB, of course, can create installation packages for the entire variety of components that it supports, as well as standard .EXE programs. It's to the VB Setup Wizard that you can now turn your attention.

How to Give Your Controls to Others

Okay. You've written a great ActiveX component. Now you want to package it so its component parts, dependencies (files or servers it needs), and everything is neatly tied up and delivered to developers or coworkers without any problems. You want to make it easy for them to install your component. By far the best way to ensure that everything is registered on their system correctly and all elements of the component are accounted for is to use VB's Setup Wizard.

Using the Setup Wizard

To demonstrate the options and features of the Setup Wizard, try creating a setup package for a sample UserControl by following these steps:

1. Start a new project by pressing Ctrl+N and choosing ActiveX Control.

2. Put a TextBox on the Form. This elementary control is merely for the purpose of illustrating how to use the Setup Wizard.

3. Click **File** → **Save** to save this project to a disk file. You'll create a .CTL and a .VBP file.

4. Save them both with the name **STest**.

Collecting Dependencies

The Setup Wizard will later want to know the location of this Visual Basic project file. The Wizard will check through the .VBP file, the .CTL file, and any other descriptive files in your project to find out if any special DLLs or other objects are required by your project and must therefore be bundled with it into the finished installation package. For example, if you've used any special controls that aren't in the basic VB controls group — or perhaps a control from a third-party vendor — these *dependencies* must be noted and bundled when your component is distributed to others. It's always possible that others don't have the dependencies your component requires already registered on their system. Also, note that the Microsoft controls — such as a TextBox — are yours to distribute embedded on your component at no cost to you. However, third-party vendors might require a fee for your use of their controls or other products. Check with them to see.

You also have to compile an .OCX file for your project prior to running the Setup Wizard, so choose Make STest OCS from VB's File menu. Save it into the same directory that you saved the .CTL and .VBP files. Now you're ready to call upon the assistance of the Wizard.

 To find out more about all the options available to you when you compile a project in VB, see the Bonus section of Chapter 14.

Mysteriously, the Setup Wizard isn't on the Add-Ins menu with all the other Wizards. You can't call it up from inside either VB or VBCCE. Instead, you'll find it in your VB5 directory in the `\setupkit\kitfil32` subdirectory (or in your VBCCE directory, if you're using that version of VB). The Wizard's filename is SETUPWIZ.EXE. Double-click it in Windows's Explorer to start it running. After reading the introduction screen, click Next. You'll see the dialog box shown in Figure 15-5.

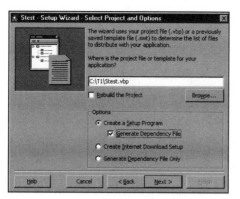

Figure 15-5 The Wizard wants to know where your project is on disk, and whether this component will be used on a regular computer system or on the Internet.

Fill in the path for your component's .VBP file on the dialog box shown in Figure 15-5. The Rebuild the Project option shown in Figure 15-5 should be used if you've made any improvements to the source code since you last compiled an .OCX version. In other words, the existing .OCX isn't the latest, best version.

TIP It's considered good practice to always select the Generate a Dependency File option shown in Figure 15-5. This file, with the extension .DEP, lists all the support files that your ActiveX component requires. The .DEP file also specifies where dependent files should be located when installed (such as the Windows\System directory) and the versions of the dependencies. (VB itself has a dependency file, VB5DEP.INI, located in the Windows directory. This file lists the standard, basic dependencies required by compiled VB components. This file is used by the Setup Wizard to determine the rock bottom necessary support file.)

Leave the option set to Create a Setup Program. This means that your STest UserControl is intended to be installed on an ordinary computer's hard drive, as opposed to being deployed on the Internet. You'll find out about the Internet option shortly in the Bonus section. When your dialog box looks like the one in Figure 15-5 (except for the file path), click the Next button and you'll see the distribution dialog box shown in Figure 15-6.

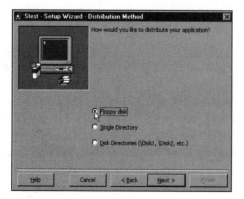

Figure 15-6 Here you select how you want your component distributed.

Choosing Distribution Methods

The options in the distribution dialog specify how you want others to access the setup. Choose Floppy Disk. This means that you'll send your UserControl to customers on floppy disk(s), or give it to coworkers to install on their personal computers via floppy. The alternative, to store SETUP.EXE and all the files needed for your project onto a single directory on your hard drive, is useful if you plan to make many copies of your installation package (and the entire package will fit on a single floppy). However, you're merely making a single, test installation package, so just choose Floppy Disk.

The third option, Disk Directories, is for large projects where you want to store the setup package on your hard drive, but want the package divided into floppy-sized subdirectories. If you're planning to make many floppy copies of a large project, this would be a good choice (as opposed to running the Setup Wizard to create each copy of your installation package). You would just insert Floppy1, Floppy2, and so on, copying the appropriate subdirectory onto each floppy in the package.

Click the Next button and choose the floppy drive where you want the Wizard to build your installation package. Stick a blank floppy disk into the drive and click Next.

Adding Other Dependencies

The Wizard, after checking the source code .VBP file in your project, has decided that you don't use any ActiveX server components within your UserControl. That's true, but if you know of any dependencies that the Wizard didn't catch, here's where you can add them. Use the Add Remote option to include .VBR files, Remote ActiveX components for intranetworks. If you want to add components on your local machine (.OCX, .DLL, or .EXE dependency files), click the Add Local button. In practical terms, the Wizard finds all references so you likely won't need to add any of your own. (This isn't the place to add READ.ME files.) However, if you're giving your component to someone that you know already has some of the dependencies, *deselect* it by clicking the checkbox next to its name. This way it won't be included unnecessarily in the installation package.

Click Next, and you'll see an announcement that the Wizard is processing VB support files — in particular the main one, weighing in at 3.1M — MSVBVM50.DLL (the VB virtual machine), plus assorted OLE (ActiveX) support and miscellaneous other files (such as updated basic VB controls). At this point you'll be notified that if your control is to be used in an IDE other than VB, you have to include support for Property Pages. Answer no.

Adding Miscellaneous Files

Now you come to the dialog box shown in Figure 15-7. Here is where you should add any README.TXT files or other custom files you want to include.

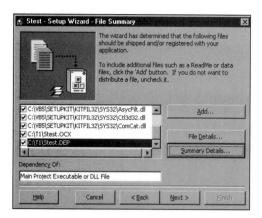

Figure 15-7 This is a list of all the files that will be bundled into the installation package. Notice that the Wizard has included a dependency .DEP file, as you requested.

If you're curious about the size, version, creator, date of creation, or other details about a given file, click File Details. If you want to see a summary of your installation bundle — especially the size — click Summary Details as shown in Figure 15-8.

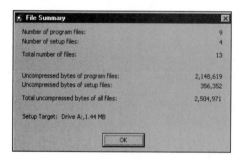

Figure 15-8 This synopsis tells you that you're probably going to need two floppies to distribute your UserControl.

The Summary Details tell you that the uncompressed size of your installation bundle is about 2.5M. After the Wizard compresses these files, at 1.58M it is still a bit too large for a single diskette. Click Next, and you'll see the final dialog box, asking you if you want to save the template that the Wizard has created. Just click Finish. That's it. Now you can give your fabulous STest UserControl to anyone, and they can just click SETUP.EXE on Diskette 1 to safely install and register the component on their system.

In fact, you may want to try testing the installation bundle now. Shut down VB and any other applications or utilities that you've currently got running in Windows. Setup prefers that nothing else use any dependencies during the installation of new dependencies. Put Diskette 1 into the floppy drive and use Windows's Start button to select the Run option. Type **a:\setup** or whatever your floppy drive letter is.

Not too much will happen, because setup will detect that your system already has all the correct dependencies installed. It will merely install your .OCX and .DEP files into the WINDOWS\SYSTEM directory, and then register them.

Try running VB now and choose a Standard EXE file. Right-click the Toolbox and choose Components. Locate Project1 (it will be named C:\WINDOWS\SYSTEM\STEST.OCX in the Location description in this dialog box, but named Project1 in the Controls list). Click it to select it and add it to the Toolbox. Then close the Components dialog box by clicking OK, and then double-click the STest control on the Toolbox to add it to the Form. There it is. It doesn't do anything — you didn't provide much in the way of functionality to this test object. Nor does it have many properties. But it did successfully install, and that was what you wanted to see.

BONUS

Deploy on the Internet

Now try following the same steps to start the Wizard running again, except this time you'll build an installation package for Internet deployment. Close VB. Run SETUPWIZ.EXE and click the Next button. If necessary, type in the path to your STEST.VBP file (it's probably already there, by default, because it was the source of the last setup package you generated).

However, this time, click Create Internet Download Setup. A What's New button appears, as shown in Figure 15-9. Click that button to see the latest information on Internet deployment from Microsoft.

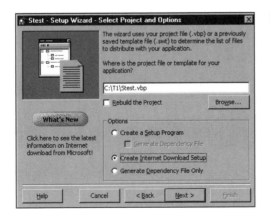

Figure 15-9 When you package a component for the Internet, no dependency file is required.

The Internet Is Cheap but Slow

Notice, too, that because your ultimate goal is to send this file out onto the Internet, the Wizard creates no .DEP file. When, earlier in this chapter, you packaged STEST for distribution to friends in your office or on a network, the Setup Wizard tried to include every imaginable file that the user might need to run your component. Floppies are cheap and relatively fast.

The Internet is cheap and relatively slow. It has a bandwidth problem at the present time — things download slowly as you must have noticed every time a graphic clogs up the pipeline and slowly, oh so slowly, unfolds on your screen. It makes sense to first download just the .OCX or other compiled component file. These files are usually quite small. The STEST.OCX is only 9216 bytes and will download over the Internet in a flash.

When you bundle a component for Internet deployment, the Setup Wizard provides *descriptions* of dependencies, not the actual dependency files themselves. These descriptions are checked against the registered files on the user's system, and only those dependencies that the user doesn't have are then downloaded (if the user gives permission by answering yes in a dialog box, or by having set Options/Security to a low enough level).

If your dependencies are exclusively from Microsoft (as is the case with your STEST component), you need not even keep the dependency files on your Web site. Instead, if it turns out that a user who downloads your STEST component needs some Microsoft support files, Microsoft provides the latest versions of many support files on its Internet site. So these dependencies can be downloaded from there rather than from your site.

Click Next, and you'll be asked where on your system you want to store the files that comprise the package you're deploying on the Internet, as shown in Figure 15-10. Choose any directory, or if you have a Web server, put them where it can get to these files. In any case, you can always copy the files onto the Web server directory later.

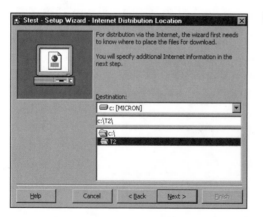

Figure 15-10 Specify the location of your Web server or any handy directory where you want the component's files to be stored.

Click Next and leave the option describing from what location dependencies (run-time components) should be downloaded set to its default: Download from the Microsoft Web site, as shown in Figure 15-11.

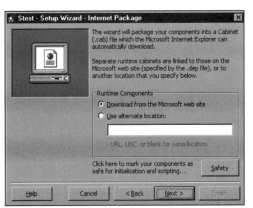

Figure 15-11 Normally you'll leave this option set at the default, pointing to the Microsoft Web site.

Click the Safety button, and you can reassure some users that your component is not going to harm their system if some person bent on destruction writes a harmful script or provides bad parameters. It doesn't reassure me. The Safety dialog box is shown in Figure 15-12.

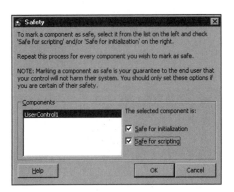

Figure 15-12 The Safety dialog box is where you mark your control(s) as safe for scripting and initialization.

Click OK, and then click Next twice to get to the File Summary dialog box. Notice that the huge MSVBVM50.DLL file evidently cannot be downloaded from the Microsoft Web site. Also note that there are far fewer files in this setup bundle than you got earlier when you were bundling the same STEST component, but for deployment on personal computers or intranets, rather than the Internet. The idea is to keep dependencies to a minimum when offering components on the Internet. Also, some dependencies aren't even necessary because when the user installed Internet Explorer, several general-use dependency files were installed along with the browser itself.

Click Next and then click Finish. Look in the directory where you asked that the files be stored. You'll see the .CAB file, a compressed version of your component (and any essential dependencies), and an .HTM (an ordinary Web page file) that contains an OBJECT reference to your component. This is the .HTM file that the Wizard generated for the STEST component, including the OBJECT reference:

```
<HTML>
<! -      If any of the controls on this page require licensing,
   you must create a license package file. Run LPK_TOOL.EXE to
   create the required LPK file. LPK_TOOL.EXE can be found on the
   ActiveX SDK, http://www.microsoft.com/intdev/sdk/sdk.htm. If
   you have the Visual Basic 5.0 CD, it can also be found in the
   \Tools\LPK_TOOL directory.

   The following is an example of the Object tag:

<OBJECT CLASSID="clsid:5220cb21-c88d-11cf-b347-00aa00a28331">
   <PARAM NAME="LPKPath" VALUE="LPKfilename.LPK">
</OBJECT>
   - >


<OBJECT ID="UserControl1" WIDTH=320 HEIGHT=240
CLASSID="CLSID:0E72833D-E332-11D0-B607-307005C10000"
CODEBASE="Stest.CAB#version=1,0,0,0">
</OBJECT>
</HTML>
```

.CAB and .INF Files Are Generated

When a user arrives at your Web page, Internet Explorer downloads the .HTM file to the user's system, along with the referenced .CAB file. If it's been signed, your component is verified. Then it's decompressed, registered, installed, and finally displayed and executed.

In a subdirectory named SUPPORT, you'll find three additional files. The .INF file contains information about safe-for-scripting, safe-for-initialization, registry details, and, among other specifications, addresses where, if necessary, dependencies can be downloaded to the user's system. For example, here's the address on Microsoft's Web site where the massive MSVBVM50 DLL can be found:

 `http://activex.microsoft.com/controls/vb5/MSVBVM50.cab`

The SUPPORT subdirectory also includes the original uncompressed version of your component's compiled .OCX file and a .DDF that contains specifications used during the compression process when a .CAB file is created.

At the current time, the Wizard leaves out the <BODY> tags that Internet Explorer expects to find. So load the STEST.HTM file into Notepad and add the <BODY> tags. You can also remove that commented section about licensing if you wish. This is the final HTML code that will display your UserControl in Internet Explorer:

```
<HTML>
<BODY>

<OBJECT ID="UserControl1" WIDTH=320 HEIGHT=240
CLASSID="CLSID:0E72833D-E332-11D0-B607-307005C10000"
CODEBASE="Stest.CAB#version=1,0,0,0">
</OBJECT>

<BODY>
</HTML>
```

Save this file as STEST.HTM. Now run Internet Explorer and load the STEST.HTM file by choosing Open from the IE's File menu. You'll see your UserControl in the browser, as shown in Figure 15-13.

Figure 15-13 Your UserControl loads successfully into the Internet Explorer browser.

Summary

In this chapter you explored two related topics: security and installation packaging. Although current security measures offer minimal real protection from viruses or invasion of privacy, efforts are ongoing to make interacting with the Internet as safe one day as watching TV. At this point, though, there's not too much you can do to certify to a user that your component is 100 percent safe. Most of the steps you learned in this chapter amount to one variation or another on the old phrase *trust me*.

In addition to calming user's fears, you also learned of the various options offered by Visual Basic's excellent Setup Wizard. The Wizard makes it easy to bundle your component and all related support files into a pack of setup diskettes, or create a setup package designed to be used on the Internet.

CHAPTER SIXTEEN

ADVANCED ACTIVEX TECHNIQUES

IN THIS CHAPTER YOU LEARN THESE KEY SKILLS

This book concludes with an exploration of three advanced topics: the operating system's Application Programming Interface, user-drawn controls, and variations of code containment. In this chapter you learn how to tap into the Windows operating system's huge collection of API functions. You find out how to create a control from scratch, programming its appearance as well as its behavior. Finally, you see how to use various kinds of hierarchical organization to strengthen the encapsulation in, and add a kind of polymorphism to, your ActiveX components.

Tap into the Massive API

The *Application Programmer's Interface* (API) is a part of the Windows and NT operating systems. It's filled with functions that you can use from within your ActiveX controls. There are three primary reasons that you will sometimes want to go beyond the functionality built into VB and resort to the API:

* The API can provide services that VB doesn't include.
* The API can be faster.
* The API can be more efficient.

You've already used the API once in this book when you created the TimeMinder component in Chapter 12. In creating that component, you wanted to permit the user to play any .WAV file when a TimeItem was elapsed, so you included the API function sndPlaySound. VB by itself can't play .WAV files.

Now you can explore the API further and, in the process, learn how to use VB's API Viewer utility to avoid typos. VB provides no syntax-checking when you're calling the API, yet API calls are frequently long and complex (and remember: The Declare statement that adds an API function to your VB program *must be on a single line — do not press the Enter key*.) Difficult to type in, API Declares are not in VB's vocabulary, so it can't warn you of any syntax errors.

How to Use the API Viewer

Fortunately, VB's API Viewer assists you by providing lists of all API Constants, Declares, and Types. You can directly insert these elements into your VB source code, eliminating the problem of typos from the Declares. This doesn't, of course, prevent typos in the *arguments* you provide to your API calls from the main source code.

If you're having problems with an API call, double-check the *arguments* following your call to the API in your main source code. The arguments' *names* need not match, but all the variable types must match. You can't use an Integer variable argument in the location where a Long variable type is called for in the Declare, for example.

To see how to use the API Viewer and how to make a highly efficient ActiveX DLL, you can try creating a different version of a UserControl you created earlier. In Chapter 7 you experimented with a framing control. To create it, you subclassed a PictureBox and a CommandButton. This approach works well enough if a developer is only using a couple of these frames in a project. But if the developer wants to use dozens of your frame controls, system resources and memory will suffer. CommandButtons, especially PictureBoxes, put a strain on the computer. They require that the system check for many events and support dozens of properties. And, of course, they eat up memory as well. (PictureBoxes are notorious resource hogs. For that reason Visual Basic added the lighter, though less feature-full, Image control.) The DLL component you'll build now provides framing services at a greatly reduced cost in run-time and memory overhead.

Try the following easy, fast, and efficient way to draw frames. You can use the API to get the current system colors (for such things as shadows and highlights) and combine that with VB's Line command to draw three different kinds of frames, at any position around any control.

Follow these steps to build the Framing object:

1. Start VB running and choose ActiveX DLL as the component type.

2. Change the name *Class1* to **Frame**.

3. Click | Project | → | Project1 Properties |.

4. Change the project name to **FrameDLL** and then click OK to close the dialog box.

Create Three Methods

Your DLL is going to provide three kinds of frames so you can create three methods for the Frame class: Extruding, Intruding, and Etched. When a developer displays them, they will look like the three examples in Figure 16-1.

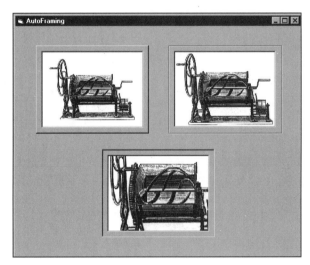

Figure 16-1   Three drawn frames: (from top left) extruding, etched, and intruding.

To create three methods for the Frame class, follow these steps:

1. Click | Add-Ins | → | Class Builder Utility |.

2. Click Frame to select it.

3. Click the flying green eraser icon to add a new method.

4. Name this method **Extruding** and give it three arguments: Container As Object, Them As Object, and Fudge as Integer. Click OK to close the dialog box.

5. Click the flying green eraser icon again to add a second method named

Intruding and give it the same three arguments.

6. Finally, add a third method named **Etched** and give it those same three arguments, too.

7. Close the Class Builder and agree to update the project.

There should now be three Subs in your source code, one for each method. You did not request a Return data type when creating these methods in the Class Builder, so the methods were made into Subs rather than Functions. Usually it's good practice to raise errors or return an error message if the developer or user provides the wrong data type to one of your functions. However, for purposes of illustration in this example, you'll display a message box instead.

You'll want the frame to conform to whatever system color settings the user has chosen as his or her personal Windows settings. The highlight, background (Window color or Buttonface color — by default the standard Windows battle-ship gray), and shadow colors can vary, depending on what desktop color scheme the user has selected. VB has no provision for getting this color scheme, so you'll have to resort to an API call.

The API call you employ to retrieve the user's system colors is named GetSysColor. Use VB's API Viewer utility to insert the necessary API Declares.

Follow these steps to insert an API Declare into your source code:

1. With the code window open, click at the very top (above all three Subs) so you create an insertion point (in the General Declarations section of the code window) where the Declare will be copied into your source code.

2. Click `Add-Ins` → `API Viewer`. (If it's not on the list of available Add-Ins, click Add-In Manager and select it from the list. If it's not on the list, use Explorer to locate it on the VB5 CD-ROM in the VB\WINAPI subdirectory. Double-click APILOAD.EXE to run it.)

3. Select `Load Text File` from the API Viewer's `File` menu.

4. Locate the text file WIN32API.TXT in your VB5\WINAPI subdirectory (or on the CD-ROM).

5. Load the text file into the API Viewer.

6. Click the Search button and type **GetSysColor**.

7. When GetSysColor appears in the Available Items list, double-click it to move it to the Selected Items list.

8. Click the Insert button and agree to insert it into your Frame class by clicking the Yes button, as shown in Figure 16-2.

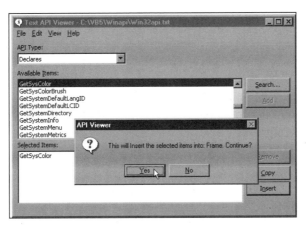

Figure 16-2 Say yes, you do want to insert the GetSysColor Declare into your source code.

Declares Must Be Private

VB wants Declares within class modules (or within Forms) to be Private, so type **Private** right before the word *Declare*. (Only within Modules can you make Declares, Constants or Type variables Public.) At this point, your source code should look like this:

```
Private Declare Function GetSysColor Lib "user32" (ByVal nIndex As
   Long) As Long

Public Sub Etched(Container As Object, Them As Object, Fudge As
   Integer)
End Sub

Public Sub Intruding(Container As Object, Them As Object, Fudge As
   Integer)
End Sub

Public Sub Extruding(Container As Object, Them As Object, Fudge As
   Integer)
End Sub
```

Just below the Declare Function line in the General Declarations section of your code, create the following four private variables that will hold the current system colors you'll use to draw frames:

```
Private HiLite As Long
Private DarkColor As Long
Private ShadowColor As Long
Private WindowColor As Long
```

You can get these system colors, if you wish, in the Initialize event, so type in the following:

```
Private Sub Class_Initialize()
HiLite = GetSysColor(20)
DarkColor = GetSysColor(16)
ShadowColor = GetSysColor(21)
WindowColor = GetSysColor(15) 'normal background
End Sub
```

Now to complete this DLL project, fill in the programming for each of the three methods. First do the Extruding method, like this:

```
Public Sub Extruding(Container As Object, Them As Object, Fudge As
    Integer)
' Container is the form on which the Them object resides
' Them is the control to frame
' Fudge is the number of pixels away from Them to draw the frame


'The caller's AutoRedraw should be set to True and its scalemode
    to 3.

If Container.ScaleMode <> 3 Then
MsgBox "You must set the Form's ScaleMode to 3, pixels"
Exit Sub
End If

If Container.AutoRedraw <> True Then
MsgBox "You must set the Form's AutoRedraw to True"
Exit Sub
End If

scw = Them.Width + Them.Left + Fudge
sch = Them.Height + Them.Top + Fudge
startx = Them.Left - Fudge
starty = Them.Top - Fudge


Container.Line (startx, starty)-(scw, starty), HiLite 'across top
Container.Line (startx, starty)-(startx, sch), HiLite 'down left

Container.Line (scw - 1, starty)-(scw - 1, sch), ShadowColor
    'right side
Container.Line (scw - 1, sch - 1)-(startx - 1, sch - 1),
    ShadowColor 'bottom line
```

```
Container.Line (scw - 2, starty + 1)-(scw - 2, sch - 2), DarkColor
    'right side
Container.Line (scw - 2, sch - 2)-(startx, sch - 2), DarkColor
    'bottom line

End Sub
```

What the Developer Provides

The developer provides three arguments: `Me`, `Me.control`, and `Fudge factor`. Whenever you pass the Me command, you are passing an "object variable" that refers to a particular object. In this case, the Me command passes the developer's Form object, and the developer should put the Me command into the argument Container.

NOTE   **The Me command is often useful as a way of passing a reference to a particular Form. Also, if you've instantiated more than one instance of a class, passing Me is a way of identifying which instance is calling.**

The developer also passes an object reference to the control that is to be framed on the Me Form. This is the *Them* argument, and it is passed from the client in this fashion: Me.Text1 or Me.Label1. Finally, the developer passes an Integer to the argument *Fudge*. This argument tells your method how many pixels out from the border of the control you want the frame drawn.

Next you check to see that the developer has set AutoRedraw to True on the Form that will contain the frame (so the frame won't be erased after being covered up by another window). You also ask that the ScaleMode be set to Pixels.

Then you calculate how wide to draw the frame by adding the Fudge factor to the Left and Width properties of the control being framed. The height of the frame is similarly calculated. Finally, the six lines necessary to create an extruded frame are drawn.

I arrived at the specifications for these lines by doing a screen capture of a CommandButton (it has an extrusion frame) and enlarging it in a drawing application so I could see the colors of the various frame lines and, in particular, how these lines intersected at the lower-left and upper-right corners. I used a TextBox to determine the calculations for an intruding frame (there are eight lines necessary for that effect). For an etched frame, a VB Frame control was examined.

A Quick Test

Before completing the other two methods, you can test this first method if you wish, just to make sure you're on the right track. Test it the same way you test most ActiveX components, by adding a Standard EXE-type project to the existing component project.

Follow these steps to test the Extruding frame method:

1. Click File → AddProject .

2. In the Project Explorer, right-click Project1 and choose Set as Start Up.

3. Click Project → References .

4. Click FrameDLL to activate it within Project1 (the Standard EXE that you'll use to test your DLL).

5. Click OK to close the dialog box.

6. Put a CommandButton on Project1's Form.

7. Double-click the CommandButton to get to its Click event and type in the following:

```
Private Sub Command1_Click()
Dim objFrameit As New FrameDLL.Frame
objFrameit.extruding Me, Me.Command1, 2
objFrameit.extruding Me, Me.Text1, 2
End Sub
```

8. Press F5 to run the Standard EXE, and you get the error message that you must first set Form1's ScaleMode to Pixels.

9. Stop the program and use the Properties window to change Form1's AutoRedraw Property to True and its ScaleMode to 3.

10. Press F5 again, and you see the extruding frame created around your CommandButton, as shown in Figure 16-3.

Figure 16-3 Success. Extruding frames are drawn two pixels out from your CommandButton and ten from the TextBox.

The other two methods are similar. Here's the source code for the Intruding method:

```
Public Sub Intruding(Container As Object, Them As Object, Fudge As
    Integer)

If Container.ScaleMode <> 3 or Container.AutoRedraw <> True Then
MsgBox "You must set the Form's ScaleMode to 3, pixels and its
```

```
    AutoRedraw to True"
Exit Sub
End If


scw = Them.Width + Them.Left + Fudge
sch = Them.Height + Them.Top + Fudge
startx = Them.Left - Fudge
starty = Them.Top - Fudge
Container.Line (startx, starty)-(scw, starty), DarkColor 'across
    top
Container.Line (startx + 1, starty + 1)-(scw, starty + 1),
    ShadowColor
Container.Line (startx, starty)-(startx, sch), DarkColor
Container.Line (startx + 1, starty + 1)-(startx + 1, sch),
    ShadowColor

Container.Line (scw - 1, starty)-(scw - 1, sch), HiLite 'right
    side
Container.Line (scw - 1, sch - 1)-(startx - 1, sch - 1), HiLite
    'bottom line
Container.Line (scw - 2, starty + 1)-(scw - 2, sch - 2),
    WindowColor 'right side
Container.Line (scw - 2, sch - 2)-(startx, sch - 2), WindowColor
    'bottom line


End Sub
```

And finally, here's the Etched method. It requires that only five lines be drawn:

```
Public Sub Etched(Container As Object, Them As Object, Fudge As
    Integer)

If Container.ScaleMode <> 3 or Container.AutoRedraw <> True Then
MsgBox "You must set the Form's ScaleMode to 3, pixels and its
    AutoRedraw to True"
Exit Sub
End If


scw = Them.Width + Them.Left + Fudge
sch = Them.Height + Them.Top + Fudge
startx = Them.Left - Fudge
starty = Them.Top - Fudge
Container.Line (startx, starty)-(scw, sch), DarkColor, B 'make box

Container.Line (startx + 1, starty + 1)-(scw, starty + 1), HiLite
```

```
'top
Container.Line (startx + 1, starty + 1)-(startx + 1, sch), HiLite
   'left
Container.Line (scw + 1, starty)-(scw + 1, sch + 1), HiLite 'right
   side
Container.Line (scw + 1, sch + 1)-(startx - 1, sch + 1), HiLite
   'bottom line

End Sub
```

You'll notice a certain amount of source code duplication among the three methods Extruding, Intruding, and Etched. The test for ScaleMode and AutoRedraw and the calculations of the height and width of the frames are repeated in each method. If you prefer, you could collapse all three Subs into a single method. You'd have to add a fourth argument that the developer would be required to supply (call it *FrameType* or something), and then, based on the requested frame type, you would use an If. . .Then or Case structure to branch to the correct line-drawing code segment.

Extra Styles

The Frame component can be used in various ways. You can combine frames to create classic, molded frames, as shown in Figure 16-4.

Figure 16-4 Call several methods at once to draw molded frames like this.

This code created the framing effect shown in Figure 16-4.

```
Private Sub Form_Load()
Dim objFrameit As New FrameDLL.Frame
objFrameit.etched Me, Me.Image1, 2
objFrameit.intruding Me, Me.Image1, 10
objFrameit.extruding Me, Me.Image1, 15
objFrameit.extruding Me, Me.Image1, 18
```

```
objFrameit.extruding Me, Me.Image1, 28
End Sub
```

In commercial Windows applications, you often see several controls grouped together into a logical zone. This is often done to create a visual grouping of controls that, working together, accomplish a single job or set a user preference. It's easy enough to frame a group of controls by first enclosing them within a Frame control, as shown in Figure 16-5.

Figure 16-5 To frame a group of controls, enclose them within an invisible control.

Set the Frame's Visible property to False so it won't show up during run time. You're merely interested in using it to establish the position of the frame you're drawing. Notice that the VB Frame control measures its top from the top of its caption, so bunch the enclosed controls upward, as shown in Figure 16-5. Also, be sure to create the controls *on the Form* not within an existing Frame (or they'll be invisible during run time). Move the group of controls onto the Frame. Then pass Frame1 as the Them argument, like this:

```
Private Sub Form_Load()
Dim objFrameit As New FrameDLL.Frame
objFrameit.intruding Me, Me.Frame1, 1
End Sub
```

You'll get the result shown in Figure 16-6.

Figure 16-6 A framed group tells the user: These controls work together logically.

Colored Frames

What if you want colored frames? Adding color is not that hard to do — you just need to use some additional API calls. Create a "solid brush" (an API feature that provides a solid color). Then use the API FillRect function to pour the color into the frame.

Add these three API Declares in boldface to the Frame class, so the General Declarations section looks like this:

```
Private Declare Function CreateSolidBrush Lib "gdi32" (ByVal
    crColor As Long) As Long
Private Declare Function DeleteObject Lib "gdi32" (ByVal hObject
    As Long) As Long
Private Declare Function FillRect Lib "user32" (ByVal hdc As Long,
    lpRect As RECT, ByVal hBrush As Long) As Long
Private Declare Function GetSysColor Lib "user32" (ByVal nIndex As
    Long) As Long
Private HiLite As Long
Private DarkColor As Long
Private ShadowColor As Long
Private WindowColor As Long
```

The FillRect API function requires a Type structure that defines the dimensions of the rectangle you want to fill. You have to put a user-defined Type variable in a Module (you can't declare it in a class module). So select Add Module from VB's Project menu, and then type the following into the Module:

```
Type RECT
    Left As Long
    Top As Long
    Right As Long
    Bottom As Long
End Type
```

Go back to the Frame class module by clicking it in the Project Explorer. To fill an Intruding-style frame, you'll want to change the arguments to add a color argument that the user can pass. If the Colr argument is zero, the frame will not be colored. Change the arguments line like this:

```
Public Sub Intruding(Container As Object, Them As Object, Fudge As
    Integer, Colr As Long)
```

Now add the following code that appears in boldface to the Intruding method to describe the rectangle you want filled:

```
scw = Them.Width + Them.Left + Fudge
sch = Them.Height + Them.Top + Fudge
startx = Them.Left - Fudge
```

```
starty = Them.Top - Fudge

Dim rec As RECT
rec.Left = startx + 2
rec.Top = starty + 2
rec.Right = scw - 2
rec.Bottom = sch - 2

Container.Line (startx, starty)-(scw, starty), DarkColor 'across
   top
Container.Line (startx + 1, starty + 1)-(scw, starty + 1),
   ShadowColor
Container.Line (startx, starty)-(startx, sch), DarkColor
Container.Line (startx + 1, starty + 1)-(startx + 1, sch),
   ShadowColor

Container.Line (scw - 1, starty)-(scw - 1, sch), HiLite 'right
   side
Container.Line (scw - 1, sch - 1)-(startx - 1, sch - 1), HiLite
   'bottom line
Container.Line (scw - 2, starty + 1)-(scw - 2, sch - 2),
   WindowColor 'right side
Container.Line (scw - 2, sch - 2)-(startx, sch - 2), WindowColor
   'bottom line
```

The Intruding-style frame uses up two pixels on all four sides to draw the frame. You can see this in the preceding Container.Line commands. Therefore, the RECT is defined as Startx (the left side of the frame) + 2 and Starty (the top) + 2. Likewise, you subtract 2 from the right side and the bottom of the frame.

Then insert the following lines at the bottom of the Intruding Sub:

```
If Colr = 0 Then Exit Sub 'they don't want any fill
Dim z As Long
z = CreateSolidBrush(Colr)
n = FillRect(Container.hdc, rec, z) 'paint in the color
f = DeleteObject(z) 'kill the brush
End Sub
```

When the developer calls the Intruding method, the color should be supplied as the final argument if a fill is desired:

```
Private Sub Form_Load()
Dim objFrameit As New FrameDLL.Frame
objFrameit.intruding Me, Me.Image3, 10, RGB(2, 34, 111)
End Sub
```

Or the developer could supply *vbMagenta* or one of the other color constants built into VB.

If you decide to add a color-fill feature to the Extruding method, make all the changes you made to the Intruding method. But the RECT structure is different: Add and subtract 2 from the right and bottom, but add and subtract only 1 from the top and left, like this:

```
Dim rec As RECT
rec.Left = startx + 1
rec.Top = starty + 1
rec.Right = scw - 2
rec.Bottom = sch - 2
```

To add a color-fill to the Etched method, reverse the RECT assignments made for the Extruding method: add and subtract 2 from the top and left, but only 1 from the right and bottom, like this:

```
Dim rec As RECT
rec.Left = startx + 2
rec.Top = starty + 2
rec.Right = scw - 1
rec.Bottom = sch - 1
```

Pure API

In the preceding examples you've used the Basic Line command to draw the frames. If you prefer, you can go directly to the API for frame line-drawing. The API includes several useful functions you can call to draw various kinds of frames. The GetClientRect function tells you the size and position of the client (container). In the example that follows, you'll pass the hWnd (the handle to the window of the Form); you want the measurements of the Form itself. GetClientRect then puts the Form's dimensions into the special user-defined variable named RECT. RECT contains four interior variables: Left, Top, Right, and Bottom.

Once you have the position and size of the Form, you can adjust that RECT by using the InflateRect API call. Provide negative values (or even 0 or 1) and the RECT specifications will shrink (reverse inflation). Set the two values within InflateRect to specify the size of the frame you want to display.

Finally, the DrawEdge call creates the frame, based on the RECT specifications, and the edge type specified (bump, etched, raised, or sunken — as defined by four API Constants). You also supply the start positions (topleft and bottom-right) for the frame drawing.

```
Private Declare Function GetClientRect Lib "user32" (ByVal hwnd As
    Long, lpRect As RECT) As Long
Private Declare Function DrawEdge& Lib "user32" (ByVal hDC As
```

```
Long, qrc As RECT, ByVal edge As Long, ByVal grfFlags As Long)
Private Declare Function InflateRect Lib "user32" (lpRect As RECT,
    ByVal x As Long, ByVal y As Long) As Long


Private Const EDGE_BUMP = &H9&
Private Const EDGE_ETCHED = &H6&
Private Const EDGE_RAISED = &H5&
Private Const EDGE_SUNKEN = &HA&
Private Const BF_TOPLEFT = &H3
Private Const BF_BOTTOMRIGHT = &HC


Private Type RECT
        Left As Long
        Top As Long
        Right As Long
        Bottom As Long
End Type


Private Sub Form_Load()
    AutoRedraw = True
    Dim r As Long, rx As RECT
    r = GetClientRect(hwnd, rx)
    r = InflateRect(rx, -12, -12)
    r = DrawEdge(hDC, rx, EDGE_ETCHED, BF_TOPLEFT)
    r = DrawEdge(hDC, rx, EDGE_ETCHED, BF_BOTTOMRIGHT)

End Sub
```

For a layered frame, just repeat the final three lines, adjusting the InflateRect variables and, perhaps, the edge specification in the DrawEdge call.

User-Drawn Controls

Sometimes called *other-drawn,* this is the most radical kind of ActiveX component. You build it from the ground up. You start out with a blank UserControl and *you*, the creator of the component, write programming that draws the appearance of the control. You can subclass existing controls into a user-drawn control, but they must remain invisible. You *can* use the invisible subclassed control's methods and properties (by mapping them). However, if you make a subclassed control visible, your user-drawn surface can no longer get the focus at run time.

When you create a user-drawn control, you have great freedom. In the UserControl's Paint or ReSize events, you write programming that creates the appearance of the control. This programming, and additional programming that defines methods and properties of the user-drawn component can, of course, make use of both the facilities built into VB as well as the vast storehouse of functions available via the Windows API described earlier in this chapter.

Make an Improved Label from Scratch

To see how to create a user-drawn control, you can create an improved Label control. You won't subclass (map) the existing VB Label control. Instead, you'll create a new Label, called SuperMsg, from scratch. When you work at this low level, you can build in any kind of appearance or behaviors you wish. The UserControl object itself has many built-in properties, methods, and events that you can map (borrow). You'll map its AutoRedraw, ForeColor, BackColor, and Font properties.

A UserControl also has a BorderStyle property that, when set to 1, draws a recessed 3D frame like the one around a standard TextBox. This is the kind of frame you created earlier in this chapter, calling it *Intruding*. This isn't a good border style for a label-type control, though. Windows has a convention (often violated) that a recessed control (TextBox, OptionButton, or CheckBox) indicates that the user is expected to type something in or provide some information. These *input* controls also usually feature a white backcolor. By contrast, controls that provide information to the user (output) usually feature a gray backcolor and, somewhat less often, an extruding frame. You'll create an extruding frame for your SuperMsg control.

A UserControl has no Caption or Text property, so you'll use an API call to create a Message property for the SuperMsg component.

Grant Your Own Wishes

When you're designing a control from scratch, you get to grant yourself wishes. You're not just inheriting existing features (and limitations) of an existing control; you're authoring a brand new control. What do you want in a Label? One thing that always bothers me about VB's Label control is that its Alignment property centers the Label's text horizontally, but not vertically. Your SuperMsg control will center its message in both directions.

Let the Developer Specify Size and Position

The SuperMsg will be single-line (no line wrapping). You'll leave the positioning of the SuperBox to the developer. It's usually preferable to let the developer (programming in the container) define the size of a UserControl. It's *always* preferable to let the developer define the position within the container or Form.

Follow these steps to user-draw your control:

1. Start VB running or press Ctrl+N to start a new project.

2. Choose ActiveX Control.

3. To map the Font, ForeColor, and BackColor properties of the UserControl, Click **Add-Ins** → **ActiveX Control Interface Wizard** .

4. Click Next to get to the Select Interface Members dialog box.

5. Move all the members in the right list (Selected Names) to the left list (Available Names) by clicking the lowest button with the << symbol on it.

6. Now hold down the Ctrl key while clicking the following available names: AutoRedraw, BackColor, Font, ForeColor, TextHeight, and TextWidth. TextHeight and TextWidth provide you with the precise measurement of the current Message in the current FontSize. This information enables you to center the message within the SuperMsg control.

7. Click Next, and then click New and add a custom member named **Message**. Make it a property. Click OK and then click Next.

8. Map all the members to UserControl except Message. Click Next.

9. Define the Data Type of the Message property as a String and set the default to "SuperMsg" (erase the default 0).

10. Click Next and then click Finish.

    Your source code should now include all the members you mapped, plus a WriteProperties/ReadProperties pair that preserves the settings of the properties, and finally, your custom Message property.

11. Use the API Viewer (described earlier in this chapter) to insert the following API Declares at the very top of the UserControl's code window (in the General Declarations section):

```
Private Declare Function TextOut Lib "gdi32" Alias "TextOutA"
(ByVal hdc As Long, ByVal x As Long, ByVal y As Long, ByVal
lpString As String, ByVal nCount As Long) As Long
Private Declare Function CreateSolidBrush Lib "gdi32" (ByVal
crColor As Long) As Long
Private Declare Function DeleteObject Lib "gdi32" (ByVal
hObject As Long) As Long
Private Declare Function GetSysColor Lib "user32" (ByVal nIndex
As Long) As Long
Private Declare Function FillRect Lib "user32" (ByVal hdc As
Long, lpRect As RECT, ByVal hBrush As Long) As Long
Private HiLite As Long
```

```
Private DarkColor As Long
Private ShadowColor As Long
Private WindowColor As Long
'Default Property Values:
Const m_def_message = "SuperMsg"
'Property Variables:
Dim m_message As String
Use a Windows Brush
```

Notice that the various framing colors are also given Private variable names here. The TextOut API call paints text onto the screen, so it will be used to display the Message within the SuperMsg control. The CreateSolidBrush API call assigns a color to a Windows "brush" that will be used to fill in the BackColor of the UserControl. This filling is necessary, or remnant lines will appear within the SuperMsg when the developer resizes it. The DeleteObject API call gets rid of the brush (much as you Set Object = Nothing when you're finished using an object). Finally, the FillRect API function fills a rectangular area on the screen with the current brush color and pattern, if any. You're using a solid brush.

The following code assigns Windows the default color scheme to the various frame-drawing colors. It also changes the UserControl's ScaleMode from the default twips to pixels. The API uses pixels for its graphics functions:

1. Type the following into the Initialize event:

```
Private Sub UserControl_Initialize()
HiLite = GetSysColor(20)
DarkColor = GetSysColor(16)
ShadowColor = GetSysColor(21)
WindowColor = GetSysColor(15) 'normal background
ScaleMode = 3 'set to pixels
'The UserControl's AutoRedraw should be set to True
End Sub
```

2. Select Add Module from VB's Project menu, and then type the following into the Module:

```
Type RECT
    Left As Long
    Top As Long
    Right As Long
    Bottom As Long
End Type
```

3. Close the Module and go back to the UserControl's code window.

4. Use the Property window to set the UserControl's AutoRedraw property to True and change its Name to SuperMsg.

Most of the action takes place in the Resize event:

```
Private Sub UserControl_Resize()

scw = UserControl.ScaleWidth
sch = UserControl.ScaleHeight

'calculate center for message
tw = UserControl.TextWidth(message) / 2
th = UserControl.TextHeight(message) / 2
tw = (scw / 2) - tw
th = (sch / 2) - th

Line (0, 0)-(scw, 0), HiLite 'across top
Line (0, 0)-(0, sch), HiLite 'down left

Line (scw - 1, 0)-(scw - 1, sch), ShadowColor 'right side
Line (scw - 1, sch - 1)-(0 - 1, sch - 1), ShadowColor 'bottom line
Line (scw - 2, 0 + 1)-(scw - 2, sch - 2), DarkColor 'right side
Line (scw - 2, sch - 2)-(0, sch - 2), DarkColor 'bottom line


Dim rec As RECT
rec.Left = startx + 2
rec.Top = starty + 2
rec.Right = scw - 2
rec.Bottom = sch - 2

Dim z As Long, flgs As Long
z = CreateSolidBrush(BackColor)
n = FillRect(UserControl.hdc, rec, z) 'paint in the color
f = DeleteObject(z) 'kill the brush


z = TextOut(UserControl.hdc, tw, th, message, Len(message))

End Sub
```

Most of this code will be familiar to you from the discussion on framing earlier in this chapter. The calculation of the variables *tw* and *th* provides an x,y coordinate used by the TextOut function to print the Message property in the center of the SuperMsg control.

Now you want to add a line to the Let BackColor, Let ForeColor, Let Message, and Set Font procedures that will trigger the Resize event. This way, when the developer changes any of those properties — either during design time or at run time — the change will be displayed at once in the SuperMsg control.

5. At the bottom of those four procedures, just above the End Property command, type **UserControl_Resize**, like this:

```
Public Property Set Font(ByVal New_Font As Font)
   Set UserControl.Font = New_Font
   PropertyChanged "Font"
UserControl_Resize
End Property
```

TIP Note that in the ReadProperties procedure, the line that reads the message should be near the top. If it's at the bottom of that procedure, the Resize event won't display a message during run time (unless it is changed in the source code). Remember that properties set during design time in the Properties window are saved to a "PropertyBag" and then read back at the start of run time. If the line that reads the message is near the bottom of the ReadProperties procedure, the Resize event will have done its job before the default message is read. So the Resize event will see an empty message (""). The ReadProperties procedure should look something like this:

```
'Load property values from storage
Private Sub UserControl_ReadProperties(PropBag As PropertyBag)
   m_Message = PropBag.ReadProperty("Message", m_def_Message)
   UserControl.ForeColor = PropBag.ReadProperty("ForeColor",
   &H80000012)
   Set Font = PropBag.ReadProperty("Font", Ambient.Font)
   UserControl.BackColor = PropBag.ReadProperty("BackColor",
   &H8000000F)
   UserControl.AutoRedraw = PropBag.ReadProperty("AutoRedraw",
   True)
End Sub
```

Test the User-Drawn Control

You can test this UserControl the usual way. Select Add Project from the File menu and then add a Standard EXE-type project. Close the SuperMsg design window so its icon appears on the ToolBox. Add a SuperMsg to Form1 of the Standard EXE project. Try adjusting its properties in the Property window, and then try running it. You'll see something like Figure 16-7.

TIP Figure 16-7 shows gradient and drop-shadow effects. To create them, take a screen capture of the Form (with Alt+PrintScrn), use a graphics application to add the shadow, and save the result as a .BMP file that you then load into the Picture property of the Form. The shadow appears behind the SuperMsg control (see the Bonus at the end of Chapter 3).

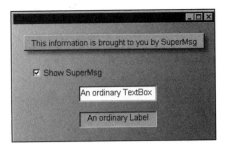

Figure 16-7 The SuperMsg control centers its text automatically. Notice that a regular Label cannot center text vertically.

BONUS

Containment and Aggregation

The topics in this Bonus section are rather subtle and abstract. However, you may find that they help you strengthen the encapsulation of your code and demonstrate useful ways to organize your ActiveX components.

Recall that all objects are not created equal. Sometimes you have a class that uses another class. A collection class is often used by a separate class — as a way of providing or storing data.

Say you have a method in one class that several other classes need to use. If you're thinking in the older, procedure-oriented way, you might say, "Why not make that method into a Public function instead of burying it as a method in one particular object?" Creating a Public function is not good OOP; it causes maintenance problems similar to those engendered when you use Public variables. It represents a failure to encapsulate and protect a function.

Another possible solution when several objects need to use a single method would be to copy and paste the method's code into each object that needs it. In other words, several objects might have identical code copied into Private, duplicate methods. However, this, too, is not good OOP practice. The problem is, if you have to make a change to that code, you'd have to make the same change in each of the various locations where it is duplicated. And you might neglect one or make an error typing. You're inviting difficulties.

Containment Is One Solution

There are several OOP solutions to the problem of sharing methods or properties. One way to do it is called *containment*. This solution means you make one object's members available only to its "container" object. If another component wants to use some of the members of the inner component, it must request these services from the outer, container component.

To see containment in action, follow these steps:

1. Start off with a Standard EXE project.

2. Click Project → Add Class Module .

3. Click Add-Ins → Class Builder Utility .

4. Click Class1 to select it, and then click the button at the far left to Add New Class. This new class, automatically named Class2, will be *contained* within Class1 (because Class1 was selected when you created Class2).

5. Give Class2 a method named **WriteIt**.

6. Close the Class Builder and type in the following line to give Class2's WriteIt method something to do:

```
Public Sub WriteIt()
MsgBox "Written."
End Sub
```

Now look at Class1's code. Here is how VB creates a contained class:

```
Private mvarClass2 As Class2

Private Sub Class_Initialize()
   'create the mClass2 object when the Class1 class is created
   Set mvarClass2 = New Class2
End Sub

Public Property Get Class2() As Class2
   Set Class2 = mvarClass2
End Property

Public Property Set Class2(vData As Class2)
   Set mvarClass2 = vData
End Property

Private Sub Class_Terminate()
   Set mvarClass2 = Nothing
End Sub
```

VB has turned Class2 into *a property of Class1*. Therefore, if a client wants to use the Write property of Class2, it must go through Class1 to get to Class2.

7. Type the following into Form1's Click event, and then press F5 and run the project:

```
Private Sub Form_Click()
Dim objClass1 As New Class1

objClass1.Class2.WriteIt

End Sub
```

Recall that VB calls a structure like this Class2-within-Class1 hierarchy an *object model*. Though similar, containment is not true OOP inheritance.

A collection class, however, demonstrates a slightly different kind of containment. You explored this technique in Chapter 12 when you created a collection class to hold the TimeItems. Remember that you didn't make that collection available to the client. That project's Contact class interacted with the client. You didn't give the developer any direct access to the collection class. When the client wanted to make a new TimeItem and add it to the collection, the client had to *go through* Contact.

Note that when you go through one object to get to another (containment), there is some overhead. Execution speed can slow down, and, what's more, during design time clients must work with a more complex syntax. However, containment is a highly flexible programming technique. Less flexible is the similar technique called *aggregation*. When you aggregate two classes, one object is still contained within another, but you have no design-time or run-time inefficiencies because (unlike with containment) the inner object is exposed directly to clients.

Aggregation Exposes Itself Directly to a Client

As with containment, when employing the aggregation technique you instantiate an inner object every time the outer (container) object is instantiated. However, with aggregation you don't make the inner object a property of the outer object.

Let's say you have a Public class that produces objects called *OuterClass* and a Private class that produces objects called *InnerClass*. The InnerClass object can't be contacted directly by a client (the object is Private and can only respond to requests from other objects within its own component — its own project). However, InnerClass has a method that multiplies a number by two, and this job is sometimes needed by clients. A client can get to InnerClass only by going through OuterClass. The following is the code of InnerClass:

```
Public Function MultiplyByTwo(TheNumber As Variant) As Variant
MultiplyByTwo = TheNumber * 2
End Function
```

Note that although this Function is Public, no client can get to it. That's because the Instancing property of InnerClass is Private — sealing off all its members from everyone except other classes within the same component. And, in this same component, is a class named OuterClass.

OuterClass's Instancing is Public (MultiUse), so clients can indeed make use of any of its Public members. And OuterClass has a way for clients to get to InnerClass's MultiplyByTwo method. Here's OuterClass's code:

```
Private objInner As New InnerClass

Public Function MultiplyByTwo(TheNumber As Variant) As Variant
MultiplyByTwo = objInner.MultiplyByTwo(TheNumber)
End Function
```

THE CONTAINER AUTOMATICALLY GENERATES THE CONTAINED

Whenever OuterClass is created (by a client), it automatically creates an InnerClass object. This creation is the basis of both the containment and aggregation techniques: one object (an object that's instantiated as Public) generates another, inner object that isn't instantiated as Public. Remember that this generation is automatic and takes place any time an OuterClass object is instantiated.

As you can see, aggregation is quite similar to the collection class technique and also similar to the containment technique. The key difference is that with aggregation, a *method* in the outer class directly calls a method in the inner class. (With containment, a *property* in the outer class passes an object variable pointing to the InnerClass and thereby, indirectly, permits access to a method in the InnerClass.)

In this example of aggregation, when OuterClass's MultiplyByTwo method is requested by a client, it merely passes on the number that the client wants multiplied. OuterClass passes this number as the argument to InnerClass's MultiplyByTwo method. (These methods of the OuterClass and InnerClass objects could have different names, and so could their arguments.) Then the real work is done by InnerClass (TheNumber * 2) and the result goes back up the hierarchy to finally reach the client.

ERROR-CHECK OR MODIFY DATA

OuterClass could do some error-checking, or even modify the data that the client was presenting, if it wanted to.

Here's what the client's request looks like when contacting the server component (to test this component, put the following code in a Standard EXE project):

```
Private Sub Form_Load()
Dim objThing As New Project1.OuterClass
n = objThing. MultiplyByTwo (5)
MsgBox n
End Sub
```

The client instantiates OuterClass, and then sends the number 5 to OuterClass's MultiplyByTwo method. Of course, OuterClass doesn't do anything with that 5. It merely passes it through to InnerClass where the actual multiplication takes place. If you repeatedly press F8 to step through this Client-OuterClass-InnerClass-OuterClass-Client maneuver, you'd see the source code executed in the following steps:

The Client
```
Private Sub Form_Load()
Dim objThing As New Project1.outerclass
n = objThing.multiplybytwo(5)
```

OuterClass
```
Private objInner As New InnerClass
Public Function MultiplyByTwo(TheNumber As Variant) As Variant
MultiplyByTwo = objInner.MultiplyByTwo(TheNumber)
```

InnerClass
```
Public Function MultiplyByTwo(TheNumber As Variant) As Variant
MultiplyByTwo = TheNumber * 2
End Function
```

OuterClass
```
End Function
```

The Client
```
MsgBox n
End Sub
```

At the end, the message box in the client displays the number *10*.

Note that a public object like OuterClass can delegate a method to an InnerClass method, but OuterClass doesn't have to delegate. The OuterClass object might delegate some of its members to the InnerClass while providing source code of its own for other members. Or, OuterClass might simply choose not to present some members to the outer world at all.

Implements, a Powerful New Command

Finally, VB5 introduced yet another way to contain one object within another: the *Implements* command. Recall that a major reason to contain one object within another is that you avoid having to duplicate code. Instead of copying and pasting duplicate code into each object that needs to use it, you create a "lower-level" (contained) object that holds the code in only that one place. This is similar to the old procedure-oriented tactic of creating a global (Public) procedure that can be accessed by all areas within a project. However, OOP style prefers that you use one of the containment techniques instead.

A Simpler Technique

There are two ways to use the Implements command. The easiest to understand is when you use Implements to contain an inner class that has ordinary methods and properties. This kind of class is the normal object-factory you've been using throughout this book — it has source code for its various methods and properties.

The second way you can use Implements to contain an inner class is called an *abstract class*. This is a novel kind of class: It has *empty* methods and properties; there's no code in them. This is a way of implementing polymorphism. Abstract classes will be discussed shortly. First consider the simpler use of Implements.

To see how to use the simpler form of Implements, follow these steps:

1. Start a new project.

2. Make it a Standard EXE type.

3. Click Project → Add Class Module .

4. Leave its Name set to *Class1*, the default.

5. Look at Class1's code window. Drop the left (objects) list down and see two entities: General (Declarations) and Class1, as shown in Figure 16-8.

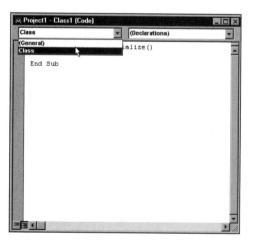

Figure 16-8 BEFORE: The objects list for Class1 lists only General and Class1.

Assume this program frequently needs to add 3 or subtract 3. Various places in your program will need to do this. You don't want to copy duplicate code in all those various places, so you create a class that does this adding and subtracting.

6. Start VB and select the Standard EXE project type.

7. Click Project → Add Class Module .

8. Change its Name from *Class1* to **MathObj**.

9. Type this into MathObj's code window, or use the Class Builder Utility to create these two methods:

```
Public Function AddThree(N As Variant) As Variant
AddThree = N + 3
End Function

Public Function SubtractThree(N As Variant) As Variant
SubtractThree = N - 3
End Function
```

10. Now go back to Class1's code window and add the Implements command to the General Declarations section of Class1:

```
Implements MathObj
```

11. Drop down the Class1's object list again and see that MathObj has been added to Class1 (*implemented* in Class1) and that Class1 now has all the Public members of MathObj identified as MathObj_AddThree and MathObj_SubtractThree (this underscore punctuation is customary when identifying implemented members of an inner class). You also see the MathObj's Public members listed in the right drop-down list, as shown in Figure 16-9.

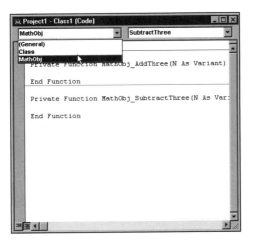

Figure 16-9 AFTER: MathObj has now been implemented in Class1.

12. You can now use aggregation to create an instance of the MathObj within Class1:

```
Implements MathObj
Private obj As New MathObj
Public Function MathObj_AddThree(N As Variant) As Variant
MathObj_AddThree = obj.AddThree(N)
End Function
```

13. Change the MathObj_AddThree method to **Public** and then pass the actual job to the obj.AddThree (the instance of MathObj) to carry out the work. This way, you can call this MathObj_AddThree method from a client. In Form1, type this:

```
Private Sub Form_Load()
Dim o As New Class1
MsgBox o.MathObj_AddThree(4)
End Sub
```

The value of this reusable interface is that you can insert MathObj (Implement it) into many other classes. Add a Class2 module and type **Implements MathObj** into Class2's General Declarations section. Now Class2 also has that pair of MathObj_AddThree and a MathObj_SubtractThree methods. This way you have created a kind of *polymorphism*. Different objects have members (methods or properties) with the same name and require the same arguments (though the objects might behave in individual ways when one of these members is invoked).

The Abstract Technique

This example has illustrated how you can combine Implements with aggregation to use the actual code within the MathObj class. As mentioned, there is a second way to use the Implements command.

Polymorphism means that several objects have a method (or property) that has the same name in each object and takes the same arguments. However, this method (or property) is specialized for each object and might behave in a different way for each object. The developer or client doesn't know anything about the low-level code that you've written to make each object behave in ways appropriate to its own nature. You could make this varying behavior happen in the preceding example by providing individual code in Class1 and Class2 for the MathObj_AddThree method (and not delegate the task to the MathObj at all). Or you could modify the result passed back after the MathObj finishes its work.

For example, what if you write an object that calculates a simple, graduated sales tax. The rule is: If something costs under $10, add $3. But if it costs over $10, add $4. Your SalesTax object can still Implement the MathObj. You can make use of MathObj's AddThree member, but you'll have to modify it a little, combining both delegation and some code of your own:

```
Public Function MathObj_AddThree(N As Variant) As Variant
MathObj_AddThree = obj.AddThree(N)
If N > 9 Then MathObj_AddThree = MathObj_AddThree + 1
End Function
```

Note that you can also Implement a class that's entirely abstract — it's going to be implemented by various other classes, but it contains no code of its own at all. It is a pure abstraction, a specification of members (an interface) but with no actual computational abilities of its own. An abstract class merely exists to provide an interface template for other classes to use.

Whenever a class includes the Implements command, that class must always provide some code within each Public member of the implemented class. For instance, in the preceding example, Class1 implemented the MathObj class. Therefore *Class1 must make sure that something happens when a client calls upon the implemented members MathObj_AddThree and MathObj_SubtractThree.* (Such is the case for Class2, since it also implements the MathObj.)

Class1 can simply pass the argument down to the inner object (MathObj) directly, delegating the job as you did in the preceding example. Or Class1 might execute some lines of code of its own before delegating. Or Class1 might execute some code of its own without delegating at all. That's up to you. But each member of an Implemented class's Public interface must be dealt with in some fashion. And, of course, if you're Implementing an *abstract* class, you cannot delegate — you're merely using the members' names. In an abstract class, there's no code that you can delegate to: an abstract class is pure interface.

Summary

In this chapter, you learned that if you want to go beyond the capabilities of Visual Basic itself, you can access a huge collection of functions built into the API, part of the Windows operating system. You learned how to use the API Viewer to avoid typos when inserting API Declare statements. Then you found out how to build controls from scratch, even how to create their appearance. Finally, you learned about some subtle ways to strengthen encapsulation in your projects.

ActiveX is a significant part of Microsoft's current strategy. As you've seen, ActiveX is a technology, a set of operating system features, a programming system, and a collection of objects you can plug into programs or Web pages. Whatever aspects of ActiveX interest you, I hope that this book has provided a solid foundation in the techniques, principles, and possibilities of this exciting and many-faceted technology.

16

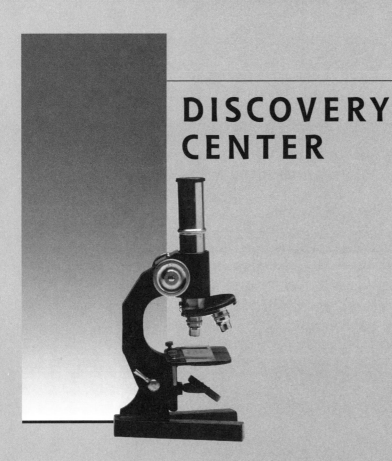

DISCOVERY CENTER

The Discovery Center serves as a handy reference to many of the significant points and step-by-step instructions that are key to mastering ActiveX. In this section, you'll find a review of some of the important elements covered in each chapter of Discover ActiveX. You also find page references to help you locate any additional information you might need on a particular topic.

CHAPTER 1

The first thing most people want to learn about ActiveX is how to use ActiveX controls in a Web page. Learning to create ActiveX components can be useful in most kinds of programming — not just for Internet documents. However, there's no doubt that ActiveX can be a valuable addition to your Web programming toolkit, so here's how to place several controls onto a Web page.

Adding ActiveX Controls to a Web Page (page 8)

Follow these steps to add TextBoxes and a Label to a Web page:

1. Start the ActiveX Control Pad. Follow the steps described in the Quick Tour at the beginning of this book to insert a Layout control into a Web page. Now display the Layout: Click the small icon next to the words <OBJECT CLASSID in the document in your ActiveX Control Pad. A Toolbox and a Form appear.

2. Pause your mouse pointer over the various controls in the Toolbox to see their names.

3. Click the item third from the left (the TextBox icon) in the top row of the Toolbox. Then drag your mouse on the Form to create a new TextBox. (Note that the icon will be third from the left if you haven't resized the Toolbox.)

4. Repeat this three more times so you have four TextBoxes on the Form.

5. Click the item second from the left (the Label icon) in the top row of the Toolbox. Drag a Label control onto the Form. Repeat three times for a total of four Labels.

6. Now drag and resize these TextBoxes and Labels so they're in the positions shown in the following figure. You can also resize the Layout if you wish.

7. To adjust the font and font size of each Label and TextBox, hold down the Ctrl key while clicking on each of the eight controls. This selects them all.

8. Right-click one of the controls and click Properties.

9. In the Properties window, double-click Font and change it to Arial. Then select 12 for Size. Click OK and then click the x icon in the upper-right corner to close the Properties window.

10. Close the Layout control. Then save the entire Page1.Htm file by clicking File → Save All .

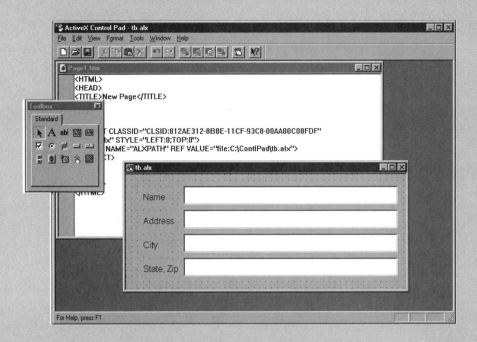

How to Test Web Pages Efficiently (page 16)

Even complicated Web pages can be tested directly in your browser. You don't have to post the pages onto an Internet site to test most features of Internet pages. When you load a page into your browser you'll see precisely how it looks, hear any audio, view any animation, interact with any controls or programming, and so on.

To take advantage of this useful and efficient testing loop, follow these steps:

1. Make an adjustment in the ActiveX Control Pad (or another page-creation editor).

2. Save the document to disk as an .HTM file.

3. Load that .HTM file into the Internet Explorer browser and try out its various features as an Internet surfer would.

4. Make further adjustments in your editor.

5. Press F5 to refresh (reload the document into) the browser.

6. Repeat Step 4 to make further improvements.

7. Repeat Steps 4 and 5 until the control works precisely the way it should.

This testing cycle is quite efficient because you can quickly test changes by just clicking the Refresh button in Internet Explorer (or pressing F5). This will reload and display the latest version of your page, including your recent changes.

CHAPTER 2

All versions of Visual Basic, and several other Microsoft products, including the ActiveX Control Pad's Layout control, feature a Toolbox with a basic set of useful controls. You can double-click any of these controls to place them onto the Layout control (or onto a Visual Basic Form). So if you intend to work with ActiveX, or Windows programming in general, you'll want to understand the properties and behaviors of this essential set of controls.

The Essential Toolbox Controls (page 22)

Follow these steps to get the ActiveX Control Pad Toolbox up and running:

1. Start the ActiveX Control Pad.

2. Click ⌊ File ⌋ → ⌊ New HTML Layout ⌋ (or press Ctrl+E).

You'll see the Layout control and Toolbox shown in the following figure.

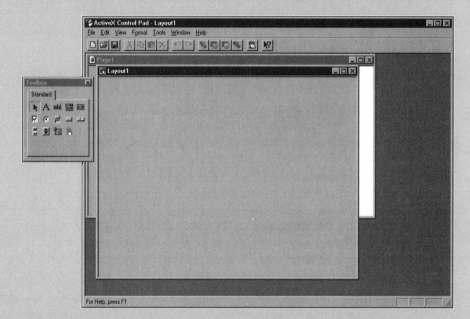

Now for a close-up of the Toolbox and its 13 controls.

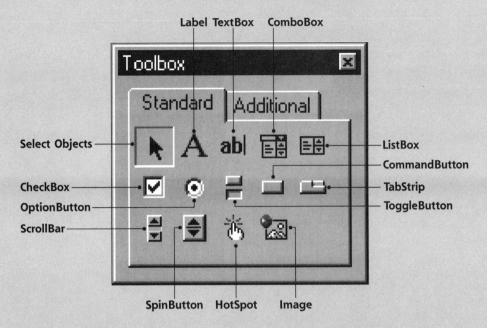

Label TextBox ComboBox

Select Objects

CheckBox

OptionButton

ScrollBar

ListBox

CommandButton

TabStrip

ToggleButton

SpinButton HotSpot Image

CHAPTER 3

A primary reason to use the ActiveX Control Pad to create a Web page or intranet site is that it includes the Layout control. With the Layout, you can easily position and size the Layout's collection of controls (from the Layout's Toolbox).

How to Add VBScript Programming to a Layout Control (page 50)

When you insert a Layout control into an HTML document using the Control Pad and then save that document, an .ALX file is automatically created. The .ALX file contains a definition of the Layout control, any additional controls contained by that Layout, and, optionally, some VBScript programming that you want carried out when the document containing the Layout is loaded into a browser.

You can add VBScript within the ActiveX Control Pad's main HTML document (the .HTM file), by using the Layout control's OnLoad event, like this:

```
<HTML>
<HEAD>
<TITLE>Page</TITLE>
</HEAD>

<SCRIPT LANGUAGE="VBScript">

Sub Layout1_OnLoad()
```

```
ListBox1.FontSize = 12

For i = 1 to 10
ListBox1.AddItem "Choice #" & i
Next
end sub

</SCRIPT>

</BODY>
</HTML>
```

But there's a simpler way to add programming to a Layout control. Any VB-Script commands that you put into the .ALX file of a Layout control will *automatically* be carried out when that Layout is loaded into a browser. It's not necessary to use an OnLoad event as a trigger. To accomplish the same thing as the preceding code (to fill the ListBox with ten choices), just add your programming directly to the Layout control's source code.

Follow these steps to insert programming directly into a Layout control's source code:

1. Start the ActiveX Control Pad. Click Edit → Insert HTML Layout . Name it **Test** and click the Open button. Click Yes when asked if you want to create a new Layout.

2. Click the icon next to the Layout HTML definition <OBJECT CLASSID. Put a ListBox onto the Layout control. Right-click the Layout control.

3. Select View Source Code.

4. The ActiveX Control Pad displays a message box informing you that it is about to save any changes you've made to the Layout. Click the button labeled Yes.

5. Windows' Notepad opens with the .ALX file loaded.

6. Type the following code into the .ALX file, at the end, below the final </DIV> command:

```
<SCRIPT LANGUAGE="VBScript">
ListBox1.AddItem "Printemps      $240"
ListBox1.AddItem "Fair Day       $350"
ListBox1.AddItem "Sandy Shores    $800"
ListBox1.AddItem "Alabama        $1200"
ListBox1.AddItem "Shrikes & Wrens $900"
ListBox1.AddItem "A Mid-day Repast  $400"
ListBox1.AddItem "Creatures      $200"
ListBox1.AddItem "Creatures #2     $200"
```

```
ListBox1.AddItem "Last Year's Snow $1800"
ListBox1.AddItem "Salamanders    $850"
</SCRIPT>
```

7. Save the results by clicking File → Save . Then close the Notepad.

8. From the ActiveX Control Pad's main window (with the .HTM document showing), click File → Save to save the entire .HTM document as **TEST.HTM**.

9. Load the TEST.HTM file into Internet Explorer by clicking File → Open .

CHAPTER 4

Anyone creating ActiveX controls must know the meaning of the three elements of any control: properties, methods, and events.

Properties Are Qualities (page 64)

To build a control, the designer first defines the set of qualities — the properties — that make up the control. Properties are things like color, font size, width, and other qualities.

Methods Are Behaviors (page 64)

Methods are jobs that a control knows how to accomplish. For example, if your control is supposed to be a cash converter, you'll teach it how to translate dollars into yen, and vice versa. Your converter control will have a DollarsToYen method and a YenToDollars method (or whatever other names you want to give these methods). You'll teach the converter how to perform the DollarsToYen method by writing some VBScript programming that looks at the digits the user types in, and then does the math to convert the user's dollar figure into yen. In other words, methods are procedures that a control can carry out.

Events Are Sensitivities (page 64)

You *sensitize* your control by giving it events to which it can react. Common events are: Click, Double-Click, Change, KeyDown, MouseDown, and Mouse-Move. You, the creator of a control, don't provide programming within an event. An event is a location where developers or programmers who use your control can, optionally, place some programming of their own. Perhaps a developer wants your converter calculator to change color every time it's clicked. Into the Click event, that developer places a line of VBScript programming that will assign a random color value to the control's BackColor property.

An ActiveX control has three levels of people interacting with it, and at each level there are more restrictions than the previous level.

LEVEL 1

The creator of a control has permission to do anything to it. At the creator level there are no restrictions. The creator defines what the control is, what it does, and what any subsequent user can do to or with it. This intimate relationship with all the nuts and bolts of an object is often called *low-level programming*. That doesn't mean it's simple, or somehow less significant than other levels of interaction. In fact, it means the opposite: Like an auto mechanic, a low-level programmer can get down into and under the object and has the understanding, and the permission, to make adjustments to virtually every aspect of the machine.

LEVEL 2

Developers who are using a prebuilt control are at the second level. Perhaps you're using the control as part of a Web page you're constructing, or maybe you're using it in a Windows application you're writing. You can define the control's behaviors and qualities only to the extent that the creator gave you permission. The creator decides which elements of the control to make available to programmers who later use this control by defining some properties, events, and methods as *Public.* Other elements of the control are not made Public and thus reside hidden within the control and beyond the reach of all programmers other than the creator.

Leaving some elements hidden is called *encapsulation* and it makes sense. When you buy a microwave oven, you, the user, expect to be able to control the power between the settings low, medium, and high. These settings have been made public by the engineer who designed the oven. You're *not* expected to yank off the case and try to double the power of the magnetron tube. Not only would that void your warrantee, it would also endanger all life forms in your vicinity.

When using a prebuilt control, you can insert some programming of your own into places that the creator permitted you access: the *events* that the creator gave to this control. If, for example, the creator gave the control a KeyDown event, then you can detect (and react to by your programming) any keys the user presses on the keyboard.

LEVEL 3

On the highest level is the ordinary end user, someone who uses Windows applications or Web pages, but doesn't do any programming. The people on this level can click a control, but cannot define what happens when that control is clicked. If the programmer has written some VBScript programming within the Click event, that programming defines what happens when the button is clicked. The user can activate, but not define, behaviors. Likewise, if the programmer has included a preferences or customization feature, perhaps the user can adjust colors, choose fonts, or make some other decisions about the qualities of the control. But all this depends on what permission the programmer has granted the user. Again, the user can activate, but not define, qualities. Obviously, describing the user as being on the highest level doesn't imply any superiority over the programmer or the creator. The word *highest* in this sense means least-involved-with, and most-abstracted-from.

VBScript Versus HTML (page 73)

VBScript puts the *active* in ActiveX, when ActiveX controls are added to a Web page. When you put a control onto a Web page, that control can contain considerable built-in functionality. A ListBox, for example, displays items of data within a vertical grid, and can tell you which items the user has selected. However, there are jobs a ListBox cannot, by itself, accomplish. For instance, if you want to add items to a ListBox, you must use the VBScript command *AddItem*. And if you want to change a picture in response to the user's click, you have to add some VBScript programming to adjust an Image control's PicturePath property.

In other words, HTML is largely a *page description* language. It's mostly devoted to describing size, position, color, typeface, and other formatting issues. There's little in HTML that's *dynamic*. HTML can't even add 2 + 2. HTML isn't designed as a way of *computing;* it's supposed to describe how a Web page will look, where things are positioned, their width, and so on. VBScript, by contrast, can add numbers together and accomplish many other jobs that come under the general heading of information processing. VBScript is a true computer language. HTML is a way of describing how a document will look to the user. ActiveX controls, supplemented by VBScript programming, make Web pages active and energetic. Stock ticker displays roll by, music plays, animation attracts the eye.

CHAPTER 5

Here's a sample of how easy it is, using the VBCCE, to design and compile an ActiveX control of your own devising.

How to Use Visual Basic Control Creation Edition (page 84)

Say you're designing a Web page that requires the user to enter a password. You want to create a small, single-line TextBox-type control that will permit the user to type in only nine characters, and will display ********* rather than the characters themselves.

Follow these steps to create a password-entry control:

1. Start the VBCCE running. If you've not yet installed it, you can find it on this book's CD-ROM.

2. Choose ActiveX control and the VBCCE will display the UserControl template shown in the following figure. The VBCCE programming design environment is virtually identical to the commercial version of Visual Basic.

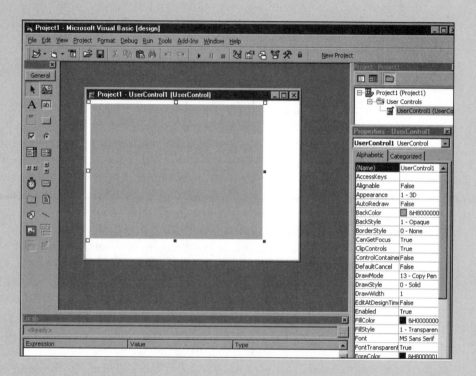

3. In the Properties window, change the Name property to **PWordEntry**. If you don't see the Properties window, press F4 to bring it up.

4. Select Properties in the Project menu.

5. Change the Project Name to **Entry**.

6. Click the OK button to close the Properties window.

7. Put a TextBox onto the Form. A *Form* is the VBCCE equivalent of the Layout control used in the ActiveX Control Pad. A Form is the primary unit of organization in VB, both visually and as a way to segregate a project's programming into various logical containers.

8. Remove the word Text1 that's displayed by default inside the TextBox. Just double-click the Text property in the Properties window, and then press the Del key to remove the unwanted *Text1*.

9. In the Properties window, change the TextBox's MaxLength property to 9 and its PasswordChar property to *.

10. Reduce the size of the Form so it just embraces the TextBox, as shown in the following figure.

11. Close the design window.

As soon as you close the design window, take a look at the Toolbox. There, down in the corner. It's your new PWordEntry control, sitting there among the other ActiveX controls such as the ListBox and Image control. This way, you can test your new control without even leaving the VBCCE integrated design environment (IDE).

How to Test a Custom ActiveX Control (page 86)

Follow these steps to test your new password-entry control:

1. Start a *regular* VB project (as opposed to an ActiveX .OCX user-control-type project) by clicking File → AddProject .

2. Double-click *Standard EXE.*

3. Double-click your PWordEntry control on the Toolbox and it will appear on Project1's Form.

4. Press F5 to run Project1.

You can now type into your PWordEntry custom TextBox and notice that it only permits you to type nine characters. It also refuses to display any characters other than the asterisk. Just what you wanted the control to do.

Once you're satisfied that your new control is well-tested and ready for general use, you can compile an official .OCX version. This compilation adds your new control to the components available for use with the ActiveX Control Pad or any version of Visual Basic (including VBA, built into Microsoft Office applications such as Word, VBCCE, and the commercial versions of VB).

To compile a control you've designed, double-click its name in the Project Explorer window, so the design window of your component becomes the active window. Then choose Make Entry.Ocx from the File menu (this assumes that you named this project *Entry*). Click the OK button. When VBCCE finishes the compilation, the new ActiveX control is *registered* by Windows and, thereby, becomes available for use by any ActiveX-capable language or application. To verify that your control has been registered and is now available for use, choose New Project from the File menu and double-click Standard EXE. Right-click the Toolbox and choose Components (or press Ctrl+T) to bring up the Components window shown in the following figure.

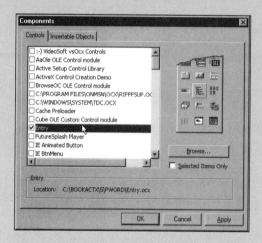

Click the OK button and check it out: There's your custom ActiveX password-entry control on the Toolbox, ready to be added to any future Visual Basic applications or Web pages you design.

CHAPTER 6

There's no reason for you to figure out how to program the low-level complexities of displaying a font or color on a UserControl that you create. VB and its existing set of controls contain loads of properties, methods, and events that can accomplish those jobs and much more. For example, if you want your UserControl to enable users to type in text, you needn't write the code that accepts and displays text.

All you have to do when designing your custom UserControl is to plug a VB TextBox into your UserControl. This way you can get all the functionality that dozens of Microsoft programmers took dozens of man-years to create. Borrowing the features of existing objects is one meaning of the term *subclassing*.

Defining the Term Class (page 110)

The concept of a *class* has been variously compared to a template, a recipe, and a blueprint. In other words, a class isn't a thing in itself; it's abstract. A class is a *plan* that describes how to create something real, how to create an *object* like an ActiveX control that actually does something in the real world.

If you look at a control's icon, such as the TextBox icon on the VBCCE Toolbox, you're looking at a class, a symbol of a *description*. If you double-click that TextBox icon on the Toolbox, an *actual control* is then inserted on the current Form. So, a class is a plan that describes the qualities and behaviors of an object. From one class you can stamp out as many identical objects as you want.

Subclassing means taking an existing class and modifying it in some way. It's like buying a set of blueprints for a house, but changing the size of the den or adding a sunroom to the original floor plan. Then you can use that subclass to stamp out as many identical objects *of the new, modified object* as you want. In its broadest definition, to *subclass* means to create a new ActiveX control out of an existing control. UserControls created out of existing controls are called *aggregate* controls.

CHAPTER 7

The VB Control Creation Edition (a version of which is found on the CD-ROM that accompanies this book) and the commercial version of Visual Basic contain a lifesaver: the ActiveX Control Interface Wizard.

Using the ActiveX Control Interface Wizard (page 136)

You'll rely on this Wizard to do the clerical work when you add a property to a UserControl you're building. (It's easy enough to add a couple of code lines to create an *event* in a UserControl. And a method is nothing more than a Sub or Function. But properties require quite a bit of housekeeping code.)

The ActiveX Control Interface Wizard is probably the most useful of all Visual Basic wizards. Whether you're borrowing an existing property (from an existing control that you're subclassing into your UserControl) or creating an entirely new property, the ActiveX Control Interface Wizard will be of considerable assistance in creating all the necessary code.

Follow these steps to practice adding a property with the ActiveX Control Interface Wizard:

1. Start the VBCCE.

2. Click `Add-Ins` → `ActiveX Control Interface Wizard`. If the Wizard isn't listed in the Add-Ins menu, choose Add-Ins Manager from the Add-Ins menu and select ActiveX Control Interface Wizard.

3. Click Next to get to the Select Interface Members dialog box.

4. Click the << button to send all Selected Names back to the Available Names list. Then double-click BackColor to return that one property to the Selected Names list, as shown in the following figure.

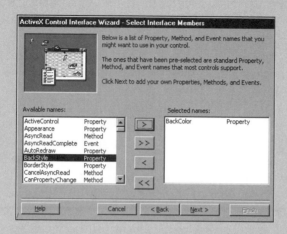

5. Click Next twice to the Set Mapping dialog box, and then change the Maps To list so the BackColor maps (borrows functionality from) the UserControl's BackColor property.

6. Click Next and then click Finish to close the Wizard.

7. Double-click the UserControl in its design window to reveal the source code that the Wizard has created for you. This source code gives the UserControl a BackColor property:

```
'WARNING! DO NOT REMOVE OR MODIFY THE FOLLOWING COMMENTED
LINES!

'MappingInfo=UserControl,UserControl,-1,BackColor
Public Property Get BackColor() As OLE_COLOR
    BackColor = UserControl.BackColor
End Property


Public Property Let BackColor(ByVal New_BackColor As OLE_COLOR)
    UserControl.BackColor() = New_BackColor
    PropertyChanged "BackColor"
End Property


'Load property values from storage
Private Sub UserControl_ReadProperties(PropBag As PropertyBag)

    UserControl.BackColor = PropBag.ReadProperty("BackColor",
&H8000000F)
```

```
End Sub

'Write property values to storage
Private Sub UserControl_WriteProperties(PropBag As PropertyBag)

   Call PropBag.WriteProperty("BackColor",
UserControl.BackColor, &H8000000F)
End Sub
```

Making Controls Sensitive to Size (page 132)

You'll often create a UserControl and permit developers who later use it to resize it. That way they can make it look right on their Forms and projects. While designing their programs, they may well prefer a different size or aspect ratio than the size and shape you originally created. Programmers expect to be able to drag your control to resize it, just as they can resize any other control, such as TextBoxes or CommandButtons, during design. There are even some cases where controls are resized during run time.

You can program the interior controls to respond to a developer's resizing of the container UserControl. Remember that no matter how many controls you place onto a UserControl, the developer will see only a single Width and a single Height property representing the entire UserControl — not the other controls inside it. In many situations, it's quite easy to make a control responsive to developers' dragging the container UserControl to a different size. All you normally have to do is put code that resizes contained controls into the UserControl's Resize event, like this:

```
Private Sub UserControl_Resize()
Command1.Height = Height
Command1.Width = Width
End Sub
```

In this example, every time the developer resizes the UserControl, that interior CommandButton is automatically resized along with it.

Using the Property Page Wizard (page 145)

There's another Wizard that comes with VBCCE, the Property Page Wizard. It allows you to add a nice touch to the Properties window, making it more efficient when a developer goes to adjust some of a UserControl's properties.

Here are the steps to take to invoke and use the Property Page Wizard:

1. Click Add-Ins → Property Page Wizard . If you don't see this Wizard listed, click Add-Ins → Add-In Manager and select VB Property Page Wizard.

2. Click Next to get past the introduction screen. You'll see the selection dialog box. Note that the Wizard has chosen to include one classic Property page: StandardColor (because your UserControl has a BackColor property from the previous example under the section entitled "Using the ActiveX Control Interface Wizard").

3. Click Next and then click Finish to close the Wizard.

Now your Property page has been added to the UserControl in your project. To see the Property page, close the UserControl's design window (thereby enabling the UserControl's icon on the Toolbox). Choose File → Add Project and choose a Standard EXE. Put a UserControl onto the Standard EXE's Form. At the top of the Properties window, double-click Custom. The Property page for Back-Color appears, as shown in the following figure.

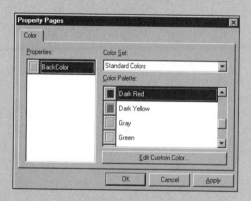

CHAPTER 8

How to Reference an ActiveX Control (page 168)

When you are referencing a control in Visual Basic, you can normally just provide its name: `Text1.Text`, `Picture4.BackColor`, or `List3.ForeColor`. However, if the control is on a different Form, you must attach the Form's name to the control's name, separated by a period: `Form3.Text1.Text` or `Form2.Picture4.BackColor`.

Likewise, if you are referencing an ActiveX control on a Layout control, you must add the Layout's name (*not its filename*) to the start of the control's name. You use this syntax as you would in Visual Basic to query or assign value to a property. For example, here's how you would delete any text in a UserControl named *SSInput1* that had been placed on a Layout control named *s_alx*:

```
s_alx.SSInput1.Text = ""
```

CHAPTER 9

Many programmers have a hard time switching from traditional programming to object-oriented programming (OOP). And what bothers most people migrating to OOP is the *planning* stage, the time before you write any code. In particular: *How do you break a programming task down into objects?*

Most books on OOP either ignore this planning problem or fog it up with unnecessary jargon and convoluted abstraction. The issue is simply this: Programmers used to traditional procedure-based programming *think in terms of the jobs that have to be done.* Back when the first engineer built the first little wooden bridge over a creek, the engineer likely made a mental list of the smaller tasks that, taken together, would result in a bridge. That list might include the following tasks:

1. Use dead, dry trees.

2. Cut trees into logs, flat on two sides.

3. Cut trees into pegs.

4. Use dried hemp for ropes.

5. Weave ropes 1-inch thick, for fastening the logs.

6. Drag logs and ropes to creek.

7. Tie logs together using ropes.

8. Sling the whole thing across the creek and fasten it to pegs.

But computers are fundamentally different from any tools we've had before. Object-oriented programming takes advantage of those differences: You try to break a job down into objects rather than tasks.

Programming differs from ordinary work in several ways. For example, when using a computer you can create objects at will — making *virtual* things that pop in and out of existence as often as needed. When building a bridge, you can't create logs at will. But in a computer program you can make as many virtual objects as you want — dropping them off the end of your assembly line with no additional cost. Five hundred computer objects cost precisely the same as only one object: in energy (electricity) and man-years (your programming time). Once you've written the class that contains all the programming to replicate the objects, producing hundreds of them at run time is free.

A second major difference between computer jobs and traditional work is that computer objects can contain intelligence. They can know methods (to accomplish tasks), react to outside stimuli (such as the Click event) and embody qualities (properties and data). In this way, computer objects differ from conventional tools. A hammer doesn't know how to hit a nail; a library card file doesn't know how to locate a book. But computer objects can move themselves, change color, grow larger, or display messages on command. A computer object is therefore more like a robot than a traditional, real-world tool like a hammer.

When you've decided to create a program using the OOP approach, start out as you always have: list the tasks. But take it one step further. Divide the tasks into three categories: the nouns, verbs, and adjectives. *The nouns will be your objects.* Then, with the objects identified, you can go on to put the verbs (methods) and adjectives (properties) into the objects. Let's try it with the bridge example. The following table diagrams the tasks.

The Elements of Building a Bridge

Nouns	Verbs	Adjectives
Tree		Dead, Dry
Log	Cut	Flat on two sides
Peg		
Hemp, Rope		Dried
Rope	Weave	1-inch thick
Log, Rope	Drag	
Log, Rope	Tie	
Log, Rope, Peg	Sling, Fasten	

You now have to make a mental leap from real-world objects (such as trees) to the virtual objects inside a computer. Computer objects can self-modify their qualities (such as their color property) and carry out tasks (such as moving themselves with their Move method).

As you collapse the bridge-building project into objects, remember that the objects can do things to themselves. So simplify things by deciding which properties and methods should be located within which objects. Because trees produce logs and pegs, you can consider Logs and Pegs *methods* of a Tree object, along with Cut and Drag. Likewise, and for the same reason, the Hemp object has a Rope method, along with Weave, Tie, Sling, and Fasten.

Now you have only two objects: Tree and Hemp. They can produce other objects and carry out various other jobs leading to the production of bridges. The Tree and Hemp objects know how to do things. They have methods built into them.

Now for the properties. A Tree has Dead, Dryness, and Flatness properties. Hemp has Thickness and Dryness properties. You can reconstruct your table to account for these properties, as in the following table.

	Tree Object	**Hemp Object**
Methods	Logs, Pegs, Cut, Drag	Rope, Weave, Tie, Sling, Fasten
Properties	Dead, Dryness	Thickness, Dryness

In this way, you've organized the job as an OOP project and now you can fire up VB's Class Builder or ActiveX Control Interface Wizard and specify the methods and properties of your objects. The next time you start a programming project, try writing out the tasks as sentences, and then "diagram" the sentences to extract the nouns, verbs, and adjectives.

CHAPTER 10

How to Set the Instancing Property (page 206)

The Instancing property of your component defines how client applications can interact with your component. *Can* a client instantiate (create) an object from this class? And if objects can be instantiated, will they be out-of-process servers or in-process servers? Recall that the terms *client* and *server* are used to illustrate the relationship between an application such as Word (the client) when it's using the services of an ActiveX component (the server).

Setting the Instancing property to SingleUse means that each time a client instantiates your component, a separate component is created. This creation is similar to what happens when you put five TextBoxes onto a Form — each TextBox is a *separate, independent* instance of the TextBox class. This kind of multiple-component creation is often necessary, but it does consume memory. However, you can prevent this memory use by setting the Instancing property to MultiUse. That way, only one instance of the component is created, no matter how many instances the client requests. For example, say that your component calculates the days between dates. Obviously only one instance of such an object is necessary. It can service any number of requests. There's no reason for multiple objects of this kind. Having several such calculators sitting around would be redundant. Notice that a DLL-type component is not even allowed to use the two SingleUse Instancing settings, so it's impossible for a client to create multiple instances of a DLL.

The following table shows you which settings of the Instancing property can be used with each of the three primary kinds of ActiveX components:

Settings for the Instancing Property

Instancing	ActiveX EXE	ActiveX DLL	ActiveX Control
Private	X	X	X
PublicNotCreatable	X	X	X
MultiUse	X	X	
GlobalMultiUse	X	X	
SingleUse	X		
GlobalSingleUse	X		

Setting the Instancing property to Private means that the objects can only be used within the DLL project. No clients can create objects from this class. (Remember that there can be several ClassModules in a given DLL project, but at least one of them *must* be MultiUse or GlobalMultiUse.) You would use the Private setting when a class provides procedures only for use within the server project itself. The PublicNotCreatable setting also prevents clients from creating objects. However, once your DLL project has instantiated an object, clients can then access any members that are declared Public. For example, if in your ClassModule set to PublicNotCreatable you have a method defined like this:

```
Public Function MyMethod()
End Function
```

clients can use this Method if *your project* instantiates that ClassModule. The restriction is that the *client* cannot itself instantiate the ClassModule.

Setting the Instancing property to SingleUse means that every time a client instantiates this class, a new, independent object is created (as just described). **GlobalSingleUse** is the same as SingleUse except that a client can use a simplified syntax when accessing the members of the class.

If an object's Name is WeatherObj and it has a Rainfall property, a client would normally access this property using this syntax:

```
WeatherObj.Rainfall = 3
```

However, if the class has been defined as GlobalSingleUse, a client need not add the class name when reading or writing to a member. Clients can access it in these two simplified ways:

```
Rainfall = 3
```

or

```
Inches = Rainfall
```

MultiUse is the default setting for the Instancing property. When a client attempts to create more than one instance of a class, new instances are not produced. Once an object exists, that same, single object can be used by more than a single client. UserControls (such as a TextBox) obviously cannot be set to MultiUse.

If you *can* use MultiUse, though, remember its advantage: You'll conserve memory. A single server object exists, but can serve several clients at the same time. However, if your object is doing a complex, time- or processor-intensive job, choose SingleUse so that separate servers will be created for each client. In that situation, SingleUse is, in fact, the more efficient choice.

How to Create a Collection Class (page 218)

Whenever you're planning to work with a group of simple objects (that would, in traditional programming, be put into an array for easier manipulation), consider building a collection instead.

Assume that you are given the job of organizing a university's collection of classic films. They want you to computerize the collection so they can search quickly for combinations of stars, directors, or other criteria. A procedure-oriented approach would focus on the writing of the search function and the other data-management tasks involved in this job. But an object-oriented approach would think in terms of *film objects,* one for each movie. And each object, as objects do, can include data (properties) and processing techniques (methods) to act on that data.

Because there are going to be many instances of the film object, you'll want a way to manage this set of objects collectively, perhaps to give each a serial number (ID), or to find out the total number of objects (the collection's Count property tells you), and other collective chores. Solution: Put all the film objects into a collection.

But you also want to prevent accidental damage to this collection, such as someone adding the wrong kind of data to the collection. A collection, by nature, will accept *any kind of variable* and yet you want this to be a collection of film objects and *only* film objects.

To be able to guarantee precisely how this collection will be used, you must encapsulate it — insulating it from the outside world. To do that, you can create a *collection class* that will produce collection objects — with specific ways that new objects can be added to the collection (nothing but film objects allowed).

Like any other class, a collection class acts like a factory that builds new objects (in this case, new collections) on demand. However, the purpose of a collection class is to encapsulate a collection (or several).

In the following example, you'll see how to use the Class Builder Utility to create a collection class. You can imagine how useful this kind of collection class would be in encapsulating data objects. If you can't, follow this next example.

To create a collection class, follow these steps:

1. Start Visual Basic. You should have a Standard EXE project with the default name Project1 and a Form1.

2. Run the Class Builder Utility.

3. Click File → New → Collection .

4. Select the New Class option button.

5. Click the New Class Properties button and name it **Film**.

6. Change the name of the collection itself to **Films** (type this name into the TextBox just above the Label *Based On* in the Properties tab of the dialog box).

7. Click OK to close the dialog box.

8. Close the Class Builder Utility.

9. Answer *Yes* when queried if you want to update the project with changes.

Now look at the methods the Class Builder has added to your Films collection class. Your project should now have three modules listed in the Project Explorer: Form1, Film, and Films. Film is the class for each film object and Films generates the collection of these film objects. Double-click Films in the Project Explorer, and you should see the following source code:

```
'local variable to hold collection
Private mCol As Collection

Public Function Add(Key As String, Optional sKey As String) As
  Film
 'create a new object
Dim objNewMember As Film
Set objNewMember = New Film


'set the properties passed into the method
objNewMember.FName = Key

If Len(sKey) = 0 Then
 mCol.Add objNewMember
Else
 mCol.Add objNewMember, sKey
End If
```

```vb
 'return the object created
 Set Add = objNewMember
 Set objNewMember = Nothing
End Function


Public Property Get Item(vntIndexKey As Variant) As Film
 'used when referencing an element in the collection
 'vntIndexKey contains either the Index or Key to the collection,
 'this is why it is declared as a Variant
 'Syntax: Set foo = x.Item(xyz) or Set foo = x.Item(5)
 Set Item = mCol(vntIndexKey)
End Property


Public Property Get Count() As Long
 'used when retrieving the number of elements in the
 'collection. Syntax: Debug.Print x.Count
 Count = mCol.Count
End Property


Public Sub Remove(vntIndexKey As Variant)
 'used when removing an element from the collection
 'vntIndexKey contains either the Index or Key, which is why
 'it is declared as a Variant
 'Syntax: x.Remove(xyz)

 mCol.Remove vntIndexKey
End Sub


Public Property Get NewEnum() As IUnknown
 'this property allows you to enumerate
 'this collection with the For...Each syntax
 Set NewEnum = mCol.[_NewEnum]
End Property


Private Sub Class_Initialize()
 'creates the collection when this class is created
 Set mCol = New Collection
End Sub


Private Sub Class_Terminate()
 'destroys collection when this class is terminated
 Set mCol = Nothing
End Sub
```

The only change you should make to the preceding VB-Wizard-generated code is to change one line in the Add method from

```
objNewMember.Key = Key
```

to

```
objNewMember.FName = Key
```

because you're soon going to create a FName property for Film class. Every time a new Film object is added to the collection, the FName (film name) must be passed to the Add method. By default, the Wizard expects you to create a unique ID key for each object in the collection, so it provides a parameter named *Key*. You can just replace the Key parameter with whatever parameter you wish (in this example, FnNme).

You can see that the Class Builder constructed Add, Remove, Initialize, and Terminate methods for this collection, as well as two properties: Item and Count. Note that these two properties are read-only. Outside programming cannot change them (there is no Let or Set procedure). These two properties are managed by the collection itself.

CHAPTER 11

Avoid Hard Coding (page 230)

When you create a traditional array, you must specify how many items the array will hold. This way, the computer then knows how much memory to set aside for your array:

```
Dim myarray(1 To 100)
```

But one of the advantages of using a collection instead of an array is that you don't need to specify the number of items in the collection; a collection can expand indefinitely. This is one of the significant advantages of OOP: You can often avoid the limitations of *hard coding* like setting an upper limit of 100 on a group of items. OOP is more relativistic than classic programming.

You can see this trend toward relativity in Internet programming. When you describe a font size in HTML (the primary Internet programming language), you'll use commands that are not specific. The HTML commands essentially say: big, bigger, biggest rather than specifying a particular, precise point size such as 14, 28, and 88.

How do you, the programmer, know in advance the size of the user's screen or browser? You don't. So you specify that this piece of text is just *bigger* than that piece, but what "bigger" actually means (in absolute measurements) depends on local conditions in the user's system and the settings the user has chosen for his browser's text-display preferences.

Likewise, how do you, the programmer, know in advance how many stamps a collector might want to catalog, or how many movies are in a university's collection of classic films? Collections don't place an upper limit on the number of items they contain.

How to Save and Load Collection Data (page 244)

You can give a collection the ability to save itself to disk. Unless you make provisions to store the items (objects) in a collection on a hard drive or other long-term storage device, those items won't be persistent. As soon as a project is shut down, all the objects will evaporate.

One way to make the items in a collection persistent is to create a Load method and a Save method for that collection's collection class. Because methods are so elementary (merely Subs or Functions), you don't need to run the Class Builder if you don't want to. There's no particular reason to fire up that Wizard with something so simple. Assume that this collection is named *mCol* and that each item in the collection has only one property, named *pSalary*. Here's what to type in for a cSave method that stores this collection on a hard drive:

```
Public Function cSave(Optional fName As Variant) As Variant

Dim intg As Integer, str As String
On Error Resume Next

If IsMissing(fName) Then 'client didn't pass path so provide
  default
fName = App.Path & "\clients.bin"
End If

Kill fName 'eliminate existing file

fnumber = FreeFile

Open fName For Binary Access Write As #fnumber
  If Err Then
    If Err <> 53 Then ' Ignore "file not found" errors
    MsgBox Error(Err): Close: Exit Function
    End If
End If

c = mCol.Count 'how many objects?

For i = 1 To c
  str = mCol(i).pSalary
  intg = Len(str)
```

```
        Put #fnumber, , intg
        Put #fnumber, , str
    Next i

    Close #fnumber
    End Function
```

This is mostly straightforward, standard VB file-saving code. The client can optionally pass a path and filename argument, or if they don't, the method generates a path\filename based on the location of the .EXE file of this project (App.Path). You Kill (delete) the existing file, if any, and then find out how many objects the collection, *mCol*, currently holds. Then you save each one's data in turn, first saving the length of the string (the salary is the only property, but in a real project you'd have many more properties). After the length is stored, you then save the actual data as text.

Retrieving a collection from the hard drive is quite similar to saving it. The primary difference is that you keep testing for End of File (EOF) as you draw in the data. The number of data items determines how many objects will be created, by using Add CCur(str). Recall that this collection's Add method accepts a single argument, the Salary (pSalary) of the client.

```
Public Function cLoad(Optional fName As Variant) As Variant
Dim intg As Integer, str As String
On Error Resume Next
fnumber = FreeFile

If IsMissing(fName) Then 'client didn't pass path so supply
  default
fName = App.Path & "\clients.bin"
End If

Open fName For Binary Access Read As #fnumber

Do While Not EOF(fnumber)
Get #fnumber, , intg

If Not EOF(fnumber) Then
str = String(intg, " ")
Get #fnumber, , str
Add CCur(str) 'create an object in the collection
End If
Loop

Close #fnumber
End Function
```

When creating a project in the real world, you'd want to add more error-trapping within the cSave and cLoad methods. Error-trapping is important whenever contacting the user's disk.

CHAPTER 12

How to Send a Message from a Server to a Client (page 250)

Conversations between a client and a server are nearly always one-sided. Most messages are requests, from the client to the server, to activate the server's methods or manipulate the server's properties.

There are times, though, when the server needs to send a message back to the client. Such a message from the server will usually be something to the effect "I'm finished with the job you gave me." Server-to-client messaging can be necessary in two situations: the client requested a time-consuming job (such as downloading a graphics file) and wants to know when the job is finished. Or, the client wants to be told when a certain amount of time has elapsed (the server is acting as an alarm clock).

You know how to have a client instantiate a server object. How, though, do you send a message back to the client from the server? You might argue that a Function-style method in the server sends something back to the client. True enough, but this kind of messaging is still instigated *by the client*. The client is requesting the services of the server and the server responds. But what if the server itself must generate a message without any involvement from the client?

If the client's language is Visual Basic or Visual Basic for Applications, sending a server-to-client message is easy. You can use the WithEvents command in the client. This adds an *event* to the client. The event will trigger whenever the server wants to trigger it. (Technically, the event is actually an attribute of the instantiated server object, as you will see.)

So if both client and server languages are VB or VBA, you notify a client from a server by "raising" an event in the server. That event *will appear in the client's list of events, along with Form Load and all the usual events.*

ActiveX UserControl (.OCX files, when compiled) components are the simplest of all to program when you want to communicate server-to-client because you don't even need to use the WithEvents command. Here's an example.

Follow these steps to see how to raise an event:

1. Start VB and choose ActiveX Control (UserControl) as the project type. If you've changed VB's options so when it starts running it doesn't display the dialog box showing the various kinds of projects, press Ctrl+N. Then choose ActiveX Control.

2. Put a CommandButton and a Timer control on the UserControl's Form.

3. Type the following into the UserControl's General Declarations section:
   Event timeup()

4. Type the following into the Timer's Timer event:

```
Private Sub Timer1_Timer()
RaiseEvent timeup
End Sub
```

This RaiseEvent command means that when the Timer has counted down to zero, the *timeup* event will trigger in the client.

5. Finally, in the CommandButton's Click event, type this:

```
Private Sub Command1_Click()
Timer1.Interval = 20000
End Sub
```

6. Now close both the design and code windows of this UserControl, thereby enabling its icon on the Toolbox.

7. Click [**File**] → [**AddProject**] and choose Standard EXE.

8. Double-click the UserControl icon on the Toolbox, to place an instance of it on Form1. Remember the kink in VB that occurs when you're testing: Make sure that in the Properties window you change the name of the UserControl to **UserControl1** (not *UserControl11* as VB, at the present time, automatically names it).

9. Double-click Form1 to bring up its code window and look for the UserControl1_timeup event. If it says UserControl11, change it to UserControl1 too. (This UserControl11 issue is discussed in a Caution in Chapter 7.)

10. Type the following into the UserControl1_timeup event:

```
Private Sub UserControl1_timeup()
MsgBox "TIME'S UP, TURKEY BOY!!"
End Sub
```

11. Now press F5 to run the project and click the CommandButton to trigger the countdown. After 20 seconds you'll see the message appear.

How to Add Any .WAV File to an ActiveX Component (page 266)

If you ever want to ring a bell or play some other sound in a project, use a .WAV file. Visual Basic can't play .WAV files itself, but whenever you need to do something VB can't do, you can contact the Windows Application Programming Interface (API). It's a huge collection of Functions, and a few Subs, that you can trigger from within VB to do jobs VB isn't designed to do. Plus, the API is often faster than VB. Here's how to play a .WAV file:

In the General Declarations section of a Module, or Form1, type the following *all on a single line* (make sure you don't press the Enter key until you've typed the last word *Long*):

```
Private Declare Function sndPlaySound Lib "winmm.dll" Alias
    "sndPlaySoundA" (ByVal l As String, ByVal u As Long) As Long
```

Then, wherever in your source code that you want to play a .WAV file, just substitute the name of a file on your hard drive for the filename *reminder.wav* in this example. In the following code, change *reminder.wav* to the name of a .WAV file on your machine:

```
x = sndPlaySound("c:\reminder.wav", 0)
```

CHAPTER 13

Early- Versus Late-Binding (page 282)

When a client declares a new object, *by naming it directly*, that object is said to be early-bound (as opposed to using the generic command *As Object*). For example, after you create a reference to Word's object library:

```
Set objWord = New Word.application
```

you can then use a line of programming like this to cause early-binding:

```
Set objWord = New Word.application
```

The phrases *early-* and *late-binding* describe how a server is connected to a client when the server is first instantiated in the client. What happens when a class you want to use isn't contained within your project or referenced by using VB's References feature on the Project menu? Say that it's an ActiveX component that's registered in your Windows Registry, but you don't want to be bothered using the References dialog box on the Project menu. In cases when a client uses the *As Object* and *CreateObject* commands, an object is said to be late-bound:

```
Dim New_Object As Object
Set New_Object = CreateObject("excel.application")
```

Late-binding occurs because when a project is compiled (compile-time, as it's called) VB cannot yet determine the members of the object that your object variable points to. References to members (such as New_Object.Text) must be checked later, during run time when the object is finally bound to your component.

If your client can refer to objects using the early-bound technique, the server will perform more efficiently. The reason for this is that when VB compiles a project (when you select Make Project in the File menu) containing a late-bound object reference, VB cannot check to see if there are any incorrect members.

For example, it's safe to assume that Excel has no Rftpdq property:

```
Public ObjExcel As Object
Set ObjExcel = CreateObject("Excel.Application")
ObjExcell.Rftpdq = "Fury"
```

When VB compiles this example, no error will be generated. VB doesn't check and doesn't know that Excel doesn't have this Rftpdq property. VB does not check the object library of a late-bound object reference. This void means that VB must add code in the compiled project's .EXE file that will have to check *during run time* for the validity of each reference to any members of the object. Clearly this retards the speed of execution. An early-bound reference, by contrast, simply and directly codes the pointer to the object's member, eliminating the necessity of having to check the validity of that reference during run time.

CHAPTER 14

Understanding the Document-Style Component (page 294)

When you press Ctrl+N in VBCCE or Visual Basic to start a new project, you are asked to specify what *kind* of project. There's the familiar "Standard EXE" executable — a typical Windows program. But there are also several additional kinds of projects such as ActiveX Control, ActiveX Document DLL, and ActiveX Document EXE. The Document-type ActiveX component is designed to run within (and be dependent on) a container. The container/contained relationship is somewhat different than the client/server relationship. The main difference between an ordinary ActiveX server component and an ActiveX Document-type component is that a Document is a *specialized* ActiveX component, designed to be activated within an Internet browser or another container application such as Word.

A Document Is Designed to Be Contained (page 295)

Think of a classic document, a Word .DOC file. It has data (text) and some information about how it should look (italic, or whatever). When you load it into Word, the .DOC takes on a particular appearance — Word, the container, displays it. So you're dealing with two entities: the data file (.DOC) and the application that displays it (Word.exe). Similarly, when you create an ActiveX Document component, two files are deposited on the hard drive: a Visual Basic Document file (.VBD) and an associated .EXE or .DLL file (the container).

An ActiveX Document is not an independent entity. Like all other ActiveX components except the ActiveX EXE, the ActiveX Document requires a client. With ActiveX Documents, the client is a *container* like the Internet Explorer browser. When an ActiveX Document is attached to a container, the process is called *siting*. Once the ActiveX Document has been sited, properties of the container (the Parent property, for example) then become available to the Document.

When you ask VB to create a Document component, VB displays a *UserDocument*. Try it now: Press Ctrl+N to start a new VB project. Choose ActiveX DLL Document. You'll see the new UserDocument in the Project Explorer, as shown in the following figure.

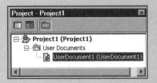

As you can see, a UserDocument is similar to the familiar VB Form. However, a UserDocument is in several ways dependent on its container in ways that a Form never is. For example, the container determines when and how a User-Document is displayed. Therefore, unlike a Form, a UserDocument has no Show, Hide, Load, or Unload methods of its own. You cannot write programming like this: UserDocument1.Hide.

Moving Between Documents with the NavigateTo Method (page 303)

With ordinary VB Standard EXE applications, you can use simple Load or Show commands to hide or reveal the various Forms within your project. You can start other applications or utilities with the Shell command, or switch to other applications that are already running by using the AppActivate command.

In a browser, though, transferring focus to a different Document requires somewhat different techniques. A person surfing the Internet often navigates by clicking hyperlinks — jump-off points within a document that take them to a different Web site or a different area within the current Web site or even locally to a different zone within the currently displayed document. So you won't be surprised to find out that a UserDocument component (an ActiveX Document DLL or Document EXE) requires what's called a *Hyperlink object* to switch to other ActiveX Documents. The target of the Hyperlink object can be any URL (universal resource locator, more commonly known as an Internet address).

The Hyperlink object has a NavigateTo method. You use that method to jump somewhere out on the Web (or to display a different UserDocument).

Follow these steps to learn how to use the NavigateTo method, and then test it:

1. Press Ctrl+N to start a new ActiveX Document DLL.

2. Double-click *User Documents* in the Project window.

3. Double-click UserDocument1 to display its design window.

4. Put a CommandButton on the Document.

5. Double-click the CommandButton to get to its code window.

6. Type the following into the code window:

```
Private Sub Command1_Click()
UserDocument.Hyperlink.NavigateTo "http://www.usatoday.com/"
End Sub
```

7. Now test it by pressing F5 to run your Document component.

8. Start a new instance of IE.

9. Click `File` → `Open` .

10. Type in: **C:\VB5\USERDOCUMENT1.VBD**. (Or use whatever path instead of C:\VB5 points to your copy of VB5.)

11. Click the CommandButton and you'll jump to the USA Today site.

You can also use the Hyperlink command to point to a .VBD file (another ActiveX Document DLL or EXE) or to a Word or Excel document. If you have a second .VBD file on your computer, try this:

```
UserDocument.Hyperlink.NavigateTo "file://c:\VB5\TestDoc.vbd"
```

You can also move back or forward through IE's cache of documents — as if the user had clicked the Back or Forward buttons on IE's toolbar. Note that the error-trapping in the following code is necessary in case you're at an end of the cache and no other document is available:

```
Private Sub Command1_Click()

  On Error GoTo Quit
  UserDocument.Hyperlink.GoForward
  Exit Sub

Quit:
  Resume Next
End Sub
```

Native-Code Compilation Options (page 304)

After all your designing, coding, and testing, you've finally built an ActiveX component and you're ready to send it out into the world. You're usually not going to release it as source code. One of the points of encapsulation is that developers, much less users, need not know the low-level details about how your component does its job.

When you're ready to distribute a component, it's time to *compile* it. You select Make *NameOfYourProject* from the VB File menu, click Options, and then click the Compile tab.

If you decide to compile into native-code, you're offered a set of six options. Here is a list of those options and what each means:

* **Optimize for Fast Code**   The compiler will choose speed over filesize whenever that tradeoff comes up during the compilation process. You should select this option in nearly all cases. Memory is cheap, but time is money.

* **Optimize for Small Code**   The opposite of Optimize for Fast Code, this option produces the smallest possible executable file, at the expense of speed.

* **No Optimization**   You should avoid this choice, unless you want a compromise between the two previous optimizations.

* **Favor Pentium Pro**   If you're sure that your component will be used only on a Pentium Pro machine, go ahead. Otherwise, you'll create a component that runs inefficiently on other computers — though it will still run.

* **Create Symbolic Debugging Info**   This option can be useful if you use Visual C++ or a debugger that can work with the .PDB files that are deposited on your hard drive if this option is selected. However, VB's IDE (integrated design environment) is world-famous for its excellent debugging facilities.

* **DLL Base Address**   Normally, you'll just leave this option set to the default. When your component is loaded into memory, Windows will try to insert it into the address specified. If Windows can't put it there, it will put it elsewhere in memory (this slows down the loading, and usually prevents the code in your component from being shared by different clients). If you're concerned about this issue and want to try to prevent memory conflicts between your components (they'll all, by default, be compiled to that same address), see the suggestions in VB's Books Online (on the Help menu).

CHAPTER 15

How to Provide Security for the User (page 311)

The Script languages, JavaScript and VBScript, were designed to compute locally. Like ordinary applications, documents containing these languages run on a user's computer and therefore could do damage to the user's machine. And embedded objects — ActiveX controls for example — upped the stakes even further. An ActiveX control is a complete Visual Basic *program* that is downloaded into a user's system. It can do to the user's system whatever a Visual Basic .EXE program can do: pretty much anything it wants. No reputable software store, no shrink-wrapped box, no famous manufacturer — just a running program slipping silently into your system from who-knows-whom and who-knows-where over the Internet.

Various strategies have been introduced to protect the innocent. For one thing, VBScript and JavaScript are emasculated languages. They've been stripped of potentially harmful commands available in their parent languages (VB and Java). The Script languages contain no disk reformatting or file deletion commands; they cannot directly contact any operating system features, such as the Windows Registry (just mucking that up can immobilize a computer); they cannot create objects.

The Script languages cannot directly communicate with peripherals or the computer's memory. They can't even print a page to the printer. This neutering of these Script languages to make them safe for Internet surfers is called *sandboxing*, though *sandbagging* might be a more accurate term.

But, Microsoft thought, what if we could authenticate downloadable objects (ActiveX controls) and assure the user that what was coming in over the Internet was, yes, an executable like any other application, *but it's been verified as having no harmful viruses*. In other words, run a virus-checker at the source rather than on the user's system.

This idea gave rise to three variations:

✳ **Digital Signing**   Add a *digital signature* that identifies the source of the control. Then, if the control does harm, somebody can be held responsible. A third-party company authorizes you (the control's creator) to "sign" your control (using VB's Setup Wizard to embed the signature, as described later in this chapter. This third-party maintains your name and address so if anything goes wrong, everyone knows where to pin the blame: on you.

✳ **Safe for Scripting**   Mark a control *safe for scripting*. When you select this option in the Setup Wizard, you are saying to users: Look, relax, I'm telling you that nothing in this control can be activated by a Script language (some VBScript or JavaScript in the document you're downloading), triggering the control to do something damaging. This control is safe.

✳ **Safe for initialization**   Mark a control *safe for initialization*. This Setup Wizard option tells users: Nothing in this control can harm your system if some malign individual tries to use HTML (<PARAM> tags) to send strange data when the control is being initialized in your browser. For example, allowing a <PARAM> command to change the color of your control is safe for initialization. Allowing a <PARAM> command to save something to the user's disk drive is not. So, when marked safe for initialization, the user can take it easy and just let this kind of "guaranteed" control into the browser.

Of course any deranged virus designer can buy a copy of Visual Basic and easily create ActiveX components. This book demonstrates just how easily. Then, using the Setup Wizard, it only takes a couple of mouse clicks to "mark" a nasty, deadly component as safe. What kind of protection is this? We might as well require that before entering a bank, everyone sign a card reading: "I promise I don't have a gun. Honest."

But any shelter in a storm I guess. Internet Explorer is by default set to warn the user of any incoming component that has not been marked "safe" for scripting and initialization. You'll still be notified if you choose "Medium," but at least the protection won't automatically turn away all incoming executables. To set these levels, run Internet Explorer and then choose Options from the View menu. Click the Security tab and then click the Safety Level button.

No one has yet reported a virus attack resulting from downloading a Script or component from the Internet. But it's only a matter of time. The user's best defense against viruses, or other problems such as a hard drive crash, is a sensible backup strategy. It doesn't take long to save your irreplaceable data files.

CHAPTER 16

How to Use the API (page 327)

The Application Programmer's Interface (API) is a part of the Windows and NT operating system. It's filled with functions that you can use from within your ActiveX controls. There are three primary reasons you will sometimes want to go beyond the functionality built into VB and resort to the API:

* The API can provide services that VB doesn't include.
* It can be faster.
* It can be more efficient.

Typing in the source code for an API call, though, can be tough. VB provides no syntax checking when you're calling the API, yet API calls are frequently long and complex (and the Declare statement that adds an API function to your VB program *must be on a single line — do not press the Enter key.*) They are difficult to type in, but API Declares are not in VB's vocabulary so it can't warn you of any syntax errors.

Fortunately, VB includes an API Viewer that assists you by providing lists of all API Constants, Declares, and Types. You can copy and paste these elements into your VB source code, so the problem of Declare typos is eliminated.

Follow these steps to insert an API Declare into your source code:

1. With the code window open, click at the very top of your source code (above all three Subs) so you create an insertion point (in the General Declarations section of the code window). This is where the Declare will be copied into your source code.

2. Click `Add-Ins` → `API Viewer` (If it's not on the list of available Add-Ins, click Add-In Manager and select it from the list. If it's not on the list, use Explorer to locate it on the VB5 CD in the VB\WINAPI subdirectory. Double-click *Apiload.exe* to run it.)

3. Select Load Text File from the API Viewer's File menu.

4. Locate the text file *Win32api.Txt* in your VB5\WINAPI subdirectory (or on the CD-ROM).

5. Load the text file into the API Viewer.

6. Click the Search button and type a Declare you're interested in, such as **GetSysColor**.

7. When GetSysColor appears in the Available Items list, double-click it to move it to the Selected Items list.

8. Click the Insert button and agree to insert it into your source code by clicking the OK button.

Note that the API Viewer inserts Declares into your source code without specifying that they are Private. It merely leaves out the Public or Private commands, thereby allowing the default to be Public. However, VB requires that Declares in a Form be Private, so you must change this code

```
Declare Function GetSysColor Lib "user32" (ByVal nIndex As Long)
    As Long
```

to this code:

```
Private Declare Function GetSysColor Lib "user32" (ByVal nIndex As
    Long) As Long
```

VISUAL INDEX

Using the ActiveX Control Pad

How to run
the ActiveX
Control Pad
page 2

Simplify Adding Controls to a Web Page

How to add
controls to
a Layout
control
page 16

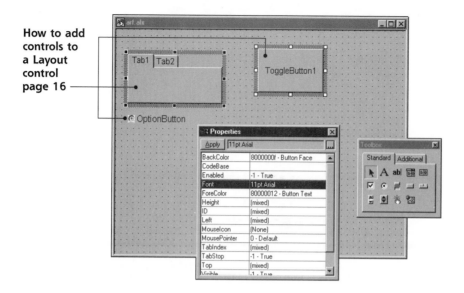

How to Create Specialized Visual Effects

How to
create drop-
shadows
page 52

How to create
etched
lettering
page 55

Using the Control Pad's Script Wizard

How to use the Script Wizard page 69

How to insert an action into an event page 70

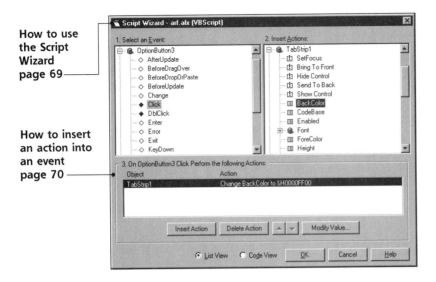

Create Your First Control Using the VBCCE

How to set options in the VBCCE page 78

How to run multiple projects in a single IDE page 89

How to use the VBCCE page 78

How to compile an ActiveX control page 81

How to use Forms page 93

How to use the Properties window page 78

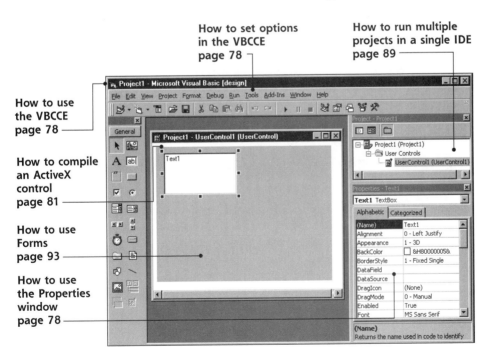

Debugging in the VB IDE

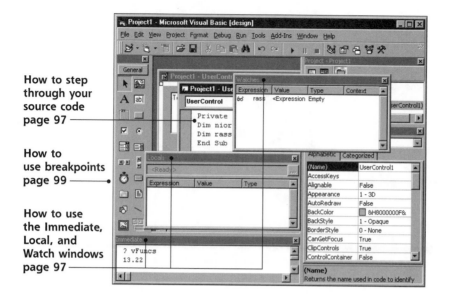

Using the ActiveX Control Interface Wizard

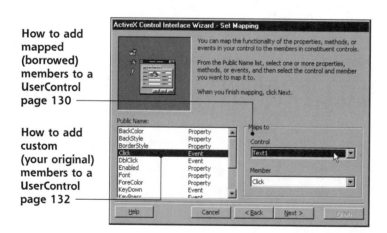

Using the Procedure Attributes Dialog Box

How to refine
a member's
qualities
page 187

How to hide
members
from a
developer
page 190

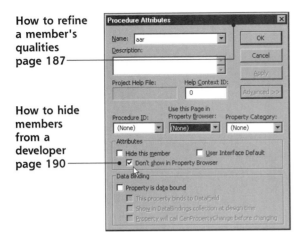

Using the Class Builder Utility

How to add new methods
page 204

How to add
new classes
page 202

How to
add new
collections
page 211

How to add
new events
page 245

How to add
new properties
page 215

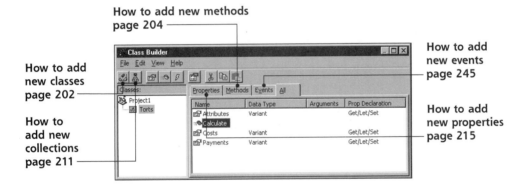

Providing Documentation to a Developer

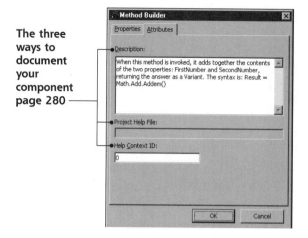

The three ways to document your component page 280

How to Use ActiveX Documents

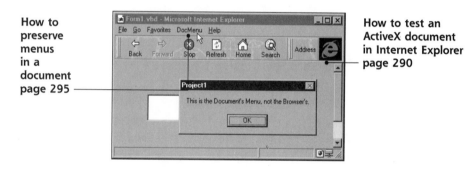

How to preserve menus in a document page 295

How to test an ActiveX document in Internet Explorer page 290

Choosing Between Compilation Options

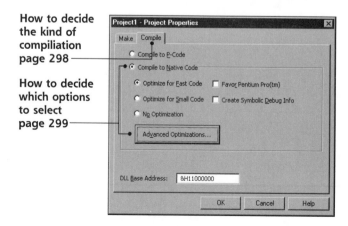

How to decide the kind of compiliation page 298

How to decide which options to select page 299

Using the Setup Wizard

How to
distribute
an ActiveX
component
to others
page 310

How and why
to use a
dependency
file
page 311

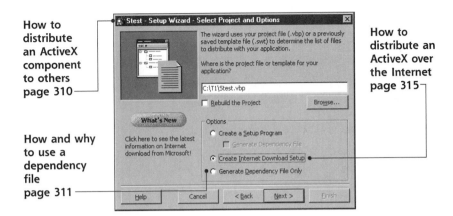

How to
distribute an
ActiveX over
the Internet
page 315

Using the Windows API

How to use
the API Viewer
utility to
avoid typos
page 322

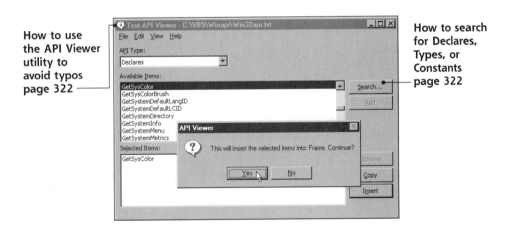

How to search
for Declares,
Types, or
Constants
page 322

Creating User-Drawn ActiveX Components

How to improve on existing controls (greater speed, less use of resources, complete originality) page 337

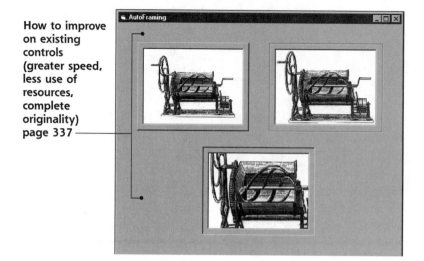

USING THE CD-ROM

Sealed in plastic on the back cover of Discover ActiveX is a CD-ROM that includes all the programming code in this book; Microsoft's ActiveX Control Pad and Visual Basic 5 Control Creation Edition; and a select group of demos of commercial ActiveX controls.

Organization

The CD-ROM includes several folders. All the source code from the book is located in the Source Code folder, divided by chapter. The ActiveX Control Pad is located in the ControlPad folder and VBCCE is in a folder named Vbcce. Each commercial ActiveX control manufacturer is in its own folder as well.

Contents

The reason for including all the source code from the book on the CD-ROM is that there are many examples throughout the book, and you'll likely want to copy and paste some of them into your programming applications or browser to experiment with them.

The CD-ROM also includes Microsoft's ActiveX Control Pad, an application that makes it easy to insert ActiveX controls into HTML source code. The Control Pad also simplifies sizing and positioning controls on Web pages. To install the Control Pad on your computer, double-click the SETUPPAD.EXE file in the ControlPad folder on the CD-ROM.

The Visual Basic 5 Control Creation Edition is a remarkable application. With it, you have access to a large subset of the features of the commercial version of Visual Basic 5. You can use the VBCCE to create fully functional ActiveX components. To install VBCCE, double-click the VB5CCEIN.EXE file in the Vbcce folder on the CD-ROM.

Finally, the CD-ROM also includes a select group of commercial ActiveX control demos. Most of the demos are activated by double-clicking an .EXE setup file (Black Diamond, Data Dynamics, Farallon, Platinum, ProtoView, and Starfish). You can activate the Vivo demo by double-clicking the VIVOPROD.EXE file in the Producer subfolder. Following is a brief description of the demos that are included on the CD-ROM.

Black Diamond Consulting offers an ActiveX control called **Surround Video**. With Surround Video, you can view 360 panoramic images. These pictures can be taken with a special rotating camera, or alternatively can be created in various 3D software rendering packages. The Surround Video control processes Surround Video Image files (*.svi) and Surround Video Link files.

The ActiveX control from Data Dynamics, Ltd. is called **DynamiCube**. It helps with data mining or analysis through instant filtering, drill-down, roll-up, and pivoting of virtually unlimited amounts of relational data.

Farallon Communications, Inc., offers an ActiveX control called **Look@Me** that permits you to observe another user's screen anywhere in the world over the Internet in real time. Look@Me is based on Farallon's Timbuktu Pro for Networks.

Platinum Technology, Inc., presents **Platinum Wirl**, a virtual-reality control that enables users to experience VRML content. It can be deployed on the Internet, within intranets, or on standalone computers.

Several demos of various useful tools are provided by ProtoView Development, Co. Their **DataTable** is a grid component — a powerful database interface designed to work like a spreadsheet. It enables you to display, manage, and edit rows, columns, and cells — even of large data sets. ProtoView's **Data Explorer** is a clever database interface that looks and acts like the Windows 95 Explorer. Users can easily browse through data, even complex data, using the hierarchical TreeView along with a ListView or a text-editing view. Finally, ProtoView's **InterAct** component has a wealth of features to help you convey data efficiently, including many tools for transforming static data and displaying it to a user within an interactive diagram.

Starfish Software, Inc., offers **EarthTime**, a control that displays the correct time for all time zones. A world map, clocks for eight cities, statistics about the cities (telephone codes, currencies, and more), a time-difference calculator, a feature that synchronizes your computer's clock with an atomic clock, and more.

Vivo Software, Inc., presents **VivoActive Producer**. It lets you develop — and view — on-demand video for the World Wide Web. The company says this product offers the simplest, fastest way to put video content on your Web pages. The VivoActive Producer lets you create VivoActive content from .AVI or .WAV files.

System Requirements

To run the applications, demos and examples in this book, your computer should meet at least the following minimum requirements:

* At least a 486 microprocessor
* Microsoft Windows 95 or later, or Microsoft Windows NT 4.0 or later.
* 16MB of RAM.
* 30MB free disk space on your hard drive.
* Internet Explorer 3.0 or later.

TROUBLESHOOTING GUIDE

After I use the Class Builder to build a collection class, the Add method created by the Class Builder appears in red (syntax error) within the source code. Or, when I try to run this source code, I get a "Compile error, Expected identifier" message.

At the time of this writing, the Class Builder has a slight problem when creating the Add method within a collection class. It leaves out the first argument, merely providing a comma, like this:

```
Public Function Add(, Optional sKey As String) As Client
```

To fix this, change it to something like this:

```
Public Function Add(Key As String, Optional sKey As String) As Client
```

Any graphics I add to a CommandButton (or Checkbox or OptionButton) when using the ActiveX Control Pad look strange — like they're washed out or missing some details.

At the time of this writing, some graphics do not display correctly when added to a CommandButton (or Checkbox or OptionButton) in the ActiveX Control Pad. They do, however, work fine in the other versions of Visual Basic covered in this book: VBCCE and the commercial versions of VB.

Any graphics I add to a CommandButton (or Checkbox or OptionButton) when using VBCCE or VB aren't visible. There is a graphics file listed in the Picture property, but still no visible graphic in the CommandButton.

Make sure you've set the CommandButton's (or Checkbox's or OptionButton's) Style property to Graphical. Even though a control's Picture property contains a reference to a bitmap, you must set its Style property as well.

I find it difficult to think in terms of zero-based arrays. It's hard to always make the mental shift to remember that the third item in an array has an index of 2. Is there any solution? Thank goodness that collections begin with an index of 1.

All versions of Visual Basic except VBScript have an Option Base command that you can use to force arrays to begin with an index of 1 rather than 0. However, VBScript doesn't include this feature. But remember, even when you use the Option Base command, it only affects arrays. It has no effect on other zero-based lists, such as the ListIndex property of a ListBox. Zero-based lists is just one of those things you have to put up with: some lists in computer programming are one-based (like collections) while other lists, like arrays, are zero-based.

I can't figure out how to use the Common Dialog control. In particular, since it's not a function, how do I get information back from it?

You query the properties of a CommonDialog control to get information back. The Common Dialog control is *modal*. Therefore, like other modal dialog windows (for example the VB MsgBox and InputBox), the CommonDialog will halt your program until the user responds. A modal window remains up there on the user's screen until the user makes some selection or, at the very least, clicks the OK or Cancel buttons and, thereby, shuts the modal window.

So if you want to permit users to open a disk file, first show them the standard CommonDialog window, then use the *FileName property* of the CommonDialog to find out the path of the file they chose. To see how this works, put a CommandButton, a CommonDialog control and a TextBox on a Form. Set the TextBox's MultiLine property to True, then type in the following code:

```
Sub Command1_Click()
On Error Resume Next
CommonDialog1.ShowOpen
Open CommonDialog1.filename For Input As #1
If Err Then MsgBox Error(Err): Exit Sub
n = Input(LOF(1), 1)
Close
Text1 = n
End Sub
```

I prefer the original VB IDE (integrated design environment), where it had individual windows on the Windows desktop rather than the new, VB5-style multiple-document-interface where VB5 takes over the entire screen. Can I change back to the pre-VB5 IDE?

By default VB5 and VBCCE display a multiple-document-interface (MDI) — windows within windows. MDI is as if you opened several documents within a word processor. You can resize them and rearrange them, but these child windows can't be dragged outside the parent window. Before VB 5, the VB IDE was a single-document-interface: a set of windows that are independent and reside on the Windows desktop as individual windows. If you prefer the single-document-interface, select Options from the Tools menu. Then click the Advanced tab and click SDI development environment.

When I finally get controls sized and positioned just as I want them to appear on a Form or Layout, they get moved accidentally when I double-click them to get to their code window. Is there a way to freeze a finished user interface?

In VB and VBCCE there is a Lock Controls option on the Format menu. Once you're satisfied with the alignment and sizing of all the controls on a Form, select Lock Controls. This way, when you're double-clicking on a control in the future (to get to its code window) you won't accidentally nudge the control out of alignment. The ActiveX Control Pad doesn't have the Lock Controls feature.

I know that I've got an ActiveX control on my hard drive, but when I select Components from VB's Project menu, the control isn't listed there. How can I add it to my Toolbox?

If an ActiveX control is available on your hard drive, but doesn't show up in the list in the Components window, click the Browse button in the Components window (Controls tab) and locate the control on your drive. This will add the control to your Components list, and also register it with Windows.

When single-stepping through my source code to debug a project, I sometimes go into a procedure that I'm sure isn't causing the problem. How can I skip this procedure? I don't want to single-step every line in it.

There are three ways to step past a known-good procedure.

* The first way is to Step Over (Shift+F8) which is like single-stepping but it will skip over a procedure (if you're about to step into one). This way you can skip stepping through a procedure that's been tested and is known good.

* The second way is to use the Step Out (Ctrl+Shift+F8) feature, new to VBCCE and VB5. It speeds through any remaining lines of programming in the current procedure, then stops on the next line in your program outside the current procedure. If you're within a procedure that you're confident isn't causing the bug, Step Out and then resume single-stepping once you're past the current procedure.

* The third way is to use the Set Next Statement feature. Pressing Ctrl+F9 (or selecting Set Next Statement in the Debug menu) will cause VB to restart running from the line you click (selecting that line as the insertion point). Set Next Statement skips all the programming between the current line and new cursor insertion point you specify by clicking it. It then resumes executing lines at the new cursor point. You can therefore specify an insertion point in your source code just beyond the current, known-good procedure that you want to skip. Set Next Statement is also useful if there's a large For...Next Loop, for example, that you want to skip over rather than try to single-step through.

I can't figure out how to create a read-only property in a class.

Just make the Property Let procedure Private (or don't even create a Property Let procedure at all).

How do you create a write-once procedure in a class?

Maybe you'll want to use unique ID numbers with items in a collection. (The index numbers of a collection are unreliable, they can shift around as the collection is added to or as items are removed.) An ID number is, however, persistently associated with a particular member of the collection. This is an example of a property that should be written once, and not written a second time. Here's the programming to create a write-once property procedure:

```
Private mID as String

Property Let ID(TheID As String)
  Static IDExists As Boolean
  If Not IDExists Then
  IDExists = True
  mID = TheID
  End If
End Property
```

**When I try to test a UserControl (an ActiveX Control project type) by cre-
ating a second project (Standard Exe project type), then adding my
UserControl to the test Standard EXE, I get very strange results. For example, if I put in a line of programming like this:**

```
UserControl1.BackColor = vbBlue
```

I get an "Object Required" error message. What gives?

You'll find this unfortunate perplexity in the VBCCE and the commercial
version of VB as well. You must memorize this oddity to avoid headaches trying
to figure out why things are not working. Technically, the error message is correct: there is no object named UserControl1, even though that was its default
name when it was created and you never changed that name.

By default, a UserControl when first created is given the name is *UserControl1*
by VB. That is as you would expect. However, when you close the design and code
windows of the UserControl, then add it from the ToolBox to a Standard EXE
Form to test it, VBCCE renames it to *UserControl11*. This can cause you no end of
confusion. For example, the VBCCE's ActiveX Control Interface Wizard will create
programming that will not work because it's using the name UserControl1. And
any programming you write to test the UserControl that involves naming it
(UserControl1) will fail because there is no UserControl1 any more.

One solution to all this is to use the Properties window to change the Name
property of the UserControl back to UserControl1. Note that this isn't technically
a bug. VB sees *UserControl1* as the name of the UserControl and, therefore, each
time you add a new instance of this UserControl to a Form, each new instance
gets the next higher default number: UserControl11, UserControl12,
UserControl13 and so on. VB is merely appending 1, 2, 3 as it always does to the
actual Name of the object. So VB is behaving as it always has.

The Visual Basic Books Online feature suggests that you can avoid this confusing situation by renaming a UserControl as soon as you start working on it.
Name it something like *Framer* or *Framit* or whatever, but don't use any digits at
the end. This way, when you add them to a Form they'll be named Framer1,
Framer2 and so on.

When I add a Standard EXE project to test a DLL component or a UserControl I have problems when I press F5 to try to test the component. It doesn't work.

Be sure that the *client* (the test Standard EXE project you just added to the existing DLL project) is the Startup project, the one that runs first. The client will contact and use the members of your DLL server or UserControl, to test it. To make it the Startup project, right-click Project2 in the Project Explorer, then choose Set As Startup. Newer versions of Visual Basic and VBCCE won't permit a DLL or UserControl to be the Startup project, so there will be no problem.

I'm having trouble making a TextBox data-aware. I've put a TextBox onto a DLL component's Form and a Data control onto the Form. I think I've got everything right with their properties, but nothing shows up in the TextBox when I run the project.

There are four properties that must be set to display data from a database in a TextBox:

* **DataBaseName** (a property of the Data control)
* **RecordSource** (a property of the Data control)
* **DataSource** (a property of the TextBox; it's the Name of the Data control)
* **DataField** (a property of the TextBox; provides the name of a field in the database)

I'm confused about how to use scripting to modify or manipulate Internet Explorer itself. Where can I find out more?

IE's Scripting Object Model allows you to contact and modify the qualities or behaviors of Microsoft's Internet Explorer browser. You insert VBSCRIPT (or JScript) into an HTML document that can then manipulate the browser itself as if it were an object. This way you can change properties of the HTML page, such as its backcolor. One of the exposed members of an HTML page within the Internet Explorer Scripting Object Model is *Document*. Therefore, if you want to display a message directly on the HTML page, you can do it within VBScript this way:

```
<SCRIPT LANGUAGE="VBScript">
document.write("This isn't HTML. It comes from VBScript.")
</SCRIPT>
```

When using Internet Explorer 4.0's scripting model, you enjoy rather complete *programmatic* control over a Web page. You can use VBScript to manipulate most aspects of an HTML page: the tags, images, text and other objects. For example, there are dozens of methods (Add, Blur, Clear, Focus, Navigate, Select, StartPainting and many more). For more information on the Internet Explorer Scripting Object Model, see this address on the Internet:

```
http://www.microsoft.com/Workshop/prog/inetsdk/docs/inet0474.htm
```

I'm having problems getting an API call to work.

If you're have difficulty with an API call, and you haven't used the VB API Viewer (if it's not on your Add-Ins menu, click the Add-In manager on the Add-Ins menu), then use it. The API Viewer utility isn't available in the VBCCE, but you've got no excuse for not using it in the commercial version of VB. API calls must include no typos, and VB cannot point them out to you if you type in a complex Declare wrong. If you use the API Viewer to insert a Declare into your source code, no typos are possible.

However, it is your responsibility to make sure that when you call the API from within your source code you match the same number, order and variable type of the arguments listed in the Declare. Double-check the arguments following your call to the API. The arguments' *names* need not match, but all the variable types must match. You can't use an Integer variable argument in the location where a Long variable type is called for in the Declare, for example. And the arguments must be in the same order as they are in the Declare. For example, if you insert the following Declare (type this on a single line):

```
Declare Function GetSysColor Lib "user32" (ByVal nIndex As Long)
    As Long
```

You cannot use this mismatched call in your code:

```
Dim Valu as Single
Valu = 20
HiLite = GetSysColor(Valu)
```

Or this mismatch (of the function's variable type):

```
Dim HiLite as Integer
HiLite = GetSysColor(20)
```

Finally, there's an outside possibility that you're using the 16-bit version of VB (VB4 has both 16- and 32-bit; earlier versions are always 16-bit). API calls for 16-bit versions of VB employ a different syntax from the 32-bit versions.

GLOSSARY

ActiveX — Microsoft's name for what used to be called *Dynamic Data Exchange* (DDE) and later, *Object Linking and Embedding* (OLE). ActiveX is a technology, a set of operating system features, a way of programming, and a collection of objects you can plug into your own programs or Web pages. The term *ActiveX* made its appearance in December 1995, as Microsoft was repositioning itself in response to the exploding popularity of the Internet. ActiveX Controls can be embedded into traditional Web pages (which are, all too often, dull and static), adding color, animation, sound, and — above all — efficient interactivity.

ActiveX Component — Previously called an *ActiveX control*, an ActiveX Component is an object that may or may not have a visible user interface, and may or may not run as a server providing features to a client application. In practical terms, most ActiveX components are of the DLL type; they run in-process and act as servers (the second largest group of ActiveX components are UserControls). A Visual Basic control such as a TextBox is an example of an ActiveX component. There are now several kinds of ActiveX components — ActiveX DLLs, ActiveX EXES, ActiveX Document DLLs, ActiveX Document EXES, and ActiveX controls (UserControl).

ActiveX DLL — The commercial version of Visual Basic (VB) can produce several types of components that the VBCCE cannot. VB can produce the following project types: ActiveX.EXE, ActiveX.DLL, ActiveX.Document DLL, ActiveX.Document EXE, and Add-Ins. A DLL differs from other kinds of components in several ways. An ActiveX DLL component is always *in-process;* it always resides within the address space and stack space of a client that's using it. A DLL component therefore loads quickly, compared to an ActiveX EXE component (which is always out-of-process). The DLL doesn't have the overhead of causing run-time DLLs to be loaded. Messaging between the client and the DLL is faster, and *procedures* (methods) in a DLL can run up to ten times faster than they would in an out-of-process, ActiveX EXE-type project.

ActiveX Document DLL — An ActiveX Document is a disk file that contains an OLE link (or several). Once fired up, an ActiveX Document can manipulate data within its own file or access other files. An ActiveX Document works within an ActiveX Document container (the client) that is capable of hosting an ActiveX Document. This technology used to be called object linking and embedding in the past, and was seen as a move toward *docucentric* computing. The fundamental difference between an ordinary ActiveX DLL server and an ActiveX Document DLL is that the Document is specialized; it's designed to be activated within an Internet browser or other container application, like Microsoft Word.

Microsoft applications such as Word, Excel, and the Internet Explorer browser — as well as languages such as VB — can act as ActiveX Document containers and host Document-style ActiveX components. (In addition to Microsoft, many other software houses have made their applications capable of hosting ActiveX Documents.)

ActiveX Document EXE — A Document-style version of the ActiveX EXE component.

ActiveX EXE — An ActiveX component designed to be run either as a server (but out-of-process with its client) or as a standalone Windows executable. In practice, people rarely find any use for ActiveX EXE-type components.

API — Application Programmer's Interface, the operating system's huge collection of functions (and a few subs) that you can tap into if Visual Basic doesn't have a feature you need, or VB does something too slowly. Windows 95 has an API, as does NT. Java includes its own API in the form of a group of objects the programmer can access.

Browser — Internet Explorer and Netscape Navigator are the two giants among browsers. A browser is the application with which you contact and navigate the Internet.

Cache — A storage area. Operating systems often set aside some RAM in the computer to hold the most recently accessed files from the (slower-than-RAM) hard drive. Studies have shown that up to 80 percent of hard drive accesses are to files that were recently accessed. Therefore, if you can keep this data in a RAM cache, it will reappear within a requesting application much faster. Internet browsers cache the most recently visited Web documents. If the user clicks the Back or Forward buttons, the cache (fast) is accessed rather than the Internet address (slow).

Class — A class is a template, a design, that describes an object. You specify the qualities, features, and behaviors of an object when you write the programming that defines a class the same way that an architect specifies the qualities, features, and behaviors of a building when he or she works up a blueprint. The blueprint is later used to create the actual, real building. Likewise, a running application or Web page can create an object (such as a particular TextBox) based on your specifications when you described the class.

Component — An ActiveX project, nearly always a server of the DLL type. Microsoft prefers the term *component* to *control* given that there are several kinds of components of which only some are what most people think of as *controls* (UserControl) or have a visible user interface. The term *control* suggests a visible interface, like a TextBox. An ActiveX project might be simply a group of functions collected together into a library-like server, a DLL (Dynamic Link Library).

Data Hiding — See *Encapsulation.*

Early-binding — When a client declares a new object *by naming it directly*, that object is said to be *early-bound* (as opposed to using the generic As Object command). For example, suppose you create a reference to Word's object library:

```
Set objWord = New Word.applicationsadasda
```

You can then use a line of programming like this to cause early binding:

```
Set objWord = New Word.application
```

The phrases early- and late-binding describe how a server is connected to a client when the server is first instantiated in the client.

When a client uses the As Object and CreateObject commands, an object is said to be late-bound:

```
Dim New_Object As Object
Set New_Object = CreateObject("excel.application")
```

With late-binding, when VB compiles the project, the members of the object that your object variable points to cannot be checked. References to members (such as New_Object.Text) must be checked later, during run time when the object is finally bound to your component. If your client can refer to objects using the early-bound technique, the server will perform more efficiently. An early-bound reference simply and directly codes a pointer to the object's member, eliminating the necessity of having to check the validity of that reference during run time.

Encapsulation — Encapsulation refuses to allow outsiders — or even you the programmer or other objects in your own project — access to the Private variables or procedures within an object. This tactic, sometimes called *data hiding*, can decrease the number of bugs and increase the modularity of an object. *Modularity* means not only subdivision, but also the reusability of an object. If it's sufficiently modular, you or others should be able to easily plug the object into other, client programs, with no unexpected side effects. When you use the Private command to define a property or method, you limit access to that property or method to only those other procedures contained within the same module (or Form).

Technically, encapsulation means that the data (such as the value of the current BackColor property) within an object is never directly made available to a client. The data in an object is manipulated only within that object. Clients never know how the data is stored (all the variables within a class are Private) nor do they know how the data is manipulated. All a client needs to know is which members of the class have been made available (or *exposed*, as it's sometimes called), the parameters they require, and what information they return, if any.

Event — A procedure in a client or control triggered when something outside happens — like the user pressing a key or clicking the mouse. A developer or programmer can write programming within the Event procedure to specify a response — how the client or control should react if the user, for example, presses the Enter key while typing something into a TextBox.

HTML — *HyperText Markup Language*, the page-description language that is the basis of Internet documents. Web pages are described by HTML (telling a browser how to display text and graphics — their size, color, position, and so on). For action, multimedia, or other dynamic or computational behaviors, HTML is useless. VBScript, ActiveX, or Java can compute and add animation, instant feedback, and other benefits to Web pages.

Inheritance — A class can provide its offspring (other classes generated from a class) with its methods, events and properties. *Subclassing* is another word for inheritance. Both terms mean that you take an existing class and modify it by making it more specialized. In this sense, when you extend a generic TextBox control to modify it to make it into a TextBox that accepts only passwords, you've created a more specialized form of the original, generic TextBox class. VB doesn't permit "true" inheritance, as defined by strict OOP enthusiasts, because there is no real parent-child relationship between the original class and the subclass. You can, however, be grateful for this "lapse," because by ignoring that technical parent-child relationship, VB avoids certain problems inherent in strict OOP. In VB, for example, the original (or "parent") class is isolated from the subclass (or "child"). This means that if you change an original class, there is no way that you will cause problems in the subclass — they have no dynamic relationship in VB. That they don't is, all things considered, a blessing.

In-process — See *Out-of-process*.

Instance — See *Instantiate*.

Instantiate — When you create a class, it's a design, a set of specifications, for an object. This description of the class happens at design time (while you're writing the program). Then, when you (or a client) use that class to create an actual object, the object is said to be *instantiated*. This instantiating happens while your program runs (during run time). Each object that's created is said to be an *instance* of the class that describes it.

Late-binding — See *Early-binding*.

Mapping — Borrowing the functionality of members of an existing control. For example, if you're including an existing VB TextBox control in a new ActiveX component of your own creation, the TextBox has both a Text and a ForeColor property. You might want to pass the functionality of these properties through from the original VB TextBox to your new, subclassed ActiveX component. Borrowing existing features of original controls is called *mapping*.

VB and VBCCE make mapping relatively painless because the ActiveX Control Interface Wizard provides considerable help. It assists you by writing the programming code to map properties.

Members — The properties, methods, and events of a particular object. Taken together, these three entities are referred to as an object's *members*.

Method — A job that a component knows how to do. For example, a VB PictureBox has a Circle method because when you, the programmer, use the Circle method, the PictureBox knows how to draw circles and display them. You can also provide methods (behaviors) to components or classes you design — just write the programming code, for example, to calculate mortgage interest and put it into a Function or Sub. Then your component has a CalcMortgage Method — or whatever you decide to call it.

Object-Oriented Programming (OOP) — An approach to programming that stresses hiding data (encapsulation). OOP also endeavors to enclose data, along with methods that process that data, into objects. OOP shifts the focus from the traditional procedure-oriented (Subs or Functions) programming style to an object-oriented style. Instead of merely listing the tasks that a project must accomplish, OOP asks that you then collapse (factor) those tasks into objects. Objects are identified as the *nouns* when you diagram the sentences in a task list:

1. Get the age of the user of this program.

2. Ask the annual salary of the user for the past ten years.

3. Calculate the user's probable social security compensation.

The object in this project is the user; it's the primary noun in each sentence. So you'll make a class out of the User. In this User class you'll create some properties and a method. The user has two properties: age and annual salary. The user has one method: calculating social security. You would build this project using OOP techniques by creating a User class (from which you can generate as many specific users as you might need). Then you would give this User class Age and Salary properties. Finally, you would include (in the User class), a CalcSS method that would check the Age and Salary properties, and look up the probable monthly retirement check the user can expect at age 65.

Object — A thing, an entity, a self-contained phenomenon. Fog, patriotism, the color blue, love, flying, and honey are not objects. They have no specificity, no discrete boundaries that distinguish them from other entities. Fog has a vague boundary; blue and love are nebulous, abstract concepts; honey flows. All these concepts are either abstract notions or something that has no particular start and end. An object is concrete. A specific stamp is an object; a stamp collection enclosed within a stamp album is also an object. The abstract concept of stamps, though, isn't an object — it's an idea. In programming, when you define a *class* (an abstract plan), that class is capable of creating (concrete, specific) *objects* during run time.

Out-of-process — The term *out-of-process* means that a component is not running in the same address space (and sharing a stack) with its client application. UserControls and DLL-type components run in-process, thereby simplifying and speeding things up when the client manipulates properties and methods in the server. See Chapter 13 for more information on in-process and out-of-process options.

Polymorphism — One of the three elemental characteristics of OOP is called *polymorphism*, as in *polymorphous perverse*, one of Freud's more antic concepts. Literally, polymorphous means many forms, like a shape shifter. (The other two elemental characteristics of OOP are inheritance and, most important of all, encapsulation.) But alas, as the word is used in computer programming, polymorphism is a more difficult idea to grasp than encapsulation or inheritance.

Here's one way to understand polymorphism. Consider Mom saying, "Everyone sit down for dinner, now." The command to sit down is a single command, a single idea — yet, in practice, various people do somewhat different things when they hear the command. Family members go to their various chairs around the table. In OOP terms, several objects can be given the same command, but each object carries out that command in a way appropriate to it.

It's safe to assume that each family member is derived from the People Class and each member has inherited many behaviors from the original Class. However, each has modified some of those behaviors as necessary because each person is a *particular* object, a member of the BrotherBilly class, SisterSue class, or DaddyJoe class. Each person has different chairs to go to when getting the message to sit.

The ultimate benefit of this individualized polymorphic reaction to a single command (method) is that Mom doesn't have to worry about what class each family member belongs to when making a request. Mom doesn't have to say, "Sue, sit in your chair over there, and Brother Dan, go around the table until you find your usual chair there in the middle of the left side of the table . . . "

Translated into the idea of polymorphism in the programming world, a developer who uses your objects doesn't have to know each object's particular class when sending a command, a message, to the object. *The object has the built-in sense to interpret the message correctly*, freeing the developer from worrying about the actual behaviors. The developer merely wants all of the objects to fall in or sit down. The developer doesn't want to worry about the details of just how each object will accomplish the job. You, the creator of an object, have given it the elemental intelligence needed to behave properly when it's requested to sit down or fall in.

For example, the VB property BackColor is polymorphic. A developer might change the BackColor of a Label and a PictureBox to pink. The Label changes colors immediately, but the PictureBox behaves differently. First look at its Picture property. If a graphic is being displayed by the PictureBox, the Box won't turn pink and cover up the graphic. A graphic overrides any BackColor. So the PictureBox interprets a change in BackColor differently than a Label. But the command from a developer, in both cases, is identical. The developer doesn't have to worry about how each object will end up implementing the command.

Project — A computer program. A project can mean an ActiveX component or a full, large computer application. For some reason, Microsoft has decided to replace the traditional word *program* with the term *project*. The words are synonyms.

Program — See *Project*.

Property — A quality of a component, like its color, font size or width. A component's properties, methods and events are called, collectively, its *members*.

Subclassing — Deriving one thing from another. See *Inheritance*.

VBCCE — *Visual Basic Control Creation Edition*. A fully functional programming environment, very similar to the commercial versions of Visual Basic. The VBCCE, however, is only capable of producing compiled (runnable) ActiveX Controls (UserControls). It cannot create runnable Standard EXEs (typical Windows programs), or ActiveX Documents.

Wizard — A utility that steps a user, programmer, or developer through the stages necessary to complete a task. Wizards can save considerable amounts of time and trouble (like VB's Class Builder or VBCCE's ActiveX Control Interface Wizard) or be of quite limited usefulness (like the ActiveX Control Pad's Script Wizard).

INDEX

(continued)

W

Z

IDG BOOKS WORLDWIDE, INC.
END-USER LICENSE AGREEMENT

READ THIS. You should carefully read these terms and conditions before opening the software packet(s) included with this book ("Book"). This is a license agreement ("Agreement") between you and IDG Books Worldwide, Inc. ("IDGB"). By opening the accompanying software packet(s), you acknowledge that you have read and accept the following terms and conditions. If you do not agree and do not want to be bound by such terms and conditions, promptly return the Book and the unopened software packet(s) to the place you obtained them for a full refund.

1. **License Grant.** IDGB grants to you (either an individual or entity) a nonexclusive license to use one copy of the enclosed software program(s) (collectively, the "Software") solely for your own personal or business purposes on a single computer (whether a standard computer or a workstation component of a multiuser network). The Software is in use on a computer when it is loaded into temporary memory (RAM) or installed into permanent memory (hard disk, CD-ROM, or other storage device). IDGB reserves all rights not expressly granted herein.

2. **Ownership.** IDGB is the owner of all right, title, and interest, including copyright, in and to the compilation of the Software recorded on the disk(s) or CD-ROM ("Software Media"). Copyright to the individual programs recorded on the Software Media is owned by the author or other authorized copyright owner of each program. Ownership of the Software and all proprietary rights relating thereto remain with IDGB and its licensers.

3. **Restrictions on Use and Transfer.**

   (a) You may only (i) make one copy of the Software for backup or archival purposes, or (ii) transfer the Software to a single hard disk, provided that you keep the original for backup or archival purposes. You may not (i) rent or lease the Software, (ii) copy or reproduce the Software through a LAN or other network system or through any computer subscriber system or bulletin-board system, or (iii) modify, adapt, or create derivative works based on the Software.

   (b) You may not reverse engineer, decompile, or disassemble the Software. You may transfer the Software and user documentation on a permanent basis, provided that the transferee agrees to accept the terms and conditions of this Agreement and you retain no copies. If the Software is an update or has been updated, any transfer must include the most recent update and all prior versions.

4. **Restrictions on Use of Individual Programs.** You must follow the individual requirements and restrictions detailed for each individual program in the appendix, "Using the CD-ROM" of this Book. These limitations are also contained in the individual license agreements recorded on the Software Media. These limitations may include a requirement that after using the program for a specified period of time, the user must pay a registration fee or discontinue use. By opening the Software packet(s), you will be agreeing to abide by the licenses and restrictions for these individual programs that are detailed in the appendix, "Using the CD-ROM" and on the Software Media. None of the material on this Software Media or listed in this Book may ever be redistributed, in original or modified form, for commercial purposes.

5. **Limited Warranty.**

   (a) IDGB warrants that the Software and Software Media are free from defects in materials and workmanship under normal use for a period of sixty (60) days from the date of purchase of this Book. If IDGB receives notification within the warranty period of defects in materials or workmanship, IDGB will replace the defective Software Media.

   (b) IDGB AND THE AUTHOR OF THE BOOK DISCLAIM ALL OTHER WARRANTIES, EXPRESS OR IMPLIED, INCLUDING WITHOUT LIMITATION IMPLIED WARRANTIES OF MERCHANTABILITY AND FITNESS FOR A PARTICULAR PURPOSE, WITH RESPECT TO THE SOFTWARE, THE PROGRAMS, THE SOURCE CODE CONTAINED THEREIN, AND/OR THE TECHNIQUES DESCRIBED IN THIS BOOK. IDGB DOES NOT WARRANT THAT THE FUNCTIONS CONTAINED IN THE SOFTWARE WILL MEET YOUR REQUIREMENTS OR THAT THE OPERATION OF THE SOFTWARE WILL BE ERROR FREE.

   (c) This limited warranty gives you specific legal rights, and you may have other rights that vary from jurisdiction to jurisdiction.

6. **Remedies.**

   (a) IDGB's entire liability and your exclusive remedy for defects in materials and workmanship shall be limited to replacement of the Software Media, which may be returned to IDGB with a copy of your receipt at the following address: Software Media Fulfillment Department, Attn.: *Discover ActiveX*, IDG Books Worldwide, Inc., 7260 Shadeland Station, Ste. 100, Indianapolis, IN 46256, or call 1-800-762-2974. Please allow three to four weeks for delivery. This Limited Warranty is void if failure of the Software Media has resulted from accident, abuse, or misapplication. Any replacement Software Media will be warranted for the remainder of the original warranty period or thirty (30) days, whichever is longer.

   (b) In no event shall IDGB or the author be liable for any damages whatsoever (including without limitation damages for loss of business profits, business interruption, loss of business information, or any other pecuniary loss) arising from the use of or inability to use the Book or the Software, even if IDGB has been advised of the possibility of such damages.

   (c) Because some jurisdictions do not allow the exclusion or limitation of liability for consequential or incidental damages, the above limitation or exclusion may not apply to you.

7. **U.S. Government Restricted Rights.** Use, duplication, or disclosure of the Software by the U.S. Government is subject to restrictions stated in paragraph (c)(1)(ii) of the Rights in Technical Data and Computer Software clause of DFARS 252.227-7013, and in subparagraphs (a) through (d) of the Commercial Computer — Restricted Rights clause at FAR 52.227-19, and in similar clauses in the NASA FAR supplement, when applicable.

8. **General.** This Agreement constitutes the entire understanding of the parties and revokes and supersedes all prior agreements, oral or written, between them and may not be modified or amended except in a writing signed by both parties hereto that specifically refers to this Agreement. This Agreement shall take precedence over any other documents that may be in conflict herewith. If any one or more provisions contained in this Agreement are held by any court or tribunal to be invalid, illegal, or otherwise unenforceable, each and every other provision shall remain in full force and effect.

INSTALLING THE PROGRAMS FROM THE CD-ROM

The CD-ROM that accompanies this book contains a select group of demo and trialware versions of commercial ActiveX controls. The appendix, "Using the CD-ROM," provides a short description of each demo. You'll also find installation information for each demo on the CD-ROM itself. Each program folder includes a file called README.TXT that you can double-click to find out how to install the demo.

Most of the demos include a setup (SETUP.EXE) program, and each demo is in its own folder. If you don't find SETUP.EXE, take a look at README.TXT file for further instructions.

To install the demo programs from the CD-ROM, follow these steps:

1. Insert the *Discover ActiveX* CD-ROM into your CD-ROM drive.

2. Click the Start button.

3. Select Programs → Windows Explorer .

4. Double-click the CD-ROM drive icon to view the contents of the CD-ROM in the right window. Or, click the plus icon next to the CD-ROM drive icon to open the DiscActiveX folder.

5. Select the folder containing the demo you'd like to install.

6. Double-click the SETUP.EXE program. If you don't find a SETUP.EXE program, read the README.TXT file for instructions.

7. If you find an ActiveX component that you want to use, contact the manufacturer (information about purchasing each component can be found in the demos themselves).